DAYS
in the LIFE of
ATLANTA

By Norman Shavin

Published by
Capricorn Corporation / 4961 Rebel Trail, NW / Atlanta, Georgia 30327
United States of America
A Joint Venture with Norman Bloom Enterprises

"Days In the Life of Atlanta" is published and distributed by Capricorn Corporation, Inc., 4961 Rebel Trail, NW, Atlanta, Georgia 30327 (United States of America). Phone: (404) 843-8668. An illustrated list of Capricorn's products will be sent free on receipt of a self-addressed stamped, No. 10 envelope.

Copyright ©1987 to "Days In the Life of Atlanta" is held by Capricorn Corporation, Inc., and Norman Bloom Enterprises. To those two entities all rights are reserved except the color photographs which are the property of Steve Hogben.

Many of the black-and-white photographs are from the Atlanta Historical Society, that excellent repository to which we give deep thanks. Others were loaned by Webb Garrison, Tracy W. O'Neal, Jr., and The Atlanta Gas Light Co. Many came from the files of Capricorn Corp.

First edition, September, 1987.
ISBN 0-910719-21-7.
Book designed by Kathleen Oldenburg King
Mechanicals by Olio-2 Advertising
Typography by Clopton Typography & Graphics, Inc.
Printing by Phoenix Communications Company
Binding by National Library Bindery of Georgia.

"Days In the Life of Atlanta" is a joint venture of Capricorn Corporation, Inc., and Norman Bloom Enterprises.

First permanent settler in downtown Atlanta was Hardy Ivy, whose cabin occupied part of the ground which includes the present intersection of Courtland Ave. and International Blvd.

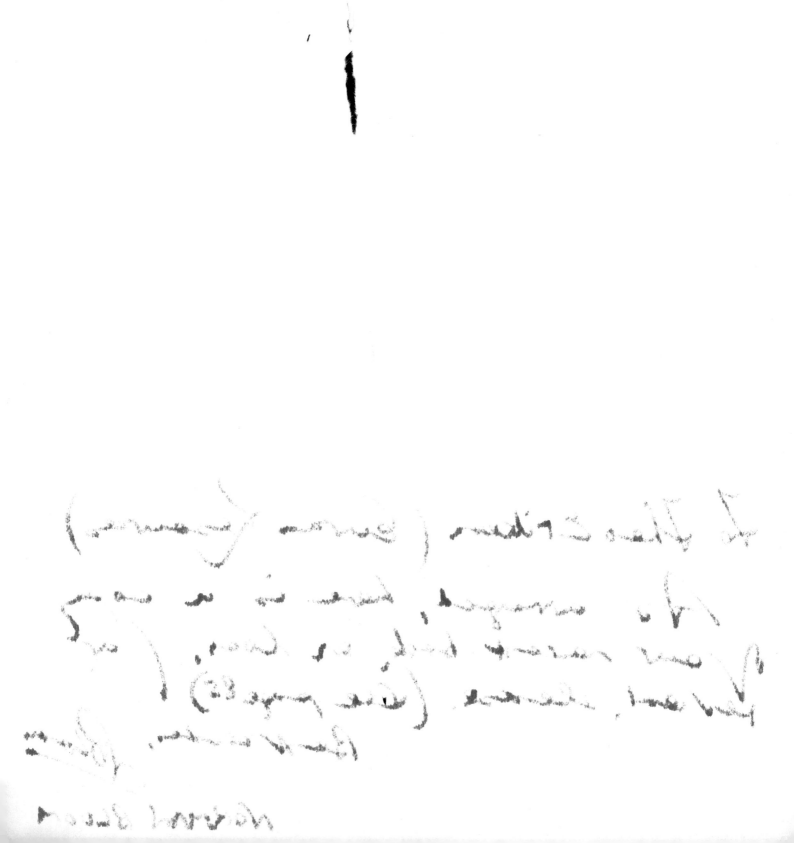

Capricorn Corporation

404-934-0256
[404] 843-8668

4961 Rebel Trail, NW • Atlanta, Georgia 30327

"DAYS IN THE LIFE OF ATLANTA"
RETAIL PRICE : $24-95 plus sales tax

DISCOUNTED PRICES FOR QUANTITY ORDERS:

10 - 24 : $23.00 EACH   ⎫ INCLUDES
25 - 49 : $21.00   ⎬ DELIVERY
50 - 99 : $19.00   ⎬ (ATLANTA REGION)
100 + : $17.00   ⎭ BUT ADD SALES TAX

To Theo Erikon (Human Resources)
As arranged, here is a copy
of our recent book on loan, for
review, please. (see page 85)
Best wishes,

NORMAN BLOOM

Publishers   Editorial Services   Marketing

Acknowledgements

The genesis of "Days In the Life of Atlanta" was hardly as historic as its subject matter.

The seed for the book was sown during an amiable conversation between Norman Bloom, my valued and long-time associate, and me one afternoon as we explored ways to mark Atlanta's sesquicentennial, celebrated in 1987.

The basic motivation was to develop a product both unique and permanent. We believe our readers will confirm that "Days In the Life of Atlanta," an illustrated chronology of Atlanta's 150 years, fulfills our ambition.

From the beginning this project has been a joint venture whose development has depended, in great measure, on the dedication and energies of Norman Bloom of Norman Bloom Enterprises.

We have conceptualized and brought to fruition other projects which have won public, corporate and civic support. And in every enterprise I have marveled at Norman's expertise and innovations in development, marketing and promotion. Beyond that, Norman's personality exudes such warmth as to envelope every contact in an aura of good spirits. His unflagging energy astonishes me, and leaves me grateful for our rewarding association.

There are others who deserve credit in the shaping of this book:

— The Sales Team, Roy Wilkes, Fran Wilkes and Jim Maggard's Binks Co. were instrumental in developing co-sponsor support. Special thanks are accorded to Roy for his devotion to this project while it was in its infancy.

— Artist Kathy King again applied her talents to one of our books. My respect and gratitude to her, for her great care under pressure of deadlines, is tremendous.

— Audrey Williams, owner of Clopton Typography & Graphics, Inc., and typesetter Ann Phillips deserve our thanks for quality work performed under strict conditions.

— Steve Hogben has again provided the color photographs, which (as usual) illustrate his skill. We worked with Steve earlier on development of our striking architecture book, "Building Atlanta," published in March, 1987.

— I was aided by four researchers: Webb Garrison, Prof. David N. Thomas of Oglethorpe University, Stephen Goldfarb and David Harmon. Each performed with dedication, and Webb is due special thanks for additional services.

I hope "Days In the Life of Atlanta" finds public acceptance. Its concept was viewed with favor by many of Atlanta's fine corporate entities and institutions, which lent their support to this book. Their confidence in it is a marvelous statement of faith, herewith repaid, and their contributions to the city's history are worthy of detailing in a special section beginning on page 175.

We are grateful for their support, without which "Days In the Life of Atlanta" would not have been possible.

NORMAN SHAVIN

Charner Humphries' White Hall Tavern, which stood at present-day Gordon and Lee Sts., was a major crossroads meeting place that was in business in 1835. Union troops used it in 1864.

Foreword

The odyssey that is a city's history can be traced in a variety of modes. One of the most inviting is by casting the drama as a year-by-year illustrated chronology of highlights of its past.

This is what "Days In the Life of Atlanta" does by re-tracing the city's 150 years from 1837 to mark its sesquicentennial.

The definition of "highlights" is, in part, a matter of the author's subjective choice. I have tempered a strict definition of that term by listing some events and incidents that reflect more mood of the times than major event. The purpose was to create an atmosphere.

Beyond that relaxation of strict interpretation of "highlights," I had to make allowances, which the reader will accept, for periods when little of moment was transpiring in a place variously called, in its earliest years, Terminus and Marthasville.

The balance between amount of text and illustrations was also juggled to keep the pages both appealing and informative. Some illustrations are related to events, depicting actual incidents or individuals involved in them. To create a sense of comprehensiveness, each year includes a brief section of events of national import.

With few exceptions each page of the chronology is concerned with only one year. Because certain illustrations demanded more space, double pages were allowed for the years 1847, 1864 and 1895.

At the center of "Days In the Life of Atlanta" is a 16-page section of color photographs designed to reflect dimensions of Atlanta in 1987, its sesquicentennial year.

Starting on page 175 is a section devoted to corporate and institutional profiles: These stories are vital parts of Atlanta's odyssey.

The city's oldest corporate citizen, Atlanta Gas Light Co., came into being in 1856, and the Company proved to be the first to become a co-sponsor of this book. We appreciate that dual leadership.

A bibliography of sources of this book's material is on page 232.

While 1837 is properly defined as Atlanta's birth year—for that was when work began on the railroad at whose juncture with other lines Atlanta would emerge—there were earlier signs that the area would become prominent.

An Indian village called Standing Peachtree was already known by 1782 and near its site on the Chattahoochee River was built, in 1813, Ft. Gilmer. In 1826 Wilson Lumpkin (later governor) and Hamilton Fulton surveyed the territory between Milledgeville (then the capital) and the future site of Chattanooga, and reported that a railroad between the points would be practicable.

In 1833 the Legislature, prodded by Gov. Lumpkin, chartered three railroad lines, but not one of them connected middle Georgia to the North. Months after the establishment of a tavern near Atlanta called White Hall and the arrival of Atlanta's first settler, Hardy Ivy, a Macon railroad convention confirmed that "an excellent route for the (rail) road . . . can be obtained from Ross' Landing [later, Chattanooga] to some point on the Chattahoochee in DeKalb County."

On Dec. 21, 1836, the Legislature's bill creating the state-financed Western & Atlantic Railroad, to tie middle Georgia to the North, was signed into law by Gov. William Schley.

Within seven months actual work began on the railroad. At its juncture with other lines would come the rustic place known first as Terminus (and White Hall), then Marthasville (for Gov. Lumpkin's daughter) and, finally, Atlanta.

Within a few years braggarts were referring to the place as the "center of creation." It was a heady boast, but when you look upon Atlanta today surely you will concede that, if not the "center of creation," it is at least a thrusting, creative center.

Proof of its progress to that estate lies among the pages of "Days In the Life of Atlanta."

NORMAN SHAVIN

Introduction

By Mayor Andrew Young

During this sesquicentennial celebration of the birth of Atlanta, it gives me pleasure to introduce a new addition to the works of Norman Shavin.

Created in the tradition of previous publications, including "Atlanta: Triumph of a People," "The World of Atlanta," and "Building Atlanta," Shavin's newest work places the growth and development of our fine city in an historic perspective.

In the course of expanding from the sleepy railroad crossing of Terminus, to the bustling young merchant center of Marthasville, to the booming modern capital of the entire Southeast, there have indeed been some wonderful "Days In the Life of Atlanta."

The day which we celebrate this year is the historic driving of a railroad stake or zero mile post at the terminal point of the Western & Atlantic Railroad in 1837. From this embryonic beginning, the city and people of Atlanta have forged ahead toward greatness.

Sometimes slowed in our progress by fatal days like Nov. 14, 1864, when General Sherman set out successfully to consume the city with fire, we have always recovered from the adverse and returned to a leadership role in the progress of mankind.

By 1870 the city was well on the road to recovery, rising like the mythical phoenix from the ashes of Sherman's fire just six years before.

On one hot May day in 1886, an Atlanta pharmacist mixed the first Coca-Cola for patrons at a local drugstore and a highly significant and ongoing chapter in this city's history had begun.

The city prospered through the early days of the 20th Century and by 1927 could claim to be the home of the largest black university complex in the nation, the conglomeration of black colleges and universities known as the Atlanta University Center.

Mayor Andrew Young

Atlanta's progress may have never been as evident as in the heady days of the Civil Rights Movement when Dr. Martin Luther King, Jr., a native son, led us on the road to desegregation and non-violent social change.

Once a portrait of the slave labor society of the Old South, in 1974 we had come of age as the capital of the New South, inaugurating my predecessor, Maynard Jackson, as the city's first black mayor.

In my own terms as mayor, the city has continued to grow and prosper, having perhaps more than our share of good days.

We have seen unprecedented economic growth, revitalization of the downtown area and a continued tradition of racial harmony. Atlanta Hartsfield International Airport has become the busiest air terminal in the United States, the rebirth of Underground Atlanta is underway and the city has been selected to host the first national political convention in its history.

As we celebrate these good old days, I commend Norman Shavin on his latest publication and look forward with him to the year ahead when we will no doubt experience the best of all "Days In the Life of Atlanta."

1837

January 5
Regarding building of the new railroad, Gov. William Schley writes: "If zeal, perseverance and industry can effect anything, they shall not be wanting."

March 2
John E. Thomson, chief engineer of the Georgia Railroad, recommends Col. Stephen H. Long as chief engineer of the new line. Long, "an officer of high standing in the [Army] Engineer Corps," had been assistant professor of mathematics at West Point Military Academy.

May 12
Long accepts the position at $5,000 for a period of not less than six months. He wanted $9,000, for which he was willing to resign his commission. [The Hopkinton, NH, native was a Dartmouth University graduate who had been part of Western explorations, worked on the Baltimore & Ohio Railroad, and who wrote a railroad-building manual. He died September 4, 1864 — two days after Atlanta surrendered to Union troops.]

May
Surveying begins for the railroad line between Chattanooga and the southern terminus.

July 4
Work begins on the railroad line for the southern terminus, at Pittman Ferry, but is soon abandoned because creeks and valleys intervene, and the gradients do not satisfy Long's specifications. [If the site had been chosen, Atlanta would have been built in the vicinity of Hog Mountain and present-day Norcross.] Engineers choose a new site: Montgomery's Ferry at old Ft. Gilmer near the Indian village of Standing Peachtree.

November 7
Long's final report is submitted to the Legislature: "The route leading from Montgomery's Ferry proved the more economical and favorable, in all respects, and has been fixed upon as the adopted route." [As it turns out, $18,000 per mile less.]

December 23
Legislature amends railroad act of 1836 to allow for a slight extension of the line so that the "Western & Atlantic Railroad shall continue from the southeastern bank of the Chattahoochee River to some point not exceeding eight miles, as shall be most eligible for running branch (rail) roads…" Thus, the original terminus of the W&A was in a lot owned by Reuben Cone where present-day Foundry St. crosses the NC & St. L. tracks.

Also this year: Establishment of the town of Roswell, named for Roswell King, a coastal planter who moves to the area with his family and some friends, including the families of John Dunwody and James S. Bulloch. Bulloch's daughter Mittie marries Theodore Roosevelt on December 23, 1853, in Roswell's Bulloch Hall. Mittie and Theodore become the parents of Theodore, Jr., later a president. Another son of Mittie and Theodore, Elliott, becomes the father of Eleanor, later Mrs. Franklin D. Roosevelt.

John E. Thomson (see Mar. 2)

Col. Stephen H. Long (see May 12)

Wilbur Kurtz, Artist
Col. Long drives a stake (see July 4)

THIS YEAR IN THE NATION

Panic of 1837 caused by wild speculation in railroads, canals and banking ... **Jan. 26:** Michigan admitted into the Union as 26th state ... **Mar. 3:** Pres. Jackson recognizes Texas as an independent country ... **Mar. 4:** Number of Supreme Court justices increased from 7 to 9 by Congress ... **Mar. 4:** Martin Van Buren inaugurated as 8th President ... **Oct. 21:** Federal troops seize Seminole chief Osceola during a parley under a flag of truce ... **Nov. 7:** Elijah P. Lovejoy, abolitionist newspaper editor, murdered by a proslavery mob in Alton, IL ... **Dec. 21:** Canadian militia destroy American-owned steamboat "Caroline" in American territory killing American citizen Amos Durfee.

Pres. Martin Van Buren (see This Year In the Nation/Mar. 4)

1838

January 1   Sixty miles of railroad bed, prepared by workmen including Indians, is ready for the builders.

April 6   Gen. Winfield Scott is sent to the vicinity to forcibly remove the Cherokee Indians, by terms of an 1802 agreement with the U. S. government, and reinforced by the Treaty of New Echota (1835). The forced march west becomes known as the "Trail of Tears."

Gen. Winfield Scott (see Apr. 6)

April 10   Aaron McCloud, of McDonough, is engaged in erecting a tower or observatory on the top of Stone Mountain, and is determined to raise it to 300 feet. It ultimately rises to only 165 feet as an octagonal pyramid of wood, and costs about $5,000. A storm blows it down, and a second tower also "went to the discard."

May 24   Georgia officially takes possession of the Cherokee country.

June 3   The major part of the removal of 15,000 Cherokee Indians is finished. They are taken first to Ross' Landing (Chattanooga), and thence to the Indian Territory [in what was then Arkansas]. More than 4,000 die en route.

December 18   Daniel Johnson deeds to Henry Irby the 202½ acres which becomes the heart of Buckhead; Irby pays $650. He erects a tavern and grocery at the northwest corner of what becomes the Roswell Road-West Paces Ferry intersection. [In 1840 the head of a buck, shot nearby, is mounted on a post at a nearby spring and the locale, including the tavern, becomes known as Buckhead. A U. S. postoffice is established at the Irby settlement and designated as Irbyville on October 5, 1841. In 1877 Irby sells his 202½ acres for 44,000 to son-in-law R. B. Hicks; Irby dies in 1879.]

December 31   Legislature incorporates Stone Mountain Academy, an educational institution.

THIS YEAR IN THE NATION

Feb. 14: John Q. Adams presents to the House of Representatives 350 petitions opposing slavery ... **Apr. 23:** Steamship service established between U.S. and Great Britain ... **May 29:** Americans burn Canadian steamship "Sir Robert Peel" in St. Lawrence River ... **June 12:** Iowa territory organized ... **Aug. 18:** First American overseas exploration expedition authorized by Congress leaves Hampton Roads, VA ... **Oct. 30:** Following riots in northwestern Missouri and the death of 17, Mormons flee to Illinois ... **Dec. 11:** A "gag rule" providing for the tabling of all anti-slavery petitions passes House of Representatives.

1839

April 6	On the road between Marietta and Montgomery's Ferry there is a riot among railroad workmen. Two females are killed, eight workmen wounded; 34 of those held responsible for starting the fracas are jailed.
Spring	John Thrasher arrives in Terminus and opens a general store. His partner is named Johnson (possibly Lochlin Johnson), and their enterprise, the first store in Terminus, is situated on the site of the present-day Federal Reserve Bank.
June 22	John Ridge and two other men are murdered by dissident Cherokees who condemn the sale of tribal lands.
Summer	Alexander H. Stephens, then 27, stops at the terminus of the railroad, and is heard to observe that, "I was just thinking what a magnificent inland city will at no distant date be built here." [Stephens later becomes Vice President of the Confederacy and governor of Georgia.]
Fall	Thrasher and Johnson are the successful bidders to construct the (Monroe) railroad embankment between the end of the former Union Station and present-day Foundry St. Each partner clears about $10,000 for grading the embankment.
December 7	Joseph Walker leads other citizens in organizing the Decatur Baptist Church (later called Indian Creek Church).
Winter	Mrs. Mulligan, wife of the W&A Railroad foreman, hosts a ball in her home, the first Terminus house with wooden planks for flooring. This is Atlanta's first social event. [The next day a delegation of men say their wives want plank flooring, too.]

THIS YEAR IN THE NATION

Border dispute between U.S. and Canada dominates foreign affairs adding to tension of earlier "Caroline" affair ... **Feb. 7:** Kentucky senator and presidential hopeful Henry Clay denounces abolitionists and declares that Congress has no power to interfere with slavery ... **Feb. 20:** Dueling in the District of Columbia declared illegal by Congress ... **Aug. 26:** Spanish ship "Amistad," which has been seized by blacks, captured by American ship off Long Island ... **Dec. 6:** Whig Party nominates William H. Harrison of Ohio for president and John Tyler of Virginia for vice-president.

Wilbur Kurtz, Artist

Johnson & Thrasher store (see Spring)

Roswell Cotton Mill, incorporated 1839

Alexander H. Stephens (see Summer)

8

1840

May 3 Col. Long resigns as chief engineer of the W&A Railroad after declining the opportunity to obtain half interest in 200 acres along what is now Marietta St. Long says, "The Terminus will be a good location for one tavern, a blacksmith shop, a grocery store, and nothing else."

December 22 The Legislature designates "the house of Henry Irby, at the place known as Buck Head," as an election district.

Terminus (the future Atlanta) is part of DeKalb County, and the census for 1840 shows that the County has 4,314 white males, 4,142 white females, six "free persons of color," 952 male slaves, and 1,052 female slaves. Total: 10,466.

THIS YEAR IN THE NATION

Census shows U.S. population is 17,069,453, a four-fold increase since the first census in 1790, and an increase of almost a third since the census of 1830 … **Jan. 8:** House of Representatives adopts rule not to receive antislavery petitions and resolutions … **Mar. 31:** A 10-hour workday is established for federal government employees by executive order of Pres. Van Buren … **Apr. 1:** Liberty Party, the first national convention of abolitionists, nominates James G. Birney of Kentucky for president … **May 5-6:** Pres. Van Buren nominated for a second term by Democratic national convention … **July 4:** Independent treasury bill signed into law by Pres. Van Buren … **Dec. 2:** Whig nominee William H. Harrison elected President; John Tyler elected Vice-President.

Barrington Hall, residence of the Roswell King family in Roswell, erected 1840

MONTGOMERY'S FERRY 1840

Wilbur Kurtz, Artist

Montgomery's Ferry across the Chattahoochee River near Atlanta (1840)

Wilbur Kurtz, Artist

The Buckhead house of Henry Irby (see Dec. 22)

9

1841

After four years of grading and surveying, not one iron rail has been laid for the W&A Railroad.

December 4   Under newly-elected Gov. Charles J. McDonald, the Legislature—finding finances at a low ebb—passes an act suspending all work on the W&A Railroad except for that part of the line extending from the southern terminus (the future Atlanta) to the approximate location of present-day Cartersville.

Gov. Charles J. McDonald (see Dec. 4)

Pres. William H. Harrison
(see This Year In the Nation/Mar. 4)

THIS YEAR IN THE NATION

Mar. 4: William H. Harrison inaugurated as ninth President ... **Mar. 9:** Supreme Court, upholding decision of lower court, frees black slaves who had taken over the Spanish ship "Amistad" in 1839 ... **Apr. 4:** Pres. Harrison dies of pneumonia; John Tyler becomes the tenth President, the first to succeed to the office not by election ... **Apr. 10:** Horace Greeley begins publication of the "New York Tribune." ... **Aug. 13:** Independent Treasury Act of 1840 is repealed ... **Sept. 4:** Distribution-Preemption Act, which allows for the sale to settlers of up to 160 acres of public land, passed by Congress ... **Sept. 11:** All cabinet members except Secretary of State Daniel Webster resign to protest Pres. Tyler's veto of national bank ... **Dec. 27-29:** "People's Constitution," with greatly expanded franchise, adopted by convention.

Pres. John Tyler
(see This Year In the Nation/Apr. 4)

Horace Greeley
(see This Year In the Nation/Apr. 10)

1842

June — Willis (21) and Julia Carlisle (17), recently married, arrive from Marietta, becoming among the earliest permanent settlers. Their home is on present-day Marietta St. (in front of the current Federal Reserve Bank). Willis opens a grocery in that home. The first Atlanta-born child is their daughter (delivery was on August 17, 1842, in Marietta). Also named Julia, that child dies in 1919.

July 11 — Samuel Mitchell donates five acres for the W&A Railroad's southern terminal station and yards. [Pioneer John Thrasher, enraged because that facility is not on part of the 100 acres he'd bought by the Monroe embankment, sells it for $4 an acre and moves to Griffin.]

Summer — Terminus is now being called Marthasville, named for the daughter of Gov. Wilson Lumpkin, major proponent of railroad expansion. [Samuel Mitchell and others want to call the place Lumpkin; the governor demurs, and even suggests the name Mitchell.] At this time the hamlet has about 30 persons living in six buildings.

Fall — A plank depot is built—a two-story frame structure (first building of such height in the town). It is used initially as the engineer's office, and later as a boarding house for railroad employees. The house, originally on Wall St., is moved several times over succeeding years, and is finally demolished about 1917.

December 24 — An excursion train, the first to depart for Marthasville, is brought from Madison (60 miles away), pulled by 16 mules. To the train engine (named Florida) a passenger car and a freight car (brought to Marthasville from Milledgeville) are connected for the slow, 20-mile trip to Marietta. Regular train service remains three years distant.

THIS YEAR IN THE NATION

Mar. 3: Law limiting factory work to 10 hours per day for children under 12 passed by Massachusetts legislature ... **Mar. 30:** Georgia's Crawford W. Long is first to use ether as an anesthetic for surgery ... **Mar. 31:** Sen. Henry Clay of Kentucky resigns his seat ... **June 10:** Wilkes expedition returns after four years spent exploring the Pacific and the coast of Antarctica ... **Aug. 9:** Webster-Ashburton Treaty signed between U.S. and Great Britain settles boundary between Maine and Canada and includes other adjustments in the U.S.-Canadian border ... **Aug. 26:** Beginning of fiscal year changed from January 1 to July 1 by Congress ... **Aug. 30:** Pres. Tyler signs tariff bill which raises import duties to those in effect in 1832 ... **Dec. 30:** Secretary of State Daniel Webster, with the advice of Pres. Tyler, states that the U.S. opposes any foreign power taking possession of the Hawaiian Islands.

Gov. Wilson Lumpkin (see Summer)

Martha Lumpkin (see Summer)

The plank depot (see Fall)

The excursion train (see Dec. 24)

Wilbur Kurtz, Artist

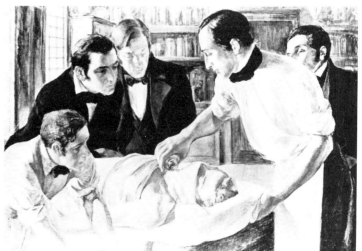
Dr. Crawford Long (see This Year In the Nation/Mar. 30)

1843

Spring	Several families, including Thomas Kile's, arrive to settle. Others are Edwin Pyne, Stephen Terry and Ambrose and William Forsyth.
Summer	Rev. John Thurman delivers the first sermon in Marthasville, at the home of a Mr. Wells (near present-day Five Points).
November 7	The governor reports that 33 miles of track are now laid north of Marthasville.
December 23	Gov. George W. Crawford signs the act incorporating the town of Marthasville, and names five commissioners as its governors: L. V. Gannon, John Bailey, Willis Carlisle, John Kile, Sr., and Patrick Quinn.

Gov. George W. Crawford (see Dec. 23)

Daniel Webster
(see This Year In the Nation/May 8)

John C. Fremont
(see This Year In the Nation/May 29)

THIS YEAR IN THE NATION

Mar. 3: Congress repeals bankruptcy act of 1841 ... **May 8:** Secretary of State Daniel Webster resigns due to differences with Pres. Tyler over the annexation of Texas ... **May 22:** First wagon train bound for Oregon leaves Elm Grove, MO ... **May 29:** John C. Fremont sets out on expedition to explore region between Rocky Mountains and the Pacific ... **June 17 :** Bunker Hill Monument dedicated ... **July 5:** American settlers meeting at Champeog in Oregon adopt local government laws, which are to function until U.S. makes area into a territory ... **Aug. 30:** Liberty Party renominates James G. Birney as president and adopts party platform that condemns further expansion of slavery.

1844

February

Lt. William T. Sherman, then 23, passes through Marthasville en route to Marietta on an Army assignment. His knowledge of the area over a two-month period becomes very useful 20 years later when he sweeps through North Georgia as commanding general of armies.

The attempt by the Marthasville commissioners to levy a tax to open new streets is rebuffed by residents, who advise them to clear the ground themselves, adding that the existing seven streets are enough: Peachtree, Marietta, Decatur, Whitehall, Pryor, Alabama and Loyd (now called Central).

This year also sees the arrival of pioneers such as Jonathan Norcross, James Loyd and James A. Collins.

In 1844 John Thrasher returns from Griffin, and Jonathan Norcross arrives to establish a sawmill to provide lumber for the railroads. Norcross' mill is Marthasville's first manufactory (at Decatur and Pratt Sts.) and is powered by a blind horse. Norcross gives lumber slabs to the poor to help them build shanties in an area that becomes known as "Slabtown."

Jonathan Norcross

Lt. William T. Sherman

Pres. James K. Polk
(see This Year In the Nation/Dec. 7)

Henry Clay
(see This Year In the Nation/Dec. 7)

THIS YEAR IN THE NATION

Jan. 15: University of Notre Dame receives its charter from the Indiana legislature ... **Feb. 28:** Secretary of State Abel P. Upshur and Secretary of the Navy Thomas Gilmer are killed aboard the U.S.S. Princeton when a gun explodes ... **Mar. 6:** John C. Calhoun of South Carolina appointed Secretary of State ... **Apr. 12:** Treaty is signed between the United States and the Republic of Texas that provides for the annexation of Texas and the assumption by the U.S. of the public debt of Texas ... **May 24:** Inventor Samuel F. B. Morse sends first telegraphic message, between Washington and Baltimore ... **May 29:** Democrats nominate James K. Polk of Tennessee as president; platform calls for the annexation of Texas and occupation of Oregon ... **June 26:** Pres. Tyler marries Miss Julia Gardiner and becomes the first president to marry while in office .... **July 3:** First treaty between the U.S. and China signed, granting U.S. trading privileges ... **Dec. 3:** Repeal of "gag rule" on antislavery petitions adopted by the House of Representatives ... **Dec. 7:** James K. Polk elected president, beating Henry Clay.

1845

May 31	George Washington Collier buys a lot and opens a grocery [at present-day Five Points] which serves as Atlanta's first postoffice beginning in 1846.
Summer	Residents begin calling the hamlet Atlanta, and within weeks that name appears on railroad circulars. The name Atlanta is coined from "Atlantic" by John E. Thomson, chief engineer of the Georgia Railroad and later president of the Pennsylvania Railroad.
September 14	First train of the Georgia Railroad (a freight conducted by engineer William F. Adair) arrives from Decatur after an hour's run.
September 15	The Georgia Railroad's first passenger train to reach Atlanta arrives from Augusta, with William Orme as conductor, assisted by George Washington Adair. The train brings Judge John P. King, the Railroad's president, who, arriving here in the dark, falls into a 10-foot hole being dug as a well. Says one observer: The Judge "was highly disgusted, and for years would not buy Atlanta real estate."
Fall	Dr. Joshua Gilbert arrives; Atlanta's first physician.
October 15	The U. S. Postoffice Department changes the name of its local office from Marthasville to Atlanta.
November 13	John C. Calhoun, chairman of the Southeastern Convention meeting in Memphis, predicts greatness for a town (Atlanta) "where railroads unite."
December 26	Legislature confirms Atlanta as the official name of the town.

Also this year: The first Jewish families—those of Jacob Haas and Herman Levi—come to Atlanta, opening a dry goods store on Whitehall St.... Mrs. Martha Reed organizes a small private school, the first in Atlanta... The second doctor in Atlanta, Stephen T. Biggers, arrives, as does the first lawyer, Leonard C. Simpson.

THIS YEAR IN THE NATION

With the annexation of Texas tensions between the U.S. and Mexico increase; at the same time tensions between the U.S. and Great Britain grow over Oregon ... **Jan. 23:** By act of Congress uniform day for presidential elections is adopted ... **Mar. 3:** Florida admitted as the 27th state with provision for slavery in its constitution ... **May 4:** James K. Polk inaugurated as the 11th President; George Dallas becomes Vice-President ... **June 8:** Former Pres. Andrew Jackson dies at 78 ... **July 5-7:** First national convention of the Native American Party, which will become the American or "Know-Nothing Party," meets and passes resolutions opposing then-current liberal immigration law ... **July 19:** Six million dollars of property destroyed in New York City fire ... **Dec. 29:** Texas admitted into the Union as the 28th state.

George W. Adair (see Sept. 15)

Judge John King (see Sept. 15)

Richard Peters, who pushed for a new name for Marthasville and asked J. Edgar Thomson for a suggestion (see Summer)

G. W. Collier's grocery at Five Points (see May 31)

Wilbur Kurtz, Artist

1846

March 21   Jonathan Norcross pays $200 for half-acre lot which is now the site of First Atlanta Tower (at Five Points).

Spring   Atlanta Hotel, the city's first, opens in a two-story brick building in the block bounded by Whitehall, Pryor, Decatur and Wall Sts. Destroyed by war in 1864; site later occupied by the Kimball House, a major hotel begun in 1870.

May 31   First sermon preached in Atlanta (after its name was changed from Marthasville); by Rev. Francis Haygood (Baptist).

July 14   First Atlanta newspaper, The Luminary, launched by Rev. Joseph S. Baker and partner Thomas Wilson. They sell it December 9 and it dies in 1848, being then known as the Tribune.

August 7   Organizational meeting of the Southern Central Agricultural Society Fair held at Stone Mountain Hotel.

August   Atlanta's second paper, the weekly Enterprise, begins publication; owners W. H. Royal and C. H. Yarbrough sell it in 1847, and it dies later that year.

September 4   The Macon and Western becomes the third railroad to enter Atlanta; service begins in October on 101 miles of track.

November 1   First Episcopal Service in Atlanta (at the home of Samuel G. Jones).

Also this year: Atlanta's second hotel, Washington Hall, opens, facing Loyd (now Central) St. Destroyed by war in 1864... Early this year (or late 1845) the first Roman Catholic mass is said in Atlanta, probably by Father John Barry, in the home of Michael McCullough.

Washington Hall, Atlanta's second hotel (see Also this year . . .)

THIS YEAR IN THE NATION

Tensions between the U.S. and Mexico over Texas result in the outbreak of the Mexican War; differences between the U.S. and Great Britain over Oregon are settled peaceably ... **Feb. 10:** Mormons leave Nauvoo, IL, under the leadership of Brigham Young ... **May 13:** Pres. Polk signs declaration of war with Mexico ... **May 24:** American army under Gen. Zachary Taylor captures Monterey, Mexico ... **June 19:** First baseball game played, in Hoboken, NJ ... **July 31:** Pres. Polk signs Walker tariff bill which lowers tariffs, reversing a trend toward protectionism ... **Aug. 10:** Smithsonian Institution chartered by Congress ... **Sept. 10:** Sewing machine patented by Elias Howe ... **Dec. 28:** Iowa becomes the 29th state.

1847

April 13   Samuel Mitchell deeds to Stephen Elliott Jr., Bishop of the Protestant Episcopal Diocese of Georgia, land for the Church's use; by various transactions this becomes the Parish of St. Philip.

April 13   Masonic Lodge #59 holds its first meeting; its charter dates from October 26.

June 10   The first Sunday school, known as the Atlanta Sabbath School, is organized.

June 23   Terrence Doonan conveys to Ignatius A. Reynolds, Roman Catholic Bishop of Charleston, SC, an acre for use as a church.

July 2   Atlanta's fourth newspaper, the Southern Miscellany, is a weekly edited by Cornelius Hanleiter, and arrives this date from its former home, Madison.

December 4   A town meeting develops support for moving the state capital to Atlanta from Milledgeville. (This campaign finally succeeds in 1868.)

December 29   Atlanta is incorporated as a town. The town limits are defined as a circle with a one-mile radius from the depot's mile marker.

December 30   William R. Howell is authorized to build a bridge across Nancy Creek on the Paces Ferry Road, and is to be paid $99.75 provided he keeps the bridge in repair for five years.

Also this year: Atlanta can boast a population of about 2,500, with 30 stores, a handful of hotels and private schools...Early this year the first house of worship is erected on a triangular lot bounded by Peachtree, Pryor and Houston Sts. Weekdays the weatherboard building is used as a school...Dr. N. L. Angier opens a private school (Angier's Academy) at Forsyth and Garnett Sts. His wife teaches there...The town's third newspaper, the Democrat (with Dr. William H. Fonerdon as editor and publisher) is launched, but dies in three months.

Dr. N. L. Angier (see Also this year . . .)

The first Sunday school (see June 10)

THIS YEAR IN THE NATION

War with Mexico continues; opposition to it grows at home ... **Feb. 22-23:** American troops under Gen. Zachary Taylor win the battle of Buena Vista, neutralizing opposition in northern Mexico ... **Mar. 3:** Congress authorizes the printing of postage stamps so the cost can be paid for in advance and not by the recipient of a letter ... **Mar. 9:** Army under Gen. Winfield Scott lands at Vera Cruz, the first large amphibious landing in American history ... **Apr. 26:** Massachusetts legislature passes resolution calling war with Mexico "wanton, unjust and unconstitutional" .... **July 24:** Brigham Young and Mormon pioneers arrive at the valley of the Great Salt Lake ... **Sept. 14:** American army under Gen. Scott captures Mexico City.

The Southern Miscellany of Dec. 4, 1847 (see July 2)

1848

January 8	Nineteen Presbyterians organize the Presbyterian Church of Atlanta.
January 29	In the town's first municipal election Moses Formwalt, a 28-year-old operator of a tin-and-copper shop (and still-maker), is chosen Atlanta's first mayor over Jonathan Norcross. The sole polling place is Thomas Kile's grocery (on the site of the present William-Oliver Building by Five Points); 215 votes are cast (all by men).
February 2	At the city council's first meeting German M. Lester is chosen marshal, and the council approves installing wooden sidewalks and a ban on Sunday business.
March	The Methodists dedicate Wesley Chapel, an outgrowth of the Union Sabbath School. The Chapel is built (in 1847) on Peachtree, just south of the present-day Candler Building.
May 28	St. Philip's Episcopal Church building is consecrated; the 28x42-foot structure costs $700.
July 5	The building of the First Baptist Church (organized January 1) is dedicated by Rev. D. G. Daniel.
September 3	In a personal grudge fight at the Atlanta Hotel, Judge Francis Cone stabs Alexander H. Stephens with a knife; latter recovers, and later serves as Georgia's governor.
September 14	Atlanta's first recorded homicide caps a long family feud: William Terrell stabs James McWilliams, and is sentenced to four years at hard labor.
October 7	Atlanta's first International Order of Odd Fellows chapter, Central Lodge #28, is organized.

November — Austin Leyden erects Atlanta's first foundry and machine shop (Atlanta Machine Works), later seized by Confederate authorities to cast shells. It is destroyed in 1864.

Also this year: The first jail is erected, at Pryor and Alabama Sts., but it is so flimsy that prisoners can burrow out from under it or topple it…Mrs. George C. Smith opens a "select school for young ladies" at the corner of Marietta and Forsyth Sts.…James McPherson opens the town's first bookstore …The Sandy Springs Methodist Church, South, is organized on what is now Mt. Vernon Highway…Atlanta has the reputation of being a rowdy town where violence, cock-fights, robbery and drunken rows are common, especially in the Murrell's Row area (near Five Points).

THIS YEAR IN THE NATION

Jan. 24: Gold is discovered at Sutter's Mill in California … **Feb. 2:** Treaty of Guadalupe Hidalgo ends war with Mexico; Mexico gives up claim to Texas and cedes New Mexico and California to the U.S. for $15 million … **Feb. 23:** Former Pres. John Q. Adams dies at 80 … **May 22-26:** Democrats nominate Sen. Lewis Cass of Michigan for president and William O. Butler of Kentucky for vice-president … **May 29:** Wisconsin becomes 30th state … **June 7-9:** Whigs nominate Gen. Zachary Taylor of Louisiana for president and Millard Fillmore of New York for vice-president … **July 4:** Cornerstone of Washington Monument is laid …. **July 19:** First Women's Rights convention, in Seneca Falls, NY … **Aug. 14:** Pres. Polk signs legislation prohibiting slavery in Oregon and establishing a territorial government … **Nov. 7:** Gen. Zachary Taylor elected President; Millard Fillmore elected Vice-President.

Wesley Chapel (see March)

Wilbur Kurtz, Artist

*Pres. John Quincy Adams
(see This Year In the Nation/Feb. 23)*

Atlanta's first election—and only polling place (see Jan. 29)

1849

January 17   Dr. Benjamin F. Bomar, elected second mayor, is sworn into office. He represents moderate, church-going elements who hope for better law enforcement.

February 7   City Council approves a property tax of 30 cents on each $100 in value, but little money is ultimately collected.

April 14   Atlanta issues its first municipal bonds in units of $500, payable in six months.

May   The town's first telegraph line goes into operation, connecting Atlanta to Macon.

June 1   The Southern Miscellany newspaper, published sporadically since 1847 and sold to businessmen including Jonathan Norcross, reappears as the Atlanta Intelligencer, with the Rev. Joseph Baker as editor.

December 1   The W&A Railroad completes 138 miles of track to Chattanooga.

Also this year: Typhoid is rife in the city, and yet there is a popular bit of boasting doggerel that runs: "Atlanta, the greatest spot in all the nation, the greatest place for legislation, or any other occupation—the very center of creation." ... Residents buy eggs for 8 cents a dozen, butter for 10 cents a pound, corn for 40 cents a bushel, "fine" apples for 40 cents a pound, sweet potatoes for 15 cents a bushel, brown sugar for six cents a pound ... The annual Fair of the Southern Central Agricultural Society is held at Stone Mountain and features the presence of showman P. T. Barnum, his animals and freaks, and Tipo Sultan, reportedly the largest elephant in captivity.

Dr. Benjamin F. Bomar (see Jan. 17)

Howell Cobb
(see This Year In the Nation/Dec. 22)

THIS YEAR IN THE NATION

Feb. 28: First boatload of 49ers arrives at San Francisco .... **Mar. 3:** Minnesota territory organized .... **Mar. 5:** Zachary Taylor inaugurated as 12th President .... **Mar. 10:** Missouri legislature endorses "popular sovereignty" which holds that only citizens of a territory can prohibit slavery, not Congress .... **Aug. 11:** Pres. Taylor issues a proclamation that disapproves of attempts to liberate Cuba from Spain .... **Sept. 1-Oct. 13:** Convention meeting at Monterey adopts constitution for California that prohibits slavery .... **Dec. 20:** Treaty of amity and trade concluded between U.S. and Hawaiian Islands .... **Dec. 22:** Rep. Howell Cobb of Georgia elected speaker of the House of Representatives after acrimonious debate and 63 ballots.

1850

January 23   William (or Willis) Buell is inaugurated as Atlanta's third mayor.

January 28   The circus comes to Atlanta—and is taxed $25 for the privilege.

January   Railroad schedules confirm that the "fast passenger train" from Atlanta to Dalton, GA (99 miles), requires only seven hours.

February 23   Legislature charters Atlanta Fire Company #1. Despite its motto, "Prompt to Action!," it doesn't go into operation for a year.

March 1   A tax of $1 is levied on every slave sold in the town.

April 10   The City Council promises $1,000 and a 10-acre lot to the Southern Central Agricultural Society to hold its next fair in Atlanta. It does, in August.

April 21   Two night watchmen are assigned by City Council to patrol the city from 10 p.m. to daylight. They are to be paid $20 each per month.

June 6   The city buys a six-acre tract ($75 per acre) from Alfred W. Wooding as the nucleus for a cemetery, years later known as Oakland. Ultimately 79 more acres are added. Tradition holds that its first occupant is Dr. James Nissen who, fearing being buried alive, arranges for another physician to slit his throat after he dies—just to make sure—before the coffin is lowered.

November 19   Atlanta census completed; population is 2,058 white persons, 493 slaves, and 18 "free" blacks. Primary occupations of some heads of household include 70 carpenters, 38 merchants, 11 clerks, 10 farmers, 10 grocers and eight clergymen.

December   In the mayoral election the contest is between the "Free and Rowdy" party (represented by Leonard Simpson) and the "Moral" party led by Jonathan Norcross. The latter wins.

Also this year: Dr. Crawford Long, first to use ether as an anesthetic in surgery, moves to Atlanta, but leaves for Athens the next year.

THIS YEAR IN THE NATION

Political life of the nation is dominated by the slavery question; after months of debate the Compromise of 1850 is enacted; it resolves the issue of slavery for the time being .... **Mar. 31:** Sen. John C. Calhoun, spokesman for the South, dies at 68 .... **July 1:** First regular mail service established west of the Mississippi River between Independence, MO, and Salt Lake City, UT .... **July 9:** Pres. Taylor dies at 65 .... **July 10:** Millard Fillmore takes the oath of office, becoming the 13th President .... **Sept. 9:** California enters the Union as 31st state; territories of New Mexico and Utah organized .... **Sept. 18:** Pres. Fillmore signs Fugitive Slave Bill .... **Sept. 20:** Slave trade abolished in the District of Columbia .... **Sept. 20:** First federal land grant for railroads approved .... **Sept. 28:** Flogging prohibited in the U.S. Navy and merchant marines by Congress.

Dr. Crawford W. Long (see Also this year . . .)

Home of William Ezzard, onetime mayor, which was completed in 1850 on the corner now occupied by the downtown Equitable Building

1851

Mayor Jonathan Norcross
(see Also this year . . .)

Pres. Millard Fillmore
(see This Year In the Nation/Apr. 25)

February 13 Father James O'Neill becomes the first pastor of the Roman Catholic Church of the Immaculate Conception.

February 14 City Council adopts an ordinance requiring each building within the city limits, kitchens and other small houses excepted, to be furnished with a ladder, and each store and house to have two fire buckets.

March 12 East Point becomes a U. S. postoffice.

July 29-31 Nine men arrested to halt a suspected slave uprising.

December Dr. T. F. Gibbs elected mayor.

Also this year: Mayor Norcross proves effective in establishing better law and order in the town, and survives personal threats from the town "toughs" ... Another newspaper, the Republican, is launched by brothers, the Rev. Russell and Jesse Reneau; it is combined in 1855 with another paper, the Discipline, which is succeeded in 1857 by yet another paper, the National American ... Seven more private schools open in Atlanta.

THIS YEAR IN THE NATION

With the Compromise of 1850 sectional conflict subsides; the South, wishing to expand slavery, looks to the annexation of the Spanish colony of Cuba .... **Feb. 10:** Illinois Central Railroad granted 2.7 million acres to build a railroad from Cairo to Galena .... **Apr. 25:** Proclamation issued by Pres. Fillmore orders U.S. citizens not to participate in hostile acts against Spanish rule in Cuba .... **May 29:** Former slave Sojourner Truth acclaimed for her presentation to the second Women's Rights Convention at Akron, OH ... **Aug. 3:** Expedition of some 400 armed men headed by Venezuelan Narciso Lopez sails from New Orleans for Cuba to liberate the island from Spanish rule .... **Aug. 16:** After being captured, 50 Americans from Lopez' expedition are tried by a Spanish military court and found guilty and executed in Havana .... **Sept. 18:** The "New York Daily Times" is founded (becomes the "New York Times" in 1857) .... **Nov. 14:** First American edition of "Moby Dick" by Herman Melville published .... **Dec. 20:** First American branch of the Y.M.C.A. opens in Boston.

1852

January 26   Mrs. T. S. Ogilby opens the city's first school of music.

January 27   The first bank is chartered for Atlanta, the Bank of Atlanta. It is organized with $300,000 capital stock available, but after eight months not a share is sold. In 1853 a Chicagoan buys most of the shares; the bank dies toward the end of 1855 following publicity attacking its paper-money policies.

May 21   City Council rules that slaves are required to have written permission to possess liquor. If found violating this order, the slave is to suffer 39 lashes to the back.

May   Moses Formwalt, Atlanta's first mayor, is stabbed to death by a prisoner while doing his duty as deputy sheriff.

July 4   First Presbyterian Church dedicated by Rev. John Wilson.

September 18   Led by Howell Cobb, Union Democrats decide, in an Atlanta meeting, not to flee the Democratic Party to join the Southern Rights movement.

Also this year: Thomas G. Healey and partner Julius A. Hayden open a brick-manufacturing firm … Operational also is the freight car manufactory launched by Joseph Winship (it is destroyed by fire in 1856, at which time he has already started a machine shop and iron works).

THIS YEAR IN THE NATION

Mar. 20: "Uncle Tom's Cabin" by Harriet Beecher Stowe published … **Mar. 29:** Ohio passes a law setting 10-hours as a maximum workday for women … **June 1-5:** Democratic Party nominates Franklin Pierce of New Hampshire for president and William R. D. King for vice-president … **June 17-20:** Whig Party nominates Gen. Winfield Scott of Virginia for president and William A. Graham for vice-president … **June 29:** Henry Clay dies at 75 … **Aug. 11:** Free Soil Party nominates John P. Hale of New Hampshire for president and George N. Julian of Indiana for vice-president … **Oct. 24:** Daniel Webster dies at 70 … **Nov. 2:** Franklin Pierce and William R. D. King win election … **Nov. 24:** Commodore Perry sails for Japan to open Pacific to American trade.

First Presbyterian Church (see July 4) stood on part of the downtown Marietta St. site now occupied by the Federal Reserve Bank.

The home of architect John Boutell, erected in 1852, stood on the southwest corner of Courtland and Ellis Sts.; demolished in 1938.

Howell's Mill was erected in 1852 several hundred yards below the old Howell Mill Road crossing of Peachtree Creek by Judge Clark Howell.

1853

January 17 By a vote of 369 to 193 John F. Mims defeats Dr. T. F. Gibbs for mayor.

January 28 City Council approves formation of a three-man police force.

February 16 City Council authorizes Edward Vincent to create a city map, its first. Vincent's fee: $100 and ownership of any copyright.

March 25 City Council approves oil-burning street lights; residents are required to supply the fuel.

June 20 Richard Peters sells the city a four-acre lot ($5,000), now site of Capitol.

July Atlanta's first hospital is opened, mainly to contend with the smallpox problem.

July 1 Edward Parsons' central market, Atlanta's first, takes shape on Market Street.

Fall The Holland Free School, Atlanta's first public school, opens.

November 12 Special election held to choose a mayor to fill the unexpired term of John F. Mims, who resigns due to ill health. William Markham selected.

November 28 William Butt leads Atlantans in an unsuccessful petition to the Legislature to have the state capital moved here.

December 20 Fulton County created, and Atlanta is designated as its seat.

Also this year: Atlanta's population exceeds the 6,000 mark.

THIS YEAR IN THE NATION

Mar. 2: Washington Territory organized ... **Mar. 4:** Franklin Pierce inaugurated as 14th president ... **Mar. 7:** Jefferson Davis appointed as Secretary of War in Pierce cabinet ... **Apr. 18:** Vice-pres. King dies ... **May 18:** First black YMCA organized by Anthony Bower in Washington, D.C. ... **July 4:** New York Central Railroad established by merger of 10 smaller railroads ... **July 8-14:** Commodore Matthew Perry reaches Tokyo with letters from American president to the Japanese emperor ... **Nov. 12:** "Clotel," by William Wells Brown, first novel by an American black, is published in London ... **Dec. 30:** Gadsden Purchase secured from Mexico.

Edward Vincent surveys town to create first map (see Feb. 16)

William M. Butt (see Nov. 28)

Mayor William Markham (see Nov. 12)

Gov. H. V. Johnson (1853-57)

1854

January	William Butt elected mayor.
February 3	City Council approves doubling of the night police force—to six men.
February 14	Legislature grants charter to found the Atlanta Medical College. Cornerstone of its first building (at a corner of Butler and Armstrong Sts.) is laid June 21, 1855. Its first class (31 doctors) is graduated September 1, 1855.
February 18	The Georgia Western Railroad is chartered.
March 1	First issue of a monthly medical publication, the Georgia Blister and Critic, is issued under editor Dr. H. A. Ramsay. It dies a year later.
March 3	Council authorizes the Mayor to have created a city seal. Jeweler Er Lawshe gets the assignment to make it (and a clock), and on May 19 presents his bill; $21 for both … Council action also bans hogs from the streets, approves the creation of a system to light the streets by gas, and pledges to continue its attempts to get the state capital moved from Milledgeville.
May 2	Ex-Pres. Millard Fillmore, the nation's 13th Chief Executive, visits Atlanta for an overnight, and is royally feted at a reception and ball.
June 30	Council gives the Atlanta Medical College faculty permission to hold lecture sessions in City Hall, until their own quarters are ready.
August	The Examiner begins publication as the city's first daily; a week later the Intelligencer becomes a daily newspaper also.
September 1	The 2nd Baptist Church is formed by 19 former members of the First Baptist who reportedly seek more liberal theology and music in their services … Trinity Methodist Episcopal Church opens this same month.
October	The new City Hall opens, and a ball is held October 17 to celebrate the new structure's completion (on the site now occupied by the state Capitol).
November	A new hotel, The Trout House, opens. It is erected by Jeremiah F. Trout on a corner of Decatur and Pryor Sts. Destroyed by Sherman in 1864.
Fall	A brick building on Decatur St. (between Peachtree and Pryor) is rising, and its second floor becomes the home of The

Athenaeum, Atlanta's first theatre, for which City Council issues a license February 16, 1855.

Also this year: A new, spacious brick railroad passenger depot is opened. It is 100x300 feet and is served by four railroads. The depot is destroyed in the fall of 1864.

THIS YEAR IN THE NATION

Slavery again becomes a major issue; debate centers in whether slavery will be allowed in the territories of Kansas and Nebraska … **Jan. 23:** Sen. Stephen Douglas of Illinois introduces a bill that would allow for "popular sovereignty" in the Kansas and Nebraska territories … **Feb. 28:** A meeting opposing Douglas' proposal held in Ripon, WI, urges the formation of a political organization which becomes the Republican Party … **Mar. 31:** Treaty of Kanagawa signed between the U.S. and Japan … **April 26:** Massachusetts Emigrant Aid Society organized to encourage non-slave owning settlers to move to the Kansas territory … **Apr. 29:** Ashmun Institute (later Lincoln University), first college in the U.S. devoted to the education of blacks, is chartered by Pennsylvania … **May 25:** Kansas-Nebraska Act passes Congress; provides for "popular sovereignty" on the slavery issue … **May 26:** Fugitive slave Anthony Burns apprehended in Boston with aid of federal and state military forces … **Aug. 9:** "Walden," by Henry D. Thoreau, published.

City Hall officially opens (see October) on site later occupied by state Capitol.

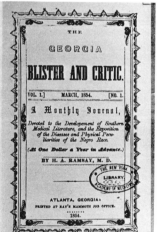

Georgia Blister and Critic (see Mar. 1)

City Council Seal (see Mar. 3)

Brick passenger depot (see Also this year . . .)

1855

January 15	Allison Nelson defeats Know Nothing Party nominee Ira McDaniel for mayor, by a narrow margin of votes, 425-415.
March 3	Basil Overby becomes first Atlantan to be candidate for governor.
March 23	William Helme (Philadelphia) proposes to City Council that he erect a gas works (using coal) to illuminate streets and buildings, with Council putting up at least 50 street lamps, and to pay for lighting them at a cost of $30 each per year. Council agrees to buy 40% ($20,000) of the stock in Helme's operation.
July 6	Mayor Nelson resigns after the City Council reduces a sentence he had levied in mayor's court.
July 20	John Glen (or Glenn) is chosen mayor for the balance of 1855.
September	Atlanta is host to the Georgia Agricultural Society Fair.
October	The city's first privately operated infirmary opens, and charges "the usual fees adopted by the physicians of the city ... with 15 cents per day for board, etc."
December 25	Atlanta's first gas lamps are illuminated

even though the operating company is not chartered by the Legislature until several weeks later.

Also this year: It is noted that more than 40 lawyers now practice in Atlanta ... In April the Fulton County Grand Jury calls attention to an "evil of vast magnitude, the herds of unruly and vicious boys who infest the streets of the city ... by day and night, especially on the Sabbath, to the great annoyance of (the) citizens ... and recommends to the city authorities the adoption of stringent measures to abate the nuisance."

Also this year: Atlanta Medical College established; it later joins with the Southern Medical College (established 1879) and Southern Dental College (organized 1892) to become part of Emory University in 1915.

THIS YEAR IN THE NATION

National attention focuses on "bleeding Kansas" as conflict there erupts between pro- and anti-slavery settlers ... **Jan. 16:** Nebraska territorial government organized ... **Jan. 28:** Railroad across Panama completed making this water-rail route the most convenient between New York and San Francisco ... **Mar. 30:** Pro-slavery legislature elected in Kansas territory through fraud and intimidation ... **May 3:** John M. Langston, first black to be elected to public office, addresses the American Anti-Slavery Society ... **May 21:** Massachusetts enacts a personal liberty law that negates the Fugitive Slave Act ... **July 4:** First edition of "Leaves of Grass," by Walt Whitman, goes on sale ... **Sept. 5:** Anti-slavery settlers meeting at Big Springs, KS, repudiates pro-slavery legislature and seek to be admitted as a free state ... **Nov. 10:** "The Song of Hiawatha," by Henry W. Longfellow, published.

Mayor Allison Nelson (see Jan. 15)

Mayor John Glen (see July 20)

Atlanta Medical College (see Also this year ...)

1856

January 25 William Ezzard elected mayor. (Atlanta's population grows to 8,000 this year.)

January 28 William Helme transfers to the mayor and City Council $20,000 in stock of the Atlanta Gas Light Company, incorporated this month by the Legislature, for $20,000 in city bonds. The Legislature's act incorporating the Company is approved February 16. Thus, Atlanta Gas Light Company is Atlanta's oldest functioning corporate citizen.

March 5 Legislature charters the Air Line Railroad to connect to South Carolina but it is delayed for years; Legislature also approves Atlanta's first city court, thus freeing the mayor from serving as a judge.

March 5 Atlantans hold a rally supporting movement to send emigrants, representing southern viewpoints, to Kansas.

March 6 Legislature approves chartering of the Bank of Fulton, with capitalization of $125,000. In 1864, under stress of war, it suspends operations, and never reopens.

June 3 City Council denies as "unwise" a black man's petition to open an ice cream saloon.

Summer Thomas West opens the city's first soda water manufactory; City Council buys 3,000 shares of stock in a bridge over the Chattahoochee.

October 2 Tragedy strikes a Know Nothing Party rally (supporting Millard Fillmore for President) when a man falls to his death from a flagpole.

December 10 Mechanics Fire Company #2 is given a charter to organize.

Also this year: A branch of the Georgia Railroad and Banking Agency is opened in Atlanta.

THIS YEAR IN THE NATION

"Bleeding Kansas" remains a major issue, with no solution coming from Congress ... **Jan. 15:** The election of an anti-slavery legislature in Topeka gives Kansas territory two opposing governments ... **Apr. 21:** First bridge over the Mississippi River, from Davenport, IA, to Rockford, IL, opens to railroad traffic ... **May 15:** Citizens of San Francisco organize the "Committee of Vigilance" following murder of local newspaper editor ... **May 21:** Sen. Charles Sumner of Massachusetts beaten by Rep. Preston Brooks after anti-slavery speech in which he criticized Brook's uncle Sen. Andrew Butler; event heightens tensions over slavery ... **May 21:** Pro-slavery forces attack Lawrence, KS ... **May 24-25:** In retaliation for sacking of Lawrence, John Brown leads a group that murders five pro-slavery settlers ... **June 2-6:** Democratic Party nominates James Buchanan for president ... **June 17-19:** Republican Party, in its first national convention, nominates John C. Fremont for president ... **June 29:** American adventurer William Walker elected president of Nicaragua ... **Aug. 16:** Gail Borden receives patent for condensed milk ... **Nov. 4:** Democrat James Buchanan elected president.

Mayor William Ezzard (see Jan. 25)

Volunteer fire company, photographed in 1856 with the fire engine named "Blue Dick" and the horse-drawn ladder truck (right, rear) called "Old Reliable."

1857

January	William Ezzard re-elected mayor.
March 12	Cornelius Hanleiter establishes a newspaper named the National American; in February, 1861, it is renamed the Gate City Guardian in deference to Georgia's secession from the Union.
May	Atlanta is first referred to as the "Gate City, the only tribute which she requires of those who pass through her boundaries is that they stop long enough to partake of the hospitality of her citizens."
October 30	Fulton Lodge #216, Masons, receives its charter.
	Also this year: The first Atlanta unit of the Young Men's Christian Association is founded this winter ... Alpharetta is incorporated by legislative act ... Edward E. Rawson enters the hardware business as senior member of the company called Rawson, Gilbert and Burr.

Pres. James Buchanan
(see This Year In the Nation/Mar. 4)

E. E. Rawson (see Also this year ...)

Dred Scott
(see This Year In the Nation/Mar. 6)

THIS YEAR IN THE NATION

Violence in Kansas continues; "Mormon War" breaks out in Utah Territory ... **Mar. 3:** Tariff reduced to lowest rate since 1850, in response to Southern demands ... **Mar. 4:** James Buchanan inaugurated as 15th president ... **Mar. 6:** Dred Scott case decided by U.S. Supreme Court, which declares slaves to be property which cannot be denied by an act of either Congress or a state government, making popular sovereignty unconstitutional ... **May 20:** Pres. Buchanan sends federal troops to Utah which is declared to be in a state of rebellion ... **June 17:** Commercial agreement between U.S. and Japan negotiated ... **Sept. 16:** Contract for overland mail service between St. Louis and Memphis to San Francisco and Los Angeles arranged between federal government and private company ... **Oct. 13:** Constitution adopted and application for statehood made by residents of Minnesota ... **Oct. 15:** Anti-slavery majority elected to new Kansas legislature.

1858

January	Luther J. Glenn elected mayor.
January 8	Atlanta's best-known military organization, the "Gate City Guard," is organized.
March 5	A petition signed by some 200 Atlantans, presented to City Council, protests the use of slave labor in industrial plants because "their masters reside in other places, and … pay nothing to the support of the city government, and whose Negro mechanics can afford to underbid the regular resident citizen mechanics … to their great injury …"
June 25	City Council offers $25,000 and 1,000 acres of land to get the University of the South to locate in Atlanta. The move fails and the school goes to Sewanee, TN.
December 11	The Legislature sets aside $100,000 annually from the net earnings of the W&A Railroad to build public schools for white children ages 8 to 18, but the onset of the Civil War forces years-long delays in shaping such a system.

Also this year: The Hibernian Benevolent Society and the Old Guard are organized … The city's first public park is developed, in the area bounded by the passenger depot, Decatur, Pryor and Loyd (now Central) Sts.

THIS YEAR IN THE NATION

Year of famous Lincoln-Douglas debates in which the issue of the expansion of slavery is thoroughly discussed … **Jan. 4:** Kansas voters hold elections for governor and other officials and soundly defeat pro-slavery constitution … **Feb. 3:** In a Senate debate John Hammond of South Carolina declares "cotton is king" and that the South can get along without the North … **May 11:** Minnesota becomes the 32d state … **June 17:** Abraham Lincoln opens his campaign for the Senate seat held by Stephen Douglas with a speech in which he quotes the Biblical warning that "A house divided against itself cannot stand" and adds "this government cannot endure permanently half slave and half free" … **Aug. 2:** Kansas voters again reject a pro-slavery constitution … **Aug. 21:** First of seven Lincoln-Douglas debates takes place at Ottawa, IL; debates continue with the last taking place on Oct. 15 in Alton, IL … **Oct. 16:** The poem, "The Courtship of Miles Standish" by Henry W. Longfellow, published … **Dec. 20:** John Brown heads a raid into Missouri to free 11 slaves; one man killed.

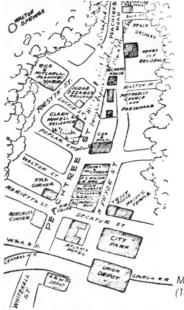

Mayor Luther J. Glenn (see January)

Map of downtown Atlanta (1858; see Also this year . . .)

Home of Lemuel P. Grant, built in 1858, used as Confederate hospital in 1864; Grant Park is named for this pioneer who supervised construction of Atlanta's defenses in 1864.

1859

January 23	Luther Glenn re-elected mayor; pledges reduction of city debt, and better police services.
February 15	New paper, Southern Confederacy, appears.
February 22	Tallulah Fire Co. #3 is organized.
April	Census reports Atlanta's population of 11,500 … An Atlanta city directory is published.
May 20	City Council issues an order requiring free blacks to post bonds of $200 to live in the city, or be liable to indenture.
July 15	City Council receives a petition from white dentists objecting to the presence in Atlanta of a black dentist (Roderick D. Badger). They request that his practice be stopped. Council ignores the petition, and Badger practices until his death in 1891.
July 19	A meeting of several Atlantans sets forth establishment of a private female institute (or college) whose first building is erected on a corner of Courtland and Ellis Sts. in 1860. The building is used as a Confederate hospital starting in July, 1863, and the girls continue their education in the Neal home (Washington and Mitchell Sts.) until the spring of 1864, when the school expires. (Gen. Sherman makes the Neal home his headquarters.)
November 28	Hook and Ladder Company #1 is organized.

THIS YEAR IN THE NATION

Feb. 14: Oregon admitted into the Union as 33d state … **May 9-19:** Commercial convention in Vicksburg, MS, calls for reopening of the slave trade … **June 10:** Gold discovered in present-day Nevada; the Comstock Lode, as it came to be known, is considered the single biggest gold strike in history … **Aug. 27:** First oil well begins producing near Titusville, PA … **Oct. 16:** John Brown, with the intention of fomenting a slave revolt, leads a raid on the U.S. arsenal at Harpers Ferry, Virginia; four of his men are killed, others captured … **Oct. 18:** Col. Robert E. Lee, leading a force of Marines, captures Brown; two of Brown's sons are among the others killed … **Nov. 2:** John Brown found guilty of murder, treason and criminal conspiracy and sentenced to death … **Nov. 8:** Ralph Waldo Emerson calls Brown "that new saint" in a lecture delivered in Boston … **Dec. 2:** John Brown hanged … **Dec. 5:** Charles Sumner of Massachusetts returns to his Senate seat after a three-year absence due to injuries sustained from blows delivered by Rep. Preston Brooks.

John Neal residence, built in 1859, was used, starting in 1873, as Girls' High School, and stood on the site of the present City Hall until demolished in 1929.

Jeweler Er Lawshe, who crafted the City Council's first seal, erected this home in 1859 on the west side of Peachtree Street next to the northwest corner of Cain. Occupancy of the house by the Lawshe family continued until his death in 1897; the structure gave way to business in 1913.

Abolitionist John Brown (see This Year In the Nation/Oct. 16)

1860

January 13	Mayor's salary raised from $500 to $1,000 per year.
January 20	William Ezzard inaugurated as mayor to third term.
January 31	Local merchants hold first meeting to consider an association to withdraw patronage from Northern merchants. On February 24 merchants form a "mercantile association" partly for the purpose of "remedying the present unjust discrimination against our city, in freights and commerce of the city." The organization is the forerunner of the Chamber of Commerce.
March 4	Central Presbyterian Church is dedicated.
April 18	Atlanta's oldest labor union, Typographers #48, is chartered.
June 24	New Masonic Lodge dedicated. Destroyed by fire May 1, 1866.
October 30	Stephen A. Douglas, U.S. Senator and candidate for President, speaks in Atlanta, arguing against secession.
October 31	Minute Men Association of Fulton County, a home military unit, organizes to defend states' rights, and defend honor and home against "a black Republican government."
November 6	In the presidential election Atlantans cast 1,070 votes for Bell, 835 for Breckinridge, and 336 for Douglas. Abraham Lincoln elected.
November 8	Minute Men, on hearing of Lincoln's election, meet and resolve that "the time has come for us to assert our rights, and we now stand ready to second any action that the sovereign State of Georgia may take in asserting her independence by separate State action, or in unison with her sister States of the South in forming a Southern Confederacy."
December 7	City Council, at the petition of David Mayer, president of the Hebrew Benevolent Congregation, donates six 15x30 foot lots to Atlanta's Jews for burials in the city cemetery (Oakland).
December 22	Minute Men fire a 15-gun salute celebrating South Carolina's secession from the Union, and Lincoln is burned in effigy.

Also this year: Various publications, all short-lived, are launched, including the Educational Repository and Family Monthly, the Hygienic and Literary Magazine, the Georgia Weekly, the Lita National, and the Southern Dental Examiner.

THIS YEAR IN THE NATION

With the election of Lincoln, the South moves toward secession ... **Feb. 22:** Shoemakers in Lynn and Natick, MA, strike for higher wages ... **Apr. 3-13:** First pony express run from St. Joseph, MO, to Sacramento, CA ... **Apr. 23-May 3:** Democratic Party convention fails to nominate a president because of withdrawal of southern delegates ... **May 9-10:** Constitutional Union Party, made up of remnants of American and Whig parties, nominates John Bell of Tennessee for president ... **May 16-23:** Republican Party convention nominates Lincoln for president and adopts free-soil platform ... **June 18-23:** Democratic Party nominates Stephen Douglas for president and adopts platform that advocates popular sovereignty ... **June 28:** Southern delegates who withdrew from Democratic convention, calling themselves National Democrats, nominate John Breckinridge of Kentucky for president ... **Nov. 6:** Republican Abraham Lincoln wins election with a majority of the electoral votes but only a plurality of the popular vote ... **Dec. 8:** Howell Cobb of Georgia resigns as Secretary of Treasury ... **Dec. 20:** Special state convention in South Carolina approves unanimously an ordinance dissolving the union between South Carolina and the U.S. ... **Dec. 30:** The seizure of the U.S. arsenal in Charleston, SC, completes the state's occupation of all federal facilities in Charleston area except for Fort Sumter.

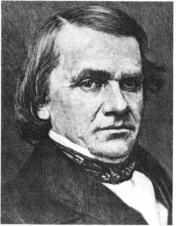

Stephen A. Douglas (see Oct. 30)

Pres. Abraham Lincoln (see This Year In the Nation/Nov. 6)

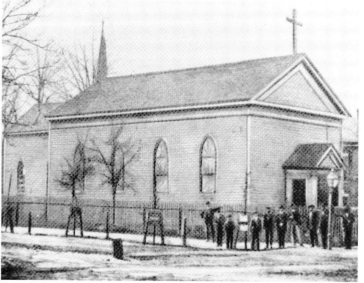

Original Church of the Immaculate Conception in 1860 (corner of present-day Central Ave. and Martin Luther King, Jr. Boulevard)

1861

January 2   Fulton County elects three delegates to the state secession convention scheduled for January 16 at Milledgeville.

January 3   In the late afternoon Atlanta sustains a 10-second shock of an earthquake … Georgia Volunteers organize.

January 17   Jared Whitaker elected mayor in a bitter contest in which he is opposed by the incumbent, William Ezzard.

January 19   Convention delegates vote 208-89 in favor of the state's ordinance of secession. Georgia becomes the fourth state to withdraw from the Union.

February 9   Georgia's Alexander H. Stephens chosen Vice-President of the Confederacy, in Montgomery, AL.

February 16   Newly-named president of the Confederacy, Jefferson Davis, visits Atlanta briefly, and attends a reception at the Trout House (near Five Points).

February 26   The first draft of men from Atlanta for the regular army of Georgia — 18 soldiers — leaves for Savannah.

March 12   Confederate Vice-Pres. Stephens is feted at the Atlanta Hotel.

April 1   Former Mayor William Ezzard, now a captain of troops, leads the Gate City Guard to garrison duty at Pensacola, FL.

April 19   An Atlanta Committee of Public Safety is organized to take care of soldiers' families.

April 27   A group of Atlanta doctors offer their services, free, to destitute families of citizens serving in the Confederate military.

June 3   A bank convention gathers to consider Confederate money problems.

August   By this time 11 companies of volunteers from Atlanta and Fulton County are in Confederate service.

November 25   Mayor Whitaker resigns to serve as Georgia's commissary-general; Thomas Lowe is elected to complete his term.

Also this year: Robert J. Lowry, 21, opens a private bank and wholesale grocery.

THIS YEAR IN THE NATION

Jan. 19: Georgia votes to secede … **Jan. 21:** Five southern senators, including Jefferson Davis, leave Washington … **Jan. 29:** Kansas is admitted as 34th state … **Feb. 4:** Six Confederate states meet in Montgomery and on Feb. 9 elect Davis president and Alexander H. Stephens of Georgia vice-president … **Mar. 4:** Lincoln inaugurated as 16th president … **Mar. 11:** Convention in Montgomery adopts Confederate constitution … **Apr. 12:** Confederates begin shelling Ft. Sumter after Union commander refuses to evacuate … **Apr. 13:** Ft. Sumter surrenders … **Apr. 15:** Lincoln proclaims state of insurrection … **Apr. 17:** Virginia secedes … **Apr. 19:** Lincoln declares blockade of the South … **Apr. 20:** Robert E. Lee resigns his commission in the U.S. Army and two days later assumes command of Virginia troops … **May 6:** Confederate Congress declares war exists with U.S. … **May 20:** Confederate capital moved to Richmond … **July 21:** First Battle of Bull Run is a Confederate victory … **Aug. 5:** Lincoln signs first national income tax law … **Oct. 24:** Transmission of first transcontinental telegraph message … **Nov. 8:** Union ship stops British vessel Trent and removes Confederate commissioners Mason and Slidell … **Dec. 26:** Trent crisis with Great Britain ends when cabinet decides to release Mason and Slidell.

Mayor Jared I. Whitaker (see Jan. 17)

Jefferson Davis (see Feb. 16)

1862

January 15	James Calhoun elected mayor.
February	Atlanta begins to fill with sick soldiers, some of the large hotels and public buildings being appropriated for hospitals.
April 12	Union spy James J. Andrews and 21 compatriots steal a locomotive, the General, at Big Shanty (near Kennesaw) and race toward Chattanooga, seeking to interrupt the rail lines as they flee. They are captured five miles short of their goal by Confederates on the pursuing locomotive named Texas.
May 14	Atlanta becomes a military post; martial law established August 11.
June 2	Union spy Andrews escapes from an Atlanta jail, but is captured the next day.
June 7	Andrews is hanged (near the present-day intersection of Third and Juniper Sts.). He is buried under a nearby pine, but in 1887 his remains are exhumed for burial in the National Cemetery at Chattanooga.
June 18	Seven other Andrews' raiders are hanged in Atlanta (near the present intersection of Memorial Drive and Park Ave.). The Union's first Medals of Honor are later awarded to all the Andrews' raiders.
September 3	Right of habeas corpus is suspended in Atlanta.
October 16	Eight of Andrews' raiders escape Fulton County jail, and reach Union lines; the remaining six prisoners are exchanged as prisoners of war in March 18, 1863.
October 16	All Atlanta conscripts between 18 and 45 years of age are called to arms.
December 3	James Calhoun re-elected mayor.
December 26	City Council orders the construction of a smallpox hospital. The disease has reached almost epidemic proportions.
	Also this year: Atlanta has become a prime center for the manufacturing of war materiel including buttons, belt buckles, spurs, saddles, canteens, tents, railroad cars, revolvers, cannon, gun carriages, knives, etc.

THIS YEAR IN THE NATION

Feb. 5: Julia W. Howe's poem, "Battle Hymn of the Republic," appears in February issue of the "Atlantic Monthly" ... **Feb. 16:** Union forces capture Ft. Donelson in Tennessee ... **Feb. 25:** Nashville occupied by Union forces ... **Mar. 9:** U.S.S. Monitor and C.S.S. Merrimac fight first battle between ironclad ships ... **Apr. 6-7:** Battle of Shiloh is a Union victory ... **Apr. 11:** Ft. Pulaski, near Savannah, falls to Union bombardment ... **Apr. 16:** Slavery in District of Columbia ended ... **Apr. 25:** New Orleans falls to Union naval forces ... **May 20:** Homestead Act passes, grants any adult settler 160 acres of government land ... **June 19:** Slavery outlawed in U.S. territories ... **July 2:** Morrill Land-Grant College Act becomes law ... **Aug. 30:** Second Battle of Bull Run, a Confederate victory ... **Sept. 17-18:** Battle of Antietam ends Lee's first attempt to invade the North ... **Sept. 27:** First unit of free black soldiers is formed in New Orleans to fight for the Union ... **Nov. 5:** Lincoln replaces Gen. George McClellan with Gen. Ambrose E. Burnside.

Mayor James Calhoun (see Jan. 15 and Dec. 3)

Capt. William A. Fuller, whose locomotive, The General, was stolen at Big Shanty, Ga., by Union spy James J. Andrews (see Apr. 12, June 2, June 7, etc.)

James J. Andrews (see Apr. 12, etc.)

1863

February 6 City Council passes a resolution requiring that a red flag be flown at every place where smallpox exists.

February 13 City Council authorizes the police committee to employ as many secret police as the committee thinks is necessary for the public good.

April 17 Military order prohibits the sale of whiskey at retail stores.

May 8 Mayor is authorized to issue a proclamation requesting citizens to organize into military companies to protect the city from such a raid as was made May 3 by Union cavalry on Rome, GA.

July 22 Col. L. P. Grant, Chief Engineer of the Department of Georgia, proposes surveys west of Atlanta as the first step in preparing defensive works for the city.

July 23 Mayor Calhoun issues a proclamation: "In view of the more than probability of an early raid on this city . . . I feel constrained for the third time . . . to call on each of our people to be prepared to defend their homes and property. I do now request every citizen able to bear arms . . . to enroll their names upon some company list . . . "

July 31 The city's police force is organized into a military company.

August 4 Col. Grant reports that fortifications have begun at the Chattahoochee ferries; weeks later he authorizes hiring black slaves from their owners to work on fortifications, at $1 per man per day.

September 22- First federal soldiers captured during fight-
September 26 ing for Chattanooga arrive in Atlanta, as do many Confederate wounded.

September 29 Gen. Howell Cobb named to command state troops, with headquarters in Atlanta.

THIS YEAR IN THE NATION

Jan. 1: Lincoln signs Emancipation Proclamation by which he declares all slaves in areas of rebellion are free ... **Mar. 3:** Conscription act drafting all males between 20 and 46 becomes Union law; allows for some exceptions and substitutions ... **Mar. 3:** National Academy of Sciences established by U.S. Congress ... **Apr. 2:** Bread riots in Richmond ... **May 1-4:** Battle of Chancellorsville is a Confederate victory, though Gen. T. J. "Stonewall" Jackson is killed accidentally by one of his own men ... **June 20:** West Virginia becomes 35th state; created out of northwestern part of Virginia ... **July 1-3:** Battle of Gettysburg; Lee's second invasion of North fails ... **July 4:** Vicksburg surrenders; Union controls all of Mississippi River, cutting Confederacy in two ... **July 11-18:** Draft riots in New York City ... **Sept. 9:** Union forces occupy Chattanooga ... **Nov. 19:** Lincoln gives Gettysburg Address at dedication of National Cemetery there ... **Nov. 23-25:** Battle of Chattanooga; Union forces drive Confederates out of Tennessee and open way to Atlanta ... **Dec. 8:** Proclamation of Amnesty and Reconstruction, a moderate plan of reconciliation for the South, issued by Lincoln.

October 30 Line of defenses around Atlanta virtually complete.

December Mayor Calhoun elected to a third term, the city's first chief executive so honored.

Also this year: City codes include the following restrictions against blacks: "Sec. 286. No person shall hire, lend or deliver any horse or horses, or any gig, sulky, buggy, or carriage of any kind to any slave or free person of color, without a written order from the owner, employer, or agent of such slave or free person of color, and any person convicted of a violation of this section of this Ordinance shall pay a fine of not exceeding fifty dollars and costs. . . Sec. 288. No slave or free person of color shall sell or hawk any beef, cake, fruit or confectionery, in any of the streets or alleys of this city; and any violator, shall on conviction, pay a fine of not exceeding five dollars and costs, or be punished by whipping, not exceeding thirty-nine lashes. . . Sec. 292. No man slave or person of color shall walk with cane, club or stick (unless blind or infirm), nor smoke a pipe or cigar in any street, lane, alley, or on the square used by the State; and, upon conviction of a violation, of any part of this section, such slave or person of color shall receive not exceeding thirty-nine lashes."

Col. L. P. Grant (see July 22)

Gen. Howell Cobb (see Sept. 29)

Gen. R. E. Lee
(see This Year In the Nation/July 1)

1864

This is the year of Atlanta's greatest trial — the year of its conquest by Union troops commanded by Gen. W. T. Sherman. The General began moving his forces from Chattanooga along the rail line south toward Atlanta in May, successfully besting Gen. J. E. Johnston's inferior numbers until the latter was removed from command by Pres. Davis in July.

February 6   Confederate cavalry Gen. John Hunt Morgan, who escaped a Union prison in Columbus, Ohio, in November, 1863, arrives in Atlanta and is tendered a hero's reception at the Trout House. (Morgan is killed Sept. 4 while on a raid in Tennessee.)

April 22   St. Luke's Episcopal Church consecrated. [It is destroyed in Sherman's burning of the city November 14-15.]

April   The Fulton County Grand Jury's presentments complain of the "insecure" jail, the "intolerable nuisance (of) the slaughter pens in the western end of the city," the fact that "a number of soldiers' families still complain that they do not receive sufficient assistance to furnish them with the necessaries of life," and that "there are a large number of idle and vicious boys strolling about the city . . . frequenting many places of vice . . . "

May 7   Sherman begins his advance south toward Atlanta.

May 15   Sherman wins the Battle of Resaca (north Georgia).

May 23   Mayor Calhoun issues a proclamation calling on "all male citizens . . . capable of bearing arms, without regard to occupation . . ." to report on May 26 to the city marshal for induction into military units. "All male citizens who are not willing to defend their homes and families," the Mayor adds, "are requested to leave the city at their earliest convenience, as their presence only embarrasses the authorities and tends to the demoralization of others."

June-July   In a series of battles on both sides of the spine of the railroad leading to Atlanta, Sherman is successful in repulsing Johnston, the biggest contest being at Kennesaw Mountain, after which Johnston is replaced as commander by Pres. Jefferson Davis, who names Gen. John Bell Hood to lead the Confederate forces.

June 10   Atlanta observes a mayor-proclaimed day of "fasting, humiliation and prayer."

June 15   The remains of Confederate Gen. Leonidas Polk, an Episcopal bishop killed in the Battle of Kennesaw Mountain, are laid on the altar of St. Luke's Episcopal Church.

July 15   Sherman's troops cross the Chattahoochee River.

July 17   Gen. Hood replaces Gen. Johnston as Atlanta's defender.

July 20   Battle of Peachtree Creek is a Union victory; shelling of Atlanta intensifies.

July 22   Battle of Atlanta; two key generals are killed — the Union's James B. McPherson and the Confederacy's William Walker.

July 28   Battle of Ezra Church is a stalemate.

August 20   Union cavalry strike at Jonesboro in an attempt to isolate Atlanta from the deeper South.

August 31-September 1   The Battle of Jonesboro is a Union victory, forcing Confederates to evacuate Atlanta. Hood sets fire to major supply dumps in Atlanta before retreating.

September 2   Mayor Calhoun leads a delegation of a few key citizens to surrender the city to Union troops (at a point marked today at Northside Drive and Marietta Street).

September 7   Sherman orders civilians to evacuate the city despite Hood's protests.

November 14-November 15   The Union army sets fire to Atlanta, and leaves on the "march to the sea." Only 400 structures remain standing, including five churches protected by the pleadings of Father Thomas O'Reilly.

November 26   Confederate troops reoccupy the devastated city.

December 7   After some Atlantans begin returning to the city, Mayor Calhoun is re-elected to office, and finds only $1.64 in the City treasury.

December 10   The Atlanta Daily Intelligencer, a newspaper which had fled weeks earlier to Macon, resumes publishing in Atlanta.

THIS YEAR IN THE NATION

Jan. 11: Sen. John Henderson proposes a constitutional amendment to abolish slavery ... **Mar. 12:** Gen. U. S. Grant made chief of all Union armies ... **Mar. 18:** Arkansas voters approve constitution abolishing slavery ... **Apr. 8:** U.S. Senate approves 13th Amendment ... **May 4-12:** Battle of the Wilderness results in no clear victor but terrible casualties ... **June 8:** National Union Party nominates Lincoln for a second term and Andrew Johnson for vice-president; platform calls for bringing rebellion to an end and the ratification of the 13th Amendment ... **June 18:** Grant begins a siege of Petersburg ... **June 19:** Confederate raider, Alabama, sunk off of France ... **Aug. 23:** With Union's capture of Ft. Morgan, Mobile Bay closed to Confederate shipping ... **Aug. 29-31:** Democrats nominate Gen. George B. McClellan for president; platform contains strong peace plank ... **Sept. 2:** Sherman's forces occupy Atlanta ... **Sept. 5:** Louisiana voters approve constitution that abolishes slavery ... **Oct. 31:** Nevada enters Union as 36th state ... **Nov. 8:** Lincoln reelected ... **Nov. 16-Dec. 20:** Sherman's march to the sea devastates Georgia.

Gen. W. T. Sherman

Gen. J. E. Johnston

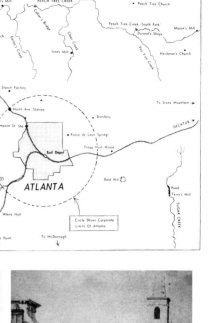

Atlanta, 1864

Confederate Fort "K," 1864 — at the intersection of today's Peachtree and Ponce de Leon Ave.

Ponder House, on Marietta St. near Bankhead Highway, shows effects of Union shelling in 1864.

Neal house (left), Sherman's headquarters in Atlanta, was on the site of today's City Hall.

Union troops tear up rails behind Atlanta's city hall/courthouse: fall, 1864.

Union troops at Five Points, 1864

Burning of a railroad roundhouse in Atlanta, Nov. 14, 1864: part of the Sherman fire which torched the city (see Nov. 14)

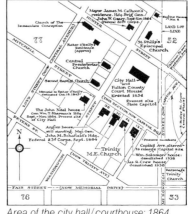

Area of the city hall/courthouse: 1864 (and later dispositions)

Father Thomas O'Reilly (see Nov. 14)

35

1865

January 6   Mayor James M. Calhoun, elected to his fourth consecutive term in the preceding month, takes office.

February 27   Rev. Henry Hornaday opens a school in the basement of the First Baptist Church.

May 13   Union Col. B. B. Egleston orders that all blacks found without passes within the city limits will be arrested and jailed.

May 16   The American flag is officially raised and then lowered to half-mast in honor of the assassinated Pres. Lincoln.

June 17   James Johnson is appointed by Pres. Johnson (no kin) as provisional governor of Georgia.

June 20   Mayor Calhoun issues $20,000 in bonds which circulate as currency.

June 24   In the first public meeting since Sherman's capture, Mayor Calhoun leads the assembly in resolving to restore commercial ties with the North, deploring Lincoln's assassination, and calling for "speedy restoration of all political and national relations."

June   The Atlanta branch of the Freedmen's Bureau establishes food distribution centers (which aid the indigent for two years).

July 7   Union Brig.-Gen. Felix Salm-Salm becomes Atlanta's military governor. (The Prussian prince dies in 1871 during the Franco-Prussian War.)

July 14   The Atlanta City Council adopts an ordinance promising equal application of laws to whites and blacks.

September 2   Former Confederate Gen. Alfred Austell organizes the Atlanta National Bank, first such institution in the South; it opens December 9 and he remains its president until his death in December, 1881.

September 14   Atlanta National Bank (predecessor to First National) chartered.

November   Atlanta Medical College resumes classes.

December   James E. Williams elected mayor.

Also this year: The Daily New Era, newspaper, begins publication . . . A school for black children opens in the fall in an old church building on Armstrong St., the first such institution for blacks.

Peachtree St., looking north from the railroad crossing, 1865

Alfred Austell (see Sept. 2)

Atlanta National Bank (see Sept. 2)

Jeweler Er Lawshe (right) stands proudly by his store, erected May, 1865, the first commercial structure built after war's end (at 47 Whitehall St.).

THIS YEAR IN THE NATION

Jan. 31: House of Representatives passes 13th Amendment ... **Jan. 31:** Lee named head of all Confederate armies ... **Feb. 17:** Sherman captures Columbia, SC ... **Feb. 22:** New Tennessee constitution abolishes slavery ... **Mar. 3:** U.S. Congress creates the Freedmen's Bureau ... **Mar. 4:** Lincoln inaugurated for the second term ... **Mar. 13:** Pres. Davis signs law allowing blacks to become soldiers in the Confederate army ... **Apr. 2:** Petersburg evacuated ... **Apr. 3:** Surrender of Richmond ... **Apr. 9:** Lee surrenders to Grant at Appomattox Court House ... **Apr. 14:** Lincoln shot while attending the theatre; dies the next day ... **Apr. 15:** Andrew Johnson takes oath of office and becomes the 17th president ... **Apr. 26:** Lincoln's assassin, John W. Booth, killed ... **May 10:** Jefferson Davis captured near Irwinville, GA ... **May 29:** President Johnson issues proclamation of amnesty for Confederates who take oath of allegiance ... **Oct. 2:** Capt. Henry Wirz, commandant of Andersonville (GA) prison, hanged for atrocities committed against Union prisoners ... **Nov. 24:** Mississippi legislature passes first black codes to control newly freed slaves ... **Dec. 18:** 13th Amendment becomes law.

1866

January 8 W. M. Bray opens his private Male and Female School (tuition: $5 per month), and Mrs. V. F. Bessent's Atlanta Female Institute (tuition $5 monthly) opens same day. By year's end Atlanta has 22 private schools, no public ones.

January 19 City Council orders temporary hospital built to contend with smallpox epidemic, and gives $10,000 to the Relief Committee for the emergency.

February 23 Legislative act authorizes incorporation of Atlanta Street Railroad Company, but reality of streetcars is years away.

March 9 Atlanta Mining and Rolling Mill Co. incorporated; business fails in 1877. Nearby streets, Gray and Kennedy, named for two of the principals, John D. Gray and Allen Kennedy.

March 12 Legislature approves act extending Atlanta's corporate limits to radius of 1½ miles from the passenger depot (alongside present-day Underground Atlanta).

April 12 Meeting held to reorganize the Board of Trade, originally launched in 1860 but dormant during war years. Board of Trade renamed Chamber of Commerce in 1871.

April 15 Atlanta Ladies' Memorial Assn. formed to recognize April 26 (the day of Gen. J. E. Johnston's surrender to Gen. W. T. Sherman) as a Confederate Memorial Day, marked by placing flowers on the graves of Confederate soliders.

Spring Capt. Tom Burnett, proprietor of the Ice House, organizes the Atlanta Baseball Club, the city's first, and challenges all comers. Rival team, Gate City Nine, wins their first contest (May 12) by 127-29, and the original Atlanta Club soon disbands. The Gate City Nine's tally for the 1866 season: 35 wins, 1 loss.

September 15 Atlanta Gas Light Co. resumes illuminating Atlanta; gas service has been interrupted since Sherman's destruction of the city in November, 1864.

October First Italian opera performs in Atlanta. "There is quite an opera fever prevailing here," one diarist records the event. "But the two dollars each stands in the way of our attendance . . . "

Fall — Georgia National Bank opens; forced to suspend operations in 1877.
— Vincent Tommey, Joseph Stewart and Gustavus Orr open hardware firm in which Lewis Beck is a "utility boy," and where William Gregg becomes bookkeeper in 1869. In 1878 Beck and Gregg purchase the firm, rename it for themselves.
— Three key hotels open this year: the American, the Planter's Hotel (both early in 1866), and the National (in May).

December 5 James E. Williams re-elected mayor.

December 12 Legislative act approves a public-school system, but it does not get underway, due to lack of funds, until 1873.

December 15 Daily Era (newspaper) reports gold found in Randall Mill Road area, but it's too little to justify serious mining.

December Legislature approves hiring of convicts by private firms; in May, 1868, first contract for such labor (100 men for a total of $2500 a year) is signed with the Georgia and Alabama Railroad. Begins chain-gain system, which is finally abolished in 1909.

Also this year: In this postwar year it's reported there are 250 businesses functioning, with annual sales of $4.5 million. Population: 10,940 whites, 9,288 blacks. Says the City Director: "This city, within the past two years, has risen out of her own ashes . . ." Among the desirable changes in street names: Crap's Alley becomes Trebursey St. (now Tatnall).

THIS YEAR IN THE NATION

Jan. 8: Rep. Samuel Shellabarger outlines in a speech to the House what will become the Congressional approach to reconstruction ... **Feb. 19:** Johnson vetos bill to expand Freedmen's Bureau ... **Mar. 17:** Johnson vetos civil rights bill that would extend equal protection to freed slaves ... **Apr. 9:** Congress passes civil rights bill over Johnson's veto ... **Apr. 30:** Race riots in Memphis between white residents and black federal troops result in 47 blacks being killed ... **May 10:** At meeting of National Women's Rights convention, Susan B. Anthony declares that "the Negro and woman now hold the same civil and political status, alike needing only the ballot" ... **June 16:** Proposed 14th Amendment passes Congress and goes to states for ratification ... **June 20:** Joint Committee of Fifteen makes its report to Congress; claims that Congress, not the president, has authority over reconstruction ... **July 24:** Tennessee restored to Union ... **July 30:** Race riots break out in New Orleans ... **Aug. 30:** National Labor Union organized to seek an 8-hour workday ... **Sept. 7:** Atlantic cable laid between Ireland and Newfoundland.

James E. Williams (see Dec. 5)

1867

January 1 — Visiting Rabbi Isaac Leeser urges Atlanta Jews attending a wedding to organize a congregation; in mid-June the Hebrew Benevolent Congregation is underway as the city's first.

March 2 — Congress passes Reconstruction Act and later makes Atlanta headquarters of the Third Military District.

March 31 — Gen. John S. Pope arrives to command the Third Military District and is honored with a dinner April 12 ("Our Pope," goes one toast, "may he be as infallible as the law has made him powerful.")

May 28 — Nineteen-year-old Morris Rich opens a modest store at 36 Whitehall St.

Spring — First Atlanta soda fountain opens in the Redwine & Fox drug store at the corner of Whitehall and Alabama Sts.

June 30 — The Young Men's Library Association is formed; first meeting is August 19.

August 11 — Following an organizational meeting this date comes the formation of the Georgia Teachers Assn.

August 12 — Gen. Pope bans City advertising in newspapers not favoring Reconstruction.

August 19 — Gen. Pope issued order giving blacks the right to serve on juries.

September 20 — When the Lincoln National Monument Assn. requests a donation from Atlanta to establish a park and monument, the city agrees to make the gift after the Association collects $750,000—a sum it never reaches.

September 21 — The U.S. Government leases the Race Track property (southwest of central city) as a site for soldier encampments; it is later the locus of Ft. McPherson, but part of the property becomes the site of Spelman College.

September — Frederick Ayer completes formation of a black public school (named after him initially, then called Summer Hill School).

October 15 — A charter is granted for the formation of Atlanta University, and Edmund Ware is named president.

December 9 — Constitutional Convention begins sessions in Atlanta (meetings run to March 11); Gen. Pope orders Mayor Williams to remain in office another year.

December 28 — Pres. Johnson issues the order relieving Gen. Pope from his command in Atlanta.

Also this year: The Atlanta Mirror of Life, devoted to amusement, romance and humor, appears in August but soon dies. The Atlanta Daily Opinion, a newspaper supporting Republicans, also begins but dies before year's end.

Atlanta's first steam fire engine, The Castalia, bought by Atlanta (Volunteer) Fire Co. #1, in 1867

Pres. Andrew Johnson (see Dec. 28)

Gen. John S. Pope (see Mar. 31)

THIS YEAR IN THE NATION

Tensions over reconstruction increase between Pres. Johnson and Congress ... **Jan. 7:** Resolution of Rep. James Ashley to empower Judiciary Committee to consider impeachment passes House of Representatives ... **Jan. 8:** Black male residents of District of Columbia given right to vote; legislation passes over Pres. Johnson's veto ... **Mar. 1:** Nebraska becomes 37th state ... **Mar. 2:** First Reconstruction Act passes over Pres. Johnson's veto; it divides the South into five military districts ... **Mar. 29:** First published account of the Ku Klux Klan appears in a Pulaski, TN newspaper ... **Mar. 30:** Treaty signed between U.S. and Russia by which U.S. purchases Alaska for $7.2 million ... **May 13:** Jefferson Davis released on $100,000 bail pending trial ... **July 19:** Second supplementary Reconstruction Act, giving military commanders in Southern states power to determine voter eligibility, passes over Pres. Johnson's veto ... **Aug. 28:** Midway Islands annexed by U.S. ... **Dec. 4:** National Grange (also known as The Order of the Patrons of Husbandry) organized in Washington, D.C.

1868

January 13	Gen. George G. Meade, who replaced Gen. Pope as military commander in Atlanta, removes Gov. Jenkins and State treasurer John Jones from office for refusing to pay $40,000 of the costs of the Constitutional Convention. (Earlier Jenkins went to Washington with the executive seal of the State and about $400,000, which he placed in New York to secure the public debt.) Gen. Meade names Gen. Thomas H. Ruger as provisional governor.
February 27	Constitutional Convention approves the idea of Atlanta as the new state capital subject to approval by citizens who vote in April on the new constitution.
March 7	Rufus Bullock receives Republican nomination for governor.
March 11	Constitutional Convention adjourns.
April 4	Former Confederate Gen. John B. Gordon nominated Democratic candidate for governor.
April 20-24	Despite Ku Klux Klan activities aimed at intimidating black voters, the new constitution is approved, Bullock is chosen first Republican governor, and Atlanta is approved as the new state capital.
June 16	Carey Styles, publisher, issues first edition of The Atlanta Constitution.
June 28	By order of Gen. Meade, Provisional Gov. Ruger is to be succeeded by Gov.-elect Bullock on July 4, the date of the first meeting of the Legislature under the new constitution.
June 30	City Councilman W. B. Cox leaves for Milledgeville with a train of 16 cars to transfer the furniture of the state Capitol to the new Capitol in Atlanta.
July 4	First meeting of Legislature draws crowds, and no real business is done until July 6.
July 21	Legislature ratifies 14th Amendment.

July 22

On this, the fourth anniversary of the Battle of Atlanta, Gov. Bullock is formally inaugurated. "We return to the Union," editorializes The Atlanta Constitution that day, "under a Constitution and a state government which has no foundations in the affection of our people . . . By the enfranchisement of the lowest class . . . and the wholesale disenfranchisement of our best citizens, we have certainly taken a retrograde movement . . . "

July 23	So-called "Bush Arbor" meeting of Democrats (near old Underground Atlanta) ventilates anger of people at the Reconstruction government. Thousands applaud five hours of speeches by such as Robert Toombs and Benjamin H. Hill.
July 29	Joshua Hill and Dr. Homer Miller elected U.S. Senators by the Legislature.
August 14	City Council proposes (and Legislature approves) use of the Kimball opera house as the temporary state Capitol.
August	Gen. Meade leaves the city, since direct military rule has been withdrawn.
September	Legislature defies Gov. Bullock and expels its black members—25 from the House, three from the Senate, on the grounds that under the State Constitution blacks are ineligible to hold office. (They are reinstated the next year by the State Supreme Court.)
October	Moore's Business College opens with nine students.
December 2	William Hulsey elected mayor.
December 17	Edwin Payne deeds a Hunnicut St. lot for a new church, Payne's Chapel.

THIS YEAR IN THE NATION

Conflict between Pres. Johnson and Congress comes to a head in an impeachment trial ... **Feb. 24:** Resolution to impeach Johnson for high crimes and misdemeanors passes House of Representatives 126 to 47 ... **Mar. 11:** Congress passes third supplementary Reconstruction Act which provides that a new state constitution may be ratified by majority of persons actually voting ... **Mar. 26:** Jefferson Davis charged with treason but trial postponed ... **May 11-26:** Impeachment trial of Pres. Johnson; Johnson is found innocent by one vote ... **May 20-21:** Republican Party nominates U.S. Grant for president; platform supports Congressional reconstruction ... **June 22:** Arkansas readmitted to the Union; six other Southern states follow three days later ... **July 4-9:** Democrats nominate Horatio Seymour for president; platform opposes Congressional reconstruction ... **July 28:** 14th Amendment to Constitution ratified ... **Aug. 11:** Radical Republican leader Thaddeus Stevens dies; he is buried, as he wished, in a black cemetery in Lancaster, PA ... **Nov. 3:** Grant elected president ... **Dec. 25:** Pres. Johnson proclaims pardon without reservations for those accused of treason against the U.S.

Gen. George G. Meade (see Jan. 13)

Carey Styles (see June 16)

William H. Hulsey (see Dec. 2)

1869

January 12	Public opening of the Kimball opera house (southwest corner of Marietta at Forsyth St.) preparatory to its use as the temporary state Capitol (a role it served until the new Capitol, present-day structure, opened in 1889).
March 18	Legislature adjourns after voting against ratification of the 15th Amendment (thus encouraging Gov. Bullock to go to Washington to seek renewal of military jurisdiction).
March 30	City purchases 47½ acres on Marietta Street to be developed as fair grounds (later known as Oglethorpe Park).
April	Georgia Railroad freight depot completed at what becomes the entrance of old Underground Atlanta (on old Alabama St.).
April	Atlanta tongues went wagging this month with the contemporary report listing 1868 incomes of some prominent citizens. Top name: John Rice, who reportedly earned $35,127.
May 3	Major civic event this date, a parade and contest among volunteer fire companies to see which one could throw water the farthest. In the hand-engine class Tallulah Company No. 3 won by tossing a stream 221 feet.
September 2	Cornerstone laid for the brick building housing the Church of the Immaculate Conception.
September 24	City Council passes a resolution to name a committee to look into establishment of a public school system (which is recommended later in the year). But such a system does not get underway until 1873.
November 7	Dedication of the First Baptist Church building, then on the site of the old postoffice (Walton at Forsyth Sts.).
December 1	William Ezzard elected mayor.
December 10	Dr. Albert Hape (whose brother later founds Hapeville) and Prof. Samuel A. King ascend in the balloon Hyperion, a local "first."

THIS YEAR IN THE NATION

Jan. 19-20: First National Women's Suffrage Convention meets in Washington, D.C. ... **Feb. 27:** Congress passes 15th Amendment and sends it to the states to be ratified ... **Mar. 4:** Ulysses S. Grant inaugurated as 18th president ... **Apr. 7:** Cincinnati Red Stockings, the first all-professional baseball team, opens its season ... **Apr. 13:** Patent for airbrakes for railroads granted to George Westinghouse ... **Apr. 16:** Ebenezer Don Carlos Basset, first black in U.S. diplomatic service, appointed Minister Resident and Consul General to Haiti ... **May 10:** First transcontinental railroad completed; tracks meet at Promontory Point, Utah ... **Sept. 1:** National Prohibition Party founded ... **Sept. 24:** "Black Friday" — financial panic caused by the manipulation of the price of gold ... **Dec. 9:** Knights of Labor founded.

December 22 The federal government returns Georgia to military jurisdiction, requiring also that it remain that way until the Legislature approves the 15th Amendment, at which time Georgia would be readmitted to the Union. "We regard the measure as an unspeakable evil," editorialized the Atlanta Constitution this date, but "we are not dismayed and ... we shall do our best to maintain the interest and welfare of Georgia in her travail and humiliation."

Also this year: The Freedman's Aid Society of the Methodist Episcopal Church organizes a coeducational black school that becomes Clark College ... Third Baptist Church (later Jones Avenue Baptist Church) is organized.

Also this year: John Smith Company founded.

Kimball opera house (see Jan. 12)

Georgia Railroad freight depot (see April)

1870

January 2   Atlanta University, officially opened last October, launches its second term. So many students appear that some dormitory rooms have five occupants.

January 10   Gov. Rufus Bullock calls the Legislature to convene with members elected in 1868 attending. Blacks then elected are later expelled.

January 14   Afraid of losing control, Gov. Bullock names a military board to investigate eligibility of legislators who oppose him.

February 3   Concerned citizens launch plans for endowment of Oglethorpe University, earlier situated near Milledgeville.

March 14   Plans are made to erect First Methodist Church, as successor to Wesley Chapel, on a site later occupied by the Candler Building.

June 3   Officials of four competing rail lines agree to build for joint use a new depot that will be 350 feet long, 120 feet wide.

June 18   Dr. Samuel Bard launches the Daily True Georgian newspaper, soon converted to a weekly.

July 15   Having ratified the 15th Amendment in February, Georgia is readmitted to the Union.

October 4   Oglethorpe University opens, with 11 instructors.

October 15   At the Capitol solemn ceremonies mourn the October 12 death of Gen. Robert E. Lee.

October 18   Newspaper stories compliment H. I. Kimball on near-completion of his splendid new hotel, equipped with central heat plus safety elevators.

October 21   20,000 persons visit the Georgia State Fair at Oglethorpe Park.

October 25   Incorporation of East Point is approved by the Legislature.

October 27   John H. James' Peachtree Street residence, called "the finest in Georgia," is acquired for use as the Governor's Mansion.

November 3   Five acres once owned by the Western & Atlantic Railroad are sold at auction; much of it goes for $300 per front foot.

November 13   Rock Springs Presbyterian Church is organized.

December 1   City Treasurer John H. Mecaslin reports assets of $841,000 — just $17,000 less than bonded debt.

December 7   Dennis F. Hammond, labeled a radical, is elected mayor; two members of the City Council are black, its first. Nine square miles in area, the city now has a population of 21,789.

December   Ex-Gov. Joseph E. Brown heads an investment group that gains control of the lucrative Western & Atlantic Railroad.

THIS YEAR IN THE NATION

Jan. 10: John D. Rockefeller and associates organize the Standard Oil Co. of Ohio with a capitalization of $1 million … **Feb. 25:** Hiram R. Revels, Republican from Mississippi becomes first black to be seated in the U.S. Senate … **Mar. 30:** 15th Amendment declared to be in effect … **May 13:** Force Bill passes Congress to oppose terrorist opposition to black advances in the South … **July 14:** Tariff bill lowering rates on mostly raw materials passes Congress … **July 15:** Georgia readmitted to the Union, the last Southern state to do so … **Oct. 12:** Robert E. Lee dies at 63 … **Dec. 10:** Wyoming gives the vote to women and allows them to hold public office … **Dec. 12:** Joseph H. Rainey of Georgetown, SC, is first black to be seated in the U.S. House of Representatives.

Gov. Rufus Bullock (see Jan. 10)

Rev. William M. Finch, one of the city's first two black councilmen (see Dec. 7)

The Kimball House (see Oct. 18)

1871

January	Atlanta Gas Light Co. establishes a rate of $5 per thousand cubic feet of coal gas; four years later that rate will drop to $4.
January	An inventory by the Western & Atlantic Railroad lists 44 locomotives valued at $166,000. One of them, #60 is named U. S. Grant.
February	Elected in 1868, Georgia Senators H. V. M. Miller and Joshua Hill are finally seated in Washington.
March 23	Irish-born Dan Lynch, 30, becomes the city's first volunteer fireman to die while fighting a blaze.
April 25	George W. Adair and Richard Peters organize a street railway company; the first two-mile line will be built to McPherson Barracks.
May 29	Contracts are let for a $130,000 waterworks. (It will be completed in 1875 at $226,000.)
May	The Baptist Orphans' Home is organized with ex-Gov. Brown serving as a trustee.
August 7	Prodded by troubles with the railroad, leading citizens organize the Atlanta Chamber of Commerce.
September 8	With Col. L. P. Thomas as conductor, the new street cars run from 7 a.m. to 10 p.m., offering today only free rides to the public.
October 2	Organization of Gate City Co. #5, equipped with a hand engine, brings the number of volunteer fire fighters 60% above the 1870 level.
October 23	Gov. Bullock, fearing prosecution for corruption, resigns suddenly and flees the state. Editor Samuel Bard of The Daily True Georgian is credited with having driven him from office.
November 15	Savannah-born Bernard Mallon begins his service as first superintendent of Atlanta Public Schools.
November 29	Legislators name a committee to examine the vacant Governor's Mansion, to make an inventory of "house and kitchen furniture, silverware, and other articles" left behind by the "absconded" governor.
December 15	By Act of Legislature, the city court is created.
December	A business census shows 76 physicians, 50 saloons, 46 lawyers and law firms, 28 butchers, 20 billiard tables, eight wagon yards, one skating rink — plus many other professional and mercantile establishments.

THIS YEAR IN THE NATION

Feb. 24: With the seating of the senators from Georgia, the South has full federal representation for the first time since the beginning of the Civil War ... **Feb. 28:** Second Force Bill, which puts national elections under the control of the federal courts, passes Congress ... **Mar. 3:** Congress creates Commission on Civil Service Reform ... **Apr. 10:** Promoter and showman P. T. Barnum opens his Great Traveling Museum, Menagerie, Caravan and Hippodrome in Brooklyn ... **Apr. 20:** Third Force Bill passes Congress; it calls for penalties for those who violate the 14th Amendment ... **Apr. 30:** Mob massacres over 100 Apaches under military protection in Camp Grant, AZ ... **May 24:** Senate ratifies Treaty of Washington which sets up commission to arbitrate claims of U.S. against Great Britain over Confederate raiders ... **Oct. 10:** Great Chicago fire ends; 300 persons killed, 90,000 left homeless ... **Dec. 16:** William M. "Boss" Tweed arrested for corruption.

Atlanta, 1871 (the view is north and the main street snaking to the top is Marietta)

Bernard Mallon (see Nov. 15)

D. F. Hammond, mayor, 1871

Grant Building (center, background) on Walton St., 1871

1872

January 30   With exercises held at the Ivy Street School, the municipal system opens. Within a month Boys High, Girls High, Crew School and Walker Street schools are in full operation. Enrollment reaches 2,090 — more than twice the estimated number.

February   Congress passes an appropriations bill that includes $100,000 for a post office and federal court building in Atlanta.

April 26   Newspaper stories bestow lavish praise upon the brand new Fulton County jail, which includes 12 cells "supplied with water and water closets."

May 14   John M. Armistead, owner of Ponce de Leon Springs, begins delivering bottled water, by wagon, from the springs "distanced about two miles from the city."

May 24   George W. Adair and Richard Peters are paid $16,000 for a lot at the corner of Peachtree and Walton Streets — a profit to them of $1,000 from a purchase made just 60 days earlier.

June 17   Ground is broken for a new building at Whitehall and Peters, for Trinity Methodist Church.

August 8   George W. Adair's Ponce de Leon Street Railway begins operation, adding to service provided by his Decatur Street and Peachtree lines.

August 22   Alexander St. Clair-Abrams launches The Atlanta Daily Herald. Within 90 days the new paper will bring Henry W. Grady to the city.

August 24   Merger of the Macon & Western Railroad with the Central Railroad and Banking Co. creates the Central of Georgia Railroad.

November 8   Citizens Bank of Georgia is organized; it will open for business on January 5 and bring first day deposits of $133,000.

October   Robert Toombs volunteers to head a team of prosecuting attorneys who will seek conviction of ex-Gov. Bullock on charges of corruption and dishonesty.

December 31   Launched this year as a municipal system, the city's two high schools and seven grade schools now serve 2,075 students.

THIS YEAR IN THE NATION

Feb. 2: First Tuesday after the first Monday in November fixed by Congress for Congressional elections ... **Mar. 1:** Yellowstone National Park established by Congress ... **Mar. 5:** Commission appointed by Pres. Grant to study plans for interoceanic canal in Colombia ... **May 1:** Liberal Republicans, dissidents from regular Republican Party, hold convention and nominate editor Horace Greeley for president ... **May 22:** Amnesty Act passes Congress; restores civil rights to all but approximately 600 former Confederates ... **June 5-6:** Republican Party nominates U.S. Grant for second term ... **July 9-10:** Unable to agree on a candidate, Democrats decide to support Horace Greeley, nominee of the Liberal Republicans ... **Nov. 5:** Susan B. Anthony arrested when she attempts to vote in presidential election ... **Nov. 5:** Grant wins a second term ... **Nov. 9:** Fire in Boston kills 13 and destroys much property ... **Dec. 11:** Pinckney Benton Stewart Pinchback becomes acting governor of Louisiana; he is the first black governor in U.S. history.

The center of Atlanta, 1872; Looking north along Whitehall from the tracks

Street railway launched (see Aug. 8)

Trinity Methodist Church (see June 17)

Robert Toombs (see October)

National Surgical Institute, 1872

The new, postwar City Hall (on the site of today's Capitol)

1873

January 1 Western & Atlantic Railroad Pres. Joseph E. Brown recommends an immediate start toward conversion of the line's locomotives from coal to wood.

January 6 A carnival, sponsored by the Mystic Brotherhood, attracts thousands. Modeled after New Orleans' Mardi Gras, it is called "a brilliant success" by newspaper editors.

February 1 Republic Block, built for commercial rental by Chicago's Republic Life Insurance Co., attracts as original tenants the Chamber of Commerce plus merchants who deal in everything from boots and shoes to diamonds.

March 1 Launched with 25 charter members, the Turn Verein offers "mental and physical development." It is a member of the nationwide Turner organization.

March 25 John B. Gordon, seated in the U.S. Senate on the 11th, becomes the first ex-Confederate to preside over that body.

May 30 Painter William Bradbury wins a contract to number all houses of the city with black-enameled tin signs. He will receive $720 for the job.

June 23 The Young Men's Christian Association is organized, with the goal of "elevation of the moral character of young men by opposition to evil influences."

July 1 Charles V. Tutwiler makes the first free delivery of a letter to grocer John C. Hallman. It is at the insistence of Postmaster J. L. Dunning that houses are numbered so free delivery could begin.

July Thomas Jones becomes first chief of police. He heads a force of 26 men who wear tin helmets and coat uniforms of Prince Albert type.

THIS YEAR IN THE NATION

Year of financial crash brought on by speculation and overextension ... **Feb. 12:** Congress stops coinage of silver when value of bullion exceeds that of the face value of the coin ... **Mar. 3:** An act promoted by Anthony Comstock that prohibits the mailing of obscene materials passes Congress ... **Mar. 4:** Pres. Grant inaugurated for second term ... **Apr. 14:** U.S. Supreme Court decides Slaughterhouse case which limits federal protection of black civil rights ... **May 1:** Post office issues one-cent postal card ... **Aug. 18:** Mt. Whitney, highest peak in the nation, climbed for first time ... **Sept. 8:** Banking house of Jay Cooke and Co. declares bankruptcy, precipitating the Panic of 1873 ... **Oct. 18:** First football conference attended by Yale, Princeton, Rutgers and Columbia drafts code of rules ... **Nov. 19:** Boss Tweed convicted on 102 counts of fraud ... **Nov. 27:** Hoosac Tunnel in Massachusetts, second longest in the world, completed.

August 26 A telegram announces completion of the Air Line Railroad, giving "unbroken iron links between Atlanta and Charlotte." Passenger service will begin at once — as far as Toccoa. September 5 will see extension of passenger service all the way to Charlotte.

September 5 Pioneer citizen William R. Venable, a resident since 1848, leaves nine children at his death. Two of them are later the owners of Stone Mountain.

December 10 Four years after laying of its cornerstone, the Church of the Immaculate Conception is dedicated after outlay of nearly $80,000 in construction costs.

December 31 A local census taken in this dark year of panic shows "a bona fide population of 30,869."

Banker John H. James Peachtree Street home, used by the state as the Governor's Mansion

John H. James: The home of this 1872 mayor became the Governor's Mansion

C. C. Hammock, mayor in 1873, 1875 and 1876

1874

February 15 An immense bridge having been built over Clear Creek, the Peachtree Street Railway extends all the way to Ponce de Leon Springs; the Whitehall Street Railway begins operation today.

February 28 Gov. James M. Smith signs legislation granting the city a revised charter. Authority of the mayor is strengthened and separate boards are created to oversee police, municipal schools and water works.

February Hannibal I. Kimball, who fled the city when the Reconstruction government fell apart, returns to face a special investigator and a grand jury. Vindicated by the jury, he is strongly supported by editor Henry W. Grady — who says Atlanta needs men with enterprise plus business skill.

March 3 Atlanta University gets from the Legislature a promise of an annual appropriation of $8,000.

March 14 Editor Henry W. Grady of The Atlanta Daily Herald publishes a statement that includes the term "The New South."

March 27 Atlanta University's first formal annual budget calls for $5,200 in salaries, $500 for fuel, $200 for farming and implements and $840 for operation of a system that forces water to the institution from the valley below.

April 26 Having raised $8,000 during four years, the Ladies' Memorial Association proudly unveils in Oakland Cemetery a granite shaft that memorializes "Our Confederate Dead."

May 28 Officials deny a formal petition that asks for instruction of Catholic pupils by Catholic teachers.

June Congress adds $175,000 to the earlier appropriation of $100,000 for erection of a federal building in Atlanta.

July 5 Newspaper publisher Alexander St. Clair-Abrams launches The Daily News. (It folds in two years.)

THIS YEAR IN THE NATION

May 8: Massachusetts passes law that limits workday for minors and women to 10 hours ... **May 16:** Collapse of Ashfield reservoir dam kills over 100 in Massachusetts ... **June 20:** Territorial government of the District of Columbia is replaced by three commissioners appointed by the president ... **July 4:** Largest arch bridge in world opened for traffic in St. Louis ... **Aug. 4-18:** First Chautauqua held in Chautauqua, NY ... **Nov. 7:** First use of the elephant as symbol of the Republican Party appears in Harper's Weekly ... **Nov. 18:** Woman's Christian Temperance Union organized ... **Nov. 24:** Patent for barbed wire granted to Joseph F. Glidden ... **Nov. 25:** Greenback party organized; platform calls for currency inflation and an end to specie payment.

August 22 Newspaper accounts laud Hapeville as "A New and Delightful Suburban Retreat, and Promising Fruit Centre."

November 4 J. H. and W. B. Seals launch The Sunny South as a literary weekly.

December 2 Cicero C. Hammock becomes the first mayor elected to a two-year term, under provisions of the new city charter.

Atlanta Street Railway (see Feb. 15)

Henry Grady (see Mar. 14)

Mayor S. B. Spencer, 1874

Hannibal I. Kimball (see February)

1875

January 4	Police Chief Thomas G. Jones, head of a 47-man force, reports that "Atlanta is no longer the rendezvous of thieves and criminals."
January 25	Chief Jones, whose report urged that pay of police lieutenants be increased to $100 a month and that of patrolmen to $75 a month, is fired.
January	Mayor Cicero Hammock works at restoration of the city's credit and simultaneous reduction of interest rates from a high of 18%. He persuades a New York brokerage house to accept 7% city bonds.
February 27	An Act of Legislature authorizes the city to pay up to $50,000 for a lot on which to construct a federal building — Postoffice plus Courthouse.
March 1	Worst downpour in the city's history, accompanied by high winds, flattens houses and barns as well as cemetery headboards and tombstones.
March 2	Atlanta Saving Bank is incorporated, with capital of $500,000.
March 23	The Atlanta Constitution reports passage of an ordinance requiring owners of cows to keep them enclosed at night. Vagrant animals, impounded, can be bailed out for $2.
March 25	A long-sought dam, essential for the municipal waterworks planned for 20 years, reaches a height of 51 feet above the bed of Poole's Creek.
August 21	Ground is broken for the Postoffice and Courthouse.
September 11	Testing the new water system, put in service today, firemen throw hundreds of gallons of water above the 153-foot flagstaff of the Kimball House hotel.
October	Transportation lines form the Southern Railway and Steamship Association. Albert Fink, first commissioner, establishes offices in the Kimball House.
November 14	Episcopal Bishop John W. Beckworth preaches the first sermon in newly-completed St. Luke's Cathedral, seating capacity 450.
November 16	The Markham House hotel opens at noon with 107 sleeping rooms — 22 of which "are heated by fire or steam as desired."

THIS YEAR IN THE NATION

Jan. 14: Specie Resumption Act, which reduces paper money in circulation to $300 million, passes Congress ... **Jan. 30:** U.S. and Hawaii sign a commercial treaty ... **Mar. 1:** Civil Rights act, guaranteeing blacks equal rights of public accommodations and conveyances and prohibits exclusion of blacks from jury duty, passes Congress ... **Mar. 15:** John McCloskey becomes first American to be named cardinal in Roman Catholic Church ... **Mar. 30:** In Minor v. Happersett, Supreme Court says that right to vote not protected by 14th Amendment ... **May 3:** U.S. joins Universal Postal Union ... **May 17:** First running of the Kentucky Derby ... **Sept. 10:** American Forestry Assn. organized ... **Dec. 6:** 44th Congress convenes; first time since 1859 that Democrats have a majority in the House of Representatives though Republicans retain majority in Senate.

Peachtree St., looking south from Auburn Ave.; buildings on left are on present-day site of Woodruff Park

Old Hunter St. (now Martin Luther King Blvd.), looking east; building in upper right is the Church of the Immaculate Conception, completed 1873.

Fulton County Prison (1875)

46

1876

January 8	A sanitary commission is established to deal with problems of waste disposal.
January 21	Actor Edwin Booth, brother of the assassin of Abraham Lincoln, plays "Hamlet" to an S.R.O. audience.
February 22	Henry W. Grady and a partner launch the Herald newspaper; it survives fewer than three weeks.
June 22	Six males form the first graduating class of the collegiate department, Atlanta University.
August 2	Democrats name Alfred H. Colquitt to run for governor, opposed by Atlanta entrepreneur Jonathan Norcross, a Republican.
August	Refugees crowd into the city by the hundreds, fleeing yellow fever in Savannah.
October 18	E. Y. Clarke sells his half interest in The Atlanta Constitution to Evan P. Howell, who immediately hires Henry W. Grady as managing editor.
October 19	Henry Grady employs Joel Chandler Harris, a yellow fever refugee, as editorial paragrapher at $25 per week.
November 15	Republican gubernatorial candidate Norcross loses to his Democratic opponent by 77,854 votes.
December 6	In an election with "no crowds, no liquor, no quarreling," Dr. N. L. Angier captures a majority of 189 votes and becomes mayor.
December 31	Busy replacing old iron rails with new ones of steel, the Western & Atlantic Railroad this year brought 200,000 tons of the tough metal from one of Andrew Carnegie's mills at Pittsburgh.
December 31	Having purchased State National Bank, whose property alone is worth $200,000, the new Merchant Bank is headed by Campbell Wallace.

THIS YEAR IN THE NATION

Feb. 2: National League of professional Base Ball Clubs is organized ... **Mar. 10:** Alexander G. Bell receives patent for telephone ... **Apr. 20:** American Chemical Society organized ... **May 10:** Centennial Exposition opens in Philadelphia ... **May 18:** First national convention of Greenback Party; platform calls for the repeal of the Specie Resumption Act ... **June 14-16:** Republicans nominate Rutherford B. Hayes for president; platform calls for sound-money policy ... **June 25:** Massacre of Gen. George Custer and his men at Little Big Horn by Sioux under Sitting Bull ... **June 27-29:** Democrats nominate Samuel J. Tilden for president ... **Aug. 1:** Colorado admitted as 38th state ... **Oct. 6:** American Library Assn. founded ... **Nov. 7:** In presidential election Tilden wins popular vote but is one vote short of victory in electoral college ... **Dec. 5:** Fire in Conway's Theatre in Brooklyn kills almost 300 ... **Dec. 14:** Wade Hampton becomes governor of South Carolina ending reconstruction in that state.

Old Alabama St. (where trolley stands) cuts across Pryor; this is the site of Underground Atlanta, 1876

Joel Chandler Harris (see Oct. 19)

Alfred H. Colquitt (see Aug. 2)

An ad of 1876

47

1877

January 25	Attorney Julius L. Brown leads in reorganization of the Beethoven Society.
March 5	A stiff ordinance provides for a fine of up to $100 for driving more than five unhaltered mules through the streets during business hours.
March 6	Portrait artist John Maier, a native of Germany dies at his residence; descendants establish Maier & Berkele.
June	A statewide election, launched by a bill sponsored by Allen D. Candler, calls for a Constitutional Convention to be held.
July 11	Under leadership of Charles Jenkins, the Constitutional Convention convenes in the State House on Marietta St.
August 11	Facing dissolution for lack of funds, the Constitutional Convention accepts a loan of $20,000 from Robert Toombs.
August 31	Its cornerstone having been laid two years earlier, the city's first synagogue is dedicated as the Hebrew Benevolent Congregation (The Temple).
September 22	Rutherford B. Hayes becomes the first incumbent U.S. president to visit the city.
November	A telephone line, first in the city, links Union Station with the depot of the Western & Atlantic Railroad.
December 5	By 110,442 to 40,947 voters of the state approve the new Constitution; by a majority of 43,946 they simultaneously decide that the Capitol will remain in the city.
December 31	Interest charges on the municipal debt amount to $168,780.37 for the year ending today; cost of fire and police protection plus schools totals $56,518 during the past 12 months.

THIS YEAR IN THE NATION

With the election of Republican Hayes, reconstruction comes to an end ... **Jan. 9:** Electoral Commission established by Congress to settle who won the contested presidential election of 1876 ... **Mar. 1:** In Munn v. Illinois, U.S. Supreme Court rules that a state can regulate a private business if it affects the public interest ... **Mar. 2:** Electoral Commission names Rutherford B. Hayes as winner of 1876 election ... **Mar. 5:** Hayes inaugurated as 19th president ... **Mar. 5:** Pres. Hayes appoints David Key of Tennessee as Postmaster General, the first southerner in the cabinet since the Civil War ... **Apr. 10:** Federal troops leave Columbia, SC ... **Apr. 24:** With departure of federal troops from New Orleans, reconstruction ends ... **June 14:** Flag Day established on 100th anniversary of first U.S. flag ... **July 17:** Large-scale strike of railroad workers begins in Martinsburg, WV.

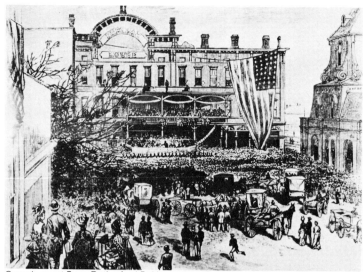

Crowds greet Pres. Rutherford B. Hayes (see Sept. 22)

Hebrew Benevolent Congregation synagogue (See Aug. 31)

Thomas G. Healey, chosen president of Atlanta Gas Light Co. in 1877

Healey Building, opened in 1877 at Marietta and Peachtree Sts. (demolished 1930)

Forsyth St., looking south (1877): in upper center is the site of today's Rich's

1878

January 1 — Ben Hill postoffice, named for the famous statesman, opens for business at Mt. Gilead Cross Roads.

January 27 — Thomas Alexander, a native of England, dies. Having made and lost and regained fortunes, he leaves behind Fulton County's first $500,000+ estate.

April 2 — Atlanta University reports cash gifts of $25 or more, totaling $25,996.41 since October 1, 1869.

April 17 — Delegates to the International Sunday School Convention begin arriving from most states and Canada for a three-day convention.

October 1 — A weather office is established in the Kimball House hotel, with Harry Hall in charge.

December 4 — With newspapers pushing for citizens to go to the polls, 4,569 cast votes in the contest for mayor. Lifelong resident William L. Calhoun, son of the wartime mayor, wins with 2,509 votes.

December 31 — Nieces of George Washington's half-brother, Lawrence, are satisfied that they did the right thing in starting a school in their home. Soon it will be called Washington Seminary.

December 31 — Sponsored by a missionary society, Atlanta Baptist College ends the year with something new—its first catalog, listing names of students who have attended since 1867.

December 31 — Having held services in a one-room house at Gammage's Crossing, the Rev. F. B. Davies — city missionary — takes pride in knowing that a church is in process of organization. It becomes Park Street M. E. Church, South.

THIS YEAR IN THE NATION

Jan. 10: Constitutional amendment giving women the right to vote introduced in Congress for the first time ... **Jan. 14:** In Hall v. DeCuir, U.S. Supreme Court rules that Louisiana law outlawing segregation on riverboats is unconstitutional ... **Feb. 19:** Thomas A. Edison receives patent for the phonograph ... **Feb. 22:** Greenback Labor Party organizes and calls for free coinage of silver, shorter work week and limitation on Chinese immigration ... **Feb. 28:** Bland-Allison Act, which requires the federal government to purchase between $2 million and $4 million of silver each month for coinage, passes over presidential veto ... **Apr. 16:** In Reynolds v. U.S., Supreme Court rules that Mormons do not have a First Amendment right to practice polygamy ... **June 11:** New government for District of Columbia denies residents right to vote in either local or national elections ... **July 11:** Pres. Hayes begins program to ferret out corruption and institute civil-service reforms ... **Aug. 21:** In Congressional elections Democrats win majorities in both houses of Congress for the first time since 1858.

December 31 — Though only eight years old, the Frank E. Block Candy Co. now has capacity to produce 40,000 pounds of candy per day plus 20,000 pounds of crackers.

December 31 — Organized this year, the White Hickory Wagon Co. will reach a production level of 8,000 drays, spring wagons, and log wagons per year.

U. S. Postoffice and Custom House (shown in 1895) was under construction in 1878. In 1910 it was purchased for use as the City Hall, serving that purpose 20 years, after which the structure at Marietta and Forsyth Sts. (now site of Bank South) was demolished.

First Presbyterian Church, at 95 Marietta St., was erected in 1878.

1879

January 29	Gen. William T. Sherman reaches the city by train in mid-afternoon; he attends an evening ball at McPherson Barracks.
February 21	Dr. Thomas S. Powell secures a charter for the Southern Medical College.
March 7	Among salaries established today by the city council is $1,350 per annum for chief of police—who is required to furnish his own horse.
April 1	Labelled "Atlanta's best drive" by the Constitution, a street is opened to link Decatur Street with Ponce de Leon. Editors are confident it will be named to honor Judge Daniel Pittman; instead, it becomes simply Boulevard, NE.
May	Gate City National Bank, with capital of $100,000, succeeds the Atlanta Savings Bank, founded in 1875.
July 26	A double ax murder, never solved, takes the lives of Martin and Susan DeFoor.
July	No longer a wanted man, ex-Gov. Bullock is back in the city to launch a movement that will result in organization of the Atlanta Cotton Mills.
August	Major W. F. Slayton is named superintendent of schools—a post he will hold for 28 years.
October	Moved from Augusta last year, Atlanta Baptist College changes it name to Seminary and finds housing in Friendship Baptist Church.
November 1	Dr. Powell's Southern Medical College begins its first term, with 64 students enrolled.
December 31	At year's end 30 patrolmen on the police force continue to draw monthly salaries of $54 each.
December 31	Readers throughout the nation have had their attention called to Atlanta by the December issue of "Harper's New Monthly Magazine."

Enjoying an outing—and the mineral water—at the Ponce de Leon springs

Interior of the Marietta St. library of the Young Men's Library Association (1879)

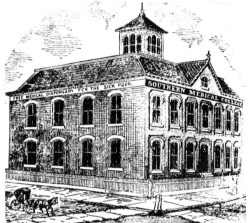
Southern Medical College (see Nov. 1)

W. F. Slayton (see August)

"The Raven," declared Harper's Monthly of December, 1879, is a character around Atlanta's Union Station who "croaks dismal forebodings of fatality and sells accident policies to travelers."

THIS YEAR IN THE NATION

Jan. 1: Federal government resumes specie payment ... **Feb. 15:** Law enacted that allows female attorneys to argue before the U.S. Supreme Court ... **Feb. 22:** First "five-cent store" opened by Frank W. Woolworth and partner in Utica, NY ... **Mar. 3:** U.S. Geological Survey established by Congress ... **May 1:** Pres. Hayes vetos bill to restrict Chinese Immigration ... **May 7:** State constitution adopted by California forbids the employment of Chinese ... **May 8:** Patent for horseless carriage applied for by George B. Seldon ... **June 16:** First Gilbert and Sullivan operetta performed in U.S. opens in New York ... **June 28:** Mississippi River Commission established by act of Congress; its function is to improve navigation on the river ... **Dec. 31:** Thomas A. Edison demonstrates first pratical incandescent lamp at his laboratories in Menlo Park, NJ.

1880

January 1   This year's municipal officers include two cemetery guards, two overseers of the chain gang, and a keeper of the powder magazine.

January   Atlanta Baptist Seminary, later Morehouse College, moves from temporary quarters in Friendship Church to its own new brick building.

February 1   Chrisman Hall, on the campus of Clark University, is dedicated.

February 28   Saints Peter and Paul, the city's second Roman Catholic church, is opened.

April 21   St. Joseph's infirmary is launched in a Collins Street residence by two Sisters of Mercy.

August 30   Officials having threatened to cut off street lights, they receive official notice that the charge for coal gas will be reduced to $23 per year per light.

August   Holding the state convention in the capital city, Democrats split and end by having a second candidate nominated by a minority faction.

September 9   A petition is filed for a new public road nearly three miles long; in time it will be West Peachtree Street.

September   School opens with 3,328 pupils enrolled; an additional 300 children between six and seven years of age find there is no room for them.

October 20   Crowds flock to the fair in Oglethorpe Park in order to see "five or six electric lights burning with great but varying brilliance."

October 28   Speaking in the Senate chamber of the Capitol, Edward Atkinson of Boston challenges the city to hold a great cotton exposition.

November 3   Having formally organized, the Legislature quickly elects ex-Gov. Joseph E. Brown to the U.S. Senate.

December 31   Year's end sees a U.S. Census count by which the city has in a decade gained 15,620 residents to become Georgia's largest, with 37,409 persons.

December   Joel Chandler Harris publishes a slim volume that is the first of a series dealing with the songs and sayings of Uncle Remus.

Also this year: Morris Brown College founded.

St. Joseph's Infirmary (see Apr. 21)

The Kimball House (hotel), depicted in 1880; it burned in 1883.

Parochial school of Sts. Peter & Paul Church; school children (seen in 1880) used the home of J. G. W. Mills (southeast corner of Marietta and Alexander Sts.) for classroom (see Feb. 28)

THIS YEAR IN THE NATION

Tenth decennial census shows that the U.S. has a population of over 50 million, an increase of over 25% since 1870 ... **Jan. 27:** Patent for incandescent lamp granted to Thomas A. Edison ... **Feb. 4:** Realistic drama "Hazel Kirke" by Steele MacKaye opens in New York; this marks the beginning of the shift away from romantic drama in America ... **Mar. 1:** Supreme Court rules that blacks cannot be barred from serving on juries ... **Mar. 24:** Salvation Army in U.S. founded in Philadelphia ... **Mar. 31:** Electricity first used for street lights in Wabash, IN ... **June 2-8:** Republican Party nominates James A. Garfield for president on 36th convention ballot ... **June 22-24:** Democratic Party nominates Winfield Scott Hancock for president ... **Nov. 2:** James A. Garfield elected president ... **Nov. 8:** Sarah Bernhardt begins her American tour in New York.

1881

January 1 Start of the new year sees an addition to the roll of municipal officers; a street lamplighter begins work at a salary of $1,700 per year.

February 16 Sarah ("The Divine") Bernhardt plays in "Camille" at the opera house.

April 10 Bishop John W. Beckwith takes charge of debt-troubled St. Luke's and makes it his cathedral.

April 11 Atlanta Baptist Female Seminary opens with 11 students; it soon moves from Friendship Baptist Church to McPherson Barracks and becomes Spelman Seminary.

May 21 Clark Howell is in the chair for the first meeting of the new county commission of Roads and Revenues; commissioners will be paid $100 per year.

July 7 Newspaper stories berate the city fathers for "Our Streets—and their miserable condition."

September 19 For the first time, hacks are required to carry license tags and to place license numbers upon driving lights for night visibility.

September 24 Southern Bell having bought a small private operation, the city's first telephone switchboard exchange is opened.

October 5 A model cotton factory 720 feet long is the main building of the long-planned exposition. With seven foreign countries represented, it is the nation's first international fair.

November 7 Responding to complaints, council members pass an ordinance providing for a fine of $100 for splitting a funeral procession.

November 18 John B. Gordon drives the first spike for the Georgia Pacific Railroad, designed to link the city with the coal fields of Alabama.

December 7 Financier and entrepreneur Alfred Austell dies.

December 31 The cotton exposition headed by Hannibal I. Kimball closes as planned in spite of pleas to continue into the new year; average paid monthly attendance was 195,518.

James English, mayor, 1881

Fulton County Courthouse, erected 1881, dedicated 1883, demolished 1911

St. Philip's Cathedral (then at the northeast corner of Washington and Hunter Sts.); erected 1881; demolished 1936.

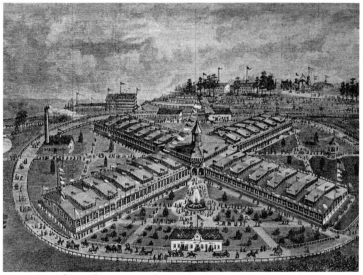

International Cotton Exposition at Oglethorpe Park (see Dec. 31)

THIS YEAR IN THE NATION

Feb. 10: Tuskegee Institute chartered ... **Mar. 4:** James A. Garfield inaugurated as 20th president ... **May 21:** American Red Cross founded by Clara Barton and others ... **July 2:** Pres. Garfield shot by disappointed office seeker Charles J. Guiteau ... **July 20:** Sioux chief Sitting Bull surrenders to Federal authorities ... **Aug. 1:** University of Texas is organized ... **Aug. 2:** Samuel Gompers and associates organize Federation of Organized Trades and Labor Unions ... **Sept. 19:** Pres. Garfield dies at 49 ... **Sept. 20:** Chester A. Arthur takes oath as 21st president ... **Nov. 14:** Trial of assassin Charles J. Guiteau opens.

1882

January 1	A newly-created board of health, with five members, takes office.
January 1	Now being assembled, the new East Tennessee, Virginia & Georgia Railroad, which will be operating before year's end, will offer competitive service linking Atlanta with Chattanooga and Macon.
January 21	Fire destroys the Block Candy Co. factory; it is the last major blaze fought by volunteer firemen.
March 4	Exposition Cotton Mills is incorporated with $250,000 capital; among the financial backers is Constitution publisher Evan P. Howell.
April	Smallpox breaks out in the black ghetto of Beaver Slide; before it ends in July, 110 cases will be reported.
April	During this spring season, newspaper agitation for more and better parks persuades Col. L. P. Grant to offer 100 acres for such use.
May	Virginia-born Woodrow Wilson, having earlier selected Atlanta as the city in which to launch a legal career, arrives and finds office space at 48 Marietta Street.
May	Volunteer firemen, 200 strong, hold their last formal banquet at the National Hotel.
August 16	Sen. Benjamin H. Hill dies at his Peachtree Street home; 20,000 march in his funeral cortege.
October 15	First services are held in St. Philip's Episcopal cathedral.
October 19	After appearing in court to take examinations, Woodrow Wilson is admitted to the bar.
November 15	Alexander H. Stephens is inaugurated as governor in DeGive's Opera House.

THIS YEAR IN THE NATION

Jan. 2: Standard Oil Trust is reorganized so that it controls 90% of the oil refining capacity in U.S. ... **Feb. 7:** John L. Sullivan knocks out Paddy Ryan to become the bare-knuckle boxing champion of the world ... **Feb. 25:** Congress enlarges size of House of Representatives from 293 to 325 ... **Mar. 24:** Henry W. Longfellow dies at 75; most popular American poet of 19th century ... **Mar. 29:** Knights of Columbus founded in New Haven, CN ... **Apr. 3:** Outlaw Jesse James killed at 36 by member of his own gang ... **May 6:** Chinese Exclusion Act, which suspends immigration of Chinese and denies citizenship to all foreign-born Chinese, passes over Pres. Arthur's veto ... **Sept. 4:** Pearl Street electric power station in New York begins operation; built by Thomas Edison, it is the first electric utility in U.S. ... **Nov. 6:** Lily Langtry makes her American debut in "As You Like It" in New York.

December 28	Seven volumes of municipal records, including deeds and mortgages, are reported stolen—and never found.
December 31	Organized this year with Jesse Rankin as president, the new Metropolitan Street Railway Co. plans to build lines into the rapidly-developing southeastern part of the city.
December 31	Oglethorpe graduate George E. King, launching what will become King Hardware Co., discovers that his first year in business has brought a loss of $1,839.
December 31	With the New Year about to begin, the city has 426 gas street lights in operation plus 51 old oil-burning lamps.
December 31	Completed and occupied during the year, the new Fulton County Courthouse is built at a cost of about $100,000.

Gov. Alexander H. Stephens (see Nov. 15)

Steam Engine Co. #4, Atlanta Fire Department, 1882

Looking north up Forsyth St. from the Walton St. intersection; First Baptist Church (with spire) stood on present site of the old postoffice.

1883

January 1   Fire Chief Matt Ryan reports that for the six months ended yesterday, cost of the 26-man paid department was $26,815.65; during the period, they fought 129 fires.

February 9   St. Luke's cathedral, a new building, holds first worship services.

February 24   Tennessee native Edward F. Hoge launches an evening newspaper, The Atlanta Journal, from 14 W. Alabama St., at 10¢ per week - payable weekly.

March 4   Gov. Alexander H. Stephens dies. Hyatt M. Patterson, founder of a distinguished funeral home, is congratulated on "the most successful large funeral" ever held in the city.

March 27   The Church of Our Father, Unitarian, is organized.

March   Organized this month, the Nine O'Clock German Club holds its first ball in the Kimball House—with dancing beginning promptly at 9 p.m.

April 16   Eighty-two business and social leaders launch the organization of the Capital City Club; they have about $4,000 with which to start.

May 17   The new Fulton County Courthouse is dedicated.

June 14   Officials of Atlanta University report that the institution owns 10 cows, four horses, some calves and "plenty of pigs."

June 16   After a successful membership drive, the Chamber of Commerce purchases new property at Pryor and Hunter Streets, for $14,340.

August 12   About 4:30 a.m., the Kimball House catches fire, leading to what some call "the biggest blaze since Sherman." Edward Hoge's infant newspaper, The Journal, scores a coup by publishing the city's first extra edition.

September 8   An act of Legislature authorizes the building of a new Capitol at a cost not exceeding $1 million.

October 5   The Chamber of Commerce wins formal incorporation.

November 12   Under the dynamic leadership of Hannibal I. Kimball, ground is broken for a new Kimball House Hotel.

December 18   At Clark University, Gammon Hall is dedicated.

December 31   With organization of the West End and Atlanta Street Railroad completed this year, the city now has four street railroad companies.

THIS YEAR IN THE NATION

Mar. 3: Congress authorizes construction of three steel cruisers, the first American warships to be built since Civil War ... **Mar. 24:** First long-distance telephone service begins, between New York and Chicago ... **May 25:** Brooklyn Bridge, longest suspension bridge in world, is opened ... **Sept. 8:** Second transcontinental railroad completed, to Portland, OR ... **Oct. 15:** Civil Rights Act of 1875 declared unconstitutional by Supreme Court ... **Oct. 22:** Metropolitan Opera House opens in New York ... **Nov. 18:** U.S. is divided into four time zones.

Mayor John B. Goodwin (1883 and 1893)

Atlanta Journal offices (see Feb. 24)

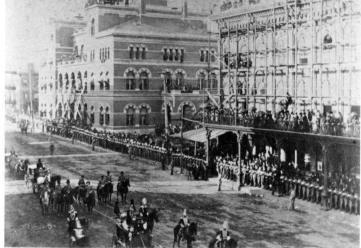

Funeral procession on Marietta St. for Gov. A. H. Stephens (see Mar. 4)

Ruins of the Kimball House (see Aug. 12)

1884

January 24	Starting with $1,500, newly-arrived Joseph Jacobs, 24, purchases a drug store that marks the beginning of a chain.
January	Construction having been completed this month at a cost of $145,000, the Gate City Bank will occupy "the finest bank building in the city."
March 30	Newspaper stories identify H. I. Kimball, George W. Adair and Richard Peters as investors behind a plan to develop Peters Park — a subdivision modeled after Chicago's Pullman subdivision.
June 28	Numerous leading citizens are among incorporators of a new cemetery, West View, located "four miles from the city" and launched with 577 acres purchased at an average of $45 per acre.
July	Newspapers announce plans to launch a Southern baseball league that will include Atlanta, Nashville, Memphis, Little Rock and other cities; an organizational meeting will be held in November.
August 6	Officials of the telephone exchange proudly announce that it now has 450 patrons; the only long-distance service, to Decatur, involves a charge of 15¢ for each five minutes.
September 12	At McPherson Barracks a temporary camp is established for the use of Florida troops during the malaria season.
October 15	The 30-year-old combination City Hall and Fulton County Courthouse building is sold at auction for $975.
November 7	News comes that the election of Democrat Grover Cleveland has been confirmed. Editor Henry W. Grady, who has had a miniature brass cannon made for the purpose, fires it. He then leads a jubilant crowd to the Capitol and forces adjournment of the Legislature.
November 13	With the old City Hall now demolished, workmen begin excavating for the new state Capitol.

THIS YEAR IN THE NATION

Jan. 1: "The Adventures of Huckleberry Finn" by Mark Twain published ... **Mar. 13:** 112 die in coal mine disaster in Pocahontas, VA ... **May 17:** Congress changes Alaska from unorganized territory to the District of Alaska administered by an appointed governor ... **June 3-6:** Republicans nominate James G. Blaine for president ... **July 8-11:** Democrats nominate Grover Cleveland for president ... **Aug. 5:** On Bedloe's Island in New York harbor, cornerstone of the Statue of Liberty is laid ... **Nov. 4:** Grover Cleveland elected president; first Democrat chief executive since the Civil War.

Also this year: Plans for 200-acre Peters Park are complete. It includes the site of the future Georgia Tech ... The new Calhoun Street School is called the finest in the municipal system; Anna D. Fuller, principal, is being paid $525 per year ... A 2,044-foot artesian well, drilled at Five Points, is providing 200,000 gallons of water per day to supplement the badly strained municipal water system.

Construction (1884) of a holding tank for manufactured gas sold by the Atlanta Gas Light Co. When this tank, between Thurmond and Foundry Sts., was removed during World War II, its structural steel was donated to the war effort.

Editor Henry Grady with Mrs. Bessie R. Johnson (left), granddaughter of Pres. Andrew Johnson, and Mrs. Henry H. Smith, in bathing attire at Cape May, N.J.

New residence of Edward Peters, 179 Ponce de Leon Ave. (1884)

1885

January	Joseph Winship, originally from Massachusetts, reorganizes the machine company he established in 1853.
March 18	Fires of undetermined origin destroy the James Bank Block and the Central Bank Block, both fronting Whitehall Street.
April 30	The now-completed new Kimball House is formally opened. Soon it will boast the city's first hydraulic elevator.
May 19	The National Commercial Convention meets in the city.
June 1	Members of the city council pass an ordinance forbidding any vehicle to cross a public bridge "at a speed greater than a walk;" violation means a fine of $100 or 30 days — or both.
June	Atlanta University reports that 10 years of contributions of 5¢ to $24.95 total $29,757.02.
July 1	The city now has 407 coal-gas street lights in use, along with 136 gasoline lamps.
July 4	Charles S. Atwood launches a newspaper called the Atlanta Evening Capitol.
July 25	Troops from Florida re-establish Camp Mitchell, three miles from the city, and remain until October.
August 10	Tennessee native Edward F. Hoge, founder of the Atlanta Journal, dies soon after having sold the newspaper to John Paul Jones of Toledo, OH.
September 2	Ceremonies mark the setting of the cornerstone of the Capitol.
September 14	By act of Legislature, corporate limits are extended to include the L. P. Grant Park.
October 15	The first class enters Morris Brown College.
October	This month sees a group of German artists arrive; Theodore R. Davis of Harper's Weekly accompanies them. They have come to make studies essential to painting a huge canvas depicting the battle of Atlanta.

THIS YEAR IN THE NATION

Feb. 21: Washington Monument dedicated ... **Feb. 26:** Contract Labor Act that prohibits the immigration of laborers who have agreed to work for the cost of their passage passes Congress ... **Mar. 3:** Post office inaugurates special delivery mail service ... **Mar. 4:** Grover Cleveland inaugurated 22d president ... **Mar. 18:** Bryn Mawr College opens near Philadelphia ... **June 19:** Statue of Liberty arrives in New York from France ... **July 23:** Ulysses S. Grant dies at 63 ... **Aug. 10:** First electric street railroad open in Baltimore.

November 25 By a majority of 228, prohibitionists win in a referendum that will bar liquor from Fulton County. (Pharmacist John S. Pemberton, fearing that his popular French Wine Coca will be affected, stirs up a new mixture he calls Coca-Cola.)

Also this year: The Y.M.C.A. has collected $75,000 toward erection of a building ... For the first time the penny is in circulation; pharmacist Joseph Jacobs brings 3,000 of them from Washington so customers can take advantage of items he offers for 17¢, 29¢, etc. Earlier, the nickel was the smallest coin available here ... Cost of lighting the streets is reported as having increased considerably, amounting to $3,212 for the year ... Year's end sees 12.5 miles of paved streets in the city, along with 56.48 miles of sidewalks.

Second Kimball House (see Apr. 30)

Cornerstone laying for the new state Capitol (see Sept. 2)

Jacobs' Pharmacy, on the site of present-day First National, at Five Points (see Also this year . . .)

1886

March	Mrs. Livingstone Mims and Miss Julia Bartlett begin organizing the South's first Christian Science congregation.
April	Gen. Philip H. Sheridan visits and inspects the 236-acre site for which Congress has appropriated $500,000 for establishment of a permanent military post near the city.
May 1	Jefferson Davis visits to participate in unveiling a monument to Sen. Benjamin H. Hill; hordes of visitors plus "practically the entire population of Atlanta" form a crowd estimated at 100,000.
May 8	Formulated by pharmacist John S. Pemberton as a headache remedy, Coca-Cola is first dispensed at Jacobs' Pharmacy—corner of Marietta and Peachtree Streets.
July 1	Last year's referendum, which gave saloon keepers a seven-month grace period, runs out today; Fulton County becomes legally bone dry.
July 28	Meeting in the city, the state Democratic convention nominates John B. Gordon for governor.
September 24	Signed today, the last of five conveyances gives military leaders clear title to the big tract of land along the Central of Georgia Railroad that will in time become Fort McPherson — honoring the Union general killed in the Battle of Atlanta on July 22, 1864.
August 31	Atlanta feels a "rocking and rolling motion throughout the city" as Charleston, SC, is hit by the worst-ever East coast earthquake.
October 4	A new ordinance provides a penalty of $25 or 30 days for wagon masters whose vehicles congregate on the Broad Street bridge.
October 15	Legislators pass a bill establishing a state technological school and appropriate $65,000—leaving site selection to be determined by competitive bids. The school becomes Georgia Tech.

THIS YEAR IN THE NATION

Jan. 18: Congress passes presidential succession act ... **Apr. 22:** Pres. Cleveland recommends to Congress establishment of a commission to arbitrate labor disputes ... **May 1-4:** Nationwide strike in support of eight-hour day staged by 340,000 union members ... **May 10:** In Santa Clara County v. Southern Pacific Railroad, Supreme Court rules that under the 14th Amendment corporations are entitled to same protections as individuals ... **May 15:** Poet Emily Dickinson dies at 56 ... **June 3:** Pres. Cleveland marries Frances Folsom ... **Sept. 3:** Apache chief Geronimo surrenders to federal authorities ... **Oct. 28:** Statue of Liberty dedicated ... **Dec. 7-8:** American Federation of Labor founded; Samuel Gompers elected first president.

October 20	Atlantans having offered to contribute $170,000 plus a site in Peters Park, the city wins the new state technological school — later Georgia Tech — in spite of bids from Athens, Macon, Milledgeville and Penfield.
November	Rockefeller Hall, 135 feet long and built at a cost of $40,000 with funds provided by John D. Rockefeller, Jr., opens at Spelman Seminary. (The institution took that name in honor of Rockefeller's mother-in-law—whose first gift was $50.)
December 21	At Delmonico's in New York City, Henry W. Grady listens to an address by Gen. William T. Sherman and to "Marching Through Georgia" played by a band; then the editor captivates Northern patriarchs with a speech — interrupted 30 times by applause — in which he declares "The New South" to be a reality.

The Legislature charters Joel Hurt's Atlanta and Edgewood Street Railway Co. — first unit in a fast-expanding transportation empire.

Also this year: Atlantans ponder a proposal that Georgia end her system of convict leasing; advocated by a Chamber of Commerce founder, Sidney Root, the reform will not be accomplished for another 22 years ... John "Doc" Pemberton spends $46 in advertising to move Coca-Cola syrup; 25 gallons sold.

107 Marietta St., home of John Pemberton, who created Coca-Cola there (see May 8)

Benjamin H. Hill statue, which stood at the southern apex of the Peachtrees (see May 1)

1887

January 4   Chartered late last year with merchant John Keely as one of its officers, the Neal Loan and Banking Co. is organized today.

January 4   Having secured pledges of $100 each from 100 white males, horse lover Joseph Kingsbery leads in organization of a Driving Club.

February   In Detroit, viewers marvel at a $40,000 painting of the battle of Atlanta that measures 50 feet in height, 400 feet in circumference, and weighs 18,000 pounds.

March 21   Members of the Driving Club vote to purchase land from George W. Collier; conditions he attaches to the sale prevent it from becoming final.

April 9   Promoters of a proposed Piedmont Exposition secure a charter for the sponsoring corporation.

April 14   Now calling themselves the Driving Park Association, horse lovers meet and agree to buy a 189-acre tract for use of the club.

June 1   Attorney Hoke Smith, 37, invests $10,000 in The Atlanta Journal and becomes president of the four-year-old newspaper.

June 28   "Doc" Pemberton registers Coca-Cola as a trademark; he will sell about 1,000 gallons of syrup this year.

August 10   By act of Legislature, East Point becomes an incorporated municipality.

October 8   The long-awaited Driving Club opens today — just two days before the Piedmont Exposition begins on its grounds.

October 17   Responding to an invitation that was engraved on Dahlonega gold, President and Mrs. Cleveland visit the Piedmont Expo.

October 22   Having attracted an estimated 200,000 visitors, the Piedmont Expo closes with a profit of $9,746.

October 24   Chartered today with a capital of $100,000, the Traders Bank is located in the city's first skyscraper office building, at 10 Decatur St.

THIS YEAR IN THE NATION

Jan. 20: U.S.-Hawaiian Treaty permits U.S. to build a naval base at Pearl Harbor ... **Feb. 2:** Electoral Count Act, which makes each state responsible for its own electoral returns, passes Congress ... **Feb. 4:** Congress passes Interstate Commerce Act ... **Feb. 8:** Congress passes Dawes Severalty Act, which allows president to terminate Indian tribal government ... **Mar. 3:** Hatch Act, which establishes agricultural experimental stations, passes Congress ... **Mar. 3:** Abolitionist and women's rights advocate Henry W. Beecher dies at 74 ... **Nov. 19:** Emma Lazarus, whose poem "The Great Colossus" is inscribed on the base of the Statue of Liberty, dies at 38.

October   The Capital City Bank, successor to a land company, begins its banking business this month — with capital of $400,000 plus a surplus of $52,000.

November 26   Prohibitionists lose in a new referendum, by which a wet majority of 1,122 carries every ward in the city.

Also this year: The city has a new official seal whose symbol is the phoenix—the mythological bird that rises from its ashes to begin a new life ... With sewer construction having received priority attention, completion of an additional 1.5 miles this year brings the city's total to about 20 miles ... Organized this year, the Gate City Coffin Co. is already employing 80 workmen who produce about 20,000 coffins per year ... Williams and Sam Venable buy Stone Mountain for $48,000.

John T. Cooper, mayor in 1887

City's second official seal, adopted in 1887

Piedmont Exposition (see Oct. 17)

Pres. and Mrs. Grover Cleveland visit (see Oct. 17)

1888

January 16	The Atlanta Philosophical Society is organized.
January	During the month, the Rev. R. H. Gammon of Batavia, IL, completes transfer of $200,000 worth of property for the benefit of Gammon School of Theology, now separated from Clark University.
March	Henry W. Grady spearheads a movement that will bring the 4-year-old Chautauqua movement to what is now Lithia Springs.
April 22	West End Baptist Church is organized and plans to erect a building on a lot given by Jonathan Norcross.
April 28	The Atlanta Bar Association is organized.
July	Withdrawal from Central Hospital of patients for whose care the city is responsible puts a financial strain upon the institution.
August	Henry W. Grady gives an address about "Cranks, Croakers, and Creditors" as the closing event of the Piedmont Chautauqua season.
August	Refugees flock into the city from Jacksonville, FL, fleeing an epidemic of yellow fever.
September	Joel Hurt's new car line to Inman Park will use electrically-propelled street cars — the city's first ... The Metropolitan Street Railway Co. inaugurates steam street car service to Grant Park.
December 7	The city enters into a contract calling for provision of 400 electric street lights of 32 candlepower at a cost of $30 per light per year.

Also this year: With classes launched in early fall, Georgia Tech's student body consists of 129 students from Georgia plus one from Chattanooga ... Bicycle riding became sufficiently popular to spur organization of The Bicycle Club of Atlanta ... Purchase of the Central of Georgia Railroad by the Richmond Terminal Co. is completed ... The Hebrew Orphan Asylum building opens ... Reorganization of the Atlanta Machine Works, producers of agricultural and mining machinery, is complete.

THIS YEAR IN THE NATION

Mar. 11-14: Blizzard strikes the East, killing over 400 ... **Mar. 16:** Louisa M. Alcott, author of "Little Women," dies at 56 ... **May 15:** Belva A. Lockwood becomes the first woman to run for president when she is nominated by the Equal Rights Party ... **June 5-7:** Democrats nominate Pres. Cleveland for reelection ... **June 19-25:** Republicans nominate Benjamin Harrison for president ... **Nov. 6:** Harrison elected president.

Georgia Tech Administration Building, erected in 1888

Hebrew Orphanage opened 1888 at 478 Washington St. and was demolished in 1974.

1889

January 1   Physical assets of the city, listed at $448,600, show the water works as most valuable at $52,000 — mules, horses, wagons and carts least valuable at $3,600.

March 20   Building commissioners deliver the new Capitol to Gov. John B. Gordon — at $118.43 under the $1 million appropriated for construction.

March 25   Joseph Hirsch, chairman of the building committee, leads in dedication of the Hebrew Orphans home.

March 28   Lumberman George V. Gress and an associate pay $4,485 for a defunct circus; shortly afterward, Gress will give its animals to the city as the nucleus of a zoo.

April 21   Thirty-four carloads of paper burn in the Jackson building; falling walls claim the lives of two firemen — first casualties of the paid department.

May 8   A site is selected for the Confederate Veterans' Home.

June 17   A charter is granted for Atlanta's Yaarab Temple.

July 4   In formal ceremonies for the opening of the new Capitol, Gov. John B. Gordon exults that "the whole enterprise is clean, credible and above suspicion."

August 8   Railroader John Williamson and attorney Patrick Calhoun clash before a committee of the Legislature; a duel ensues. Fought at the Alabama state line, the only blood flows from a bullet that takes off the little finger of a Constitution reporter.

August 14   A postoffice is established in west Atlanta — later called Battle Hill.

August 22   The city's first electric street car makes a successful run from Edgewood Avenue to Inman Park.

September 24   Decatur Female Seminary, later Agnes Scott College, opens with 57 day students and three boarding students.

THIS YEAR IN THE NATION

Feb. 9: Agriculture Department raised to cabinet rank ... **May 2:** Benjamin Harrison inaugurated 23d president ... **May 31:** Johnstown, PA destroyed by flood with more than 2,000 deaths ... **July 23:** John L. Sullivan defeats Jake Kilrain in a 75-round world champion boxing match ... **Nov. 2:** North Dakota becomes 39th state; South Dakota becomes the 40th. ... **Nov. 8:** Montana becomes 41st state ... **Nov. 11:** Washington becomes the 42d state ... **Nov. 14:** Nellie Bly sets out to beat the fictional Phileas Fogg in circumnavigating the world in less than 80 days ... **Dec. 6:** Jefferson Davis dies at 81.

December 8   Knights Templar and Scottish Rite Masons form the Ancient Arabic Order Nobles of the Mystic Shrine.

December 12   Though ill, Henry W. Grady speaks in Boston on "The Race Problems in the South"; he dies 11 days later.

December 25   Funeral services for Henry W. Grady; civic leaders are making plans to erect a handsome monument.

Also this year: The start of American Trust and Banking Co. — later Fourth National Bank.

John T. Glenn, mayor, 1889

George V. Gress (see Mar. 28)

State Capitol (see Mar. 20)

Atlanta, 1889, as seen from the top of the state Capitol

1890

January 20	An article in the Constitution notes that baskets full of Civil War bullets, found on battlefields after a rain, are being sold as lead for 3¢ to 5¢ a pound.
March 13	A three-day auction of furniture from the old Capitol starts today; it will yield $2,075.
March 24	Mrs. Benjamin Harrison, wife of the President, visits the city.
April 4	By purchasing 44 acres, the city expands L. P. Grant Park to 131.5 acres in size.
April 27	The Constitution lauds West End for plans to replace 30 oil street lights with 100 gas lights.
April	The Women's Press Club is organized.
June 15	Georgia Tech graduates its first class.
June 15	Newspaper stories announce plans for a 900-acre planned community called Manchester; eventually it becomes College Park.
August 10	Children having conducted a "penny campaign," the elephant Clio, purchased with proceeds, arrives at the zoo.
August 20	A new street railway company secures a franchise to build an electric line from Broad Street to McPherson Barracks.
September	This month, a Butler Street lot is purchased; plans call for it to be the site of a municipal hospital honoring Henry W. Grady.
September	The immense circular painting of the battle of Atlanta, sold at auction, is acquired by Paul M. Atkinson of Georgia.
October 19	Major and Mrs. John Dale of London open a Salvation Army mission.
November 9	The first inauguration of a governor takes place in the new Capitol.
November	Clark Howell, 27 and son of the publisher of the Constitution, becomes Speaker of the Georgia House of Representatives.

THIS YEAR IN THE NATION

May 2: Oklahoma territory organized ... **June 27:** Dependent Pension Act, which provides pensions for poor or disabled Civil War veterans, passes Congress ... **July 3:** Idaho admitted as 43d state ... **July 10:** Wyoming admitted as 44th state ... **Aug. 6:** First execution by electrocution in U.S. ... **Nov. 1:** Mississippi adds to its constitution a clause requiring that a voter understand parts of the state constitution ... **Nov. 17-Dec. 29:** Uprising of plains Indians in Ghost Dance War ... **Nov. 29:** First Army-Navy football game: Navy wins 24-0 ... **Dec. 29:** Battle of Wounded Knee, last major conflict between Indians and U.S. troops.

Also this year: Rapid building has brought the city's indoor toilets to 2,829 — with only 9,000 outdoor privies still in use ... Having purchased the southwest corner of Whitehall and Hunter Streets for $30,000, Joseph M. High plans to erect a department store ... Blacks make up 43% of the city's population of 65,533 ... With 100 miles of street railways in service, Atlanta has the nation's most complete system.

Center of Atlanta, 1890: looking east from the Broad St. bridge toward Union Station, which fronted Pryor St. At middle left, the second Kimball House.

Boating on Lake Abana, Grant Park, 1890

Main campus of Atlanta University, 1890

Dr. John R. Hopkins' fanciful residence, built in 1890 on the southeast corner of Peachtree and Baker Sts.; demolished in 1931.

1891

January 5   A "winged vestibule train" makes its first run from the city to Washington, DC; it will become the famous Crescent Limited.

January   Maddox Park, 81 acres, is acquired by the city for $19,045.

January   Joel Hurt and other members of the water commission publicly back plans to spend an estimated $600,000 in order to get "10 million gallons of Chattahoochee river water daily."

March   Mayor W. A. Hemphill, working quietly to avoid competition from speculators, has managed to acquire nearly 200 acres of land — needed for the proposed new water works.

April 3   Famous explorer Henry M. Stanley arrives to deliver a lecture under sponsorship of the Young Men's Library Association — which nets $387.75 from the event.

April 14   Asa Candler completes purchase of Coca-Cola, for a total of $2,300.

April 15   President Benjamin Harrison pays his second visit to the city. (He came in 1864 as a colonel in Sherman's army.)

April 15   A local chapter of the Daughters of the American Revolution is organized.

May 8   The first car runs on the river line of the Atlanta Rapid Transit Co., with receipts for the day being $33.60.

May 16   Joel Hurt organizes the Atlanta Consolidated Street Railway Company, hoping to gain a monopoly.

June 25   The eight-story fireproof Equitable Building is launched, with the cornerstone being laid "with impressive Masonic ceremonies."

July 1   Interviewed by a reporter, a sign painter employed to number buildings says that "a number is placed on every house, regardless of the protest of the owner."

September 21   An act of Legislature provides for incorporation of the Commerical Travelers' Savings Bank.

THIS YEAR IN THE NATION

Mar. 3: Forest Reserve Act, permitting establishment of national forests passes Congress ... **Mar. 3:** Federal court of appeals established ... **Mar. 4:** International Copyright Act adopted by U.S. ... **Apr. 4:** Actor Edwin Booth appears on stage for the last time ... **Apr. 7:** P. T. Barnum dies at 81 ... **May 5:** The Music Hall, renamed Carnegie Hall in 1898, opens with Peter I. Tchaikovsky conducting ... **May 18:** People's Party of the United States of America founded in Cincinnati ... **July 31:** Patent for movie camera applied for by Thomas A. Edison ... **Dec.:** Basketball invented by Canadian James Naismith.

October 1   The Edgewood Avenue theater, second in the city, opens to the public.

October 21   The completed Henry W. Grady Monument is unveiled by his daughter.

November 3   A splendid new train, the Dixie Flyer, inaugurates service that links the city with Nashville and St. Augustine.

Also this year: Massachusetts native Henry M. Atkinson buys the Georgia Electric Light Co.; soon he will acquire local rights to use Edison patents ... Year's end sees John McEachern and Isham Sheffield using an office for which they pay $5 a month rent; their Industrial Aid Association will become the Life Insurance Co. of Georgia ... Except for Broad Street, major railroad crossings are still at grade level; construction of a two-span iron bridge on Forsyth Street is under way.

Henry W. Grady monument unveiled (see Oct. 21)

Big Bethel A. M. E. Church, constructed in 1891

Joel Hurt (see May 16)

Mayor W. A. Hemphill (see March)

1892

January 29	Asa G. Candler establishes the Coca-Cola Company as a Georgia corporation; he has been sole owner since April of last year.
February 20	Meeting in the city for the state's first intercollegiate football game, Auburn trounces the University of Georgia, 10 to 0.
February 22	Owner Paul M. Atkinson places the immense painting of the battle of Atlanta on exhibition in an Edgewood Avenue building.
February 27	Philanthropist John D. Rockefeller announces a gift of $40,000 "for school for practical training," to be established at Spelman Seminary.
April 10	Mayor Hemphill, having acquired a 60-foot strip of land connecting the city with the new water works reservoir, is lauded by the Constitution; that strip becomes Hemphill Avenue.
April 24	The Seaboard Air Line Railroad runs its first train into the city, over just-completed 273 miles of track linking Atlanta with Monroe, NC.
May 25	The new Grady Memorial Hospital is dedicated; it has 100 beds plus 10 rooms for "pay patients."
June 10	A steam locomotive with no air brakes, used because lightning knocked out a dynamo, jumps the tracks and kills four and injures a score in the city's worst street railway accident.
September 20	S. M. Inman gives his Forsyth Street residence for use as the Jennie D. Inman Orphanage for helpless children.
November 1	Election of Grover Cleveland to the presidency leads to ceremonial firing of Henry Grady's brass cannon.
November 4	The Atlanta Street Railway Co. obtains its charter, leading to a franchise to build extensively.
November 14	The Hotel Aragon, built by George W. Collier and destined to be a landmark, opens on Peachtree Street.
December 8	Joel Hurt recommends that directors of the Commercial Travelers' Savings Bank "turn it into a large trust company;" it becomes The Trust Company of Georgia (now SunTrust).

Also this year: DeGive's Grand Theatre (later Loew's Grand) opens, first Atlanta theatre with electric lights; it burns in 1978.

THIS YEAR IN THE NATION

Feb. 12: Abraham Lincoln's birthday made an official holiday ... **Mar. 26:** Walt Whitman dies at 73 ... **Apr. 19:** Duryea brothers build one of the first successful cars in U.S. ... **June 7-10:** Republicans nominate Pres. Harrison for a second term ... **June 21-23:** Democrats nominate former President Cleveland ... **July 1-9:** Strike of Carnegie steel mills at Homestead, PA, turns violent; 18 die, hundreds injured ... **July 2-5:** First national convention of People's Party; James B. Weaver nominated for president ... **Sept. 7:** In first championship fight held according to the rules of the Marquis of Queensberry, which requires gloves and three-minute rounds, James J. Corbett knocks out John L. Sullivan in the 21st round ... **Nov. 8:** Democrat Cleveland elected president ... **Nov. 20:** Homestead steel strike ends with defeat of the union.

Equitable Building (center) opened in 1892 and is shown that year; demolished 1971.

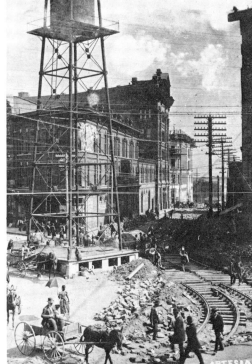

Tracks for the electric trolley cars being laid at Five Points in 1892 alongside the artesian well

Hotel Aragon (see Nov. 14)

1893

January 18 Eight inches of snow covers the city; it is so heavy that the roof of the building housing the painting of the battle of Atlanta collapses.

January 22 The Central of Georgia Railroad places in service a new fast train, the Nancy Hanks, named for a prize-winning trotting horse — (that was named for Abraham Lincoln's mother).

January 24 "Black Week" begins with a murder-suicide at 6 p.m., includes failure of Gate City Bank due to embezzlement, and ends with suicide of attorney and social leader Tom Cobb Jackson plus the shooting of youthful Florence and Minnie Force by their sister.

January 31 Coca-Cola is registered as a trademark in the U.S. Patent Office.

February 10 Laurent DeGive's new opera house, the Grand Theatre (later Loew's Grand) opens its 2,700-seat palace with a performance of "Men and Women."

April 14 Opened today at 97 N. Pryor Street, the Marion Hotel remains in business until 1951.

April 18 Residents of Wheat Street wake up to discover that, by action of City Council, they now live on Auburn Avenue.

July 22 Opened to traffic today, the elegant Forsyth St. bridge has as its first rider Fire Chief W. R. Joyner in a buggy pulled by a horse.

July 25 Water from the Chattahoochee River enters the city for the first time; the new system is fully operative by September.

August 1 Unable to pay bills, the new owner of the painting depicting the battle of Atlanta sees it sold for debts; Ernest Woodruff acquires it for $1,100.

August 13 Having proved to be too fast and too expensive for the era, the splendid Nancy Hanks train is removed from service.

August Atlanta volunteers itself as "a city for safety" to persons from Pensacola and Brunswick who are refugees from yellow fever.

THIS YEAR IN THE NATION

Financial panic begins four years of depression ... **Feb. 24:** Philadelphia and Reading Railroad enters bankruptcy ... **Mar. 3:** Grover Cleveland inaugurated as 24th president, the only one to serve two non-consecutive terms ... **May 1:** Columbian Exposition in Chicago opens ... **May 5-June 27:** Stock market declines in heavy trading ... **June 20:** American Railroad Union founded by Eugene V. Debs ... **Aug. 23-29:** Nearly 1,000 persons killed when tropical storm devastates area between Charleston, SC, and Savannah, GA ... **Sept. 16:** Six million acres of Oklahoma territory opened to settlement ... **Nov. 7:** Colorado enacts voting rights for women.

November 1 Members of the city council direct that the artesian well at Five Points be abandoned, now that Chattahoochee River water is available.

November 4 Greatly helped by Leonard Wood, later to become commander of Teddy Roosevelt's Rough Riders, Tech gridders roll over the University of Georgia, 22 to 6, in their first clash.

November 20 By act of Legislature, West End is brought within Atlanta's corporate limits and becomes the city's seventh ward.

November Having moved to the new Equitable Building, the Commercial Travelers' Savings Bank undergoes the transition that makes it The Trust Co. of Georgia.

December 20 Bolton, the community built upon the site of Standing Peachtree, wins incorporation.

Also this year: Civic leaders are intrigued by William Hemphill's suggestion that Atlanta stage "the biggest exposition ever" in Piedmont Park. By year's end business men subscribe $134,000 to the proposed exposition.

Interior of Loew's Grand Theatre (see Feb. 10)

Concordia Hall, which opened in 1893, stood on the northwest corner of Forsyth and Mitchell Sts. and was used by the Concordia Society, a social and cultural organization.

1894

January 1	Home owners rejoice that the New Year begins with a cut in the charge for water from 85¢ per 5,000 gallons to 60¢ per 6,000 gallons.
January 8	W. A. Hemphill, one-time mayor who is now business manager of The Constitution, is selected to head the organization planning a new exposition.
February 10	Newspaper employees form the Atlanta Press Club and choose Clark Howell as first president.
April 26	Oakland Cemetery sees the unveiling of the marble "Lion of Atlanta." Honoring the unknown dead of the Confederacy, it is a replica of the world-famous Lion of Lucerne, Switzerland.
June 18	Led by J. P. Morgan, several rail systems serving the city are reorganized as the Southern Railway Co.
July 21	No longer under financial stress, leaders and officers of St. Luke's agree that it become a church—with St. Philip's assuming the role of cathedral.
September 9	A newspaper story describes "The Last of Its Kind" — the mule-drawn street car serving Wheat Street, made obsolete by Joel Hurt's electric-powered cars.
October	Members of the American Street Railway Association convene in the city to study the successful electric rail system operated by Joel Hurt.
November 8	A police court judge rules that a widely-challenged poster showing Lillian Lewis can be displayed in spite of her scanty attire; she will play the title role in "Cleopatra" at DeGive's new theatre.
November 30	Joseph E. Brown dies at his Washington Street home. He was wartime governor before serving as a justice of the state

THIS YEAR IN THE NATION

With worsening economy, country is racked with bank failures, railroad bankruptcies and labor unrest … **Mar. 25-May 1:** Coxey's army of unemployed (named for Jacob S. Coxey) marches from Massilon, OH, to Washington; on Apr. 29 Coxey is arrested for trespassing on the Capitol grounds … **Apr. 14:** First public demonstration of motion pictures by Thomas A. Edison … **May 11-Aug. 6:** Strike against Pullman Palace Car Co. by American Railroad Union involves violence … **July 4:** Republic of Hawaii declared … **Aug. 7:** U.S. recognizes the Republic of Hawaii … **Aug. 18:** Carey Land Act, which grants land to eight western states to encourage immigration, passes Congress … **Aug. 28:** Wilson-Gorman Tariff lowers import duties and authorizes federal income tax … **Sept. 1:** Forest fire in Minnesota kills more than 400 persons and destroys more than 160,000 acres of timber … **Dec. 14:** Eugene V. Debs receives a six-month sentence for his participation in the Pullman strike.

Supreme Court and as a U.S. senator. (He and Mrs. Brown are represented on the Capitol lawn by a husband-wife statue — one of the few of its kind in the world.)

December 1	School executives lay the cornerstone for the new Boys High School building, scheduled for completion the next year.
December 12	Oakland City, lying between West End and Fort McPherson, wins incorporation.
December 18	Residents learn from the Constitution that the southside waterworks property and lake will be converted to recreational use. It is to include "an immense bath house, music stand, open air theatre, and a large and elegant pavilion" in addition to rowboats and electric launches on the lake. Soon it becomes widely known as Lakewood.
December 27	The old Capitol building at Marietta and Forsyth Streets, formerly Kimball's Opera House, is leveled by fire.

The Oakland Cemetery "Lion" (see Apr. 26)

Interior of Jacobs' Pharmacy at Five Points in 1894

1895

January 30	Susan B. Anthony, coming to preside over the 27th annual National American Woman Suffrage Association convention, takes up residence in the Aragon Hotel.
April 22	Workmen lay the cornerstone of the Women's Building for the upcoming expo (now called the Cotton States and International Exposition of 1895).
April 28	Maine native Hannibal I. Kimball, so exuberant an entrepreneur that he was called "a steam engine in britches," dies in Boston after having helped shape postwar Atlanta.
April 29	Thomas Bowles' New Lyceum Theater at the corner of Edgewood and Piedmont Avenues has its gala opening.
May 2	The former West End postoffice becomes Battle Hill, commemorating the site of the Battle of Ezra Church.
May	Congress votes $200,000 for a government exhibit at the upcoming expo and the bill wins presidential approval by Grover Cleveland.
June 22	Already expanding, the youthful Southern Railway Co. buys the Atlanta & Florida road.
July	Atlanta ladies organize a chapter of the United Daughters of the Confederacy — second in the state.
July	Joel Hurt becomes president of The Trust Co. of Georgia.
August 9	Opened to traffic earlier, the Broad Street Bridge is today declared completed.
August	Long-awaited Lakewood Park opens — to whites only.
September 18	At Buzzard's Bay, Mass., Pres. Cleveland pushes the button that starts machinery in motion at the great exposition. Ex-Gov. Rufus B. Bullock, master of ceremonies, introduces dignitaries and speakers. Among them is Booker T. Washington, who

delivers an impassioned plea that blacks make compromises for the sake of jobs. His "Atlanta Compromise" is cheered by white listeners, decried by many black analysts.

October 1	First played on opening day of the expo, Victor Herbert's "Salute to Atlanta" march is now generally familiar.
October 8	On a rare trip from Philadelphia, the Liberty Bell reaches Piedmont Park and is placed on display.
October 27	Pres. Grover Cleveland and his cabinet visit the exposition.
October 27	A tremendous attraction comes to the exposition — Buffalo Bill Cody's Wild West Show.
December 4	Asa G. Candler proudly announces that Coca-Cola is now sold in every U.S. state and territory.
December 7	Atlantans have begun to hum the "King Cotton March," composed for the expo by John Philip Sousa and first played here by his band.
December 16	Long called Manchester, the outlying town to which Cox Female College has moved, becomes College Park, by act of Legislature.
December 31	With the Cotton States and International Exposition closing today, backers calculate the total cost — between $2,500,000 and $3,000,000. During 100 days, 800,000 visitors came to see some of the 6,000 exhibits.

Downtown Peachtree St., 1895: Homes at left occupied sites now held by Macy's and the Westin Peachtree Plaza Hotel.

Junction of Peachtree and Pryor, 1895: DeGive's Opera House (later Loew's Grand) occupied the present site of the Georgia-Pacific Center; tall spire topped the First Methodist Church, its site now occupied by the Candler Building.

THIS YEAR IN THE NATION

Depression continues through most of the year ... **Jan. 22:** National Assn. of Manufacturers founded ... **Feb. 20:** Abolitionist Frederick Douglass dies at 78 ... **Mar. 20:** Sixty killed in coal mine explosion at Red Canyon, WY ... **May 20:** Income tax provisions of Wilson-Gorman tariff found unconstitutional by Supreme Court ... **June 11:** Patent for an automobile issued to Charles E. Duryea ... **Aug. 31:** First professional football game played ... **Sept. 18:** Booker T. Washington calls for racial reconciliation and separation in a speech at the Cotton States and International Exposition in Atlanta ... **Oct. 12:** Installation of electric generating station at Niagara Falls completed ... **Nov. 28:** First automobile race in U.S. is run between Chicago and Evanston, IL; only two cars finish.

At the Piedmont Exposition: Nellie White
(see Apr. 22 etc.)

At the Piedmont Exposition: "Streets of Cairo"

At the Piedmont Exposition: Lake Clara Meer and exhibit halls

At the Piedmont Exposition:
Philadelphia sent the Liberty Bell

At the Piedmont Exposition: The ferris wheel

At the Piedmont Exposition: The sexy (?)
"Coochee-Coochee Girls"

At the Piedmont Exposition: The "shoot-the-chute"

At the Piedmont Exposition

1896

January 15 Third National Bank opens for business at Broad and Alabama Streets.

January 25 This being the 137th anniversary of the birth of Robert Burns, admirers meet in the Aragon Hotel to organize the Atlanta Burns Club. (Eventually the Club erects the only replica of the poet's home.)

February 13 Eugene V. Debs, leader of the great Pullman strike of 1894, speaks to a packed house; later he campaigns for the presidency as an inmate of Atlanta's federal penitentiary.

March 5 Socrates Ivy, first male child to be born in the city, dies.

May 17 A fire in a Decatur Street fish market leaps to adjacent buildings and claims one life plus $300,000 in property damage.

May 26 Atlanta University Prof. W. E. B. DuBois, destined to gain fame as a founder of the N.A.A.C.P., leads the first of a series of conferences on living conditions of urban blacks.

August 16 Georgia Tech Pres. Lyman Hall proposes fencing the campus "to protect the property against tramps." (Trustees spend $500 for the project in December.)

December 2 Local contests arouse so little interest that only 2,500 persons bother to vote in an election that puts Charles Collier in the mayor's office. Collier was president and director-general of last year's great exposition.

December 22 William Jennings Bryan, famous orator defeated last year in a bid for the presidency, is greeted by a crowd of 3,000 on his arrival at Union Depot.

December 29 Austria's Prince and Princess Khevenhullar-Metch stop briefly in the city, making a tour of the world.

Also this year: The American Trust and Savings Bank successfully converts into Fourth National Bank ... Having resigned from the Cleveland cabinet during the summer, Hoke Smith has resumed management of The Journal and is crusading against the administration's monetary policies ... Municipal rules regulating bicycle traffic include: "#5 — Don't scorch, and this means you. #7 — Don't say 'Get out of my way' to any chance pedestrian who may appear in your path" ... Piedmont Driving Club is in the middle of the city's first experiment with golf, a seven-hole course having been laid out on club grounds ... Year's end sees still another significant local organization in action — the Atlanta Women's Club ... This has been a record year for building, with 360 residences having been erected at a cost of $472,491.

Victorian homes in Atlanta's first suburb, Inman Park, developed by Joel Hurt in the 1890s.

Office of the Atlanta Gas Light Company

Inside the Equitable Building

THIS YEAR IN THE NATION

Jan. 4: Utah becomes the 45th state ... **May 27:** St. Louis struck by tornado that kills 306 ... **May 28:** Supreme Court in Plessy v. Ferguson accepts the doctrine of separate-but-equal ... **June 16-18:** Republicans nominate William McKinley for president ... **July 7-11:** After his famous Cross of Gold speech, William J. Bryan nominated by Democrats for president ... **July 22-25:** People's Party nominates the Democratic nominee Bryan for presidency, but unlike the Democrats, chooses Tom Watson of Georgia for vice-president ... **Aug. 17:** Gold discovered in Yukon, setting off Klondike gold rush ... **Oct. 1:** Rural free mail delivery inaugurated ... **Nov. 3:** McKinley elected president.

1897

January 1   Organized last year with $350,000 capital, Atlanta Woolen Mills now has 350 employees.

January 18   Funded in the amount of $100,000 by the Western & Atlantic Railroad plus the Seaboard Air Line, a new freight depot is ready for use.

May 3   The City of Atlanta purchases the old Fulton County Courthouse for use as a city hall.

June 23   Georgia Tech trustees award a contract to construct a dormitory at a cost not to exceed $13,000.

July   Marist Fathers purchase land at Peachtree and Ivy Streets (where the Church of the Sacred Heart will be built).

September 9   Col. I. W. Avery — Confederate veteran, editor of The Constitution for five years, and author of the only comprehensive history of the state for the period 1850-1881 — is at his death eulogized as "one of the old cavaliers of the Old South."

September   This month has seen the city's first use of electrically-heated street cars.

October 26   Wealthy Thomas J. Healey, a pioneer citizen and builder, dies.

October 30   At Brisbane Park, University of Georgia fullback Richard Von Gammon sustains fatal injuries in a football game with the University of Virginia.

November 22   John Ryan, Sr., a pioneer dry goods merchant who was one of the city's earliest users of display advertising in newspapers, dies.

Also this year: Though established only a few months ago, the Atlanta Box Factory's 60 employees are producing 60,000 boxes a day "of the cheaper variety."

THIS YEAR IN THE NATION

Feb. 17: National Congress of Mothers (which will become the PTA in 1924) founded ... **Mar. 2:** Legislation requiring literacy test for immigrants vetoed by Pres. Cleveland ... **Mar. 4:** William McKinley inaugurated as 25th President ... **Mar. 17:** Bob Fitzsimmons beats James J. Corbett for boxing heavyweight championship ... **Apr. 22:** First workable submarine is demonstrated ... **June 15:** Social Democracy of America, a Socialist political party, founded by Victor L. Berger and Eugene V. Debs ... **July 7:** Dingley Tariff, with the highest duties up to that time, passes Congress ... **Oct. 1:** Section of Boston subway, the first in the U.S., completed ... **Oct. 29:** Henry George, advocate of the single-tax and author of the book "Progress and Poverty," dies at 58.

John H. Mecaslin, named president of Atlanta Gas Light Co., on Dec. 17, 1897; he had been a City Councilman and City treasurer.

English-American Building (The Flatiron), erected in 1897—and still standing in 1987.

Birthplace of Dr. Martin Luther King, Jr., built in the 1890s.

Three Atlanta pioneers, in 1897, John J. Thrasher (left), who opened Atlanta's first store; George W. Collier (center), who owned an 1840's grocery at Five Points; and George W. Adair, founder of a prominent real estate firm.

Charles A. Collier, mayor 1897-98

1898

January 23	Construction of the new $100,000 plant of the Atlanta Milling Co. begins.
March 4	Noted singer Anna Held fills an engagement in the city, starring in the comedy, "Gay Deceiver."
March 12	Mayor Charles Collier accepts from George V. Gress the gift of the immense painting later housed in the Cyclorama. Gress has specified that the city must spend at least $1,000 on the canvas and its building. (Repair costs total $4,066.17.)
March 12	By order of the Secretary of War, the city is made headquarters for a new Department of the Gulf — created in preparation for the invasion of Cuba.
April 18	Noted author James Whitcomb Riley visits.
April 21	War with Spain having been declared, Atlantans rush to volunteer for combat service.
April 30	John S. Cohen of the Journal, the city's first war correspondent, scores a world scoop with a dispatch describing the bombardment of Fort Cabanas, near Havana.
May 1	Bishop Thomas A. Becker, Diocese of Savannah, dedicates Sacred Heart Church.
May 1	Admiral George Dewey becomes a national hero because of his victory in the Battle of Manila Bay; for the battle, he used strategic plans developed by Flag-Lieutenant Thomas M. Brumby of Marietta.
May 1	Local cracker factories owned by Frank Block and Thomas Lewis have converted their operations to manufacture hardtack for troops fighting the Spanish.
May 4	Fort McPherson having been designated as a prison for captured Spanish, it receives the first contingent — 15 officers and privates.
May 7	First Atlanta volunteers for the war, 47 in number leave the city for training at Camp Northen, in Griffin.

May 30	Society girls organize a relief association, soon collect $702 for aid to fighting men.
May 30	Atlanta Title Co. issues its first policy.
July 20	Thirty thousand Confederate veterans launch a three-day reunion on the 34th anniversary of the Battle of Peachtree Creek.
August 1	The Constitution publishes a sketch of "the new county jail on Butler Street" — destined to gain lasting fame as Fulton Tower. It is described as a colossal structure "that is perhaps the finest Jail on earth."
August 15	The Atlanta Athletic Club is organized.
September	Having been created by a recent merger between Atlanta Medical College and Southern Medical College, the new Atlanta College of Physicians and Surgeons begins its first term.
September	Col. J. C. Woodward makes plans to launch the Georgia Military Academy, at College Park.
December 4	North Avenue Presbyterian Church is organized.
December 14	Pres. McKinley and members of his cabinet are in the city for a two-day Peace Jubilee celebrating victory in the Spanish-American War.

Joel Chandler Harris (left) is visited by poet James Whitcomb Riley (see Apr. 18).

THIS YEAR IN THE NATION

Feb. 15: U.S.S. Maine explodes in Havana harbor killing 260 and arousing strong anti-Spanish sentiments in U.S. ... **Apr. 11:** Ignoring Spanish concessions, Pres. McKinley sends war message to Congress ... **Apr. 20:** Congress adopts resolution authorizing intervention in Cuba by U.S. forces ... **Apr. 25:** War declared between U.S. and Spain ... **May 1:** American fleet under Admiral George Dewey destroys Spanish fleet in Manila Bay ... **May 12:** Louisiana constitution adds grandfather clause which drastically reduces black voting ... **June 20:** Guam captured by U.S. Navy ... **July 1-3:** U.S. and Spanish troops battle each other near Santiago, Cuba, including Rough Riders storming of San Juan Hill ... **July 7:** U.S. annexes Hawaiian Islands ... **Aug. 12:** Fighting ceases as Spain surrenders ... **Nov. 8:** Theodore Roosevelt nominated to be governor of New York by Republican Party ... **Dec. 10:** Treaty of Paris signed by U.S. and Spain, ending 105-day Spanish-American War.

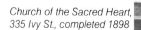

Church of the Sacred Heart, 335 Ivy St., completed 1898

1899

January — Eugene M. Mitchell, president of the Young Men's Library Association, sees newspaper accounts of Andrew Carnegie's gifts to other cities and contacts him.

February 2 — Carnegie writes that it will give him "great pleasure to present Atlanta with $100,000 to build a free public library," if the city will provide a site plus $5,000 a year for operating costs.

March 5 — The new Baptist Tabernacle is dedicated at the corner of Luckie and Harris Streets.

March 22 — The Retail Credit Co. is launched in a one-room office in the Gould Building; it will become internationally powerful Equifax Corporation.

April 2 — Temporary quarters for the new Christian Science congregation are dedicated.

April 18 — U.S. Atty.-Gen. J. W. Griggs inspects the site of the proposed federal prison.

April — Completion of the Mitchell Street viaduct gives the west side a fast and safe link with downtown.

May 6 — Andrew Carnegie having boosted his gift to $145,000, the Carnegie Library is organized.

May — Coca-Cola hires a salesman to cover Cuba and Puerto Rico — the company's first markets outside the U.S.

July 21 — Benjamin Thomas and Joseph Whitehead are given the go-ahead to launch a system of franchised bottling of Coca-Cola.

September 1 — George M. Brown, son of the wartime governor, organizes the Georgia Savings Bank and Trust Co.

September 24 — Trustees announce selection of the corner of Forsyth and Church Streets as site of the Carnegie Library. Finding themselves $1,000 short of the $35,000 purchase price, they manage to raise the balance by public subscription; soon the street faced by the library will become Carnegie Way.

October 18 — Lakewood Park is put to good use as the site for the Georgia State Fair that begins today.

October 24 — Flag-Lt. Brumby, a hero of the Battle of Manila Bay, is given a gala banquet.

November 4 — A Spanish-American War hero, Adm. Winfield S. Schley, is greeted by 50,000 as he arrives to accept the city's gratitude.

November 11 — Workmen launch an immense new project — the bulding of Whitehall Street bridge.

December 17 — Lt. Thomas Brumby dies in Washington, D.C., at 44. Admirers plan to erect an obelisk to his memory; they place two cannons, equipped with slots, at the base of the Grady Monument for the convenience of contributors.

December 31 — A year-end summary indicates that 2,125 building permits have been issued in 1899 — a record at this stage in the city's history … Having established new headquarters at 130 Marietta Street, the city's Salvation Army office assumes oversight of the entire state.

THIS YEAR IN THE NATION

With Spain expelled from the Philippines, the U.S. now does battle with islands' independence movement led by Emilio Aguinaldo … **Jan. 20:** Revolutionary assembly ratifies Filipino independence from U.S. rule … **Feb. 17:** Anti-Imperialist League, which opposes U.S. expansion, founded … **Mar. 2:** Mt. Rainier National Park in Washington established … **July 18:** Author of juvenile fiction Horatio Alger dies at 67 … **Aug. 17:** First conference of National Afro-American Council held in Chicago … **Dec. 2:** European powers and U.S. agree on disposition of the islands of Samoa.

Bicycle squad of the Atlanta Police Department in 1899

1900

January 14	Capitol Avenue Baptist Church is dedicated.
February 22	Brought here by the Atlanta Concert Association, Ignace Jan Paderewski gets an ovation "the like of which probably no other musician has ever received."
May 7	A fire that started in the Ware Furniture Co. factory spreads to residences and leaves more than 200 homeless.
May 23	Dorothy High breaks grounds for the North Avenue Presbyterian Church; her mother, Mrs. J. M. High (for whom the High Museum is named) makes the first contribution to the building fund.
May	Financiers form The Atlanta Rapid Transit Co. to compete with the system owned by Joel Hurt.
June 2	Bottled Coke will soon be available locally; The Atlanta Coca-Cola Bottling Co. is licensed.
July 19	Confederate veterans plus members of the Grand Army of the Republic launch joint encampments at three battlefield sites: Peachtree Creek, Battle of Atlanta, and Ezra Church. Most fought in the Atlanta campaign.
September 9	The cornerstone of Carnegie Library is laid; earlier, Mrs. William L. Peel presented to the institution a bust of philanthropist Carnegie.
October 1	Readers see the first issue of the Atlanta Daily News, staffed largely by persons who have left The Journal.
October 5	Transit company abuses being the chief issue in the municipal election, vocal critic Livingstone Mims easily wins the contest for mayor.
October 10	At Piedmont Park the Southern Inter-state Fair — predecessor of long-famous Southeastern Fair — opens.
December 21	By act of Legislature, the state accepts the Confederate Veterans' Home and 114 acres of land from the city.

THIS YEAR IN THE NATION

Twelfth decennial census shows U.S. population over 76 million, an increase of more than 20% since 1890 ... **Jan. 29:** Baseball's American League founded ... **Mar. 5:** Hall of Fame for Americans founded in New York ... **Apr. 30:** Casey Jones dies at the throttle of his Cannon Ball Express while trying to save the train from collision ... **May 11:** By knocking out James J. Corbett in the 23d round, James J. Jeffries defends his heavyweight championship ... **June 19-21:** Republicans nominate Pres. McKinley for a second term and Theodore Roosevelt for vice-president ... **July 4-6:** Democrats again nominate William J. Bryan for president ... **Aug. 8-10:** First Davis Cup competition held in Longwood, MA ... **Sept. 8:** More than 6,000 killed when hurricane strikes Galveston, TX ... **Nov. 6:** William McKinley elected for a second term.

December 31 Year's end sees the powerful Journal under new management; Hoke Smith sold it a few weeks ago to James R. Gray and associates for $300,000.

Also this year: Coca-Cola executives decide to expand the advertising budget; in the new year it will for the first time exceed $100,000 ... It is now certain that a federal prison will be located here; the city has purchased a suitable site for $25,000 and will give it to the federal government ... Figures reveal that Atlanta has become third in size among Southern cities, topped only by New Orleans and Louisville. Of 89,872 Atlanta residents, 39.8% are black.

First home of the Atlanta Coca-Cola Bottling Co. opens in 1900 at 125 Edgewood Ave. (see June 2).

Groundbreaking for the Carnegie Library on May 15, 1900 (see Sept. 9)

Marietta St., looking west from Five Points, 1900

1901

February 21 Fire destroys the Markham block; loss is set at $500,000.

February 28 Atlanta's first "horseless carriage" appears. Bicycle dealer William Dawson Alexander assembles a trio of "Locomobile steamers," each weighing about 650 pounds. Easily finding a sale for the vehicles, Alexander soon forms a partnership with C. L. Elyea to become Atlanta's agent for Oldsmobiles.

March 5 Atlanta realtor George Washington Connors secures articles of incorporation for the Atlanta Steel Hoop Company. Before 1901 southern farmers had to purchase the steel bands for holding their cotton bales from Pittsburgh. Within a year the Connors enterprise employs 120 workers and produces 50 tons of steel bands a day.

March 12 The first Home for Incurables is dedicated. Since 1893 the King's Daughters and Sons had conducted a program of caring for the poor. The facility is one of the city's most successful charities.

June 3 Confederate soldiers home opens, but is destroyed by fire September 30.

October 9 After years of waiting Atlanta has a viaduct over the railroad crossing between Peachtree and Whitehall streets. No longer is it necessary to dodge locomotives and wait for trains to pass. Northern and southern parts of the city are now joined.

October 25 Atlanta railroads agree to spend up to $25,000 to refurbish the city's 30-year old car shed used as a depot. For months the press agitated for improvement, complaining over a live alligator in the waiting room and a crowded passageway filled with a "seething mass of disgusted humanity." Georgia humorist and journalist Frank L. Stanton, writes the "Ballad of the Car Shed," in which he declares: "I've faced all the greatest dangers in every land and clime / Married two buxom widders—I mean, just one at a

time! An' J'ined the old-time ku-klux, that made you get up an' get / But the ol' Atlanty car shed is the toughest I've tackled yit!"

November Baptist Tabernacle Infirmary and Training School for Christian Nurses is launched. (Predecessor to Georgia Baptist Medical Center.)

Banker John W. Alexander goes for a ride in his 1901 Locomobile, Atlanta's first "horseless carriage."

Empire Building, erected 1901, became the home of C & S National Bank, at Broad and Marietta Sts.

Livingstone Mims, mayor in 1901-02.

THIS YEAR IN THE NATION

Jan. 10: First significant discovery of oil in Texas as Spindletop gusher blows ... **Feb. 25:** United States Steel, largest industrial corporation with a capitalization of more than $1 billion, formed ... **Mar. 2:** Platt Amendment, calling for the end of U.S. occupation of Cuba but providing for U.S. intervention, approved by Congress ... **Mar. 4:** Pres. McKinley inaugurated for a second term ... **Mar. 23:** Filipino rebel Emilio Aguinaldo captured ... **July 4:** William H. Taft made governor of the Philippines ... **Sept. 6:** Pres. McKinley shot by American anarchist Leon Czolgosz ... **Sept. 14:** Pres. McKinley dies; Theodore Roosevelt sworn in as 25th president ... **Nov. 18:** U.S. and Great Britain sign Hay-Pauncefote Treaty which opens the way for the U.S. to build a canal across the Isthmus of Panama ... **Nov. 27:** Army War College established ... **Dec. 3:** In his first message to Congress Pres. Roosevelt calls for broad economic and social reforms.

1902

January 1 Twenty-five men are added to the Atlanta Police Force, bringing its membership to a total of 150.

January 31 The Atlanta Journal reports that the new Atlanta Federal Penitentiary is open. Fourteen officials and six convicts transferred from Sing Sing arrive. The new facility is lauded as the finest institution of its kind in the world.

February 8 The long rivalry over control of Atlanta utility and street car companies between Joel Hurt and Harry M. Atkinson is over. Emerging from their settlement is the Georgia Railway and Electric Company, the forerunner of the Georgia Power Company.

March 3 Carnegie Library opens.

May 16 The North Georgia Electric Company is formed to construct a power plant on the Chattahoochee River near Gainesville. It is to be the first hydro-electric project in Georgia.

May 16 A former Atlanta policeman, Samuel A. Kerlin, is set upon by blacks in the Pittsburgh area of the city. In the ensuing melee, known as the "Pittsburgh Riot," three policemen, two blacks and one white are killed.

August 2 Alhambra Hotel burns.

August 4 The Atlanta News, penny daily newspaper, first appears.

October 25 Joseph M. Terrell is inaugurated Governor of Georgia.

November 3 Work begins on a new passenger depot, Union Station, on Forsyth Street.

December 9 Large sections of the central business district are destroyed by fire which begins at 4 a.m. in the basement of the Snook and Austin Furniture Company. Spread by high winds, the fire causes $325,999 in property damages before it's brought under control.

THIS YEAR IN THE NATION

Jan. 1: First post-season college football game, the Rose Bowl, played ... **Feb. 18:** Sherman Antitrust Act used for the first time, against the Northern Securities Co. ... **Apr. 11:** Confederate general and former governor of South Carolina Wade Hampton dies at 84 ... **May 12-Oct. 13:** Strike of anthracite coal miners settled through presidential intervention ... **May 20:** U.S. withdraws troops from Cuba ... **June 2:** Oregon is first state to adopt initiative and referendum under which voters can legislate directly ... **Oct. 2:** Women's suffrage advocate Elizabeth C. Stanton dies at 86 ... **Nov. 23:** Army bacteriologist Walter Reed dies at 49 ... **Dec. 8:** Oliver Wendell Holmes appointed to the Supreme Court.

Also this year: Georgia Power Co. acquires all trolley lines ... The Atlanta Freight Bureau organizes, plays key role in removing discriminatory rates that have hampered Southern industrial growth.

Carnegie Library (See Mar. 3)

Piedmont Driving Club, 1902

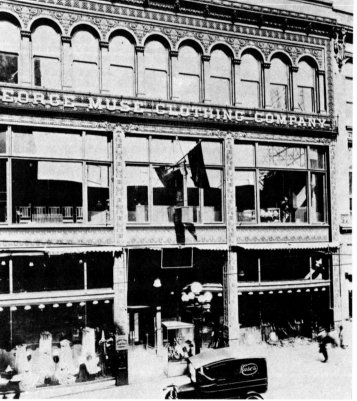
George Muse Clothing Co., downtown, in 1902

1903

January 15 Atlanta's newest hotel, the Piedmont, is opened. It is hailed as "our New York hotel," suggesting a facility operated according to national standards in appointments and cuisine.

February 10 The Atlanta Terminal Company is launched to build a train shed.

March 15 The Lutheran Church of the Redeemer, the first English-speaking Lutheran Church in Atlanta, is organized in the old railroad Y.M.C.A. on Hunter Street.

April 11 The cornerstone is laid for All Saints Episcopal Church on the corner of West Peachtree and North Avenue.

June 21 The obituary for George Washington Collier, Atlanta's oldest pioneer, is carried in The Constitution on the day of his burial.

September 10 The newly-authorized Georgia State Board of Health is organized with an Atlanta physician, Dr. Henry F. Harris, as the first secretary.

Also this year: The Atlanta Independent, a black weekly that is published until 1932, makes its appearance.

Also this year: Edwin Ansley begins development of Ansley Park.

THIS YEAR IN THE NATION

U.S. acquires land necessary for a canal across the Isthmus of Panama by supporting Panamanian rebels against Columbia ... **Feb. 14:** U.S. Army General Staff Corps established by Congress ... **Feb. 14:** Dept. of Labor and Commerce with cabinet rank established by Pres. Roosevelt ... **May 23:** Wisconsin provides for first direct primary election system in U.S. ... **July 17:** Painter James McN. Whistler dies at 69 ... **Aug. 1:** First transcontinental automobile journey ends after 52 days on the road ... **Nov. 6:** U.S. recognizes the Republic of Panama as an independent nation ... **Nov. 18:** Hay-Bunau-Varilla Treaty between U.S. and Panama, which gives U.S. right to a 10-mile-wide strip of land across Panama to build a canal, is signed ... **Dec. 17:** Wright brothers achieve first flight of heavier-than-air machine at Kitty Hawk, NC.

Piedmont Hotel (see Jan. 15); it occupied the site of today's Equitable Building.

Piedmont Hotel lobby (see Jan. 15)

Alonzo F. Herndon's Tonsorial Palace at 66 Peachtree St.

Alonzo F. Herndon, founder of the firm which became Atlanta Life Insurance Co.

Evan P. Howell, mayor, 1903-04

1904

May 23	The Atlanta City Council passes a resolution calling for the purchase of Piedmont Park from the Piedmont Park Exposition Company for $99,000. At the same time the city limits are extended to include the Park.
June 12	One of the first accidents involving a motor car is reported in The Journal. At about 3 p.m. there is a collision involving an automobile, a horse-drawn surrey and a streetcar running on Peachtree Street. The automobile is badly damaged, but the horse escapes without injury.
June 20	City Council passes an ordinance regulating the operation of automobiles. It sets an eight miles-per-hour speed limit, provides for the licensing of operators with the city clerk, and requires the conspicuous display of a number four inches high and two inches wide.
July 1	Atlanta, Knoxville & Northern (L&N) begin operating trains into Atlanta from Knoxville.
August 3	Atlanta's first traffic fatality occurs when Marietta chemist Frank Reynolds is killed after losing control of his White Steamer on Marietta Road. His wife is seriously injured.
December 5	The first train departs from the new Seaboard freight station on Spring Street.
December 20	An announcement is made of the development of Ansley Park, originally called Peachtree Garden. Edwin P. Ansley, the principal developer, stages a street-naming contest. Among the winners are La Fayette Drive and The Prado.
	Also this year: The Rucker Building is constructed on Auburn Ave., the first in Atlanta be built by a black man (Henry Rucker).

Rhodes Hall, erected in 1904 by furniture dealer A. G. Rhodes at 1516 Peachtree St.

Peachtree Street, from just north of Ellis St.; homes on left occupied the site now held by Macy's.

Edwin P. Ansley (see Dec. 20)

THIS YEAR IN THE NATION

Jan. 2: Confederate general James Longstreet dies at 83 ... **Feb. 7-8:** Fire destroys central business district of Baltimore ... **May 4:** First Olympic games to be held in U.S. open in St. Louis ... **June 21-23:** Republicans nominate Pres. Roosevelt for his first full term ... **July 6-9:** Democrats nominate Alton B. Parker ... **Oct. 27:** First section of New York City subway accepts passengers ... **Nov. 8:** Theodore Roosevelt elected President ... **Dec. 6:** Pres. Roosevelt extends meaning of Monroe Doctrine by giving U.S. sole responsibility for Western Hemisphere.

1905

January 1   The Fourth National Bank Building, a 16-story palatial structure of Italian Renaissance design, is finished on the corner of Peachtree and Marietta streets.

February 3   A record snow and ice storm virtually closes down the city. All services including telephone communication are disrupted.

March 2   The formal organization of the Standard Club, a prominent institution of the Atlanta Jewish community, is launched with Isaac Liebman as president.

May 13   The new Terminal Station opens at the intersection of Mitchell Street and Madison Avenue. After presiding over festive ceremonies, Capt. James W. English leads the Sixteenth U.S. Infantry Band into the waiting room playing "Dixie."

June 28   The Atlanta Art Association is chartered. Spearheading the project, Mrs. Isaac S. Boyd. This marks the beginning of a movement that leads to the opening of a museum of art on land donated by Mrs. Joseph Madison High in 1926.

August 16   The Wesley Memorial Hospital, with a capacity of 50 beds, opens. Bishop Warren A. Candler is the first president of the Board of Trustees. Later rebuilt on Clifton Road, it becomes a gift to Emory University and is named Emory University Hospital.

October 20   Pres. and Mrs. Theodore Roosevelt visit the Roswell home of his mother. Later, the presidential party arrives in Atlanta for festive appearances.

Also this year: The Atlanta Life Insurance Company is organized (first called Atlanta Mutual Association) under the leadership of Alonzo Herndon.

Also this year: Louisville & Nashville Railroad connects to Atlanta.

THIS YEAR IN THE NATION

Feb. 20: Supreme Court rules that states have the right to require vaccination ... **Feb. 23:** Rotary Club founded by Paul Harris ... **Mar. 4:** Pres. Roosevelt inaugurated for a full term ... **May 31:** Japan asks Pres. Roosevelt to mediate in the Russo-Japanese War ... **June 28-July 8:** I.W.W. founded by Eugene V. Debs, William Haywood and others ... **July 1:** John Hay, Secretary of State under Presidents McKinley and Roosevelt, dies at 66 ... **July 22-Oct.:** Yellow fever epidemic in New Orleans results in 400 deaths ... **Sept. 5:** Through mediation of Pres. Roosevelt, Treaty of Portsmouth ending Russo-Japanese War is concluded ... **Oct. 31:** "Mrs. Warren's Profession," by G. B. Shaw, closes after only one performance in New York due to its alleged indecency.

Terminal Station (see May 13)

Pres. Theodore Roosevelt (in front of woman; see Oct. 20)

Mounted city police in 1905

Chain gang with guard, 1905

A 1905 view, looking south from the corner of Peachtree and Houston Sts.: The hole in the ground becomes the Candler Building.

1906

January 4 — Dedication ceremonies are held for the 17-story Candler Building on the corner of Houston and Peachtree Streets. For years the expression, "as tall as the Candler Building," was used to describe high structures in Atlanta.

January 11 — Fire destroys two 1895 Exposition buildings and damages the Piedmont Driving Club. Frightened horses, elephants and buffaloes in a nearby circus threaten to escape but are kept in place by skillful animal keepers.

January 16 — During the demolition of the 52-year-old Medical College on Butler Street, the cornerstone is opened. It contains a number of objects including a Bible, a bottle of alcohol and a pea whistle that is still blowable.

February 6 — The Central Bank and Trust Company opens in the Candler Building.

April 1 — Trains begin running from Cincinnati to Atlanta.

April 25 — A daily newspaper, The Atlanta Georgian, begins publication. Editor John Temple Graves crusades against open saloons and the convict lease system, and champions child labor laws. After six years the Georgian becomes part of the Hearst chain of newspapers.

June 3 — The First Baptist Church is dedicated on Peachtree Street.

September 22 — On the heels of a bitter gubernatorial campaign in which black disfranchisement was promised by the victor, Hoke Smith, black attacks on white women are reported in several places about the city. The news sparks the worst disturbances since the Civil War: For four days mobs of whites and blacks battle. Twelve Atlantans — 10 blacks and two whites — are killed. The Chamber of Commerce issues a report blaming the riots on whites.

October 1 — Eighteen locomotives are put out of commission as fire destroys the Western & Atlantic Railroad roundhouse and shops.

State militia rests on Marietta St. near Peachtree St. during the race riot of 1906 (see Sept. 22); inset shows building in Brownsville surrounded by a white posse.

How the cover of Parisian magazine depicted the Atlanta race riot of 1906

Candler Building (see Jan. 4)

Horse race at Piedmont Park

THIS YEAR IN THE NATION

Mar. 13: Susan B. Anthony, pioneer in women's rights, dies at 86 ... **Apr. 18:** San Francisco suffers earthquake, fire follows; damage, $400 million ... **May 14:** Statesman and reformer Carl Schurz dies at 77 ... **June 4:** Reynolds and Neill report discloses insanitary conditions in meat-packing industry ... **June 29:** Hepburn Act, which authorizes the federal government to set railroad rates, passes Congress ... **June 29:** Pres. Roosevelt signs legislation authorizing a lock-type canal in Panama ... **June 30:** Pure Food and Drug Act passes Congress ... **June 30:** Meat Inspection Act passes Congress ... **Sept. 24:** Devil's Tower in Wyoming named as first national monument by Pres. Roosevelt ... **Nov. 9:** Pres. Roosevelt sails for Panama to inspect work on canal and in doing so becomes first president to leave the country while in office ... **Dec. 10:** Pres. Roosevelt receives Nobel Peace Prize for his efforts in ending Russo-Japanese War ... **Dec. 12:** Pres. Roosevelt appoints Oscar S. Strauss as Secretary of Commerce and Labor, the first Jew to hold a U.S. cabinet post.

1907

January 1	The Georgia judicial system is enlarged with the addition of a Court of Appeals with jurisdiction of all cases not assigned by the State Constitution to the Supreme Court.
February 7	The Atlanta Auditorium-Armory Co. is launched to build a convention facility.
May 25	The statue of Gen. John B. Gordon is unveiled on the Capitol grounds. It is the work of Solon H. Borglum, brother of Gutzon Borglum, first sculptor of Stone Mountain.
June 29	Hoke Smith inaugurated governor.
November 1	The Piedmont Driving Club, which burns in early 1906, reopens amid festive ceremonies.

Gov. Hoke Smith (see June 29)

W. R. Joyner, mayor, 1907-08

THIS YEAR IN THE NATION

Jan. 22: First American performance of "Salome" by Richard Strauss given at the Metropolitan Opera House; further performances canceled due to shocking nature of the opera ... **Feb. 12:** 113 die when steamer Larchmont sinks in Long Island Sound ... **Mar. 13:** Financial panic begins with sharp drop in stock prices ... **Mar. 14:** Pres. Roosevelt concludes Gentlemen's Agreement with Japan to exclude Japanese laborers from U.S. ... **Apr. 1:** Lt.-Col. George W. Goethals named to direct construction of Panama Canal ... **Sept. 12:** World's largest ship, the Lusitania, docks in New York on her maiden voyage ... **Nov. 16:** Oklahoma becomes 46th state ... **Dec. 10:** Albert A. Michelson receives a Nobel Prize for physics, the first American to be so honored ... **Dec. 16:** Great White Fleet leaves West Coast for a round-the-world cruise to demonstrate U.S. naval strength.

1908

January 1 — Prohibition returns to Atlanta after a state-wide referendum, but in March Atlanta saloons win the right to sell "near beer."

April 25 — A tornado sweeps through Atlanta causing heavy wind and water damage.

May 1 — Fire in the Terminal district causes $1 million damage.

June 19 — Atlanta, Birmingham and Atlantic (SCL) operates first train to Atlanta from Manchester.

June 24 — The Atlanta Constitution hails the election of Gov. Joseph M. Brown over Hoke Smith as a return to "sanity, justice and conservatism." Two years earlier Smith defeated Clark Howell, publisher of The Constitution.

June 25 — The DeKalb County Superior Court grants a charter for Druid Hills, a subdivision on Moreland Avenue.

July 3 — Joel Chandler Harris dies at 59; he is world famous as the author of "Uncle Remus: His Songs and His Sayings."

July 10 — The Uncle Remus Memorial Association is proposed at a meeting called by Mayor W. R. Joyner. The movement leads to the purchase of author J. C. Harris' home, the "Wren's Nest," as a memorial. Formal transfer of the property to the association occurs January 18, 1913.

December 2 — A general mayoral election, normally routine in Georgia's one-party politics, attracts unusual attention. In the September 25 primary James G. Woodward defeats two opponents, but two months later his public drunkenness arouses such public indignation as to cause a citizens' committee to nominate Robert Maddox as Woodward's opponent. Maddox wins 7,719 to 4,530.

THIS YEAR IN THE NATION

May 28: Congress passes legislation regulating child labor in the District of Columbia ... **May 30:** Aldrich-Vreeland Currency Act, establishing the National Monetary Commission, passes Congress ... **June 16-20:** Republicans at the behest of Pres. Roosevelt nominate William H. Taft for president ... **June 24:** Former Pres. Grover Cleveland dies at 71 . **July 7-10:** Democrats nominate William J. Bryan for president for the third time ... **Oct. 1:** Model T introduced by Ford Motor Co. ... **Nov. 3:** William H. Taft elected President ... **Dec. 26:** Jack Johnson wins heavyweight boxing championship by beating Tommy Burns.

Forsyth St. (1908), from Luckie St., looking south toward the old postoffice.

Gov. Joseph M. Brown (see June 24)

Steel magnate and library philanthropist Andrew Carnegie (left) visits Joel Chandler Harris (see July 3).

Robert F. Maddox (see Dec. 2)

1909

January 1   An Atlanta expansion embraces the 10-year old town of Edgewood whose officials turn over its municipal properties and indebtedness to the city government. Atlanta's population is thus increased by 8,000, its area by six square miles and its taxable property by $2.4 million.

January 15   Pres.-elect William H. Taft is the first visiting dignitary in Atlanta history met by a welcoming committee that comes to the Union Depot by automobiles.

February 11   Atlanta's first taxicabs appear. The Atlanta Taxicab Company displays its eight units along Pryor Street. The passenger pays 30 cents for the first half-mile and 10 cents for each additional quarter mile.

February 22   The $250,000 Masonic Temple on the corner of Peachtree and Cain streets is dedicated.

April 19   Oakhurst is incorporated as a town by order of the Superior Court of DeKalb County.

May   First Atlanta Music Festival held; soprano Geraldine Farrar stars, and urges citizens to invite the Metropolitan Opera to perform.

September 13   Oglethorpe University re-established; after Atlanta donates a 137-acre site and a $250,000 endowment is raised, it reopens in 1916.

September   Atlanta Crackers win the Southern League pennant, repeating their success of 1907.

November 6   The South's first Automobile Show opens in the new Municipal Auditorium. Among the cars on exhibit are Cadillac, Oldsmobile, Packard, Stoddard-Dayton, Maxwell, Pierce-Arrow, Franklin, Peerless, Brush, Pennsylvania, Hudson, Stearns, Elmore, Marmon, Woods, Aperson, Overland, Austin, Reo, Locomobile, White, Mora, F.A.L., Waverly, Black, and Rapid.

November 10   Elwood Haynes, an auto racer, displays his original 1893 automobile in a drive around Asa Candler's two-mile Hapeville speedway. The event is the highlight of a week of racing events which are a part of Atlanta's "Automobile Week."

December 24   The Georgia Comptroller of the Currency authorizes establishment of the Fulton National Bank which begins operation with $300,000.

Atlanta Crackers (see September)

Candler racetrack, where first auto races were held Nov. 9-13, 1930 (see Nov. 6); this becomes the site of Atlanta's first municipal airport.

THIS YEAR IN THE NATION

Mar. 4: William H. Taft inaugurated as 27th President ... **Mar. 30:** Queensboro Bridge over East River in New York City opened to traffic ... **Apr. 6:** Expedition led by Robert E. Peary reaches North Pole ... **June 10:** Author, clergyman and former senator Edward E. Hale dies at 87 ... **July 12:** Amendment to Constitution authorizing an income tax passes Congress and is sent to the states for ratification ... **Nov. 18:** U.S. troops are sent to Nicaragua to quell disturbances ... **Dec. 26:** Painter of the American West, Frederic Remington dies at 48 ... **Dec. 31:** Manhattan Bridge over the East River in New York City opened to traffic.

1910

January 1	City limits are extended to include the town of Oakland City.
April 4	The Mechanical and Manufacturers' Club purchases 150 acres off Peachtree Road at the DeKalb County line to build Brookhaven Country Club. Three years later it becomes part of the Capital City Club.
April 6	Wesley Memorial Church is opened to the public.
May 2	A week of performances by the Metropolitan Opera Company begins with "Lohengrin." Twenty-seven thousand persons attend these performances, producing gross receipts of $71,030.50.
May 21	The Peachtree Heights Park Company purchases land west of Peachtree Road for a development which, says The Journal, will become "a residence section excelled nowhere in beauty and desirability."
August 23	Georgia's gubernatorial primary is a repetition of the race two years earlier, Hoke Smith versus Joseph M. Brown. In 1908 Brown was the winner; now Smith wins by 2,000 votes.
October 10	Cortland Winn defeats J. G. Woodward in mayoral primary.
October 31	Fire destroys the residence of John C. Todd on Greenwood Avenue, the oldest Atlanta landmark. The Todd family had lived on the site since the 1820's.
November 8	The abandoned U.S. customshouse is purchased for $70,000 by Mayor Robert Maddox from personal funds to provide the city with a better city hall. At the time the city could not afford the purchase. City Council pledges to repay the Mayor in three years.
December	Atlanta's population is 154,839, 33.5 per cent of its citizens being black.

Metropolitan Opera tenor Enrico Caruso (left) and H. M. Atkinson during the Met's visit

THIS YEAR IN THE NATION

Feb. 8: Boy Scouts of America founded ... **Mar. 17:** House of Representatives adopts rules to reduce the power of the Speaker of the House ... **Mar. 26:** Immigration Act amended to exclude from the U.S. paupers, criminals, anarchists and diseased persons ... **Apr. 21:** Mark Twain dies at 74 ... **May 16:** Bureau of Mines established in Department of Interior ... **June 18:** Mann-Elkins Railroad Act, which gives Interstate Commerce Commission jurisdiction over telephone, telegraph and cable companies, passes Congress ... **June 25:** Postal Savings Bank system established by Congress ... **June 25:** White Slave Trade Act (the Mann Act) passes Congress ... **Oct. 26:** Philosopher and psychologist William James dies at 68.

1911

March 9   The Southern Commercial Congress attracts the incumbent and the immediate past Presidents William H. Taft and Theodore Roosevelt. Also attending about the same time was Gov. Woodrow Wilson of New Jersey.

June 15   Nine year old Robert Tyre "Bobby" Jones defeats Howard Thorn in the city junior championship golf meet. It marks the beginning of a career that brings fame to the city.

October 2   The public is invited to inspect the Georgian Terrace Hotel; 5,000 attend the grand opening.

October 10   Allen G. Newman's Peace Monument is unveiled near the 14th Street entrance to Piedmont Park. In spite of rain, more than 50,000 people witness the ceremonies that include a parade.

October 29   All of Atlanta's debutantes assemble at the Piedmont Driving Club as members of the first Debutante Club.

November 17   Atlanta's first Air Show is staged at the Atlanta Speedway (later site of the Municipal Airport). Pilot Thornwell Andrews wins the quick starting contest, leaving the ground after a run of only 225 feet.

December 17   The newly-built home of the Capital City Club opens on the corner of Peachtree and Harris Streets.

December   A report shows that 50% of Atlanta's white school children and almost 75% of the black school children suffer some physical deficiency; e.g., malnutrition, anemia, glandular disease.

Also this year: The "old" Forsyth-at-Walton St. Postoffice is completed.

THIS YEAR IN THE NATION

Jan. 21: National Progressive Republican League organized by Sen. Robert M. LaFollette ... **Feb. 3:** Electric self-starter for automobiles demonstrated by its inventor, Charles Kettering ... **Mar. 7:** U.S. troops sent to U.S.-Mexican border to protect American interests as Mexico erupts into revolution ... **Mar. 25:** Fire guts Triangle shirtwaist factory killing 145 persons, mostly women ... **May 15:** Supreme Court orders the break-up of the Standard Oil Trust ... **June 9:** Prohibitionist Carrie Nation dies at 64 ... **Oct. 16:** Progressive Republicans nominate Robert M. LaFollette for President ... **Oct. 29:** Newspaper entrepreneur Joseph Pulitzer dies at 64 ... **Dec. 18:** U.S. abrogates treaty with Russia because Russia will not honor the passports of American Jews ... **Dec. 23:** Theodore Roosevelt says that he is available to be Republican nominee for President in 1912.

Former Mayor Robert Maddox's West Paces Ferry mansion, built in 1911, was demolished in 1966 to make way for erection of the Governor's Mansion.

Courtland S. Winn, mayor, 1911-12

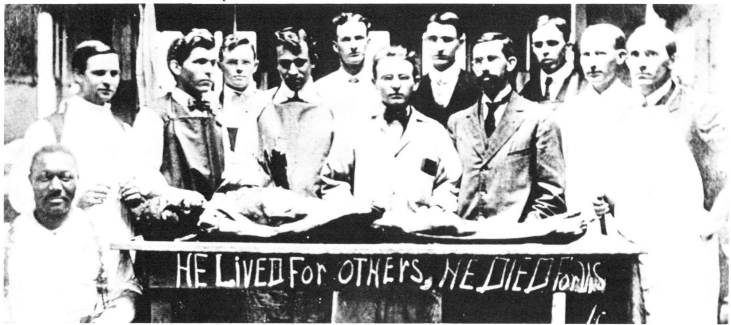

Medical students, faculty and an attendant posed with a classroom corpse in 1911; some wag inked the photo, "He lived for others, he died for us."

1912

January 1	Effective this date the Georgia Railway and Electric Co. is leased to the Georgia Power Co.
January 31	The Sunday American newspaper appears for the first time.
March 31	Prof. Thornwell Jacobs' movement to reestablish Oglethorpe University begins. Forty-two Atlantans pledge a minimum of $1,000 each to rebuild the institution that had closed in Atlanta 40 years earlier.
July 7	Druid Hills, a real estate company, closes the contract for the building of an 18-hole golf course and clubhouse on a 100-acre site on the north side of Ponce de Leon Avenue.
Summer	After the failure of a Vice Commission to secure improvement, a privately-funded drive manages to close a number of brothels.
October 15	Mayor James Woodward, having promised to isolate red-light district activities, wins the primary election.
December	The Chamber of Commerce receives a report that the health department is poorly managed and that "all cases of infection, smallpox possibly excepted, among colored people are allowed to spread." The Chamber insists on a registration of tubercular residents, and inspection of city milk.

Thornwell Jacobs (see Mar. 31)

Woodrow Wilson, former Atlanta lawyer (see This Year In the Nation/Nov. 5)

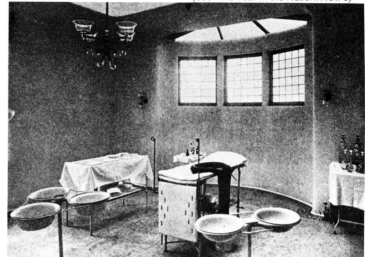

Operating room of Grady Hospital, 1912

THIS YEAR IN THE NATION

Jan. 6: New Mexico becomes the 47th state ... **Jan. 22:** Key West, FL, linked to mainland by railroad ... **Feb. 14:** Arizona becomes the 48th state ... **Apr. 15-16:** On her maiden voyage, Titanic sinks after hitting an iceberg; over 1,500 drown including many Americans ... **May 13:** Congress passes and sends to the states a constitutional amendment requiring the direct election of senators ... **May 15:** American Red Cross founder Clara Barton dies at 91 ... **May 30:** Wilbur Wright dies at 45 ... **June 5:** Marines land in Cuba to protect American lives and property during political disturbances ... **June 18-22:** Republicans nominate Pres. Taft for a second term ... **June 25-July 2:** Democrats nominate Woodrow Wilson for President ... **Aug. 5-7:** Former Pres. Theodore Roosevelt is nominated for President by the Progressive (Bull Moose) Party ... **Oct. 14:** Roosevelt shot but gives scheduled speech before taken to hospital ... **Nov. 5:** Woodrow Wilson elected President; though he carries 40 of the 48 states, Wilson receives only a plurality of the vote.

Ivan Allen, Sr. (later a civic leader and state senator) with son Ivan, Jr., who became mayor in 1960.

1913

April 26 Mary Phagan is murdered in the National Pencil Factory, a crime which ultimately leads to a major outbreak of anti-Semitism, the conviction of Factory owner Leo Frank, and his murder by a mob. Frank is pardoned 60 years later.

August 1 The Atlanta Rotary Club receives its charter.

September The initial class enters Atlanta Medical College, which was created after Atlanta Physicians and Surgeons College and the Atlanta School of Medicine merge.

October 1 The Hurt Building, reportedly the 17th largest in the world when completed, partially opens.

October 30 The Winecoff Hotel opens on Peachtree Street, downtown.

Also this year: The Healey Building, at Forsyth and Walton, opens.

Also this year: Ponce de Leon Apartments built.

THIS YEAR IN THE NATION

Feb. 25: 16th Amendment to the Constitution, which allows for the income tax, declared in effect ... **Mar. 4:** Woodrow Wilson inaugurated as the 28th President ... **Mar. 4-5:** Dept. of Commerce and Labor divided into two cabinet-level departments by act of Congress ... **Mar. 12-Apr. 21:** Strike of garment workers for higher pay, shorter hours and union recognition is won ... **Mar. 31:** Financier J. P. Morgan dies at 76 ... **May 10:** Mother's Day is designated as the second Sunday in May ... **May 31:** 17th Amendment to the Constitution, which provides for the direct election of senators, declared in effect ... **Oct. 3:** Underwood-Simmons Tariff Act passes Congress; it reduces tariffs and enacts an income tax ... **Dec. 23:** Pres. Wilson signs Federal Reserve Bank Act.

Mrs. Mary L. McLendon (left), Mrs. Hardin and Mrs. Grossman in a parade to advocate women's rights (1913)

Winecoff Hotel, 176 Peachtree St. (see Oct. 30)

Healey Building (see Also this year . . .)

Tenor Enrico Caruso and friend, here for the Metropolitan Opera season (April, 1913)

Peachtree St. (1913): The view is north from the front of today's Woodruff Arts Center.

1914

May 10 — The Shriners' Convention begins in Atlanta; delegates come in 150 Pullman cars.

June 13 — Mrs. Lois Nelms Dennis and her sister Beatrice leave Atlanta for New Orleans where they are seen once. Their disappearance is a continuing news story of national interest.

July 16 — The Educational Commission of the Methodist Church, meeting in Atlanta, announces its decision to establish a university, and Asa Candler pledges a million dollars. Emory College is designated the liberal arts division of the new university. Bishop Warren Candler is named first Chancellor of the institution.

August 14 — The city limits of Atlanta are extended to include Boulevard Park.

August 20 — Dr. Henry L. Wilson sells to the North Boulevard Park Corporation 64 acres east of Piedmont Park for $77,812.50. Promoter Aquilla J. Orme later resells the property for approximately $10,000 per acre.

September 4 — The "Buy a Bale of Cotton" movement is launched to compensate for the loss of the cotton market as a result of the outbreak of World War I a month earlier. Purchasers are asked to store the cotton and pledge not to sell it for at least a year.

October 18 — Atlanta's wealthiest citizen, Asa G. Candler, president of the Central Bank and Trust Company, offers to lend $30 million on cotton at six cents per pound.

November 16 — The newly established Federal Reserve Bank of Atlanta opens at 9 a.m. on the second floor of the Hurt Building. It begins operation with $4 million in gold. Atlanta is headquarters for the Sixth District of the Federal Reserve System.

Boys High School football team of 1914

Fulton County Courthouse: opened in 1914.

THIS YEAR IN THE NATION

War breaks out in Europe; U.S. plans to remain neutral; closer to home, U.S.-Mexican relations are strained as U.S. takes sides in Mexican Revolution ... **Mar. 12:** George Westinghouse, inventor of the air-brake for railroads and founder of the company that bears his name, dies at 67 ... **Aug. 1:** Universal Negro Improvement Assn. founded by Jamaican black Marcus Garvey ... **Aug. 4:** Proclamation of Neutrality issued by Pres. Wilson as war breaks out in Europe ... **Aug. 15:** Panama Canal opens ... **Sept. 26:** Federal Trade Commission Act passes Congress ... **Dec. 10:** Theodore W. Richards receives Nobel Prize for chemistry, the first American to do so ... **Dec. 24:** Explorer and conservationist John Muir dies at 76.

1915

January 4	Mayor Woodward inaugurated for fourth term.
January 12	Samuel Inman, known as "First Citizen of Atlanta," dies.
January 25	Charter is granted to Emory University.
March 15	Asa Candler submits the highest bid for Georgia state bonds issued to meet the state's debt. He saves the state $372,846.
June 21	The death sentence imposed on Leo Frank is commuted to life in prison by Gov. John Slaton. Mob violence forces the proclamation of martial law on June 22, and troops protect Slaton until his term expires June 26.
August 16	Vigilantes sieze Leo Frank from his cell in Milledgeville, and hang him in Marietta.
August 21	Asa Candler purchases a 40-acre tract, the Anthony Murphy property, on which to build a cotton warehouse.
September 1	The Scottish Rite Masons open a hospital for crippled children.
September 20	The Journal reports that Gutzon Borglum of New York is visiting Atlanta to inspect Stone Mountain as a site for a sculptured likeness of Confederate heroes.
October 17	The Mion Building on Luckie Street is gutted by fire.
November	William Joseph Simmons and 33 friends go to the top of Stone Mountain and revive the Ku Klux Klan which had not been active since the 1870's.
December 7	D. W. Griffith's "The Birth of a Nation" opens at the Atlanta Theater and attracts wide attention to the story of the Civil War.

Gov. John Slaton (see June 21)   Samuel Inman (see Jan. 12)

Coca-Cola bottling magnates, Mr. and Mrs. J. T. Lupton of Chattanooga, TN, were early and enthusiastic backers of reborn Oglethorpe University. They gave $100,000 to launch the Atlanta institution, and steered a plow for ground-breaking ceremonies in 1915.

THIS YEAR IN THE NATION

Jan. 28: Congress creates U.S. Coast Guard ... **Feb. 6-20:** Opening of Panama Canal celebrated in San Francisco by the Panama-Pacific International Exposition ... **Apr. 5:** Jess Willard becomes world heavyweight boxing champion by knocking out Jack Johnson in the 26th round ... **May 7:** Lusitania, a British liner with many Americans aboard, is sunk by German submarine ... **Oct. 5:** Germany apologizes and offers reparations for the sinking of the Lusitania ... **Nov. 14:** Booker T. Washington dies at 59 ... **Dec. 4:** Peace ship Oskar II with Henry Ford leaves U.S. for Europe to attempt to negotiate peace ... **Dec. 4:** Ku Klux Klan granted charter by Georgia ... **Dec. 18:** Pres. Wilson marries Edith Bolling Galt, having been left a widower in August, 1914.

1916

March 20   Sam Venable, Mrs. Coribel Venable Kellogg and Mrs. Robert Venable Roper deed the face of Stone Mountain and 10 adjacent acres to the United Daughters of the Confederacy for a proposed Confederate memorial.

April 17   Leather billies replace wooden clubs on the Atlanta police force by order of the Chief of Police.

May 20   The Venable family gives a deed to Mrs. C. Helen Plane, president of the United Daughters of the Confederacy, for a part of Stone Mountain on which to carve a Civil War memorial.

June 5   The first motor trucks replace horses in the Atlanta Fire Department.

July 19   A citizens committee of 200 asks Asa G. Candler to become a candidate for mayor in the forthcoming August 24 primary. The city is on the brink of bankruptcy.

September 30   Atlanta has its first serious labor dispute. Motormen and conductors begin a strike against the Georgia Railway and Power Company for union recognition, shorter hours and higher wages. After several weeks of striking, the workers win higher wages but the union is not recognized.

October 2   The Atlanta Junior League is formed by members of the Debutante Club at the Piedmont Driving Club.

November 2   The Atlanta National Bank becomes the city's largest financial institution by merging with American National. It has nearly $15 million in deposits.

December 6   Asa Candler defeats Arthur Corrie in the race for mayor.

THIS YEAR IN THE NATION

Jan. 28: Louis D. Brandeis becomes first Jew to be appointed to the U.S. Supreme Court ... **Feb. 28:** Author Henry James dies at 72 ... **Mar. 9:** Mexico's Pancho Villa raids Columbus, NM ... **Apr. 18:** Pres. Wilson issues ultimatum that U.S. will sever relations with Germany if she continues submarine warfare against merchant craft without warning or provision for rescuing passengers ... **June 3:** Congress passes National Defense Act, which provides for the organizing of a peace-time army ... **June 7-10:** Republicans nominate Charles E. Hughes for president ... **June 14-16:** Democrats nominate Pres. Wilson for a second term ... **July 2:** Hetty Green, the richest woman in the U.S., dies at 81, leaving an estate at $100 million ... **Aug. 4:** U.S. purchases Virgin Islands from Denmark for $25 million ... **Sept. 3:** Pres. Wilson signs Adamson Act, which provides for an 8-hour day for those working for the railroads ... **Oct. 16:** First birth-control clinic opened in Brooklyn; Margaret Sanger is arrested for this and serves a 30-day sentence for "maintaining a public nuisance" ... **Nov. 22:** Author Jack London dies at 40.

Asa Candler (see Dec. 6)

Golfer Bobby Jones, 1916

Alexa Stirling, Atlanta's first championship woman golfer, won the Women's National Golf title on Oct. 7, 1916.

Interior of the Maier & Berkele jewelry store at 31 Whitehall St. (1916)

Thomas Egleston: His will, probated after his death in 1916, left funds that led to the creation of Henrietta Egleston Hospital for Children (see 1928).

1917

January 2	Asa G. Candler is inaugurated mayor of Atlanta.
January 7	Gen. Leonard Wood visits and selects an Atlanta site for a military camp.
February 27	Among the 30 makes of automobiles available in Atlanta is the locally-made "Hanson Six," on display at the Southeastern Automobile Show. The "Hanson Six" sells for approximately $1,000.
April	Enrico Caruso sings at Atlanta's last pre-war opera season.
May 19	A long parade of soldiers marching to the strains of "Dixie" and "It's a Long Way to Tipperary" passes in review before Maj.-Gen. Leonard Wood.
May 21	Several fires are started in various parts of the city. While only one death is reported, 300 acres are laid waste, 1,938 houses are burned and 10,000 people, mostly blacks, are made homeless. Property loss amounts to $5.5 million of which about $3.5 million is covered by insurance.
June 1	Announcement is made that the Cross Keys section of DeKalb County is selected by the U.S. as the site of a military installation, later named Fort Gordon.
June 5	Draft registration is held; ultimately 7,890 Atlantans serve in the armed services during World War I.
July 11	Aviator Walter J. Carr survives a plane crash in Piedmont Park before 10,000 spectators.
August 17	The $250,000 Hemlock Telephone Exchange with 40 operators opens at the corner of 10th Street and Crescent Avenue.
September 5	Camp Gordon opens and recruits begin arriving. By the end of World War I the total number of soldiers passing through Camp Gordon include 6,153 officers and 227,312 enlisted men.

THIS YEAR IN THE NATION

Jan. 31: U.S. is notified by Germany that it will resume unrestricted submarine warfare on May 4 ... **Feb. 3:** U.S.S. Housatonic sunk by German submarine; as a result Pres. Wilson breaks diplomatic relations with Germany ... **Mar. 5:** Pres. Wilson inaugurated for a second term ... **Mar. 18:** German submarines sink three American ships; many lives lost on the Laconia ... **Mar. 20:** Cabinet recommends to Pres. Wilson that Congress declare war on Germany ... **Apr. 2:** Jeannette Rankin is the first woman to be seated in the House of Representatives ... **Apr. 6:** U.S. declares war on Germany ... **Apr. 24:** Congress passes Liberty Loan Act to finance the war ... **May 18:** Congress passes Selective Service Act ... **June 26:** First U.S. troops arrive in France ... **Nov. 11:** Constitution of New York amended to give women the vote ... **Dec. 7:** U.S. declares war against the Austro-Hungarian Empire.

November 1	Henry Mikell is consecrated Episcopal bishop of Atlanta.
November 9	Evangelist William Ashley "Billy" Sunday arrives in Atlanta for a crusade in a temporary tabernacle at Jackson and Irwin Streets.
November 9	James L. Beavers is reinstated as Chief of Police. He is exonerated of charges made in connection with his crusade against crime and vice.
November 29	Famed Irish tenor John McCormick sings before 5,000 in the Auditorium.
December 22	Margaret Wilson, daughter of the President, sings before an admiring audience.

Fire of 1917 (see May 21)

Fire of 1917: some of the ruins (see May 21)

German U-boat prisoners, confined in 1917 at Ft. McPherson

Martha Lumpkin Compton, for whom Atlanta was first named Marthasville, dies Feb. 13, 1917.

1918

January 28	Atlanta barbers unanimously agree to raise the price of a shave from 15 to 20 cents.
March 5	The Journal reports that the president of the Chamber of Commerce, W. H. White, Jr., is investigating the prospect of a landing field which will allow the city to have the benefit of airmail.
April 29	Confederate veterans of the Civil War join in a parade with soldiers going off to fight in World War I.
May 13	The five-story department store of the Chamberlin-Johnson-DuBose Company, a leader in the retail business, opens at a new location on Whitehall Street. It operates 13 more years before closing in the midst of the Depression.
May 21	On the first anniversary of Atlanta's great fire, 14 "units of motor apparatus" arrive at the Atlanta Fire Department, replacing the last of the fire horses.
July 10	James L. Key wins the Atlanta mayoral race over three opponents, including former Mayor James G. Woodward.
August 20	The State Department of Archives and History is created by the Legislature. Dr. Lucian L. Knight is the first director.
September 22	In the midst of meatless and wheatless days of World War I, City Gasoline Administrator J. W. Goldsmith, Jr., orders Atlantans to observe "joy-riderless Sundays" when only medical and military personnel could use automobiles.
October 1	The Federal Reserve Bank opens on Marietta Street.
October 7	In the midst of the national flu epidemic, soldiers at Camp Gordon sleep under the stars securely wrapped in blankets while all public facilities are closed in Atlanta.

December 31 The triangular plot at the northern apex of the two Peachtrees is named Pershing Point with the understanding that no buildings are to be constructed there. It is named in honor of Gen. John J. Pershing, commander of the American Expeditionary Force in World War I.

One of the soldiers Atlanta sent to World War I: Lt. Stephens Mitchell, brother of author Margaret.

Mayor James L. Key (see July 10)

THIS YEAR IN THE NATION

U.S. sends over a million troops to Europe, helping the Allies win war against Germany ... **Jan. 8:** Pres. Wilson outlines his peace program, consisting of the Fourteen Points, in address to Congress ... **Mar. 4:** Bernard Baruch named by Pres. Wilson to take over War Industries Board ... **Mar. 19:** Daylight Savings Time mandated by act of Congress ... **Apr. 8:** National War Labor Board established to arbitrate labor disputes ... **May 15:** Airmail service between New York and Washington begins ... **June 3-4:** U.S. and French forces at Chateau-Thierry halt German advance; first substantial role for U.S. troops in the World War ... **Sept. 14:** Eugene V. Debs receives 10-year prison sentence for advocating pacifism ... **Sept. 21-Nov. 7:** U.S. participates in major battles of the Argonne Forest and Ypres ... **Oct. 3:** Pres. Wilson is notified by Germany that it will accept the Fourteen Points as a basis for peace negotiations ... **Oct. 13-15:** About 1,000 killed as forest fires burn large areas of Minnesota and Wisconsin ... **Nov. 11:** Hostilities end on the Western Front.

1919

February	The 9th Peace Congress is held in Atlanta; former Pres. Taft presides.
April 1	Atlanta war veteran Isadore M. Weinstein establishes a shop on Walker Street to supply linen to restaurants. It evolves into the National Linen Service.
April 3	The Chamber of Commerce wins a battle in the Legislature to prevent transfer of the capital to Macon.
May	Atlanta approves women's suffrage, and 4,000 women vote in the September primary.
September 5	Asa Candler sells the Coca-Cola Company for $25 million to a group led by Ernest Woodruff and Samuel Dobbs.
September 29	Citizens & Southern National Bank opens.
November 7	The Wilson Hotel fire results in four fatalities.
November 23	Speaking before 2,000 at the Auditorium, Vice-President Thomas R. Marshall is subjected to a hoax. On a nearby phone, an unidentified caller tells a custodian that Pres. Woodrow Wilson has just died. As the audience quietly disperses, the organist softly plays "Nearer My God to Thee." When he learns of the hoax, Marshall jokes that the caller "spoiled an awful good speech."
November	The Women's Voter League is established.

Also this year: Atlantans vote down an $800,000 bond issue that would have provided for a new building for the Cyclorama and a Grant Park museum … For three months the Chamber of Commerce, in cooperation with other agencies, conducts an employment bureau for returning veterans … Mrs. Mary L. McLendon becomes "Mother of Suffrage Work in Georgia" as she succeeds in persuading the city Democratic Executive Committee to allow women to vote in city primaries … The First Presbyterian Church is completed on the corner of Peachtree and Sixteenth Streets. … Marian Anderson receives her first concert fee, $50, for singing at Atlanta University … Citizens & Southern National Bank enters Atlanta by acquiring the Third National Bank.

THIS YEAR IN THE NATION

Influenza epidemic kills more than a half million persons in U.S. and 20 million worldwide … **Jan. 6:** Former Pres. Roosevelt dies at 60 … **Jan. 29:** 18th Amendment to the Constitution, which allows for the prohibition of the manufacture and sale of alcoholic beverages, is declared ratified … **Mar. 15-17:** American Legion founded by American troops in Paris … **June 28:** Treaty of Versailles signed … **July 4:** Jack Dempsey becomes world heavyweight boxing champion by knocking out Jess Willard in 3d round … **July 10:** Pres. Wilson presents Treaty of Versailles to the Senate for ratification … **Aug. 11:** Industrialist and philanthropist Andrew Carnegie dies at 83 … **Sept. 9:** Most of the Boston police force goes out on strike; Gov. Calvin Coolidge breaks the strike with aid of the State Guard … **Sept. 25:** Pres. Wilson collapses while giving a speech in favor of the League of Nations … **Oct. 28:** Volstead Act becomes law over presidential veto … **Nov. 19:** Senate fails to ratify the Treaty of Versailles because it contains section on League of Nations.

Gen. John J. Pershing, commander of the American Expeditionary Force in Europe during World War I, was greeted with admiring smiles as he left the Georgian Terrace Hotel in 1919 to inspect army camps.

Julia Carlisle Withers: first girl born to Atlanta parents (1842), dies Oct. 29, 1919).

1920

April	Geraldine Farrar, soprano, shocks Atlantans by doing a strip during the opera "Zaza."
July 28	Proponents of Bible reading in the public schools win in a referendum, 7,631 to 1,865.
July 28	James L. Key wins reelection as mayor.
October 12	Mayor James L. Key appoints Atlanta's first Planning Commission, authorized by the Georgia Legislature.

Also this year: Atlanta joins the nation in becoming legally dry as a result of the ratification of the 18th Amendment which forbids the manufacture, transportation and sale of alcoholic beverages ... The city begins the decade with a population of 200,616. That number will soon increase as hundreds of Georgians are driven from their farms by the boll weevil ... Atlanta is one of the first places where an aviator's service is used in a political campaign. James H. Elliott flies over Atlanta dropping circulars for the political leader in Georgia, Hoke Smith, running for the U.S. Senate against Tom Watson. Elliott's fee is $200. Smith loses ... The palatial Howard Theater opens; it is built by cotton merchant George T. Howard.

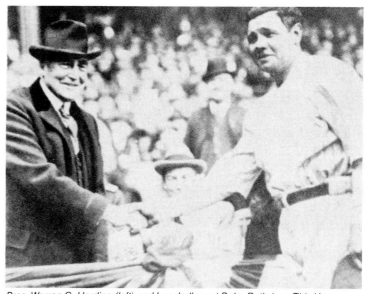

Pres. Warren G. Harding (left) and baseball great Babe Ruth (see This Year In the Nation/Nov. 2)

THIS YEAR IN THE NATION

Anti-communist scare sweeps country, Federal agents led by Attorney-General A. Mitchell Palmer conduct raids across country in which 2,700 persons are arrested ... **Jan. 16:** Prohibition amendment goes into effect ... **Mar. 19:** Treaty of Versailles fails to be ratified by Senate for the second time ... **May 5:** Nicola Sacco and Bartolomeo Vanzetti are arrested and charged with murder ... **June 8-12:** Republicans nominate Warren G. Harding for President ... **June 28-July 6:** Democrats nominate James M. Cox for President and Franklin D. Roosevelt for Vice-President ... **Aug. 26:** 19th Amendment, which gives women the vote, is ratified ... **Sept. 8:** Airmail service between San Francisco and New York begins ... **Nov. 2:** Warren G. Harding elected President ... **Nov. 8:** Judge Kenesaw M. Landis is made commissioner of baseball as a result of the Black Sox scandal of the previous year ... **Nov. 30:** Regular evening radio programming begins on station KDKA in Pittsburgh ... **Dec. 10:** Pres. Wilson awarded Nobel Peace prize.

1921

January 26	United States Vice-Pres.-elect Calvin Coolidge arrives in Atlanta to speak to the Southern Tariff Association.
January	James Key is inaugurated for his second term as mayor.
August 5	The Atlanta Girl Scout movement is chartered.
August 16	Citizens Trust Bank opens.
October 1	The fireproof Cyclorama building, at Grant Park, is dedicated.
October 27	Pres. and Mrs. Harding visit the city during an inspection trip to Ft. Benning.

Also this year: Laura M. Smith, a distinguished educator and business leader, becomes the first chairperson of the Women's Division of the Chamber of Commerce ... A landmark, the original DeGive's Opera House on the corner of Marietta and Forsyth Streets, comes down during the year. Built on the site is the Palmer Building ... Atlanta's leading tennis amateur, Frank C. "Hop" Owens, successfully defends his state title for the first of six consecutive years ... The Citizens Trust Company becomes the second black bank in Atlanta, organized by Heman F. Perry, president of the Standard Life Insurance Company. The first black bank, Atlanta State Savings Bank, was formed in 1909 ... Atlanta voters approve an $8,850,000 bond issue for schools, sewer system expansion, a downtown viaduct and waterworks improvements.

Downtown Peachtree St. held Atlanta's "theatre district." Visible in this 1921 photo are the Lyric (at the juncture of Forsyth St.), and the Howard (right). The Howard and the adjacent Paramount (not shown) occupied the site now held by the Georgia-Pacific Center.

THIS YEAR IN THE NATION

Mar. 4: Warren G. Harding inaugurated as the 29th President ... **May 19:** Emergency Quota Act, which restricts immigration to 3% of the 1910 figure, passes Congress ... **June 10:** Congress passes National Budgeting and Accounting Act, which establishes the Bureau of the Budget in the Treasury Department ... **June 30:** Former Pres. William H. Taft appointed Chief Justice of the Supreme Court ... **July 2:** Jack Dempsey successfully defends his heavyweight championship against Georges Carpentier ... **July 14:** Sacco and Vanzetti convicted of murder ... **July 21:** Gen. Billy Mitchell demonstrates the power of airplanes by sinking two battleships ... **Oct. 5-13:** First play-by-play radio broadcast of a World Series ... **Dec. 25:** Pres. Harding pardons Eugene V. Debs.

1922

March 16	The South's first commercial broadcast license is issued to The Atlanta Journal for WSB. Broadcasts originate in The Journal building.
March 17	The Atlanta Constitution begins broadcasts over its station, WGM, which is later donated to Georgia Tech with new call letters, WGST.
July 15	Atlanta's first municipal swimming pool for blacks is opened in Washington Park.
September 1	Atlanta's last hanging occurs in the old Fulton County jail. Frank B. DuPre is put to death for killing a detective in a jewelry store robbery.
September 6	Former Mayor James G. Woodward unexpectedly enters the mayoral primary. He loses his last bid for public office and dies a year later.
September 13	Bessie Kempton becomes the first woman to win a seat in the Legislature.
September 16	Rebecca Latimer Felton, of DeKalb County, becomes the first woman selected to be a member of the U.S. Senate. Chosen to fill the session upon the death of Sen. Tom Watson, Mrs. Felton serves only one day.
September	Walter Sims wins the mayoral nomination over Police Chief Beavers after a campaign in which the prime issue is police corruption.
December	Wesley Memorial Hospital opens on the Emory campus.
	Also this year: Bessie Kempton, Atlanta Constitution reporter, becomes the first woman elected to the state Legislature.

Hollywood star Rudolph Valentino, broadcasting over WSB Radio (see Mar. 16)

Social event of 1922 was the marriage of Margaret Mitchell (fifth from right) to Berrien K. Upshaw (holding her arm); before year's end he had left her, and in 1925 she married John Marsh (second from left), best man at the 1922 wedding.

THIS YEAR IN THE NATION

Feb. 18: Capper-Volstead Cooperative Act, which exempts certain agricultural associations from the antitrust laws, passes Congress ... **Apr. 7:** Secretary of Interior Albert B. Fall grants Mammoth Oil Co., owned by Harry F. Sinclair, a lease to the Teapot Dome oil reserve ... **Apr. 15:** Questions raised in Congress about lease of Teapot Dome fields by Sen. John B. Kendrick ... **May 12:** Meteorite weighing 20 tons and creating a 400 foot square crater falls near Blackstone, VA ... **May 30:** Lincoln Memorial dedicated ... **Aug. 2:** Inventor of the telephone Alexander G. Bell dies at 75 ... **Sept. 21:** Fordney-McCumber Tariff, which increases duties on both manufactured and farm goods, passes Congress ... **Sept. 22:** Cable Act, which allows women to marry aliens without loss of citizenship, passes Congress.

1923

January 30 The community of Brookhaven obtains a U.S. postoffice.

March 27 One of America's great mail robbers, Gerald Chapman, escapes the Federal Penitentiary in Atlanta. Three years later he is hanged in Connecticut for killing a policeman.

June 3 Gutzon Borglum begins the sculpture of the face of Robert E. Lee on the side of Stone Mountain.

September 9 Ponce de Leon baseball park burns.

December 12 The Police Committee of the City Council suspends Chief James L. Beavers and names Ewell Leonard Jett as "acting chief." Jett is a member of one of the city's pioneer families.

December 20 Opening ceremonies are held for the Spring Street viaduct, a million dollar project widely regarded as Atlanta's greatest civic structure up to this time.

Also this year: An enormous educational expansion is started during the year with the construction of 18 public schools ... The year is also marked by a building boom in the private sector of the city. Among the new structures are the 101 Marietta Street Building, Glenn Building, Commercial Exchange Building and Rich's department store ... The year is important in the history of Atlanta suburban development with launching of subdivisions named Morningside Park and Brookwood Hills ... The Greater Atlanta Community Chest is organized ... Robert Woodruff becomes president of The Coca-Cola Company, beginning a dominance that will last 60 years.

Robert W. Woodruff (see Also this year . . .)

Spring St. viaduct (see Dec. 20)

THIS YEAR IN THE NATION

Jan. 10: Pres. Harding orders U.S. troops of occupation be withdrawn from Germany ... **Mar. 4:** Agricultural Credits Act, which provides for a system of credit banks to handle agricultural loans, passes Congress ... **Mar. 4:** Albert Fall, Secretary of the Interior, resigns in Teapot Dome Oil scandal ... **Aug. 2:** Pres. Warren G. Harding dies at 57 ... **Aug. 3:** Calvin Coolidge sworn in as 30th President ... **Sept. 15:** Gov. J. C. Walton puts Oklahoma under martial law to combat terrorist activities of Ku Klux Klan ... **Oct. 25:** Senate hearings on Teapot Dome scandal open ... **Oct. 26:** Electrical engineer and inventor Charles P. Steinmetz dies at 58 ... **Dec. 10:** Nobel Prize in physics awarded to Robert A. Millikan.

1924

January 6   The four-story red brick Boy's High School on the corner of Courtland and Gilmer Streets is gutted by fire.

January 19   George F. Willis purchases the DeKalb County town of Ingleside and surrounding areas for the development of a model residential suburb. This marks the beginning of Avondale Estates ... Sculptor Gutzon Borglum's head of R. E. Lee, cut into Stone Mountain's face, is unveiled. (It is later blasted off when Augustus Lukeman takes over the job.)

March 17   Pres. Coolidge signs bill authorizing mintage of 5 million Stone Mountain Half-Dollars to commemorate the valor of Confederate soldiers.

April 19   The $6 million Biltmore Hotel is opened by gala ceremonies that attract a thousand guests from throughout the nation.

May 1   The municipal market opens on Edgewood Avenue to serve as an outlet for the produce grown by Georgia farmers.

May 24   Druid Hills Golf Course burns.

September 24   Mayor Walter A. Sims defeats Mayor James L. Key in the primary by about 1,400 votes.

Also this year: Gov. and Mrs. Clifford Walker move into a new mansion, a 13-room, five-bath home of Georgia granite at 205 Prado in Ansley Park ... By act of the Legislature, Fulton County officials are taken off the fee system. Henceforth they will be on salary ... The baseball season opens in a $250,000 facility, the R. J. Spiller Field, called "the most magnificent baseball park in the minor league" ... In an editorial comment on the opening of the Robert Fulton, a 15-story hotel, the Constitution declares that "Each of the 300 rooms will be outside with private bath, and will be equipped with running ice water ..."

Stone Mountain sculptor Gutzon Borglum (bald man standing at left) entertained dignitaries on the ledge of the Mountain's granite which formed the shoulder of Robert E. Lee; this year, 1924. (See Jan. 19).

THIS YEAR IN THE NATION

Feb. 3: Former Pres. Woodrow Wilson dies at 68 ... **Feb. 12:** "Rhapsody in Blue," by George Gershwin, given first public performance ... **Mar. 28:** Attorney General Harry M. Daugherty resigns under pressure from Pres. Coolidge ... **Apr. 9-16:** Dawes Plan for German reparations accepted by Germany ... **May 26:** Immigration bill based on national origins passes Congress ... **May 26:** Composer and conductor Victor Herbert dies at 65 ... **June 10-12:** Republicans nominate Pres. Coolidge for a full term... **June 15:** Native-born American Indians made American citizens by act of Congress ... **June 30:** Albert Fall, Harry F. Sinclair and Edward L. Doheny are indicted on charges related to the Teapot Dome scandal ... **June 24-July 29:** After many ballots, dark horse John W. Davis is nominated by the Democrats for President ... **July 14-18:** Progressive Party nominates Sen. Robert M. LaFollette for President ... **Nov. 4:** Pres. Coolidge elected President ... **Dec. 13:** Labor leader Samuel Gompers dies at 74.

Glimpses of Atlanta at 150

Three Atlanta mayors—a current one and two "formers"—held cheerful sway over a Fourth of July parade float: Left (foreground), Andrew Young, now in his second term; center, Maynard Jackson, and Sam Massell (in white suit).

The Moorish-themed Fox Theatre, which opened in 1929, was threatened in the 1970s by the wrecking ball until a citizens' "Save the Fox" movement protected it. Its magnificent interior is now the site of plays, movies and concerts.

Quiet reverence for the past and artifacts of civilizations long buried appeal to visitors to the Emory University Museum of Art and Archaeology.

Two playful polar bears are among the crowd pleasers at Zoo Atlanta in Grant Park. Origins of the Zoo date from the 1890s; the park is named for Lemuel P. Grant, civic leader who gave considerable acreage to develop it.

The Atlanta Botanical Gardens, one of the city's newest attractions, is situated inside Piedmont Park, a 100-year-old recreational area where the Cotton States and International Exposition drew hundreds of thousands in the fall of 1895. That was one of Atlanta's greatest self-promotions.

The Atlanta area is blessed with nearby boating opportunities: Man-made waterways, Lakes Lanier and Allatoona and others, as well as the Chattahoochee River.

A rite of spring is the annual Atlanta Steeplechase, a fund-raiser for charity and a magnet for the "horsey" set who make a festive day of picnicking at the outing.

The crowded mass of runners in the
Peachtree Road Race pace off . . . each
hoping — at least — to finish the course
and win two prizes: the satisfaction of the
conquest and a celebrative T-shirt from
the sponsor, The Atlanta Journal-
Constitution.

The Peachtree Road Race is an annual Fourth of July event
that usually draws 25,000 runners to a curving course that
stretches from Lenox Square to Piedmont Park. In motion is a
special category of competitors . . . those confined to
wheelchairs by handicaps.

The Swan House, built in 1926 in Buckhead for the Edward H. Inman family, has served for years as a central fixture of the Atlanta Historical Society. The gardens were inspired by the Palazzo Corsini gardens in Rome.

The Governor's Mansion on West Paces Ferry Road was dedicated in January, 1968. The columned, Greek Revival structure occupies the site once held by the suburban home of an Atlanta mayor, Robert F. Maddox.

Atlantans' passion for how they live is reflected in an incredible variety of architectural and landscaping styles. These two private houses typify Atlanta's homes beautiful.

High Museum of Art
opened Oct. 15, 1983.

The Fourth of July parade, a WSB-TV creation, brings tens of thousands downtown to
admire marching bands, floats and all manner of colorful displays. Angular structure
in the center is the Flatiron Building, erected in 1897.

Atlanta-Fulton County Stadium, situated between downtown and the Hartsfield
International Airport, is home for the Atlanta Braves, site of the Atlanta Falcon football
contests, and locus for other events that might require seats for more than 50,000.
Note the city's skyline above the Stadium's rim.

Suggestive of Atlanta's rich cultural life is the Atlanta Opera's performance of
Mozart's comic "Cosi Fan Tutti." The first theatre came to Atlanta in the 1850s; opera
arrived in 1866. Since then the city's life has been enriched by numerous performing
groups including the long-lived Academy Theatre, the Alliance Theatre, the Atlanta
Symphony Orchestra, and the Atlanta Ballet and others.

Nature has been kind to Atlanta, and residents have repaid the blessing by the preservation of trees and the affectionate cultivation of gardens and lawns: Autumn brings a cloak of multicolored canopies, spring delivers bouquets of flowers, and a mini-waterfall is a year-'round attraction in a city where snow is rare.

The State Capitol, which rests on a knoll close by "Underground Atlanta," the city's birthplace, was opened in 1889, and cost just under $1 million. It occupies ground once held by Atlanta's city hall and courthouse.

On a face of Stone Mountain are three Confederate "greats" in mighty sculpture: Gen. Robert E. Lee (center), President Jefferson Davis (left), and Gen. T. J. "Stonewall" Jackson. Stone Mountain Park's attractions draw millions of visitors annually.

A gawker's paradise since its opening 20 years ago, the interior of the downtown Hyatt-Regency Hotel features a floor-to-ceiling atrium (architect John Portman's first) and "bubble" elevators that ride outside a soaring column.

Atlanta's rarefied rank as one of the nation's top convention cities is solidified by its offerings of prime hotel accommodations, symbolized by this downtown stunner, the Marriott Marquis, whose soaring interior is festive to the eye.

Atlanta is a city of churches catering to major (and most minor) denominations. The Cathedral of St. Philip, dominating a rise in Buckhead, suggests the dignity in them all, and the promise of peaceful contemplation.

The tomb of Dr. Martin Luther King, Jr., native Atlantan and a winner of the Nobel Peace Prize, rests in a reflecting pool at the downtown Dr. Martin Luther King, Jr., Center for Non-Violent Social Change. The legend on the tomb of the civil rights leader slain in Memphis, TN., in April, 1968, is from an old spiritual: "Free at last, Free at last, Thank God Almighty I'm free at last . . ."

One of Atlanta's great passions is shopping, and this mall interior is typical of the inviting atmosphere which lures locals, tourists and conventioners. Ever since the grandpa of local malls—Lenox Square— opened in 1959, such centers have mushroomed in and around the city.

Inside the structure first known as the Omni (now CNN Center) are the studios and headquarters of the technologically innovative Cable News Network, brainchild of telecasting entrepreneur Ted Turner. CNN symbolizes Atlanta's history and development as a communications center.

In the middle of downtown is Robert W. Woodruff Park, named for the city's greatest philanthropist. It is surrounded by buildings ranging in age from the 1890s to the present. In the background is the Candler Building, completed in 1905, over which looms the Georgia-Pacific Center, which opened in 1983.

One of Atlanta's greatest construction projects is the years-long development of its rapid-transit system—a mixture of fixed rail and bus transportation. Pictured is part of the interior of the central city's main station, Five Points.

Fireworks over Atlanta illuminate the city's good feeling about itself as it passes the 150-year anniversary. The burst of color is a kind of exultation over the progress which has marked the city's history since its humble beginnings as a railroad town.

1925

January 1 The Atlanta city limits are extended to include Cascade Heights and Morningside Park.

February 25 Impatient over the progress of the Civil War project, the Stone Mountain Memorial Association cancels Gutzon Borglum's contract. In anger Borglum destroys the models he has made and flees; later he begins his most famous project, the Mt. Rushmore carvings.

April 1 Sculptor Augustus Lukeman (Borglum's replacement) resumes the Memorial carving at Stone Mountain; he begins by blasting away all of Borglum's work, and preparing a carving space 305 feet wide and 190 feet high.

April 6 Nearly every piece of fire-fighting equipment in Atlanta is used to contain a blaze at the Jass Manufacturing Company on Decatur Street, dealers in cotton waste. Six fire-fighters are killed.

April 25 R. H. Macy and Co. purchases Davison-Paxon-Stokes Co., and the following day announces plans for a six-story department store costing $6 million.

April 26 An all-Pullman train for the Atlanta-New York run makes its first northbound departure with its cars named for prominent southern personalities like Robert E. Lee and Patrick Henry.

Also this year: Improvements of the water works, an extension of the sewer system and 28 miles of street paving ... New Atlanta structures include the Henry Grady Office Building, the B. F. Keith Theater and the Cox-Carlton Hotel ... Partly in response to the adverse effect of the Florida land boom, Ivan Allen, Sr., and other business leaders launch the "Forward Atlanta"

campaign. It seeks to advertise the city's climate, labor supply and abundance of natural resources. The campaign reportedly brings 760 businesses to Atlanta in the next five years ... Fifty Methodist congregations form Goodwill Industries.

Municipal Auditorium interior, 1925

Famous Georgians, 1925: Golfer Bobby Jones (left) and baseball great Ty Cobb

THIS YEAR IN THE NATION

Jan. 5: Mrs. Nellie T. Ross becomes the first woman governor when she completes the term of her late husband ... **Mar. 4:** Pres. Coolidge inaugurated ... **Apr. 25:** Painter John S. Sargent dies at 69 ... **June 18:** Leader of the Progressive movement, Robert M. LaFollette, dies at 70 ... **July 10-21:** Trial of John T. Scopes for teaching evolution in the public schools of Dayton, TN ... **July 26:** Three-time presidential candidate and Secretary of State William J. Bryan dies at 65 ... **Sept. 3:** Army dirigible Shenandoah crashes in Ohio ... **Oct. 28-Dec. 17:** Col. Billy Mitchell found guilty of charges of insubordination and is court-martialed ... **Dec. 10:** Vice-Pres. Charles Dawes given Nobel Peace Prize for his plan for German reparations payments ... **Dec. 29:** Name of Trinity College changed to Duke University in order to receive a $40 million trust fund from James B. Duke, founder of the American Tobacco Co.

1926

Sears, Roebuck building on Ponce de Leon (see Also this year . . .)

January 9 Atlanta's "Master Builder," Joel Hurt, dies.

February 14 Influential Atlanta residential architect Neel Reid, 41, dies.

May 8 Atlanta accepts Mrs. J. M. High's offer of her home on condition it be used as an art museum; the museum opens in October.

June 30 The Fulton Superior Court grants a charter for the Atlanta Historical Society, an organization inspired by state Rep. Walter McElreath.

July 26 The Pullman Co. opens a plant in Atlanta.

September 15 Regular airmail service to Miami begins.

September 22 Isaac N. Ragsdale wins Atlanta's mayoral race over four opponents.

October 1 An old Five Points institution, Thomas H. Pitts' famous cigar store and soft drink establishment since 1894, closes.

Also this year: Lamartine G. Hardman, becomes governor-elect after a run-off primary victory in which he wins 228 county unit votes. At the same time Eugene Talmadge enters state politics by winning election to the office of Commissioner of Agriculture ... Asa G. Candler donates 53 acres near Druid Hills to the city. The area becomes Candler Park ... Construction begins on the nine-story Sears, Roebuck and Company plant on Ponce de Leon Avenue ... One of Atlanta's best known black athletes, Leo "Tiger" Flowers, becomes the world's middle-weight boxing champion.

Davison-Paxon Co. store, built at Peachtree and Ellis Sts. in 1926, is now Macy's.

Fans of the Georgia-Georgia Tech game in Atlanta simply abandoned their cars near Grant Field to watch the game on Nov. 13, 1926.

Gov. L. G. Hardman (see Also this year . . .)

THIS YEAR IN THE NATION

Jan. 27: Senate approves U.S. participation in the Permanent Court of International Justice at the Hague ... **Mar. 7:** First transAtlantic radio-telephone transmission between New York and London ... **Apr. 11:** Horticulturist Luther Burbank dies at 77 ... **May 5:** Sinclair Lewis refuses Pulitzer Prize for his novel "Arrowsmith"... **May 8-9:** First flight over North Pole made by Richard E. Byrd and Floyd Bennett ... **July 26:** Robert T. Lincoln, son of Pres. Lincoln and former Secretary of War, dies at 83 ... **Aug. 6:** Gertrude Ederle becomes the first woman to swim the English Channel ... **Sept. 18:** Hurricane hits Florida and other southern states, killing 372 and doing $80 million of damage ... **Sept. 23:** Gene Tunney defeats Jack Dempsey for world heavy boxing championship.

1927

January 3	Isaac N. Ragsdale, elected mayor the previous September, is inaugurated.
January 9	The first demonstration in Atlanta of a telephotograph machine capable of transmitting pictures by wire occurs in the Old Telephone Building on the corner of Pryor and Mitchell Streets.
February 20	Announcement is made that four of the older police horses — Monk, Prince, Dan and Rabbit — are retiring nearly 10 years after the police force had become motorized in 1918.
March 21	Davison's department store opens; it is the R. H. Macy Co.'s first store in the South.
September 12	Hotel Candler opens on Ponce de Leon Avenue.
September 14	Columbia Seminary, 100-year-old Presbyterian institution, completes its move from Columbia, SC, to the Atlanta area. It opens on a 7-acre campus on Columbia Drive.
October 11	"Lindbergh Day" is celebrated as the "Lone Eagle," Charles A. Lindbergh, arrives in Atlanta. Twenty thousand hear the hero's speech at Grant Field.

Also this year: William B. Hartsfield becomes chairman of the City Council's Aviation committee as Mayor Isaac N. Ragsdale calls Atlanta the recognized southeastern hub of air transportation. Candler Field is now adequate to accommodate the largest commercial and military planes ... The Frank E. Block Company, founded in 1870 on Elliott Street, is purchased by the National Biscuit Company. The old facility operates until 1940 when a new plant is constructed near Fort McPherson.

THIS YEAR IN THE NATION

Jan. 7: Commercial phone service begins between London and New York ... **Mar. 7:** In Nixon v. Herndon, Supreme Court rules that blacks cannot be kept from voting in primary elections ... **Apr. 7:** First public demonstration of television ... **May 20-21:** Charles A. Lindbergh becomes the first person to make a solo flight across the Atlantic ... **July 29:** First electric respirator (i.e., iron lung) goes into use in New York's Bellevue Hospital ... **Aug. 2:** Pres. Coolidge declines to run for another term as president ... **Aug. 27:** Sacco and Vanzetti executed ... **Sept. 27:** Babe Ruth hits his record-setting 60th home run ... **Oct. 6:** "The Jazz Singer," with Al Jolson, the first talking movie, opens ... **Nov. 13:** The Holland Tunnel, the first underwater automobile tunnel, opens between New York City and New Jersey ... **Dec. 27:** "Show Boat," adapted from a book by Edna Ferber, opens on Broadway.

Atlanta Airport, 1927

Noon meeting sponsored by the Atlanta Christian Council in the Peachtree Arcade (February, 1927).

1928

January 1	Atlanta city limits are extended to include the town of East Lake, a municipality incorporated in 1910.
January 16	The J. P. Allen store opens on Peachtree Street.
March 29	Samuel I. DuBose, of the Chamberlin-Johnson-DuBose company, makes the first transAtlantic phone call from Atlanta. It is a business call to Paris.
April 9	Augustus Lukeman's design for the Stone Mountain Civil War Memorial is unveiled. The project, however, is soon suspended once again because of the sponsor's lack of resources.
April	A Chevrolet plant begins operations.
May 20	The Venable family reclaims Stone Mountain and the unfinished carving.
June 29	Morris Rich, founder of the famed department store, dies.
August 5	The city's second black newspaper, Atlanta World, begins publication. The first had been the Independent in 1903.
September 26	Franklin D. Roosevelt of New York, former candidate for Vice-President, speaks in Atlanta in behalf of the Democratic presidential ticket headed by Gov. Alfred E. Smith.
October 28	Henrietta Egleston Hospital for Children opens.

Also this year: Fulton Federal Savings and Loan Assn. and Georgia Federal Savings and Loan Assn. launched.

Also this year: General Motors Corp. Lakewood plant opens.

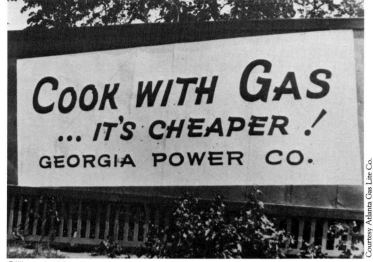

Billboard, 1928, when Atlanta Gas Light Co. was a department of Georgia Power Co.

Pres. Herbert Hoover
(see This Year In the Nation/Nov. 6)

THIS YEAR IN THE NATION

Feb. 2: Fire in Fall River, MA, causes $20 million damage ... **Mar. 10:** Pres. Coolidge signs Alien Property Act that compensates German nationals and companies for property seized during World War I ... **Mar. 13:** Santa Clara Valley, north of Los Angeles, flooded when dam collapses; 450 die ... **June 12-15:** Republicans nominate Herbert Hoover for President ... **June 26-29:** Democrats nominate Alfred E. Smith for President ... **July 30:** Movies in color demonstrated by George Eastman in Rochester, NY ... **Aug. 27:** Kellog-Briand peace treaty signed by 15 nations ... **Sept. 27:** U.S. recognizes the Nationalist Government of China headed by Chiang Kai-shek ... **Nov. 6:** Herbert Hoover elected President ... **Nov. 16:** Record day on the New York Stock exchange: 6,641,250 shares change hands.

1929

January 7	Georgia Tech's football team returns to a city-wide celebration after winning the Rose Bowl, 8 to 7.
January	Ragsdale begins his second term as mayor.
March 12	Asa Candler, the Coca-Cola Co. magnate, dies.
April 13	The City of Atlanta purchases Candler Field (297 acres) for $94,500. This transaction helps assure Atlanta's future in aviation.
July 27	The Legislature increases the length of Atlanta's mayoral term from two to four years.
September 25	A ceremony is held to mark the laying of a cornerstone of the Southern Bell Building on the corner of Ivy Street and Auburn Avenue.
November 25	The First National Bank of Atlanta, the largest financial institution south of Philadelphia, is established.

Also this year: Construction of the new City Hall is completed ... Air passenger service between Atlanta and Birmingham is established on a daily basis ... Regular bus service is inaugurated in 1929 as Atlanta becomes a main point on a line between Cincinnati and Jacksonville ... The $1.6 million, 21-story Rhodes-Haverty office building becomes Atlanta's tallest structure ... Dorothy Alexander organizes a group that becomes the Atlanta Ballet Co. ... Fox Theatre opens.

Also this year: Fourth National Bank merges with the Atlanta and Lowry National Bank to form the First National Bank of Atlanta (now known as First Wachovia).

THIS YEAR IN THE NATION

Stock market crash at the end of October begins the Great Depression ... **Jan. 15:** Kellog-Briand peace pact ratified by Senate ... **Feb. 11:** Young Plan, named for Owen D. Young, replaces the Dawes Plan for restructuring German war debt ... **Feb. 14:** St. Valentine's Day Massacre ... **Mar. 4:** Herbert Hoover inaugurated as the 31st President ... **Apr. 25:** Tornadoes in Georgia and South Carolina kill 65 ... **May 17:** Al Capone sentenced for a year for carrying a concealed weapon ... **May 27:** Pocket veto declared constitutional by Supreme Court ... **June 15:** Agricultural Marketing Bill, which establishes the Federal Farm Relief Board, signed by Pres. Hoover ... **July 22-Aug. 1:** Prison riots in New York state and Leavenworth, KS ... **Oct. 2:** Violence leads to three deaths during textile strike in Marion, NC ... **Oct. 24-28:** Stock market crash; millions of shares of stock change hands, billions of dollars of paper value lost ... **Nov. 11:** Ambassador Bridge between Detroit and Windsor, Canada, dedicated.

Fox Theatre opens in 1929; the men's lounge

City Hall (see Also this year . . .)

1930

January 1 The 125-room Jefferson Hotel is opened on the site of Temple Court, famous since 1895 first as an apartment house and later as the building in which many Atlanta lawyers had their offices.

January 4 Fulton County Grand Jury attacks allegations of graft at City Hall; later estimates it costs $1 million a year.

January 13 The Fulton County Grand Jury begins a probe of graft within Atlanta's municipal government. During the course of this investigation, 26 persons are indicted by two grand juries; 15 are convicted or plead guilty.

January 16 The William-Oliver skyscraper is erected.

January 30 Natural gas, piped in Louisiana, reaches Atlanta. This source of energy replaces manufactured gas which had been used for over 75 years.

February 22 The new 14-story City Hall, constructed for $1,000,000, officially opens.

March-May Fears of communism arise in the city as M. H. Powers of Minnesota and Joe Carr of West Virginia, American Communist party organizer, arrange interracial party meetings. On March 9 police arrest Powers, Carr, Emory student Robert H. Hart and two other whites at an integrated "party" meeting; on May 21 four more whites and two blacks are arrested at a meeting. Hart and a white couple are released. Six are charged with insurrection laws that date from the 1860's. The "Atlanta Six" are eventually released on bail and leave the state.

April 6 The four-story Marlborough Building, built in 1904 and housing the offices of many physicians, is gutted by fire.

In April of 1931, a modern fire proof building, known as the W. W. Orr Doctor Building, is built on the site. It is one of the first professional medical buildings in which doctors participated in designing the building.

April 18 Union Station is placed into service.

May 19 Publisher William Randolph Hearst gives Oglethorpe University $100,000.

June 18 At the height of The Constitution's expose of municipal graft, voters sweep out of office virtually every office-holder mentioned in the stories. At the same time former Mayor James L. Key, not mentioned in the probe, wins the mayoral primary.

July 14 Bobby Jones returns to Atlanta for a celebration of his "grand slam" victory in golf's four greatest tournaments — the American Amateur, the American Open, the British Amateur and the British Open.

August 3 Atlanta awarded a spot on the coast-to-coast air mail route.

October 31 The Southern Bell Telephone Building on the corner of Ivy Street and Auburn Avenue opens. It is primarily devoted to servicing toll lines, radio transmission and telephone transmission of photographs.

December 10 Atlanta-New York airplane passenger service begins. On January 1, 1931, service between Atlanta and Miami is inaugurated.

Also this year: Bryan (Bitsy) Grant wins the U.S. Clay Court Championship, and repeats the success in 1934 and 1935.

THIS YEAR IN THE NATION

Economic decline intensifies with increase in bank closings and unemployment; drought in Ohio and Mississippi valleys causes distress to farmers ... **Mar. 8:** Former President and Chief Justice of the Supreme Court William H. Taft dies at 72 ... **June 17:** Hawley-Smoot Tariff Act signed by Pres. Hoover, sending import duties to record highs ... **July 3:** Veterans' Administration created by Congress ... **Sept. 3:** Electric passenger train demonstrated in New Jersey ... **Dec. 11:** Largest bank failure in history of U.S. takes place when Bank of New York stops business; almost 400,000 depositors affected.

Passengers board an Eastern Air Transport plane (1930); Its full load was 18 passengers; its air speed, 120 m.p.h.

When natural gas came to Atlanta (see Jan. 30), congratulations were in order. Shaking hands over a ditch where the gas line lay were R. C. Hoffman, Jr., vice president of Atlanta Gas Light Co. (left), and J. H. White, president of Southern Natural Gas Corp.

1931

February	Two noted Atlanta landmarks are razed: the Dougherty (or Hopkins) house, a castle-like structure in the central business district, and the Ryan mansion, one of the city's few remaining antebellum homes.
March	Southern Bell installs a new telephone dial system. The Raymond dial office replaces a manual office formerly known as the West. During the year, new dial offices are also erected at East Point and Buckhead.
May 3	Cincinnati-Atlanta mail and passenger air route launched.
May 5	The Atlanta Constitution is awarded a Pulitzer Prize for exposing graft in city government.
July 25	The Southern Railway's Air Line Belle between Atlanta and Toccoa in North Georgia is discontinued. This 93-mile "commuter service" had been in operation since 1879.
Summer	Lenox Park, a residential subdivision located north of Rock Springs Road between Morningside and Druid Hills, is developed.
Fall	Rev. Martin Luther King, Sr., becomes pastor of Ebenezer Church after the death of his father-in-law, Rev. A. D. Williams.
September 16	Because of his efforts to repeal the Prohibition Amendment, Mayor James Key is removed as a Sunday School teacher at Grace Methodist Church. The next month Key starts a nondenominational Sunday School class at Capitol Theatre.
October 16-18	The Hebrew Benevolent Congregation's Temple is dedicated.
December 1	The Atlanta Trust Company Building, originally the Empire Building, becomes the Citizen and Southern National Bank Building.
December 2	Atlanta votes to retain Central Standard Time.
December	To help relief agencies, retail stores sponsor a "Good Samaritan Buying Campaign" with a grand prize of $2750 to be given to charities and churches receiving the largest number of votes from customers. A customer received a vote for every cent spent.

THIS YEAR IN THE NATION

Depression deepens; over 800 banks fail in September and October alone ... **Jan. 19:** Head of National Commission on Law Observance and Enforcement states that the Prohibition law can no longer be enforced due to high profits of liquor trade and public apathy ... **Mar. 3:** "The Star-Spangled Banner" adopted as the official national anthem ... **Mar. 20:** Gambling made legal in Nevada ... **Sept. 22:** U.S. Steel announces that it will reduce the wages of 220,000 workers by 10% ... **Sept. 29:** Episcopal Church liberalizes church stand on remarriage ... **Oct. 17:** Al Capone receives an 11-year jail sentence for income tax evasion ... **Oct. 18:** Inventor Thomas A. Edison dies at 84 ... **Oct. 25:** George Washington Bridge, the first bridge over the Hudson River and the world's longest suspension bridge, opens.

The Hebrew Benevolent Congregation's Temple has been its home since 1931 (on Peachtree St.). A bomb wrecked part of it in 1958 (see Oct. 16).

Home of Georgia Tech Evening School in 1931 (223 Walton St.), later Georgia State University

Opera star Amelita Galli-Curci performed here in 1931.

1932

January 1	As part of Georgia's program for "Bigger and Better Counties," Milton County and Campbell County merge with Fulton ... In May the Roswell Militia District, including the town of Roswell, is transferred from Cobb to Fulton County.
January	At the suggestion of Mrs. John Hope, wife of the president of Atlanta University and a black civic leader, citizenship schools are started for Atlanta's blacks. Blacks are taught the procedures involved in registering to vote in hopes that the white primary would eventually be declared unconstitutional.
March 15	In a recall election, Mayor Key retains his office. Prohibitionists and labor leaders generally favored his ouster; Key's greatest support is in the black community.
March	The 10 Pryor Street Building is erected. Because of the depression, the building is seven floors instead of 10 as first planned. (After the construction of the building, no major, privately-financed building will be constructed in downtown Atlanta until after World War II.) ... The Atlanta World becomes a daily newspaper.
April 30	Veteran Police Chief James Beavers is succeeded by Detective Lieutenant T. O. Sturdivant.
May 8	A $50,000 air terminal building is dedicated at Candler Field.
May 12	The Fox, the city's largest theatre, is closed when the local building contractor is unable to pay taxes for 1930-1931 or meet $60,000 in matured notes for 1932. (The theatre is closed for two years.)
June 30	Thousands of unemployed workers, black and white, march on the courthouse protesting the inadequacy of city relief measures. On July 1 the Fulton County Commission appropriates $6,000 to provide immediate relief for families whose grocery orders were cut off due to a curtailment of emergency relief funds.
July 12	Fulton County's "self-help plan" goes into effect. In return for light work, unemployed heads of families receive a noonday meal and $1.25 in scrip to buy groceries.
July 16	Dedication ceremonies are held for the modernized and rebuilt bridge over the railroad tracks (Peachtree-Whitehall viaduct). The original viaduct had been built in 1901.
July	7,592 needy families in Atlanta and Fulton County are receiving aid.

August	The Atlanta Negro Chamber of Commerce is organized.
Summer	Atlanta's Chamber of Commerce launches a "Back to the Farm" Movement. Land is secured for people who want to cultivate.
September 27	A direct relief loan of $315,093 is secured for the City and Fulton County from the Reconstruction Finance Corporation. Proceeds are doled out through a Central Relief Committee.
October 24	A parade to honor Franklin D. Roosevelt's visit to Atlanta draws nearly a quarter of a million viewers.

THIS YEAR IN THE NATION

Jan. 12: Oliver W. Holmes at 90 resigns from Supreme Court after almost 30 years' service ... **Jan. 20:** Reconstruction Finance Corporation, headed by Charles Dawes, attempts to prop up banking system by lending money to banks and other financial institutions ... **Mar. 1:** Amendment to the Constitution, calling for the moving of the date of the inauguration of the president to Jan. 20, sent to the states to be ratified ... **Mar. 21:** Tornadoes kill 360 in Florida, Georgia, Alabama, Tennessee and Kentucky ... **May 12:** Dead body of Charles Lindbergh, Jr., found ... **May 20-21:** Amelia Earhart becomes the first woman to fly solo across the Atlantic ... **June 14-16:** Republicans renominate Pres. Hoover for a second term ... **June 27-July 2:** Democrats nominate Franklin D. Roosevelt as president ... **July 18:** Canada and U.S. sign treaty to build the St. Lawrence Seaway ... **July 22:** Federal Home Loan Bank Act, to stimulate home construction and ownership, becomes law ... **Aug. 16:** Farmers Holiday Association asks farmers not to sell produce until prices rise ... **Sept. 1:** New York Mayor James J. Walker resigns ... **Oct. 31:** Agricultural Department report shows that average farm income after expenses drops from $847 in 1929 to $341 in 1931 ... **Nov. 8:** Franklin D. Roosevelt elected President ... **Nov. 11:** Tomb of Unknown Soldier dedicated ... **Dec. 27:** Radio City Music Hall in Rockefeller Center, the world's largest theatre, opens.

Franklin D. Roosevelt, who recuperated from polio at Warm Springs, GA, campaigned in Atlanta in 1932 for the presidency, with his daughter Margaret (center) and wife Eleanor. Driver of the car (foreground) is Atlantan A. L. Belle Isle.

1933

January 13	The city finance committee votes to cut the salaries of municipal employees by 20 per cent. Rich's department store soon announces that scrip from municipal employees will be accepted, and change be given in U.S. currency instead of scrip.
January 24	Atlanta banks refuse to give City Hall credit unless it cuts another $1 million from its $14 million budget. Stressed by the Depression and high unemployment, both City Hall and the County governments cut staff salaries.
April 7	L. W. "Chip" Robert, Jr., a noted Atlanta engineer and builder, is appointed Assistant Secretary of the Treasury in charge of public works programs. He becomes instrumental in helping Atlanta obtain government funds.
May 19	City Council passes an ordinance allowing the sale of 3.2 beer. Before nightfall, 49 new establishments have been licensed to sell beer. Sale of any stronger beverage is prohibited by state law.
May	Eastern Air Transport, the fourth largest airline in 1933 (and soon renamed Eastern Airlines), moves its general operations and headquarters to Atlanta. On Sept. 16 Eastern launches it first night flight from Atlanta to New York, though service to and from Atlanta had begun in December, 1930. Delta Air Lines begins serving Atlanta in June, 1930, and moves its headquarters to the city in 1941.
Spring	Local ministers organize the Cooperative Exchange Club to create jobs with merchants who pay workers with exchange checks redeemable for goods at any store which participates in the program.
July 6	John K. Ottley, president of First National Bank, is kidnapped for a $40,000 ransom. Ottley is eventually released unharmed.
July 11	Atlanta begins a transient bureau to help jobless drifters who travel through Atlanta. Transient facilities included two hotels for men. In addition to providing lodging and meals, the bureau also operates an infirmary, a recreation room and a library.
September 1	Due to a campaign waged by the Atlanta Chamber of Commerce, 532 employers are brought under the provisions of the National Recovery Act. These firms employ nearly 50,000 persons, added nearly 6,000 workers to their payrolls during the year, and increase wages and salaries by more than $400,000.
September 21	Atlanta voters approve of commercial amusements on Sunday. On October 19 theatre owners and managers decide to show Sunday movies. They, however, agree to donate Sunday receipts to charity and Depression relief.
October 4	An estimated 50,000 people participate in a parade honoring the National Recovery Act.
October 9	The new Hilan Theatre at 800 Highland Avenue, NE, opens in the new Franklin Roosevelt Building. It has indirect lighting and a lobby with mirrored walls and chrome fixtures.
November	The Civil Works Administration (CWA) announces $400,000 worth of improvements in Fulton County including $200,000 for improvements at Grady Hospital and $11,000 for repairs at Georgia Tech. CWA projects include the start of Atlanta's new sewer system, the paving of city streets, organizing a 45-member symphony, staffing positions in the public library, maintaining a transient shelter, and public works art projects.
December 2	A $3,000,000 postoffice opens on Forsyth Street.
	Also this year: A half-million people parade Peachtree Street in support of the National Recovery Act.

THIS YEAR IN THE NATION

Franklin D. Roosevelt becomes President just as economy hits bottom; in the Hundred Days much legislation is passed to deal with the immediate economic problems of bank failures and unemployment ... **Jan. 5:** Former Pres. Coolidge dies at 60 ... **Feb. 6:** 20th Amendment to the Constitution becomes law ... **Feb. 15:** Pres.-elect Roosevelt uninjured in assassination attempt ... **Feb. 25:** First U.S. aircraft carrier, the Ranger, goes into service ... **Mar. 4:** Franklin D. Roosevelt inaugurated as the 32d president ... **Mar. 6-9:** Pres. Roosevelt declares a bank holiday ... **Mar. 12:** Pres. Roosevelt broadcasts his first fireside chat ... **Mar. 31:** Civilian Conservation Corps established to give work to youths 18-25 ... **Apr. 4:** Navy dirigible The Akron, the world's largest, goes down in the Atlantic ... **Apr. 19:** Pres. Roosevelt announces that U.S. will go off the gold standard ... **May 12:** Federal Emergency Relief Administration established to deal with low farm income ... **May 18:** Congress establishes the Tennessee Valley Authority ... **May 27:** Century of Progress Exposition opens in Chicago ... **June 16:** Glass-Steagall Act, establishing the Federal Deposit Insurance Corp., passes ... **June 16:** Farm Credit Act becomes law ... **June 16:** National Industrial Recovery Act is passed ... **Aug. 5:** National Labor Relations Board established ... **Nov. 8:** Civil Works Administration, forerunner of the WPA, is begun to create jobs for unemployed ... **Nov. 16:** Soviet Union and U.S. establish diplomatic relations ... **Dec. 5:** Prohibition repealed as 36th state approves 21st Amendment to the Constitution.

The "old" postoffice (see Dec. 2)

1934

January 1	Construction of Atlanta's new sewer system begins. Prior to this construction, over half of Atlanta's wastes were being dumped in various streams leading into the Chattahoochee. In April this project is turned over to the Public Works Administration (PWA). When finished, this project cost over $6,000,000 of which the City paid only 14 per cent. The rest of the total is funded through government agencies.
January	The Coca-Cola Company helps Atlanta meet its deficit of $1,047,399.68 by advancing the city $800,000.
February 14	The "ride-rob" epidemic reaches Atlanta. This "technique" involves the robbing and assaulting of stopped motorists, particularly at red lights. In late February, Police Chief Sturdivant gives his officers permission to "shoot to kill" offenders and urges motorists to arm themselves for self-protection. On March 6 Sturdivant denies that crime is rampant in the city.
February	Over 15,000 people in Fulton County are working on CWA jobs.
April 4	The U.S. Postoffice announces that Atlanta will be a spot on a new transcontinental air mail line from Charleston to Los Angeles. When completed, three major air mail routes will cross the city. Atlanta is also on the New York-New Orleans and the Chicago-Jacksonville routes.
Spring	John Wesley Dobbs, retired railroad mail clerk, Grand Master of the Masons in Georgia and black civic leader, organizes the Atlanta Civil and Political League to encourage black citizens to become involved in the political process. The next year Rev. Martin Luther King, Sr., pastor of Ebenezer Baptist Church, leads a voting registration march on City Hall.
August	Interracial mass meetings protesting the inequitable distribution of relief take place at the Capitol throughout the month.
September 3- September 18	Labor unrest in Georgia's textile mills reaches Atlanta. Strikes close all but one of the city's mills. Intermittent violence results in a declaration of martial law by Gov. Eugene Talmadge. An appeal by Franklin D. Roosevelt to end the strikes eases tensions on both sides.
September 26	James L. Key is reelected mayor. At the same time decisive victories are recorded in favor of Daylight Savings Time and repeal of Georgia's "dry-bone" law.
October 1	Atlanta City Council votes for Daylight Savings Time to begin on April 28.
October	Mayor Key announces that teachers and City employees will be paid in scrip for the last two months of the year due to the depletion of finances.
November 7	The new police station and jail annex opens. This facility, which cost $350,000, is financed through funds made available by the Works Progress Administration (WPA).

THIS YEAR IN THE NATION

Jan. 30: Dollar devalued to 59.06 cents by Pres. Roosevelt under authority of Gold Reserve Act ... **Jan. 31:** Federal Farm Mortgage Corp. is established ... **Mar. 24:** Philippines Independence Bill, which provides for independence in 1946, passes Congress ... **Apr. 12:** Senate investigation of war profiteering during World War I opens with Sen. Gerald Nye as chairman ... **May 23:** Bank robbers Bonnie Parker and Clyde Barrow killed by police ... **June 19:** Federal Communications Commission established by Congress ... **July 6:** John Dillinger shot dead by federal authorities in Chicago ... **Aug. 15:** Marines leave Haiti ... **Sept. 1-Oct. 3:** One million textile workers out on strike ... **Sept. 8:** Ocean liner Morro Castle burns off coast of New Jersey with loss of 120 lives ... **Oct. 25:** Railroad record of 57 hours from New York to Los Angeles set by Union Pacific train.

Charles Lindbergh (left) gave aviation a big boost when he visited Atlanta in 1927 (not long after his solo transAtlantic flight), and again in 1934 when he was photographed with Atlanta Constitution publisher Clark Howell Sr.

1935

January 19
One of Atlanta's oldest structures, the Georgia Railroad Freight Depot (recently known as the Atlanta Joint Terminal Building), is destroyed by fire.

February 5
Despite the city's strong support of Franklin D. Roosevelt, Huey Long speaks before large crowds on his trip to Atlanta. Long advocates his "share the wealth program."

March 14
Gov. Eugene Talmadge signs the Atlanta Ward Reduction Bill. This measure provides for a reorganization of Atlanta's municipal government by reducing the number of wards (13 to six), councilmen (39 to 18), and school board members (14 to six).

April 3
Stone Mountain sculptor Augustus Lukeman dies.

May
Atlanta United Auto Workers Local 34 joins locals across the country in a nationwide auto strike. Workers strike at Lakewood Fisher Body and Chevrolet plants.

June 7
Atlanta reported to be the leading horse and mule market in the U.S.

July 1
City Council adopts a proposal for a referendum on the establishment of the eastern time zone for Atlanta. It is not until the adoption of the Uniform Time Law on March 21, 1941, that the whole state adopts eastern time permanently.

July 5
Metro Atlanta assured $4.6 million additional WPA funds for sewer projects (making total $7+ million).

September 11
County engineers suggest a belt highway around Atlanta.

September 13
The Fulton Grand Jury begins a probe of alleged misconduct within the Atlanta Police Department.

September 18
Voters approve a $175,000 bond issue for sewers and schools.

October
A national survey indicates that Atlanta's per capita debt is the lowest in the nation.

November 15
A motorcade celebrates the paving of the last link between Atlanta and Savannah.

November 29
Pres. Roosevelt dedicates Techwood Homes, the first federally-assisted public housing project in the nation. He also visits the site of the University Housing Project, the black counterpart to Techwood homes.

December 28-
January 2
A sleet and ice storm paralyzes the city. Damage costs the city $2,500,000.

December
The municipal zoo at Grant Park displays a large variety of animals. Many were purchased from Asa Candler, Jr.'s, private collection with dimes donated by city children.

Also this year: The Peoples Savings Bank, predecessor of First Georgia Bank (now First Union), chartered.

THIS YEAR IN THE NATION

New Deal moves ahead as dust storms begin in the Great Plains ... **Jan. 26:** Floods in South kill 27 and cause $5 million damage ... **Apr. 27:** Congress establishes Soil Conservation Service in Department of Agriculture to combat soil erosion ... **May 6:** Works Progress Administration established by executive order ... **May 11:** Rural Electrification Administration established to bring electricity to rural areas of the country ... **June 10:** Alcoholics Anonymous founded ... **June 26:** National Youth Administration established as part of the WPA ... **Aug. 14:** Social Security Act becomes law ... **Aug. 31:** Congress passes a neutrality act that forbids the shipment of U.S. arms to warring nations ... **Sept. 8:** Sen. Huey P. Long assassinated at Baton Rouge ... **Oct. 10:** "Porgy and Bess" by George Gershwin opens on Broadway ... **Nov. 9:** Committee for Industrial Organization set up within American Federation of Labor to organize whole industries instead of just certain crafts.

Gov. Eugene Talmadge (see Mar. 14)

1936

January 13	Atlanta's Police Committee launches a probe of the Grand Jury's charges against the Police Department.
February 13	Police Chief T. O. Sturdivant and Detective Poole are suspended by the Police Board and scheduled to face charges of incompetency and inefficiency. Lieutenant Marion Hornsby is made acting chief.
March 9	After a long trial, Police Chief Sturdivant and Detective Poole are given a Police Board reprimand and restored to duty, cleared of all charges.
March	After several days of disorder and 15 arrests, the strike at the American Hat Manufacturing Company ends when an agreement is reached between labor and management.
April 7	A group of Atlanta business leaders are quick to respond to tornado-stricken Gainesville, Ga. A relief fund drive nets more than $150,000.
April 18	The first Dogwood Festival is held.
May	Twenty-six die in Terminal Hotel fire.
June 21	"Gone With the Wind" published; one million copies printed by year's end.
June 28	Margaret Mitchell's "Gone With the Wind" goes on sale in Atlanta.
June	With funds provided by WPA, the Battle of Atlanta Cyclorama painting is turned into a three-dimensional display.
Summer	Black teachers begin meeting to discuss discriminatory pay scales. Rev. Martin Luther King, Sr., helps lead the fight. (It would be 11 years before near equality in wages is achieved.)
September	Techwood Homes opens.
September 23	William B. Hartsfield defeats James Key in the mayoral primary.
November 14	Clark Howell, Sr., an editor of The Atlanta Constitution since 1889, dies.
November 21	"Tobacco Road" plays at the Erlanger Theatre after winning a court injunction test.
November 19	Fire guts the interior of the five-story Cable Piano Building on north Broad Street. Three people are killed and six are injured. This fire causes many to question the efficiency of Atlanta's fire department.
December 10	Emory University announces a $6 million development plan.
December	The Coca-Cola Company announces it will stand behind the city's December payroll. Because of this action, city scrip, usually cashed at a heavy discount, is honored at full face value by banks.

THIS YEAR IN THE NATION

Jan. 1: Unemployment insurance begins ... **Jan. 6:** Agricultural Adjustment Act found unconstitutional by Supreme Court ... **Jan. 11-Feb. 3:** Sit-down strikes at General Motors facilities ... **Feb. 17:** Supreme Court upholds constitutionality of Tennessee Valley Authority ... **June 9-12:** Republicans nominate Alfred Landon for President ... **June 23-27:** Democrats nominate Pres. Roosevelt for a second term ... **June 30:** Walsh-Healey Government Contracts Act, which requires all companies doing business with the federal government to adopt minimum wage and restrict use of child labor, becomes law ... **July 11:** Triborough Bridge connecting Manhattan, Queens and the Bronx is dedicated ... **Aug. 9:** Journalist muckraker Lincoln Steffens dies at 70 ... **Oct. 30:** Dock strike involving 39,000 workers begins on West Coast ... **Nov. 3:** Pres. Roosevelt reelected in a landslide.

Margaret Mitchell and her father eye her book (see June 28)

William B. Hartsfield (see Sept. 23)

For young Tracy W. O'Neal the great event of 1936 was a muscle-testing meeting with former heavyweight boxing champion Jack Dempsey, in Atlanta that July to referee wrestling matches.

1937

January 5	Police Chief Sturdivant and Chief of Detectives Poole resign. Lieutenant Marion A. Hornsby is appointed new chief.
January 27	Clark Howell, Jr., is named publisher of The Atlanta Constitution.
January	Atlanta accepts the Model Budget Law of 1937. Under its provisions, only 99 per cent of the previous year's revenues may be allocated.
February	City Hall releases funds to feed the needy.
March 2	Mayor Hartsfield charges that Atlanta is a dumping ground for the underworld. He estimates that at least 3,000 persons live on profits obtained from illegal means.
March 27	Citizens protest the danger of police chases of liquor cars through congested downtown Atlanta. On March 29 the Police Department outlaws these chases.
April 11	Atlanta is designated a cathedral city.
April	University Homes, offering public housing for black residents, opens.
May 3	Margaret Mitchell wins the Pulitzer Prize for "Gone With the Wind."
August 1	The Atlanta Journal opens a radio station, WAGA.
August 18	Grady Hospital establishes the city's first blood bank.
August	Memorial Auditorium roof collapses in a storm.
September 17	Responding to Mayor Hartsfield's charges, the Fulton County Grand Jury begins a sweeping investigation of graft and organized crime.
October 5	A dental clinic for children is dedicated at Atlanta Southern College.

THIS YEAR IN THE NATION

Jan. 8: U.S. embargoes shipment of arms to war-torn Spain ... **Feb. 4:** West Coast dock strike ends with union victory ... **Feb. 7:** Former senator and diplomat Elihu Root dies at 92 ... **Feb. 11:** Sit-down strike ends at General Motors with union victory ... **Mar. 2:** Two largest steel companies, faced with a strike, recognize union and grant 40-hour week ... **May 6:** German dirigible Hindenburg explodes and is destroyed by fire at Lakehurst, NJ ... **May 23:** Industrialist John D. Rockefeller dies at 97 ... **May 27:** Golden Gate Bridge, longest suspension bridge in the world, opens ... **May 30:** Memorial Day Massacre as police open fire on steel workers demonstrating near Republic Steel plant in Chicago ... **June 22:** By knocking out Jim Braddock in the 11th round, Joe Louis becomes heavyweight champion of the world ... **July 11:** Composer George Gershwin dies at 38 ... **Dec. 12:** Japanese air force sinks U.S. gunboat Panay in China; Japan apologizes and offers to pay damages.

November 2	An estimated $25,000 worth of damage is done to the Carroll Furniture Company Building as flames sweep a section of the store.
November 17	Rev. William Holmes Borders, later an important black leader, is appointed pastor of Wheat Street Baptist Church.

Seven traffic deaths in August, 1936, set off a publicity campaign climaxed by a "Parade of Horrors" (in March, 1937) featuring vehicles in which drivers and or passengers had died.

The Hindenburg (see This Year in the Nation/May 6)

Joe Louis (see This Year in the Nation/June 22)

1938

February 5 Thomas Reed, a municipal consultant employed by Fulton County, Atlanta and the Chamber of Commerce to make a study of both county and city governments, presents his report on county/city consolidation. (While civic leaders are generally cool toward his report, many of Reed's recommendations, in whole or in part, have been adopted.)

March 30 Citizens of Fulton County vote overwhelmingly to allow liquor sales; on April 25 liquor sales in Atlanta begin.

May 14 Georgia's first four-lane "super highway" (U.S. 41) is opened between Atlanta and Marietta.

May 16 The 30-year-old, five-story Terminal Hotel catches on fire; 34 persons are killed.

May 27 A resolution creating the Atlanta Housing Authority is approved by the mayor.

June 11 Members of the Atlanta Housing Authority are appointed; Charles Palmer is its first chairman.

June 16 Ralph McGill is appointed executive editor and editorial columnist of The Atlanta Constitution.

June During the first six months of the year 93 companies locate in Atlanta.

July 2 The U.S. Housing Authority allocates $9,000,000 to Atlanta for slum clearance.

July 14 Ernest Woodruff announces the chartering of the Emily and Ernest Woodruff Foundation.

August Two of Atlanta's few remaining antebellum homes, the William Solomon and James R. Crew houses, are razed to make way for state office buildings. During the 1850s these homes were in the city's finest residential area.

THIS YEAR IN THE NATION

Recession worsens; Germany annexes Austria ... **Jan. 22:** 30 executives of 16 oil companies convicted of price-fixing of gasoline ... **Apr. 14:** In response to recession Pres. Roosevelt asks Congress for $3 billion to spend on public works and relief ... **Apr. 22:** 45 killed in explosions in mines in Buchanan County, VA ... **May 26:** House Committee on Un-American Activities under the chairmanship of Martin Dies established ... **June 22:** Joe Louis retains his heavyweight championship by knocking out Max Schmeling in the first round ... **June 24:** Food, Drug and Cosmetic Act passes Congress ... **June 25:** Minimum wage raised to 25 cents per hour by Fair Labor Standards Act ... **Sept. 15:** Author Thomas Wolfe dies at 37 ... **Sept. 21:** Hurricane hits New England causing 600 deaths and much damage ... **Oct. 30:** Orson Welles' radio adaptation of "War of the Worlds" causes brief hysteria ... **Nov. 18:** First convention of CIO elects John L. Lewis as president.

Summer The nation's first air traffic control tower goes into operation at Atlanta Municipal Airport.

November 21 The stage play "Tobacco Road" opens at the Erlanger Theatre. Because of the play's language and "earthy escapades," members of the library board's censor committee ban the play. Attorneys for the show obtain an injunction allowing it to open.

December 5 As Atlanta's auto death toll climbs to 50 (plus 1,279 injured) the City Council adopts a uniform 25-mile-an-hour speed limit.

The City of Atlanta built its first air terminal in 1932, and the tower was added in 1938.

After Prohibition was repealed in Georgia in 1938, state law required customers to sign a register when they made purchases. The most frequently used names are those of the governor and the revenue commissioner.

Dedication of the steel door for Oglethorpe University's Crypt of Civilization came during the 1938 commencement; the Crypt of artifacts was sealed May 25, 1940, and is to be opened in 8113 A.D.

1939

January	Atlanta becomes one of the first large cities in the South to enact a civil service law.
January 14	Endowment grants totaling $2,500,000 are given Emory University and Agnes Scott College. One week later, Samuel C. Dobbs, an Atlanta financier and philanthropist, gives $1,000,000 to Emory.
January 18	The Catholic Co-Cathedral of Christ the King is dedicated. Imperial Wizard Hiram Evans of the Ku Klux Klan is one of the invited guests. The Klan are former owners of the property on which the Church is built.
May 1	Robert Woodruff is elected chairman of the board and Arthur Acklin is named president of Coca-Cola.
May 28	James Key, mayor for 10 years, dies.
June 24	Nunnally's, the downtown place where a fellow bought his girl ice cream or candy after the show, closes.
July 1	Charles Palmer reports that 54.85% of all Atlanta's housing is substandard.
July 22	The Sixth World Baptist Conference opens at the Atlanta Baseball Park on Ponce de Leon Ave.
November 11	The Atlanta Housing Authority announces plans for a 15-year, $50,000,000 building program to wipe out the city's slums.
November 21	The Joseph B. Whitehead Foundation gives $450,000 to various churches and charities in Atlanta.
November 23	A complete union of the Methodist Episcopal Church, the Methodist Episcopal Church South, and the Methodist Protestant Church is declared at a conference in Wesley Memorial Chapel.
December 12	James M. Cox, former governor of Ohio and 1920 Democratic nominee for president, buys The Atlanta Journal and its

radio station, WSB. Five days later Cox purchases and folds The Atlanta Georgian and Sunday American. The Atlanta Journal thus has the afternoon market to itself.

December 15	The world premiere of the movie version of Margaret Mitchell's "Gone With the Wind" is presented at Loew's Grand Theatre.
December 26	City officials announce that Atlanta will enter 1940 free of current debt and with about $500,000 in the bank.

At the World Baptist Alliance meeting in Atlanta in July, 1939, flags representing delegates from various nations—including Nazi Germany—flew over downtown Peachtree St.

Clark Gable, author Margaret Mitchell (center) and Vivien Leigh (see Dec. 15)

Seven former Georgia governors posed in 1939 (from left): E. D. Rivers, 1937-41; Eugene Talmadge, 1933-37 and 1941-43; Richard B. Russell, 1931-33; Clifford M. Walker, 1923-27; T. W. Hardwick, 1921-23; Hugh M. Dorsey, 1917-21, and John M. Slaton, 1913-15.

THIS YEAR IN THE NATION

Roosevelt tries to build country's military strength as fascism spreads across Europe ... **Apr. 30-Oct. 31:** World's Fair held in Queens, NY ... **May 5-13:** United Mine Workers, led by John L. Lewis, close most bituminous coal mines ... **May 5:** Three Methodist Churches become one by signing Declaration of Union thus uniting 8 million members in one organization ... **June 7-12:** King and Queen of England visit U.S. ... **June 28:** Regular airplane passenger service begins between U.S. and Europe ... **July 25:** Senate ratifies treaty with Panama relinquishing right to intervene in that country's domestic affairs ... **Aug. 2:** Hatch Act, which restricts political activity of federal employees, passes Congress ... **Sept. 8:** Pres. Roosevelt declares the country to be in a limited emergency ... **Nov. 4:** Amendments to Neutrality Act of 1937 allow belligerents to purchase arms from the U.S. on a cash-and-carry basis ... **Dec. 11:** The use of evidence obtained by use of a wiretap without a warrant declared by Supreme Court to be unlawful ... **Dec. 12:** Actor Douglas Fairbanks, Sr., dies at 56.

1940

January 30 A ten inch snowfall paralyzes the city.

February 12 The City raises $10,000 for Albany, GA, hit by tornadoes leaving 1500 homeless and 12 dead.

March The Grand Jury probes an outbreak of floggings in Fulton County. These incidents are traced to the Ku Klux Klan, and 10 Klan members are indicted. Later in the year, Floyd I. Lee — "Kingpin of the East Point Klan" — and others are convicted.

May 20 The City Council orders probes of all aliens within the city.

May The Metropolitan Opera again visits Atlanta; first time since 1930.

July 3 The Council approves a $4,000,000 bond issue for schools and hospitals.

July 22 The new national headquarters of Coca-Cola open.

September The John Hope Homes, which replace 500 slum dwellings with 606 apartments, open. Also this month, Dr. Benjamin Mays becomes president of Morehouse College.

September 4 Roy LeCraw, former Atlanta Chamber of Commerce president, defeats W. B. Hartsfield by 111 votes to win the mayoral nomination.

October 10 Work begins on the Atlanta Naval Air Station (today's DeKalb Peachtree Airport). Fort McPherson, the Atlanta General Depot at Conley, and Lawson General Hospital in Chamblee were other military installations in the Atlanta area.

October 22 A $3,500,000 loan to pay Georgia's teachers is refused by Atlanta's banks unless Gov.-elect Eugene Talmadge guarantees repayment. Gov. Ed Rivers decides to borrow the money from New York banks.

October 28 The Atlanta Greek community begins collecting funds to send to Greece following invasion by Italy.

November 11 Having just had its roof repaired, the front section of the Atlanta Municipal Auditorium is severely damaged by fire.

November 23 Joel Hurt Park, first new park in the downtown area since the Civil War, is dedicated.

November 28 The Joseph B. Whitehead Foundation again helps Atlanta's charities by distributing $286,000 to various institutions.

Also this year: Atlanta's in-city population hits 302,288 persons, of whom 104,533 are black.

Hurt Park (see Nov. 23)

THIS YEAR IN THE NATION

As Germany overruns most of Europe, Pres. Roosevelt attempts to prepare at home while aiding Great Britain during her finest hour ... **Jan. 19:** Sen. William Borah, first elected in 1906, dies at 74 ... **Jan. 26:** U.S. refuses to renew trade treaty with Japan ... **Apr. 22:** Antipicketing laws of Alabama and California declared unconstitutional by Supreme Court ... **May 15:** First helicopter demonstrated by Igor Sikorsky ... **June 3:** U.S. begins to supply Great Britain with war materiel ... **June 10:** Black leader Marcus Garvey dies at 52 ... **June 24-28:** Republicans nominate Wendell L. Willkie for president ... **June 28:** Smith Act, which requires all foreigners to be registered and fingerprinted, becomes law ... **July 15-19:** Democrats nominate Pres. Roosevelt for a third term ... **Aug. 29:** Color television demonstrated by CBS ... **Sept. 3:** Pres. Roosevelt trades Great Britain 50 destroyers for the right to build bases on British territories ... **Oct. 24:** 40-hour week provision of Wages and Hours Act goes into effect ... **Nov. 5:** Pres. Roosevelt elected for third term ... **Nov. 7:** Tacoma Narrows Bridge falls into Puget Sound only four months after its completion ... **Dec. 21:** Author F. Scott Fitzgerald dies at 44.

1941

March 27	Gov. Talmadge signs a bill requiring the state park authority to take over development of the Stone Mountain Memorial.
May 1	Robert L. MacDougall of Atlanta is named Assistant Commissioner of the WPA.
May 5	Westbrook Pegler, working for The Atlanta Constitution, wins the Pulitzer Prize for reporting. His prize-winning articles were written for the New York World-Telegram.
May 10	A new $340,000 farmer's market opens and handles $6,000,000 by the end of the year. By the end of 1942, this figure rises to $10,000,000.
July 18	The Atlanta City Council denies use of City auditorium to isolationist Sen. Burton K. Wheeler.
July 21	The governor announces that he will withhold news from The Journal and The Constitution unless they "correct their attitude."
July 22	Garbage workers strike for higher wages. On July 28 City Council approves an overall wage increase to City employees totaling $52,678.
August 22	A polio epidemic delays the opening of schools until Sept. 15.
September 6	The cruiser "Atlanta" is christened by Margaret Mitchell.
October 15	One thousand students from the University of Georgia storm the state Capitol to protest Gov. Talmadge's attack on academic freedom. Ten state-supported colleges were threatened with the loss of accreditation due to "political interference."

THIS YEAR IN THE NATION

Jan. 6: In address to Congress Pres. Roosevelt urges that the U.S. supply nations fighting totalitarian aggressors with needed arms and thus becomes the arsenal of democracy ... **Feb. 15:** First B-24 bomber supplied to Great Britain ... **Mar. 8:** Author Sherwood Anderson dies at 64 ... **Mar. 11-12:** Lend-Lease Act passes Congress ... **Mar. 17:** National Gallery of Art opens ... **Mar. 19:** National Defense Mediation Board established to prevent strikes in defense industries ... **Mar. 22:** Grand Coulee Dam begins to produce electricity ... **Mar. 31-Apr. 28:** Strike by United Mine Workers wins a dollar-a-day raise ... **Apr. 11:** Office of Price Administration established ... **Apr. 17:** Automobile manufacturers agree to lower output to 1 million units per year ... **Apr. 28:** Supreme Court rules that blacks must be offered train accommodations equal to that of whites ... **May 27:** Pres. Roosevelt declares that an unlimited state of emergency exists ... **May 31:** "Tobacco Road" closes after 3,180 performances ... **June 2:** Baseball player Lou Gehrig dies at 38 ... **June 14-17:** Pres. Roosevelt freezes all Italian and German assets in U.S. ... **Aug. 14:** Pres. Roosevelt and Prime Minister Churchill draw up the Atlantic Charter ... **Aug. 18:** Selective Service Act of 1940 becomes law ... **Sept. 4:** U.S. destroyer Greer attacked by German U-boat ... **Sept. 9-22:** Three American ships sunk off Iceland by German U-boats ... **Dec. 7:** Japan attacks U.S. naval base at Pearl Harbor ... **Dec. 8:** Pres. Roosevelt addresses Congress calling for a declaration of war on Japan ... **Dec. 11:** Germany and Italy declare war on U.S. ... **Dec. 12:** Japan occupies Guam ... **Dec. 22:** Pres. Roosevelt signs new Selective Service Act requiring all males from 18 to 64 to register ... **Dec. 22:** Japan occupies Wake Island.

December 20	A gasoline pipeline from the Gulf of Mexico through Atlanta to Chattanooga, TN, is opened.
December	During this year Atlanta completes four New Deal housing projects — the Grady, Egan, Herndon and Capitol Homes. By 1941 Atlanta has eight federally-funded housing projects. Also this year: Delta Air Lines opens its $150,000 general office and hangar at Atlanta Airport.

Delta Air Lines' hangar, which could accommodate six, 21-passenger planes, opened in 1941 (see Also this year . . .)

Author Margaret Mitchell christens the USS Atlanta III on Sept. 6, 1941, at Kearny, NJ.

Academy of Medicine, built in 1941 at 875 W. Peachtree St.

1942

January 2	Rich's, Inc., celebrates its 75th anniversary.
February 9	Stores begin to stagger their hours as war hours go into effect.
February 20	A B-29 assembly plant is announced for Marietta. It is expected to bring 40,000 jobs into the area.
February 25	Capt. Eddie Rickenbacker donates funds to Cobb County to construct a school to teach aircraft workers.
March 14	City Council accepts the resignation of Mayor LeCraw. He reports as a major in the chemical warfare department of the army.
April 7	As a war measure the City Council adopts a midnight curfew on all public amusement houses.
May 27	William B. Hartsfield defeats eight opponents in a special primary, and wins the right to replace Roy LeCraw, who resigned due to military service, as mayor.
June 2	Newly-elected Mayor W. B. Hartsfield declares war on the underworld. He calls on Police Chief Hornsby to rid the city of "loafers," "idlers" and "criminal parasites."
July 21	Atlanta's 300 truck men (workers who carry garbage to the trucks) walk off their jobs. Due to failure of the white drivers to support them and the use of convict labor, the strike ends after one week.
August 25	Using flour bombs, the city of Atlanta practices a blackout air "raid."

October 22	The Washington Aircraft School, an institution to teach blacks aircraft work, opens.
November 12-13	The anti-aircraft cruiser "Atlanta" is sunk off Guadalcanal; 172 men are killed and 79 wounded.
December 11	William Alexander, coach of Georgia Tech from 1920-1945, is named "Coach of the Year."
December	The Atlanta Chamber of Commerce announces that Atlanta's population is 473,800 — a growth of 31,506 since the 1940 census.

Also this year: Due to wartime restrictions, sugar is limited for bakeries and soft drink manufacturers; businesses stagger hours to save on power and transportation; Mayor Roy LeCraw leads a bike parade to Piedmont Park to show how automobile gas can be saved; grading begins for the Marietta Bell Bomber plant; bus and streetcar stops reduced.

THIS YEAR IN THE NATION

110,000 Japanese-Americans, including 75,000 U.S. citizens, moved from West Coast to inland camps; wartime exclusion lasts three years ... **Jan. 1:** Ban on the production of new cars ordered by office of Production Management ... **Jan. 1:** 26 nations, meeting in Washington, agree to support war aims of Atlantic Charter and to make no individual peace with Axis ... **Jan. 12:** National War Labor Board established by Pres. Roosevelt to prevent strikes in defense production ... **Feb. 12:** Artist Grant Wood dies at 50 ... **Apr. 9:** Bataan Peninsula captured by Japanese; next day infamous Death March begins ... **May 6:** Fortress Island of Corregidor captured by Japanese ... **Apr. 18:** 16 bombers led by Gen. James Doolittle bomb Tokyo ... **May 5:** Sugar rationing begins ... **May 7-8:** In Battle of the Coral Sea, U.S. forces halt Japanese drive toward Australia ... **May 14:** Congress creates Women's Army Auxiliary Corps ... **May 29:** Actor John Barrymore dies at 60 ... **June 3-6:** Battle of Midway results in critical victory by U.S. over Japan ... **July 22:** Coupons for gasoline rationing issued ... **Nov. 8:** U.S. and British forces land in North Africa ... **Nov. 13:** Draft age lowered from 21 to 18 ... **Nov. 28:** 487 die in fire at Coconut Grove night club in Boston.

*Assembly line for B-29s
(see Feb. 20)*

1943

February Grace Towns Hamilton is appointed direc-tor of the Atlanta Urban League, and holds this post until 1961. During her tenure the Atlanta Urban League becomes active in the struggle for black civil rights.

March 2 The newly reconstructed Municipal Auditorium opens.

April 15 Construction of the Bell Plant is turned over to the Army Air Force. The plant begins producing B-29s in September. (Bell closed the plant in 1946 but it was reopened in 1951 as Lockheed-Georgia.)

April 30 The Georgia Works Progress Administration ceases operation.

May 3 An ordinance is passed outlawing the posses-sion on the streets of switchblade knives, razors, ice picks and similar weapons unless wrapped. Illegal knives include those open-ed with a button and those more than two inches in length. Ordinance is due to a rash of crimes committed with such weapons.

May 17 City Council appropriates $10,031.30 as the City's share of an expanded county program to wipe out venereal disease. Atlan-ta ranks second (behind Washington, DC) as the city with the most reported cases.

May 25 According to the Chamber of Commerce, 48 new concerns and manufacturing plants, 31 resident representatives, and 19 branches and agencies of the federal government located in the city between January and April, bringing 4,223 people to the area.

August 4 A biracial committee adopts a resolution establishing the Southern Regional Council. The Council was chartered January 6, 1944.

September 30 Expressing fear of postwar migration, Mayor Hartsfield asks the City to subsidize the private development of 2000 acres of unused residential land within the City. Funding would be used for the grading and extension of streets, and the installation of water mains. Previously, private developers picked up the cost.

December 3 Eight hundred truck drivers strike to pro-test a delay in putting into effect a War Labor Board-approved pay increase of three cents per hour. Nineteen companies are affected by the strike, and over three million pounds of freight pile up at local truck depots.

December 10 Thornwell Jacobs resigns as president of Oglethorpe University.

December 21 Bell Aircraft Corporation's first all-Georgia built B-29 rolls off the assembly line at Marietta.

December Atlanta ends the year in the best financial condition in its history with a cash surplus of approximately $1,000,000.

THIS YEAR IN THE NATION

Jan. 5: Agricultural scientist George Washington Carver dies at 78 ... **Jan. 12-24:** Pres. Roosevelt and Prime Minister Churchill meet at Casablanca to discuss war strategy ... **Apr. 8:** Pres. Roosevelt orders all salaries, wages and prices be frozen ... **May 27:** Racial discrimination forbidden in war industries ... **July 1:** Withholding of income taxes goes into effect ... **July 10:** Allied forces invade Sicily ... **Aug. 11-24:** Pres. Roosevelt and Prime Minister Churchill meet in Quebec to discuss the war against Japan ... **Sept. 9:** Allied forces invade Italy ... **Nov. 9:** United Nations Relief and Rehabilitation Administration established by 44 nations ... **Nov. 28-Dec. 1:** Roosevelt, Stalin and Churchill meet at Teheran and pledge cooperation in defeating Germany and Italy.

Rolling out a B-29 (see Dec. 21)

1944

January 2   The City and county planning commission announces that postwar development plans include construction of three elevated highways over the railroad lines that converge in the city, erection of a mile-long, $2,000,000 plaza, construction of a combined railroad terminal located northeast of Union Station and extension of the Hunter Street viaduct. Plans also called for expansion of Oakland Cemetery and a civic center surrounding the Capitol.

January 7   Restrictions are tightened on the renewal of pool hall licenses. Stricter regulations were due to the fear that "lawless elements" were operating some establishments. Thirty-seven pool halls were licensed by the City at this time.

January 20   Two million dollars worth of supplies is destroyed by explosions and fire at the Atlanta Ordnance Depot.

March 14   The USS Clark Howell is launched at Savannah. The ship is named after Clark Howell, Sr., late editor and publisher of The Atlanta Constitution.

April 1   Because of labor shortages in the area, a 48-hour work week becomes effective for essential and non-essential industries in Fulton, DeKalb and Cobb Counties. The increase in hours results in a 30 per cent increase in wages.

May 2   Employees of the three largest bakeries which produce 70 per cent of the bread in the Atlanta area go on strike. There are fears of bread shortages but the strike ends May 5.

June 5   Ernest Woodruff, former president of the Trust Company and head of the syndicate that bought the Coca-Cola Company from the Candler family, dies. Ernest's son, Robert W. Woodruff, prime mover at Coca-Cola since 1923, becomes one of Atlanta's most influential citizens.

July 4   Efforts are made by many blacks to vote in Georgia's all-white primary. A. T. Walden, regional council of the NAACP; Professor Clarence Bacote, head of the history department at Atlanta University; C. A. Scott, editor of The Atlanta Daily World and Rev. Martin Luther King, Sr., pastor of Ebenezer Baptist Church, are among those not allowed to vote. But all who attempted were registered to vote in the general election.

July 16   The Westside Health Center, first public health center for blacks in Georgia, opens.

August 24   According to the U. S. Department of Labor, Atlanta is paying the lowest wages in the nation.

December 3   The new cruiser "Atlanta" is commissioned. Money for this new ship is raised through a war bond drive conducted immediately after the sinking of the first "Atlanta." The original goal of this drive is to raise $35 million but Atlantans contribute $165 million. This cruiser is the fourth ship commissioned by the United States and the Confederacy to bear the name Atlanta.

December 6   Morgan Blank, a columnist with the Atlanta Journal, helps mediate a prisoner rebellion at the Atlanta penitentiary.

December 6-7   Four-page photo engraved editions of The Atlanta Journal and Constitution are published instead of normal editions because of a two-day work stoppage by printers seeking higher wages, shorter working hours and other contract revisions.

THIS YEAR IN THE NATION

Jan. 6: Muckraker Ida Tarbell dies at 86 ... **June 4:** Allied forces enter Rome ... **June 6:** Normandy invasion by American, British and Canadian forces ... **June 13:** Germans launch their first V-1 at London ... **June 26-28:** Republicans nominate Thomas E. Dewey for president ... **July 1:** Bretton Woods conference, which will establish the International Monetary Fund, opens ... **July 19-20:** Democrats nominate Pres. Roosevelt for a fourth term ... **July 21-Aug. 10:** U.S. forces capture Guam ... **Aug. 21-Oct. 9:** Plans for the United Nations made at conference at Dumbarton Oaks ... **Aug. 25:** Paris liberated by allied troops ... **Sept. 8:** First V-2 fired at London ... **Sept. 14:** Northeast hit by hurricane killing over 400 persons ... **Oct. 4:** Politican Alfred E. Smith dies at 70 ... **Nov. 7:** Pres. Roosevelt wins his fourth presidential election ... **Nov. 24:** Massive bombings from Marianas on Japan begin ... **Dec. 16-26:** Battle of the Bulge ... **Dec. 17:** Federal government announces that as of Jan. 2, 1945, Japanese-Americans no longer excluded from West Coast.

Singer Al Jolson appeared in 1944 at the Bell Bomber plant (Marietta) for a War Bond rally.

Launching ceremony for the USS Atlanta IV; the USS Atlanta III, christened by Margaret Mitchell in 1941, was sunk off Guadalcanal in November, 1942 (see Dec. 3).

1945

February 5	A Youth Orchestra of 115 players is started in Atlanta.
March	The first black kindergarten opens; a second one opens in September.
April 13	Atlanta mourns as President Franklin Roosevelt's funeral cortege passes through the city. Shops and businesses close for the day.
May 24	A ticker-tape parade is held for Gen. Courtney Hicks Hodges, a native Georgian, and 50 First Army veterans.
July 27	Atlanta and other cities in northern Georgia and the Carolinas experience earth tremors.
August 24	113 equipment operators of the sanitary, construction, parks, and health departments go on strike. The city uses strike breakers to end the walkout.
September 9	William B. Hartsfield wins the mayoral primary.
October 1	The Fulton-DeKalb Hospital Authority is created to administer all area hospitals after January 1.
October 18	A memorial honoring Father O'Reilly, hero of Sherman's 1864 fire, is unveiled at City Hall.
Fall	Plans are developed to construct a multi-million dollar Atlanta expressway.

THIS YEAR IN THE NATION

Feb. 4-12: Roosevelt, Stalin and Churchill meet at Yalta to discuss the expected problems of postwar Europe ... **Feb. 14:** Allied forces reach the Rhine River ... **Apr. 1-July 2:** Okinawa Islands captured from Japanese ... **Apr. 12:** Pres. Roosevelt dies at 63 at Warm Springs, GA ... **Apr. 18:** War correspondent Ernie Pyle killed in combat at 44 ... **Apr. 25:** U.S. and Soviet armies meet in Europe ... **Apr. 25-June 26:** Charter of the United Nations drawn up at conference at San Francisco ... **May 7:** Germany surrenders ... **July 16:** Atomic bomb successfully tested in New Mexico ... **July 17-Aug. 2:** Allied leaders meet at Potsdam to discuss the denazification and demilitarization of Germany ... **July 28:** U.N. charter ratified by Senate ... **July 28:** Airplane crashes into Empire State Building ... **Aug. 6:** Atomic bomb dropped on Hiroshima ... **Aug. 9:** Atomic bomb dropped on Nagasaki ... **Sept. 2:** Japan formally surrenders to U.S. ... **Dec. 21:** Gen. George S. Patton dies in automobile accident in Germany at 60.

Father Thomas O'Reilly (see Oct. 18)

Peachtree St., Aug. 14, 1945; Celebrating Japan's surrender to the Allies.

In early 1945 Hollywood star Tyrone Power set hearts a-flutter as he addressed a war bond rally in the headquarters of the Atlanta Gas Light Co. He was then a Marine Corps lieutenant.

After his death at Warm Springs, GA, on Apr. 12, 1945, Pres. Franklin D. Roosevelt's funeral train pauses in Atlanta, en route to Washington, as mourners turn out.

1946

February 2 A special election to fill the term of Congressman Robert Ramspeck of the Fifth District (Atlanta), who resigned, is held. With strong support from the black community, Mrs. Helen Douglass Mankin wins.

March 4 Despite the objections of more conservative black leaders, the United Negro Veterans, a small organization of returned soldiers, march on City Hall to protest brutal treatment by the Atlanta Police Department. Between 100 and 200 black veterans participate in the march.

March 6-May 4 Several black Atlanta organizations agree to pool their efforts under the local branch of the NAACP and a newly formed All-Citizens Registration Committee in a massive drive to register black citizens. When this drive starts March 6, fewer than 7,000 blacks were registered. On May 4, when the campaign officially ends, 24,137 blacks are on the registration lists.

April 1 The United States Court in the case of Chapman versus King declares the Georgia white primary to be unconstitutional.

April The first Atlanta book fair is held.

May 9 During a massive cross-burning ceremony on Stone Mountain, 227 new members are initiated into the Georgia Association of Klans. Imperial Wizard Samuel Green estimates Klan membership in Atlanta at 20,000 members, nearly half the total estimated Klan membership in the state.

August 14 Atlanta and Fulton County Citizens approve of a bond issue of over $4 million to finance new school construction and implement an express highway plan.

December 7 The Winecoff Hotel, lacking both fire escapes and sprinklers, catches fire; 119 people are killed and another hundred are injured.

December 21 Gov.-elect Eugene Talmadge dies before assuming office. Atlanta and the rest of Georgia experience the "Year of the three Governors." After much confusion over who is governor, Herman Talmadge wins the 1948 special gubernatorial election.

Also this year: Golfer Louise Suggs wins "women's grand slam," repeats the feat in 1947, and in 1948 wins the British Women's Championship.

THIS YEAR IN THE NATION

Jan. 10: Radar beam bounced off the moon by U.S. Army laboratory in Belmar, NJ ... **Jan. 21-Feb. 17:** Strike in steel industry results in increases in wages and price of steel ... **Mar. 5:** Winston Churchill gives his Iron Curtain speech at Westminster college in Fulton, MO ... **Apr. 1-May 29:** Strike in the coal industry ... **Apr. 30:** War crimes trial for Japanese leaders begins in Tokyo ... **July 4:** Philippine Islands given complete independence ... **July 7:** Mother Frances X. Cabrini becomes the first American to be canonized a saint ... **July 27:** Author Gertrude Stein dies at 72 ... **Dec. 25:** Comedian W. C. Fields dies at 66.

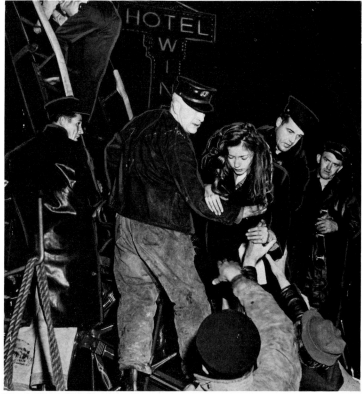

Winecoff Hotel fire (see Dec. 7)

Winecoff Hotel fire (see Dec. 7)

1947

January 19	The Atlanta Symphony Orchestra is formed from the Atlanta Youth Orchestra.
February 4	After the sudden death of Marion Hornsby on January 31, Herbert Jenkins is appointed chief of police. Jenkins promises to reduce the influence of the Ku Klux Klan within the department and build a modern-day police force.
March 18	Congress grants a press card to a reporter from the Atlanta Daily World, a black newspaper.
March 27	The Metropolitan Planning Commission is established. This Commission has the authority to recommend plans for the orderly growth and development of the Greater Atlanta area.
May	After interruption caused by the war, the Metropolitan Opera returns to Atlanta for a week's engagement.
Summer	To attract visitors to the city, Atlanta sponsors free pop concerts and places 23 historical markers in the downtown area.
August 19	Voters in Buckhead and Cascade Heights defeat Hartsfield's annexation proposals.
September 5	Atlanta ends its system of sexually segregated white high schools. Boys High and Tech High become the coeducational Grady High School. Girls High becomes the coeducational Roosevelt High School.
September	The School of Social Work becomes part of Atlanta University; the University of Georgia opens an Atlanta Division.
October 27	Delta Air Lines opens a $1,000,000 headquarters in Atlanta.
December 1	City Council authorizes the hiring of black policemen. On December 15 the police union wins a stay order preventing the implementation of this resolution.

December 7	Lester Maddox opens the Pickrick, a restaurant popular with the working class residents of its neighborhood. (In the 1950s the restaurant's weekly ads in The Constitution speak on political issues, particularly in favor of segregation.)
December 10	A Ford assembly plant opens in Hapeville. This plant contributes to a post-war boom which creates about 25,000 jobs in the greater Atlanta area.
December 29	The Atlanta Constitution moves into new headquarters.

Gen. Dwight D. Eisenhower visits Atlanta Apr. 7, 1947, and waves from the first car as residents turn out to greet the war hero.

Pres. Harry Truman (see this Year In the Nation/Mar. 12)

THIS YEAR IN THE NATION

Mar. 12: Pres. Truman announces Truman Doctrine to aid countries against communist aggression ... **Mar. 22:** Program to check loyalty of all federal employees announced by Pres. Truman ... **Apr. 11:** Jackie Robinson becomes first black baseball player in major leagues ... **Apr. 16:** Over 500 killed when ship explodes in Texas City, TX ... **Apr. 24:** Author Willa Cather dies at 71 ... **June 5:** Marshall Plan for European recovery announced at Harvard commencement ... **June 11:** Rationing of consumer goods ends ... **June 23:** Taft-Hartly Act passed over Pres. Truman's veto ... **Sept. 18:** Air Force established as an independent service ... **Sept. 20:** Former New York mayor Fiorello La Guardia dies at 64 ... **Oct. 14:** Capt. Charles Yeager breaks the sound barrier ... **Dec. 20:** Philosopher Alfred N. Whitehead dies at 86.

1948

January 1 City Council endorses a slum clearance program. Projected cost: $50,000,000.

February 2 In honor of Atlanta's 100th anniversary as an incorporated municipality, descendants of the original city officials reenact the first meeting of Atlanta's first City Council (February 2, 1848).

February 4 Control of the Bank of Atlanta passes to the Citizens and Southern Bank when the larger bank buys a majority holding of the unit's common stock.

February 26 The police union's stay is overturned, and eight black policemen are added to the Atlanta Police Department. Black officers, however, are assigned to black neighborhoods, report to the Butler Street YMCA instead of the police department on Decatur Street, and cannot arrest a white citizen.

April 3 First black policemen in Atlanta go on duty.

May 5 George Goodwin, Atlanta Journal reporter, is awarded Pulitzer Prize for disclosing voting frauds.

May 9 A new passenger terminal opens at Atlanta Municipal Airport. Total cost of the new terminal is $180,000.

June 16 A General Motors plant opens at Doraville.

July 8 To halt a price war in Atlanta, the Georgia Milk Control Board votes to revoke the license of the Atlanta Restaurant Dairy, Inc., for price cutting.

August 3 City Council passes a resolution authorizing a $150,000 radar system at Atlanta airport.

September 8 The Rich Foundation donates WABE-TV to the Atlanta public school system.

September 29 The South's first TV station, WSB-TV, begins operation.

December 19 The Atlanta Urban League issues a report on the effects of separate school systems. Blacks live mostly in an area which contains 72 per cent of Atlanta's juvenile delinquency, 60 per cent of its crime, and 69 per cent of its TB cases.

THIS YEAR IN THE NATION

Jan. 30: Aviator Orville Wright dies at 76 ... **Apr. 1-Sept. 30, 1949:** Berlin Blockade ... **Apr. 30:** 21 nations of the Western Hemisphere establish the Organization of American States ... **May 10:** General Motors and United Auto Workers sign first labor contract providing for cost-of-living increases ... **June 3:** Mt. Palomar Observatory, with the largest telescope in the world, is dedicated ... **June 21-25:** Republicans nominate Thomas Dewey for president ... **June 24:** Pres. Truman signs bill restoring Selective Service ... **July 12-14:** Democrats nominate Pres. Truman for a full term ... **July 17:** Dixiecrats nominate Gov. Strom Thurmond for president ... **July 24-27:** Progressive Party nominates former Vice-President Henry Wallace for president ... **Aug. 16:** Babe Ruth dies at 53 ... **Oct. 1:** California law that made miscegenation a crime declared unconstitutional by Supreme Court ... **Nov. 2:** Pres. Truman elected for a full term.

George Goodwin (see May 5)

City Hall marks Atlanta's 100th year since incorporation: Margaret Mitchell hands a piece of cake to Mayor W. B. Hartsfield (see Feb. 2).

1949

January 31	A paralyzing ice storm causes one death and the worst electric power shortage in the city's history.
March 5	Solicitor-General Paul Webb cracks down on the popular Pyramid clubs in the Atlanta area. He declares them in violation of Georgia's anti-lottery laws.
April 9	Atlanta's last horse-power trolley makes its final run. They have been operating in the city since 1871.
May 1-20	Transit workers strike for better wages, pensions and working conditions.
May 2	In a move against the Ku Klux Klan, City Council bans the wearing of masks except at festive occasions. Violators can be fined up to $200 and be jailed for 30 days.
August 3	The Fulton County Grand Jury launches an investigation into what is termed a million-dollar liquor traffic in the dry counties of Georgia. Atlanta is identified as the fountainhead of this traffic.
August 11	Margaret Mitchell is struck down by a taxi and dies August 16.
August 12	Plaza Park, built over the railroad gulch, is dedicated. Later it becomes hangout for Atlanta's derelicts.
August 27	Samuel Roper, a former member of the Atlanta police force, succeeds Dr. Samuel Green as Imperial Wizard of the Georgia Association of Klans. Dr. Samuel Green dies August 18.
September 7	Blacks participate in a mayoral primary for the very first time since the white primary was declared unconstitutional. Mayor Hartsfield easily reelected.
September 22	A statue of the late Gov. Eugene Talmadge is unveiled on the Capitol lawn.
October 7	Radio Station WERD, owned and operated by blacks, begins broadcasting.
October 13	Margaret Truman wows the audience in Atlanta's first all-star concert series.

Margaret Mitchell: last photo,
taken in the summer of 1949 (see Aug. 11)

THIS YEAR IN THE NATION

Jan. 20: Pres. Truman inaugurated for a full term as president ... **Mar. 2:** First nonstop air circumnavigation of the earth made in just over 94 hours by military aircraft ... **Apr. 4:** Treaty establishing NATO signed by 12 nations ... **Apr. 14:** Nuremberg trials end with conviction of 19 of 21 Nazi officials ... **Apr. 20:** Discovery of cortisone announced by Edward Kendall of the Mayo Foundation ... **June 22:** Ezzard Charles defeats Joe Walcott for heavyweight boxing championship ... **July 21:** Senate ratifies NATO treaty ... **Aug. 10:** Department of Defense established ... **Oct. 7:** "Tokyo Rose" sentenced ... **Oct. 26:** Minimum wage increase from 40¢ to 75¢ per hour.

Plaza Park (see Aug. 12)

137

1950

January	City Council adopts "The Plan of Improvement for the Governments of Atlanta and Fulton County." This plan basically calls for the annexation of 82 square miles containing nearly 100,000 residents, and a realignment of services between the city and the county which would basically remove the county from providing municipal services.
March 6	Federal Judge Neil Andrews rules that Atlanta legally censored "Lost Boundaries," a movie about "passing." On October 17, the Supreme Court upholds the city's right to local censorship.
March 18	James Cox, owner of the Atlanta Journal, obtains The Atlanta Constitution in a stock trade. The papers' production, Sunday editions and ad sales are merged.
April 16	Edward Harkness Hall, Atlanta University's Administration Building, is dedicated.
May 18	Transit workers again go on strike. During this period the city allows the use of jitneys — privately-owned vehicles — licensed by the city and permitted to charge a 10-cent fare (the same as the trolley fare). Jitneys had been banned from Atlanta streets for 25 years.
June 24	A group of businessmen purchase the Georgia Power's transit operation and incorporate it as the Atlanta Transit Company. Georgia Power Company had operated the transit system since 1902. The Atlanta Transit Company is eventually bought out by the Metropolitan Atlanta Rapid Transit Authority (MARTA).
June 29	Fulton County and Atlanta approve the Plan of Improvement and the creation of eight consolidated programs.
July	High Points Apartments, a $12,500,000 development for members of the black middle class, is dedicated. The apartment's 452 units help break the bottleneck in black housing due to an increase in black population and limited living space due to segregation.
September 19	A petition to end segregation in Atlanta's public school system is filed by some 200 black children and their parents. This petition is later denied.
October 9	The Supreme Court refuses to review a charge of discriminatory wage scales for Atlanta's black teachers.

THIS YEAR IN THE NATION

Jan. 17: Brink's holdup nets robbers over $2 million ... **Jan. 21:** Alger Hiss found guilty of perjury ... **Feb. 9:** Sen. Joseph McCarthy claims there are 205 members of the Communist party working in the State Department ... **Mar. 19:** Author of the Tarzan books, Edgar R. Burroughs, dies at 74 ... **June 5:** Supreme Court declares that segregation in railroad dining cars violates Interstate Commerce Act ... **June 25-30:** North Korean troops attack South Korea ... **June 27:** Pres. Truman orders U.S. armed forces to Korea ... **Sept. 15:** U.S. forces land at Inchon ... **Sept. 23:** McCarran Internal Security Act is passed over Pres. Truman's veto ... **Oct. 23:** Entertainer Al Jolson dies at 54 ... **Nov. 20:** U.N. forces reach Korean-Chinese border ... **Nov. 26:** China attacks across her border pushing U.N. troops back ... **Nov. 29:** 29 churches form the National Council of Churches ... **Dec. 16:** Pres. Truman declares a state of national emergency.

Atlanta from the air, 1950

The Ku Klux Klan meets at Stone Mountain in August, 1950.

The Governor's mansion in Ansley Park, in September, 1950

James Cox (see Mar. 18)

1951

January 3	According to the City Budget Commission, cost of City government operation for 1951 will be $18,821,446, largest in the city's history.
January 4	Due to the Korean War, the Marietta Bell Bomber plant, which closed after World War II, is reopened by the federal government.
January	Building permits in the city for the month reach an all-time high: 658 permits with a value of $4,590,410 are awarded.
January	The University of Georgia begins publishing the Atlanta Economic review.
February 1	Railroad workers in Atlanta begin a "sickness" walkout, causing a five-to-six-hour delay on passenger and freight trains. Due to material shortages caused by the strike, the General Motors plant here has to lay off employees and cut production schedules.
February 16	In a "power struggle," the Atlanta Journal and Constitution win a battle against Gov. Herman Talmadge as the Legislature adjourns without restricting their right to publish.
April	The Peachtree Hotel opens in the newly refurbished building which had housed the Winecoff Hotel. The latter was burned in part in 1946.
July 6	Desiring to meet in a southern city, the National Association for the Advancement of Colored People opens its convention in Atlanta.
Summer	Georgia experiences its worst drought in 25 years. While corn and truck crops die for lack of water, tobacco prices remain high.
September 25	Dedication ceremonies are held for the first completed portion of Atlanta's expressway system: Three miles of the north leg are finished.

THIS YEAR IN THE NATION

Jan. 26: Wages frozen by the Economic Stabilization Administration ... **Feb. 26:** 22d Amendment, limiting presidents to two terms, becomes effective ... **Apr. 11:** Gen. Douglas MacArthur relieved of his command in Korea by Pres. Truman ... **June 4:** Constitutionality of Smith Act upheld by Supreme Court ... **July 12:** National Guard called out by Gov. Adlai Stevenson to quell race riot that occurs when black family moves in Chicago suburb of Cicero ... **July 18:** Joe Walcott regains heavyweight championship from Ezzard Charles ... **Aug. 14:** Newspaper publisher William R. Hearst dies at 88 ... **Sept. 1:** U.S., Australia and New Zealand sign the ANZUS pact, a mutual defense agreement ... **Sept. 8:** Peace treaty between Japan and 48 nations signed in San Francisco ... **Dec. 20:** Atomic test station at Arco, Idaho, generates electricity.

September 30	WSB-TV increases its power to a maximum of 50,000 watts, making it the most powerful TV station in the nation. Along with this change, WSB-TV begins broadcasting on Channel 2 instead of 8. Atlanta's third television station, WLTV, begins operating on Channel 8.
October	Atlanta policemen begin enforcing the city's jaywalking laws. This crackdown comes after two months of oral warnings followed by two months of written warnings. Jaywalking is now included as a traffic violation and conviction goes on record. In 1950, 17 out of 20 persons killed in traffic accidents in Atlanta are pedestrians; 13 of them were jaywalking.
October 25	John R. (Fat) Hardy is arrested after the discovery that he is distributing poisonous whiskey to the black community, leading to the deaths of 45 people. Over 300 people became ill after drinking it. Later in the year Hardy is convicted of murder and given a life sentence.
November 16	The Fulton County Jury investigates the reasons for Atlanta's biggest traffic bottleneck, Peachtree Road from West Peachtree to beyond Brighton Road. City Police Chief Herbert Jenkins, County Police Chief G. Neal Ellis and City traffic engineer Karl Bevins testify. A longer green light signal is the solution proposed.

Gov. Herman Talmadge (see Feb. 16)

1952

Gen. D. D. Eisenhower
(see This Year In the Nation/July 7)

January 1   As a result of the Plan of Improvement, Atlanta's land area trebles (from 33 to 118 square miles). Population increases about 100,000.

March 16   An ordinance making drunken driving unlawful is declared unconstitutional. The district court rules that drunken driving is covered by state law; therefore, drunken driving cases must be tried in lower state courts rather than in Atlanta Municipal Court. But the Legislature in 1953 passes a bill giving the Atlanta Municipal Court jurisdiction over drunken driving cases in the city.

May 1   WSB-TV and WSB Radio become the first in the nation to win the George Foster Peabody Award for regional public service — WSB-TV wins for "Our World Today," a high school panel quiz show, and WSB Radio for "Our Pastor's Study."

Summer   As a result of the national steel strike, the local General Motors plan cuts its production schedule and begins to lay off employees; 3900 are affected.

June 15   The first parking meter in Atlanta is installed on Ivy Street. During the first five months of operation, the City earns $101,768 off meters.

June 22   The Hughes Spalding Pavilion is dedicated at Grady Hospital.

October 14   The Daily World, Atlanta's black newspaper, endorses Dwight Eisenhower for President. Both the Constitution and Journal back Adlai Stevenson.

November 9   The Ernest Woodruff Medical Research Building is dedicated at Emory University.

December 1   Mayor W. B. Hartsfield is elected president of the American Municipal Association.

THIS YEAR IN THE NATION

Feb. 27: U.S. and Japan sign treaty that allows U.S. to have military bases in Japan ... **Apr. 8:** Pres. Truman seizes steel mills to prevent strike ... **June 1:** Philosopher John Dewey dies at 92 ... **June 2:** Supreme Court declares seizure of steel mills by President unconstitutional ... **June 27:** McCarran-Walter Immigration Act passes over Pres. Truman's veto ... **July 7-11:** Republicans nominate Gen. Dwight Eisenhower for President and Sen. Richard Nixon for Vice-President ... **July 16:** Pres. Truman signs G.I. Bill of Rights ... **July 21-26:** Democrats nominate Gov. Adlai Stevenson for President ... **July 25:** Commonwealth of Puerto Rico established ... **Sept. 18:** Richard Nixon delivers "Checkers" speech ... **Sept. 23:** Rocky Marciano wins the heavyweight championship by knocking out Joe Walcott ... **Sept. 26:** Philosopher George Santayana dies at 88 ... **Nov. 1:** First hydrogen bomb exploded ... **Nov. 4:** Eisenhower elected President ... **Nov. 29:** Pres.-elect Eisenhower travels to Korea to personally assess the situation.

1953

January 1   Due to its Plan of Improvement, Atlanta enters the new year with a cash carry-over of $2,515,000, the largest in the city's history.

February 9   Fire ravages the block-long Seaboard warehouse beneath the Spring St. viaduct. Fire Chief Morris H. Dean dies, and 13 other firemen are injured. The fire's estimated damage is $2,000,000.

April 12   Abby Rockefeller Hall opens on the campus of Spelman College.

May 1   Delta Air Lines of Atlanta merges with Chicago and Southern Airlines of Memphis.

May 3   Dr. Rufus Clement, black president of Atlanta University, was nominated in a city-wide primary to the Board of Education as the representative from the third ward. In the same election, attorney A. T. Walden and Dr. Amos Miles are elected to the City Democratic Executive Committee. This election marked the first time since December 7, 1870, that Atlanta had elected black candidates to office.

June 30   Police patrol a neighborhood two blocks off Bankhead Avenue, NW, when white residents of the community protest at the homes of two black families who move into the area.

July 8   Three Atlanta youths cause excitement when they claim to have run over "a little man from outer space" and to have seen two others sail away in a flying saucer. Two Air Force representatives investigate, and hundreds phone the newspapers wanting information. One man offers $5000 for the body. The "man from space" is actually a shaved capuchin monkey. One of the youths in the hoax is fined $40 for placing a carcass on the highway.

July 10   According to Atlanta's slum clearance committee, owners spent over $8 million in a four-year period to improve 16,252 dwelling units housing 28,982 families.

Summer   Theatre of the Stars offers its first series of Broadway entertainments.

Fall   Atlanta's first postwar housing project, the 990 unit Carver Community, opens.

October 5   A new charter and code of general ordinances is approved. A coalition of blacks and whites once again elects Hartsfield mayor.

November 24   Adlai Stevenson speaks before 15,000 people on the lawn of the state Capitol.

THIS YEAR IN THE NATION

Jan. 20: Dwight D. Eisenhower inaugurated as the 34th President ... **Mar. 12:** All price controls lifted ... **Apr. 1:** Department of Health, Education and Welfare established by Congress ... **June 8:** Supreme Court rules that restaurants in Washington cannot refuse to seat blacks ... **June 19:** Ethel and Julius Rosenberg executed for espionage ... **July 27:** Armistice ends Korean War ... **July 31:** Sen. Robert A. Taft dies at 63 ... **Oct. 5:** Earl Warren becomes Chief Justice of the Supreme Court ... **Oct. 30:** George C. Marshall receives Nobel Peace prize ... **Dec. 16:** Major Charles Yeager flys experimental plane to a record 1,650 m.p.h.

Looking south from Houston (left), Peachtree (center) and Forsyth Sts., 1953. The Loew's Grand Theatre (at left) was replaced by the Georgia-Pacific Center. Building beyond the Coca-Cola sign is the Candler.

Austin T. Walden (see May 3)

Municipal Auditorium, facing Hurt Park, with construction of an addition to Grady Hospital behind the Auditorium, 1953

1954

January 1	The old bicameral system of city council and board of aldermen is replaced with a single body — a board of aldermen made up of two members from each ward.
March 25	A fire and explosion at an office building on Pryor Street also damage other businesses on the street. Firemen from the 13 counties battle the flames.
April 5	A report on black park facilities prepared by the Atlanta Urban League criticizes the pace at which the City is improving facilities. The report points out that black citizens only have access to 151 acres of the 2,178 acres of land the city devotes to park use. Only two of six swimming pools are allotted to blacks, and no golf courses.
June 3	Atlanta slum clearance officials announce that they will begin a slum clearance program beginning in 1955. Emphasis will be placed upon "elimination" instead of rehabilitation.
July 1	A major stoppage by construction workers temporarily halts all building in the Atlanta area as over 2,500 workers strike. The strike stops 1,600 projects.
July 14	Voters approve a $10,000,000 bond issue — Five million for schools; two million for street improvements, two million for improvements on sewers and one million for municipal building bonds.
July-October	Atlantans experience a spell of several dry days; for the past three summers, Atlanta has been plagued with drought-like conditions.
September 17	Four men escape the Atlanta Penitentiary — its first jail break in 31 years.
December 22	A new zoning plan is adopted for the Atlanta Metropolitan Area.
December	By the end of the year nearly 13 miles of Atlanta's new expressway system is complete.
Winter	Construction is completed on the Fulton National Bank building; it opens the following April, and has its "grand opening" in October, 1955. (The building now houses Bank South, newer name of the Fulton.)

THIS YEAR IN THE NATION

Jan. 21: Atomic-powered submarine Nautilus launched ... **Mar. 1:** Five members of Congress are wounded when Puerto Rican nationalists open fire from spectator gallery of the House of Representatives ... **Apr. 8:** At news conference Pres. Eisenhower propounds domino theory of Communist expansion ... **May 17:** In Brown v. Board of Education of Topeka, Supreme Court requires an end to racial segregation in public education ... **June 29:** Atomic Energy Commission removes security clearance from J. Robert Oppenheimer ... **July 17:** First Newport jazz festival opens ... **Aug. 24:** Communist Control Act becomes law ... **Sept. 8:** South East Asia Treaty Organization for mutual defense is formed ... **Dec. 2:** Senate censures Sen. Joseph McCarthy.

Fulton National Bank building, first postwar skyscraper (22 stories), opens (see Winter).

1955

February	Louis Lautier, a black reporter for the Daily World, is the first black elected to the National Press Club.
March 11	A five-alarm fire roars through the State Farmers' Market. Damage is in excess of $100,000; 50,000 pounds of bananas and 15,000 pounds of rutabagas are lost.
April 5	Memorial Services honoring Trevor Arnett, a promoter of black education, are held at Spelman College.
July 6	A judge lifts the ban of Mrs. Christine Smith Gilliam, Atlanta censor, on showing the movie, "The Blackboard Jungle." This movie, according to Mrs. Gilliam, is "lewd, obscene and salacious."
July 13	Despite the U.S. Supreme Court decision on integration, the Atlanta library affirms its position and denies black petitions for desegregation.
July-August	A long court battle begins when Horace Ward, a black Atlantan, tries to enter the University of Georgia's law school. The University of Georgia remains segregated until Charlayne Hunter and Hamilton Holmes are admitted under a court order in January, 1960.
August 1	Georgia orders all black teachers to quit the NAACP or lose their teaching licenses. The order is rescinded August 5.
September 1	The Atlanta Division of the University of Georgia divorces itself from its parent institution and opens as the State College of Business Administration.
October 17-October 21	The Fulton National Bank Building, first postwar skyscraper (22 stories, now Bank South), has its grand opening. It is the area's most modern bank.
October 22	The first postoffice substation manned by only black personnel opens in the city.
November 7	The U.S. Supreme Court declares segregation on Atlanta's golf courses unconstitutional.
December	By the end of the year, 44 new companies have located in Atlanta.
December 24	Atlanta's golf courses are integrated without incident.

THIS YEAR IN THE NATION

Jan. 28: Resolution passed by Congress gives President permission to use U.S. military forces to protect Formosa ... **Apr. 7:** Actress Theda Bara dies at 64 ... **Apr. 12:** Polio vaccine declared both safe and effective by discoverer Jonas Salk ... **May 31:** Supreme Court orders that public schools be desegregated within a reasonable time ... **July 11:** Air Force Academy dedicated ... **July 18-23:** Pres. Eisenhower meets with Soviet Premier Bulganin; no agreements reached but tensions relax ... **Aug. 7-21:** Hurricane Diane causes 191 deaths and billions of dollars of damage from New Jersey to Rhode Island ... **Aug. 12:** Minimum wage is increased from 75¢ to one dollar per hour ... **Sept. 24:** Pres. Eisenhower suffers a heart attack ... **Oct. 18:** Scientists at the University of California, Berkeley, announce that they have created anti-matter ... **Nov. 1:** Dale Carnegie dies at 66 ... **Nov. 7:** Supreme Court extends rule of desegregation to public parks, playgrounds and golf courses ... **Nov. 25:** End to segregation ordered on interstate buses and trains by Interstate Commerce Commission ... **Dec. 5:** American Federation of Labor and Congress of Industrial Organizations form a single organization.

Kimball Hotel, viewed from Plaza Park, was in 1955 only a few years away from destruction.

Cellist Enrico Leide (shown in 1955) conducted his own orchestra which entertained Atlantans for many years before the Atlanta Symphony.

1956

The U.S. Supreme Court ruled on Dec. 13, 1956, that the Alabama state law requiring blacks to sit in the rear of public transportation vehicles was unconstitutional after a massive boycott was led by Dr. Martin Luther King, Jr.

January 23   Blake Ragsdale Van Leer, president of Georgia Tech since 1944 and a nationally known educator, dies.

February 1   The completion of Buford Dam results in the formation of Lake Lanier. The dam and lake were a six-year project of the US Corps of Engineers.

February 7   The Fulton County Grand Jury holds its longest session in almost 10 years as it begins a probe of Atlanta's juvenile delinquency problem. Concern was due to an upswing in teenage crime in Atlanta, particularly on the northside section of the city. A detective blames the "lack of parental love" and movies which glorify juvenile criminals. He blames the upswing in Atlanta on a movie, "The Blackboard Jungle."

September 29   The Klan holds its biggest rally since World War II in a pasture not far from Atlanta. More than 3,500 members from at least 17 states attend.

November 8   The diocese of Atlanta of the Roman Catholic Church comes into being with the appointment of the Most High Reverend Francis Hyland as bishop. Prior to this time, Atlanta was part of the Savannah diocese.

November 22-
December 14   In a move against the NAACP, the Georgia state revenue commissioner demands the financial records of the Atlanta branch. John H. Calhoun, president of local NAACP, refuses. After a trial, Calhoun is found guilty of comtempt. The branch is fined $25,000. The jailing of Calhoun is the first of a NAACP leader since the southern states began a crackdown on the NAACP. On December 14 the local branch yields its records.

December 10   Rather than admit black members, the Atlanta Public Teachers Association votes to withdraw from the American Federation of Teachers, an AFL-CIO affiliate.

THIS YEAR IN THE NATION

Mar. 12: 101 Southern Congressmen call for massive resistance to desegregation ... **Mar. 20:** Longest major strike in two decades ends when 70,000 members of the Union of Electrical Workers return to work after 156 days ... **May 21:** Hydrogen bomb dropped from an airplane for first time ... **June 9:** Intestinal obstruction successfully removed from Pres. Eisenhower ... **June 25-26:** Ocean liners Andrea Doria and Stockholm collide with loss of 50 lives ... **June 29:** Pres. Eisenhower signs Federal Highway Act inaugurating the interstate highway system ... **Aug. 11:** Artist Jackson Pollock dies at 44 in an auto accident ... **Aug. 13-17:** Democrats again nominate Adlai Stevenson for President ... **Aug. 20-23:** Republicans renominate incumbents Eisenhower and Nixon ... **Aug. 25:** Sex-researcher Alfred Kinsey dies at 62 ... **Oct. 8:** Only no-hitter in a World Series game pitched by Don Larsen of the New York Yankees ... **Nov. 6:** Pres. Eisenhower reelected.

1957

January   A group of Spelman students and Prof. Howard Zinn attempt to sit in the "white only" section in the gallery of the Georgia Assembly. Periodic visits are made by black students until the gallery is desegregated in 1963.

January 9   Black ministers briefly try to integrate Atlanta's bus lines.

January 10-11   Sixty blacks from 10 southern states meet in Atlanta to discuss organizational strategy for the fight for integration in the South. On January 11 this conference issues "A Statement to the South" which praises nonviolent means to achieve integration. Originally called the "Southern Negro Leaders Conference on Transportation and Nonviolent Integration," this organization will eventually be called the Southern Christian Leadership Conference.

March-November   Investigations begin probing rumors that the Police Department is protecting the "bug," a lottery. Charges stem from a surprise raid on a Howell Mill Road garage where a million dollar ring allegedly operated. Sixteen officers are indicted; all are exonerated and return to duty.

April 17   Despite charges of police corruption, voters approve a bond issue to build a new police station.

September   Hartsfield defeats Archie Lindsey, Fulton County Commissioner, in the mayoral primary.

December 4   Hartsfield easily crushes Lester Maddox's petition campaign. Hartsfield is reelected to his sixth term.

Atlanta Police Department's first policewomen to walk a beat appeared in August, 1957; they were Mrs. Aline Mitchell (left) and Mrs. Hilda Hill.

Dr. Noah Langdale, Jr., becomes president of Georgia State University in 1957.

THIS YEAR IN THE NATION

Jan. 14: Actor Humphrey Bogart dies at 57 ... **Mar. 11:** Admiral Richard E. Byrd dies at 68 ... **Apr. 29:** First Civil Rights bill since Reconstruction passes Congress ... **May 2:** Sen. Joseph McCarthy dies at 47 ... **June 17:** Five communists are freed by Supreme Court and new trials are ordered for nine others ... **June 27:** Hurricane Audrey causes 534 deaths in Texas and Louisiana ... **July 1:** International Geophysical Year begins; for 18 months scientists from 70 countries study the earth ... **July 6:** Althea Gibson becomes the first black to win the Wimbledon tennis singles for women ... **July 31:** Distant Early Warning radar defense system becomes operational ... **Sept. 4:** Gov. Orval Faubus of Ark. calls out National Guard to prevent integration of Central High School in Little Rock ... **Sept. 23:** Black students enter Central High but are withdrawn because of the threat of mob violence ... **Sept. 24:** Pres. Eisenhower sends in federal troops to enforce court ordered integration ... **Oct. 5:** Soviets launch first artificial earth satellite ... **Oct. 17-21:** Queen Elizabeth II and Prince Philip visit the U.S. ... **Nov. 26:** Pres. Eisenhower suffers a mild stroke ... **Dec. 18:** First commercial nuclear power plant begins to produce power.

1958

January 11 Asking for an end to segregation in Atlanta's public school system, 10 black children and their parents file suit in federal court.

January 26 Grady Hospital's new $26,000,000 building is dedicated.

February 18 The Georgia Legislature names a Stone Mountain Memorial Association which has the authority to purchase the mountain and surrounding land (3,200 acres) for a state park, and complete a Confederate monument.

April 7 The Atlanta NAACP attempts to block the City's urban renewal program. The Atlanta branch charges that black areas such as Vine City and Buttermilk Bottoms are being ignored by the City. The branch also charges that the City has no effective relocation program to help black citizens.

May 7 Nine thousand workers strike at Lockheed.

June 17 The U.S. Supreme Court rejects a petition filed by Mayor Hartsfield to get a three-judge federal panel to review the constitutionality of Georgia's county unit system. Hartsfield is a vocal critic of the unit system.

October 1 The $24 million Broadview Plaza Shopping center opens, then Georgia's largest shopping center.

October 12 The Temple of the Hebrew Benevolent congregation is dynamited and five members of the National States Rights Party are indicited. The motive is believed to be Rabbi Jacob Rothschild's support for school desegregation. The trial ends with no verdict.

November 14 Hartsfield asks the General Assembly to let Atlantans decide whether to close schools or keep them open despite integration (local option). Under state laws an integrated school cannot receive public funding, thus automatically closing them.

December 12 Help Our Public Education (HOPE), the most important predominately white group which worked to mobilize support for open schools, is launched. HOPE chapters are started in other cities in Georgia.

December 31 Atlanta's retail sales have increased 600% since 1939. The city now makes 12.8% of all wholesale sales in the South.

THIS YEAR IN THE NATION

Jan. 31: U.S. launches first successful artificial earth satellite ... **Apr. 14:** Texas pianist Van Cliburn wins the Tchaikovsky competition in Moscow ... **Apr. 28-May 15:** Vice-President Nixon visits eight Latin American countries and receives hostile reception in Lima and Caracas ... **May 30:** Bodies of unknown soldiers from World War II and the Korean War interred at the Tomb of the Unknown Soldier (renamed Tomb of the Unknowns) ... **June 28:** Mackinac Bridge, second longest suspension bridge in the world, dedicated ... **July 15:** Pres. Eisenhower sends Marines to Lebanon ... **July 29:** National Aeronautics and Space Administration (NASA) established ... **Aug. 23:** National Defense Education Act passes Congress ... **Sept. 22:** Presidential assistant Sherman Adams resigns after being accused of using his position for personal gain ... **Oct. 5:** High school in Clinton, TN wrecked by bomb.

Mayor W. B. Hartsfield (left) and Rabbi Jacob Rothschild survey The Temple's bomb damage (see Oct. 12)

1959

January 9	Atlanta's segregated bus system is declared unconstitutional by a federal court.
January 10	Georgia's colleges are ordered not to refuse applicants on the basis of race.
May 4	Atlanta Constitution's editor Ralph McGill wins the Pulitzer Prize for his editorial writing. Specifically mentioned is his column, "A Church, A School," about the 1958 dynamiting of the Jewish Temple.
May 19	The Atlanta Public Library integrates when Mrs. Maynard Jackson receives a library card.
May 22	The library announces that "The Rabbit's Wedding," a story for three-to-seven year olds about the marriage of a black rabbit to a white rabbit, has been removed from open shelves.
Spring	A report by City Comptroller Earl Landers shows Atlanta is involved in 42 capital improvement projects at an estimated cost of $105,208,400. The City's share of financing these projects is $48,178,400, with federal and state funds paying the rest.
June 5	School desegregation in Atlanta is ruled illegal. Mayor Hartsfield again asks the Georgia Legislature to let "Atlantans decide the fate of their schools and the future of their children."
August 3	Lenox Square mall opens to a crowd of 50,000. Forty-seven shops open.
October 10	Metropolitan Atlanta's population reaches over one million inhabitants. To celebrate, the city prints billions of dollars in simulated million-dollar "Confederate bills" and distributes them throughout the nation.
November 29	Martin Luther King, Jr. announces his resignation at Dexter Baptist Church (Montgomery, AL) and his plans to move to Atlanta. On February 7, 1960, King gives his first sermon at Ebenezer Church as co-pastor.

THIS YEAR IN THE NATION

Jan. 3: Alaska becomes the 49th state ... **Jan. 7:** U.S. recognizes new revolutionary government of Cuba ... **Jan. 21:** Movie producer Cecil B. De Mille dies at 77 ... **Apr. 9:** Architect Frank L. Wright dies at 89 ... **Apr. 16:** Bolshoi Ballet makes first appearance in U.S. at Metropolitan Opera House ... **Apr. 25:** St. Lawrence Seaway connecting the Atlantic Ocean with the Great Lakes opens ... **May 24:** Former Secretary of State John F. Dulles dies at 71 ... **June 18:** Actress Ethel Barrymore dies at 79 ... **June 26:** Ingemar Johannson becomes world heavyweight champion by knocking out Floyd Patterson ... **July 15-Nov. 7:** Longest strike in steel industry ... **July 17:** Singer Billie Holiday dies at 44 ... **July 21:** First atomic-powered merchant ship, the Savannah, launched ... **Aug. 8:** First picture of the earth from outer space transmitted from Explorer VI and broadcast on TV ... **Aug. 21:** Hawaii becomes the 50th state ... **Sept. 15-27:** Soviet Premier Khrushchev visits U.S. ... **Oct. 16:** Military leader and diplomat George C. Marshall dies at 78 ... **Nov. 2:** Before a congressional committee Charles Van Doren discloses that he was given answers in advance on TV quiz program.

Surveying the ruins of "Tara" on Hollywood's "Gone With the Wind" set in 1959, 20 years after the film was premiered in Atlanta; at left, author Norman Shavin.

1960

January 11	Gov. Vandiver threatens to withhold all state money from integrated schools.
February	Inspired by the sit-ins at Greensboro, NC, the Committee on Appeal for Human Rights, an organization of students from the Atlanta University Center interested in bringing about racial change in Atlanta and the South, decide to model some demonstrations on the Greensboro sit-ins. Before taking action, leaders of this organization meet with Dr. Benjamin Mays and other black leaders who urge the group to publish their goals before taking action.
March 9	"An Appeal for Human Rights," listing the students' goals, is published in the Atlanta Journal and Constitution, and the Daily World.
March 15	Two hundred college students stage sit-ins in downtown cafeterias and lunch counters of state, federal, county and city buildings, as well as those of railroad and bus terminals. A total of 77 students are arrested for violation of the state's anti-trespass law.
March 23	The Georgia Committee on Schools (Sibley Committee), formed by the state Legislature to restudy the school issue and make recommendations, visits Atlanta. Atlantans overwhelmingly support to keep their schools open whether integrated or not. Later this year The Committee on Schools, in a report to the Legislature, recommends that Georgia repeal its massive-resistance laws and adopt a local-option policy that would allow communities determine their course of action.
May 17	To commemorate the anniversary of the Brown decision, students march from the Atlanta University Center to the state Capitol. Police Chief Herbert Jenkins turns them back, and the students proceed to Wheat Street Baptist Church for a rally. No violence erupts.
May	Jack Nelson of The Atlanta Constitution wins a Pulitzer Prize for his expose of conditions at the state mental health institute at Milledgeville.

THIS YEAR IN THE NATION

Jan. 23: Bathyscaphe Trieste descends 35,800 feet to the bottom of the Mariana Trench ... **Feb. 2:** Sit-in demonstrations begin when four black students attempt to be served at lunch counter in Greensboro, NC ... **Feb. 22-Mar. 6:** Pres. Eisenhower makes a two-week visit to South America ... **Apr. 1:** Tiros I, first U.S. weather satellite, launched ... **May 1:** U-2 spy aircraft piloted by Gary F. Powers of U.S. is shot down over the Soviet Union ... **May 6:** Pres. Eisenhower signs a civil rights bill that permits federal judges to send referees to supervise voter registration ... **July 13-14:** Democrats nominate John F. Kennedy for President and Lyndon B. Johnson for Vice-President ... **July 27-28:** Republicans nominate Vice-President Nixon for President ... **Aug. 23:** Lyricist Oscar Hammerstein II dies at 65 ... **Nov. 8:** John F. Kennedy elected President ... **Nov. 28:** Author Richard Wright dies at 52.

Summer	Black protest continues. On July 27 several black students are arrested for attempting to eat lunch in the state Capitol, City Hall and Fulton County Courthouse. On August 7 about 25 students are arrested for staging kneel-ins at local churches. Various stores and restaurants are picketed and boycotted for their treatment of blacks and their refusal to increase black employment.
June 1	Ralph McGill is named publisher of the Atlanta Constitution. Eugene Patterson becomes editor.
July 31	To combat the conservatism of the Daily World and act as a voice for the student movement, the black newspaper, The Atlanta Inquirer, is founded. Its editors include Julian Bond.
October 19	Martin Luther King, Jr., and 35 students (including one white man) are arrested for sitting in at Rich's department store. On the following Thursday and Friday more demonstrators are arrested. Mayor Hartsfield asks for a 30-day truce so negotiations between white and black leaders can begin.
November 28	Ivan Allen Jr. is named president of the Chamber of Commerce and the businesses endorse his Six Point Program for the development of Atlanta. These points include open schools, an acceleration in the tempo of local expressway construction, urban renewal, an auditorium-coliseum and stadium, a rapid transit system, and a "Forward Atlanta" program to promote the city.

Following the report of John F. Kennedy's presidential victory, Atlanta Constitution publisher Ralph McGill (crouching, left) and editor Eugene Patterson (arm upraised) fire late Constitution editor Henry W. Grady's miniature cannon in celebration. Similarly, Grady had fired it when the first Democratic president after the Civil War was elected. Also in the photo, former Constitution associate editor Bruce Galphin (upper left) and reporter Frank Wells (next to Patterson).

1961

February 15 The police arrest one white and seven black ministers for supporting the "jail-in" of students.

March 7 The Chamber of Commerce announces a lunch counter desegregation agreement. According to the agreement between white and black leaders, the full desegregation of downtown stores and lunch counters would occur within 30 days of the desegregation of Atlanta public schools. All picketing and boycotting will stop and charges against the students would be dropped.

May The Chamber of Commerce "kicks off" its Forward Atlanta Program, a program to promote the city and attract new industries. "Atlanta" magazine, a monthly designed to promote the city, is launched.

May The firm of (Griffith) Edwards and (John) Portman, architects, opens the Atlanta Merchandise Mart. (The firm, on Edwards' retirement in 1968, becomes known as John Portman & Associates.)

June 7 Mayor William B. Hartsfield announces he will not be a candidate for mayor. Hartsfield served almost 28 years as the mayor.

August 30 Nine black children integrate four formerly all-white high schools.

September 4 A rally to protest racial change in Atlanta is held by 250 segregationists.

September 18 Three black students integrate Georgia Tech.

September 22 The combined votes of the black community and middle-to-upper class whites helps Ivan Allen Jr. to beat Lester Maddox in the mayoral primary. The Hartsfield era ends.

Also this year: The $20 million Atlanta Airport terminal opens, as does the Atlanta Decorative Arts Center.

Atlanta Merchandise Mart (see May)

Atlanta Airport terminal (see Also this year . . .)

Mayor Ivan Allen (see Sept. 22)

THIS YEAR IN THE NATION

Jan. 3: U.S. breaks diplomatic relations with Cuba ... **Jan. 20:** John F. Kennedy inaugurated as the 35th President and the first Roman Catholic to be President ... **Mar. 1:** Pres. Kennedy establishes the Peace Corps by executive order ... **Mar. 29:** The 23rd Amendment to the Constitution giving the residents of Washington, DC the right to vote for President is ratified ... **Apr. 16-May 17:** Bay of Pigs invasion of Cuba fails; Pres. Kennedy takes full responsibility ... **May 4-24:** Biracial group sponsored by the civil rights organization C.O.R.E. travels through the South ... **May 5:** Alan B. Shepard becomes first American in space ... **July 2:** Author Ernest Hemingway commits suicide at age 61 ... **Aug. 17:** Latin American leaders declare their support for Pres. Kennedy's Alliance for Progress ... **Oct. 1:** Roger Maris of the New York Yankees hits his 61st home run of the season, breaking Babe Ruth's record ... **Nov. 16:** Sam Rayburn, first elected to the House of Representatives in 1912 and Speaker since 1940, dies at 79.

1962

January 2 Ivan Allen, Jr., is inaugurated mayor of Atlanta — the first time since 1943 that anyone other than W. B. Hartsfield has been installed as mayor.

January 15 A budget is passed to put city employees on a 40-hour week. The aldermanic board also passes a rapid transit proposal asking that the City be given equal representation on a Metro Rapid Transit Authority.

January 29 On recommendations of Police Chief Herbert Jenkins, Mayor Allen approves a resolution to wipe out all restrictions on the duties of black policemen extant since 1947. Restrictions are lifted April 30.

February 1 Commemorating the second anniversary of the sit-ins at Greensboro, NC, 100 Atlanta blacks march on the Capitol here.

February 11 One of Atlanta's first urban residential developments opens at Thomasville; residences are reserved to blacks.

February 14 Protesting the segregation of hospital facilities, students jam the halls at Grady Hospital; 23 are arrested.

February 16 The Legislature approves a constitutional amendment to allow regions or cities to establish their own public transportation systems. The amendment is defeated in the general election.

February 19 Plans for an auditorium are announced. Estimated cost, $50 million.

February 26 Pope John XXIII designates Atlanta an archdiocese. It comprises the dioceses of Charleston, SC; Miami, FL; Raleigh, NC; St. Augustine, FL; and Savannah, GA. All these cities had been part of the Baltimore province. On March 29 Bishop Paul Hallinan is made Archbishop of Atlanta.

March 28 The City Planning Commission issues a report which details $137 million in projects over the next six years for streets, sewers, parks, the police department, urban renewal and a new auditorium.

April 7 The Georgia Supreme Court rules that Atlanta's movie censorship laws violate the state constitution. One month later the city's aldermen approve a new rating system: "approved," "unsuitable for the young," and "objectionable." This rating system is also struck down by the courts.

April 28 A Federal court rules that Georgia's county unit system is unconstitutional. In May the court orders the Legislature to reapportion on the basis of population. Thus, Atlanta's representation in the state Senate rises from one to 12.

June 3 A plane crash at Paris' Orly field kills 111 Atlantans — art patrons visiting European capitals under the sponsorship of the Atlanta Art Association.

June 11 Archbishop Hallinan announces the desegregation of the 8 elementary and five high schools of the diocese.

June 27 The State Democratic Executive Committee rules that the county unit system would not be used in the primary.

November 7 Largely due to the reapportionment of the Legislature, LeRoy Johnson, a black, and Dan I. McIntyre, a Republican, are elected to the Georgia Senate.

November 10 The Atlanta postmaster is suspended because of his non-compliance with the anti-discriminatory policy of the Kennedy administration.

December 18 The city erects a barricade at Peyton and Harlan Roads in southwest Atlanta and declares the thoroughfares closed. This barricade, referred to as the "Peyton" or "Berlin" Wall by members of the black community, failed to halt the "spillover" of Collier Heights, a black subdivision, into Cascade Heights, an all-white neighborhood.

THIS YEAR IN THE NATION

The Cuban missile crisis brings the U.S. and the Soviet Union close to war ... **Feb. 10:** U-2 pilot Gary F. Powers released by the Soviet Union in exchange for Soviet spy Rudolph Abel ... **Feb. 14:** Jacqueline Kennedy narrates a 60-minute documentary on the White House for an estimated 80 million TV viewers ... **Feb. 20:** John H. Glenn, Jr., becomes the first American to orbit the earth ... **Mar. 2:** Pres. Kennedy announces the U.S. will resume atomic testing ... **Mar. 26:** In Baker v. Carr the Supreme Court rules for one-man, one-vote apportionment for state legislatures ... **Apr. 10-13:** U.S. Steel raises, then rescinds the rise in the price of steel under pressure from the White House ... **Apr. 21-Oct. 21:** Seattle World's Fair ... **June 25:** Supreme Court rules against prayer in the public schools ... **July 10:** Telstar communications satellite launched ... **Aug. 5:** Actress Marilyn Monroe dies at 36 ... **Oct. 1:** Charles Meredith becomes first black student at the University of Mississippi but only after federal troops put down riot led by whites ... **Oct. 22-24:** Cuban missile crisis ... **Oct. 25:** Novelist John Steinbeck awarded Nobel Prize for literature.

Singer Frankie Avalon visits Atlanta Jan. 17, 1962, on behalf of the March of Dimes.

1963

January 2   Emory University accepts black students in its nursing school, undergraduate, graduate and medical schools. (This year, Trinity Presbyterian School, Oglethorpe University, Smith-Hughes Vocational School and Atlanta Speech School accept black students. DeKalb Area Trade School accepts applications from blacks. In 1962 Georgia State College admitted its first black student. and Agnes Scott College trustees announced acceptance of applications from black students for the 1963-64 term.)

January   The Board of Aldermen vote 10-3 to refuse to take down "Peyton Wall," and Mayor Allen refuses to have the barrier removed by executive decree. On March 1 Fulton County Superior Court orders the wall removed.

May   A $39 million bond issue is passed. (The previous year an $80 million proposal was defeated.)

Spring   Numerous meetings occur among city administrators, black leaders and hotel and restaurant owners to solve the issue of desegregation. Black demonstrators picket, boycott and stage demonstrations at hotels and restaurants. On March 1 a "lie-in" is held at Grady Hotel.

Summer   Atlanta swimming pools and parks are desegregated.

July 22   Numerous suburban and drive-in theatres begin to integrate. Between July 22 and August 5 they agree to allow up to six black patrons per performance. After August 5 and in the event of no incidents, the theatres agree to admit black patrons generally. If incidents arose as a result of integration, the theatres had the right to resegregate.

July 25   Mayor Allen announces his support for the Civil Rights Bill pending in Congress.

July 26   At the request of Pres. Kennedy, Mayor Allen testifies on behalf of the Civil Rights Bill.

August 28   Rev. Ashton Jones, a white minister who refuses to leave First Baptist Church when refused admittance in the company of blacks, is arrested for disturbing worship. He is sentenced to 12 months in jail, but after numerous appeals, he is released after 188 days in jail.

October 19   A "summit meeting" of representatives of nine black organizations occur and a plan, "Action For Democracy," is adopted. Black leaders recommend a local public accommodations act, an open-occupancy housing law, establishment of a "fair employment" machinery, desegregation of Atlanta schools, the appointment of blacks to judgeships, and the desegregation of public facilities.

November 27   Mayor Allen appoints a biracial committee to investigate the racial situation in Atlanta. December resolutions by the aldermen and the Chamber of Commerce urge the voluntary desegregation of businesses, employment and public facilities.

December 15   The Summit Leadership Conference holds a rally in Hurt Park. It features the first public appearance of Dr. Martin Luther King, Jr., in his own hometown, at the request of the black community.

THIS YEAR IN THE NATION

Jan. 7: Price of a first-class letter goes up from 4¢ to 5¢ ... **Jan. 8:** Mona Lisa goes on exhibit in the National Gallery of Art ... **Jan. 29:** Poet Robert Frost dies at 88 ... **Mar. 18:** In Gideon v. Wainwright the Supreme Court rules that an indigent defendant must be given free legal counsel in all criminal cases ... **Apr. 3-May 12:** Massive demonstrations in Birmingham, AL protesting racial injustice ... **Apr. 5:** U.S. and Soviet Union agree to establish a hot line between the White House and the Kremlin ... **July 25:** U.S., Great Britain and the Soviet Union sign nuclear test ban treaty in Moscow ... **Aug. 28:** 200,000 persons march on Washington to support an end to racial discrimination; they hear Martin Luther King, Jr., give his "I have a dream speech" ... **Sept. 15:** Four children killed as black Baptist church is bombed in Birmingham, AL ... **Nov. 22:** Pres. John F. Kennedy assassinated in Dallas; later the same day Lyndon B. Johnson is sworn in as the 36th president ... **Nov. 24:** Alleged assassin of Pres. Kennedy, Lee H. Oswald, killed by Jack Ruby while in police custody ... **Nov. 29:** Pres. Johnson appoints a committee to investigate the assassination of Pres. Kennedy.

Nov. 25, 1963: Members of the late Pres. John F. Kennedy's family—and brothers Edward (left) and Robert (right)—watch as his funeral cortege passes. In the center are Mrs. Kennedy, daughter Caroline (left) and son John.

1964

January	Mayor Allen appoints A. T. Walden, black leader and attorney as a "stand-by" judge for both the municipal and traffic court of Atlanta. This is the highest and only judicial appointment held by a black in Georgia.
January 18	The Summit Leadership Conference requests the Student Nonviolence Coordinating Committee to launch a nonviolent campaign against segregated restaurants, the Atlanta NAACP to launch a nonviolent campaign against major hotels that are segregated, and the Southern Christian Leadership Conference and the All-Citizens Committee to launch a voter education campaign.
January 29	Because of confrontations between demonstrators and the police, Mayor Allen calls for a 30-day cooling off period.
April 8	The Atlanta Board of Education changes the requirements of black pupils who want to transfer to white schools. The list is narrowed from 17 to three: pupil preference, available facilities and proximity. Only a few students were qualifying under the old regulations.
April 15	Ground-breaking ceremonies are held for Atlanta Stadium, built in 51 weeks.
June 12	The first issue of The Atlanta Times is published. The new paper lasts only through August 31, 1965.
July 3	Lester Maddox uses a gun and ax handles to expel blacks from his Pickrick restaurant.

On July 22 the federal court upholds the Civil Rights provision that bars discrimination in public accommodations. Among those ordered to desegregate, Maddox closes his restaurant in August.

July 11	Work on the Stone Mountain Memorial resumes under sculptor Walter Hancock.
July	The J. W. Bowen Housing Project opens . . . A biracial committee reports that 908 blacks have been hired by the City during the first half of the year. In comparison, only 672 whites were hired.

Also this year: Atlanta had the nation's second largest gain in new construction. Department stores sales showed the third greatest gain among America's 25 largest cities. A constitutional amendment authorizes planning of a unified regional transit system, and the Chamber's Forward Atlanta campaign is renewed.

THIS YEAR IN THE NATION

Jan. 8: In a joint session of Congress Pres. Johnson outlines his War on Poverty ... **Jan. 17:** Riots in Canal Zone against U.S. presence there ... **Jan. 23:** 24th Amendment outlawing the poll tax in federal elections ratified ... **Feb. 25:** Cassius Clay becomes heavyweight champion by beating Sonny Liston ... **Mar. 27-28:** Earthquake hits Alaska causing 114 deaths and $750 million damage ... **Apr. 5:** Gen. Douglas MacArthur dies at 84 ... **Apr. 22-Oct. 17:** New York World's Fair ... **July 2:** Civil Rights Act of 1964 signed by Pres. Johnson ... **July 13-17:** Republicans nominate Sen. Barry Goldwater for President ... **July 31:** U.S. spacecraft Ranger 7 sends close-up pictures of the moon before crashing on the lunar surface ... **Aug. 7:** Senate passes Gulf of Tonkin resolution ... **Aug. 24-27:** Democrats nominate Pres. Johnson for a full term as president ... **Oct. 14:** Martin Luther King, Jr., awarded Nobel Peace Prize ... **Oct. 16:** Composer and lyricist Cole Porter dies at 71 ... **Oct. 20:** Former president Herbert Hoover dies at 90 ... **Nov. 3:** Lyndon Johnson elected President by a landslide.

On the 25th anniversary of the world premiere of "Gone With the Wind," the movie was "re-premiered" here. Attending were (from left) Mr. and Mrs. Stephens Mitchell (he was the only brother of author Margaret); Vivien Leigh (who played Scarlett O'Hara); actors Douglas Fairbanks, Jr., and George Murphy; "GWTW" producer David O. Selznick, and Olivia deHavilland, who portrayed Melanie.

1965

January 27	A biracial dinner honors Dr. Martin Luther King, Jr., winner of the 1964 Nobel (Peace) Prize.
April 9-11	A three-game series between the Braves and the Detroit Tigers helps dedicate Atlanta Stadium though the Braves are required to play their 1965 seson in Milwaukee. For one season Atlanta Stadium is the home of the Atlanta Crackers.
June 2	Grady Hospital begins to desegregate its facilities.
June 6	Over 500 Klan members march in Atlanta.
June 23	Mayor Allen names a commission on crime and juvenile delinquency; it is chaired by lawyer Griffin Bell.
July 3	A. T. Walden, the voice of Atlanta's black community for nearly 30 years dies.
September 13	Atlanta receives a $6,300,000 anti-poverty grant from Congress.
October 16	Mayor Allen defeats "Muggsy" Smith (53,233 to 21,907) to win another term. Q. V. Williamson is elected as the first black alderman in Atlanta in nearly a century.
December	Atlanta's employment rate increases 38 per cent since 1961. Its unemployment rate of 2.2 per cent is lowest in the nation.

THIS YEAR IN THE NATION

War in Vietnam escalates as do racial tensions at home ... **Jan. 4:** In State of the Union message Pres. Johnson discusses his plans for his Great Society program ... **Feb. 21:** Malcolm X killed ... **Mar. 7-9:** Protesters in Selma, AL are clubbed by state troopers when they attempt to begin march on Montgomery ... **Mar. 21-25:** March from Selma to Montgomery led by Martin Luther King, Jr., dramatizes lack of black voter registration in Alabama ... **Apr. 28:** Pres. Johnson announces he is sending Marines to the Dominican Republic to protect Americans and U.S. property ... **June 3:** Astronaut Edward White becomes first American to walk in space ... **July 14:** U.S. ambassador to the U.N. Adlai Stevenson dies at 65 ... **July 15:** Mariner 4 begins sending back to earth close-up pictures of Mars ... **July 30:** Pres. Johnson signs legislation creating Medicare ... **Aug. 6:** Pres. Johnson signs Voting Rights Act ... **Aug. 12-17:** Race riots in Watts section of Los Angeles; 35 killed and many more are injured ... **Sept. 29:** Bill establishing the National Foundation for the Arts and the Humanities signed by Pres. Johnson ... **Nov. 9-10:** Northeast struck by electric power failure ... **Dec. 15:** Two Gemini spacecraft rendezvous in space.

Atlanta Stadium (see Apr. 9)

Rabbi Jacob Rothschild presents a commemorative bowl to Dr. Martin Luther King, Jr. (see Jan. 27).

In October, 1965, the historic Magna Carta came to Atlanta, and was photographed with then-Mayor Ivan Allen, Jr. (left); former Pres. Dwight D. Eisenhower, and (at right) the late Hugh M. Mercer, then partner-in-charge of Price Waterhouse and president of the Atlanta branch of the English Speaking Union, which hosted the local ceremonies.

1966

January
The Atlanta Police Department organizes the Crime Prevention Bureau. Officers of this Bureau, assigned to Economic Opportunity Centers in ghetto areas, act as guides and counselors for the unemployed, assist in providing welfare services and provide law enforcement.

January 10
Because of his stand against the Vietnam war, the Georgia House refuses to seat Rep. Julian Bond.

April 12
Before 50,671 persons the Atlanta Braves play their first official National League baseball game in Atlanta Stadium.

April 16
Stone Mountain Park officially opens.

June 6
600 of Atlanta's 850 firemen strike, demanding reduction of their 60-hour week.

Summer
The Atlanta Historical Society purchases the Swan House as its headquarters.

September
The Atlanta Falcons bring the National Football League to Atlanta. No other city in its history had ever brought both professional baseball and football teams in the same year.

September 6-September 11
Blacks riot in Summerhill, triggered by the shooting of a suspected auto thief escaping a white police officer and some incitement by Stokely Carmichael; 35 are injured and 138 arrested. While trying to calm the crowds, Mayor Allen is toppled from a car. Carmichael, of the SNCC, is indicted for inciting a riot (Sept. 13). During the riot, Julian Bond announces his resignation from SNCC.

September 11
Atlanta Falcons' first regular season game; the football team loses to Los Angeles, 19-15.

November 8
Mayor Allen creates the Community Relations Commission as a means by which all citizens can state their grievances.

Fall/Winter
Rather than being forced by his party oath to support Lester Maddox for governor, U. S. Rep. Charles Weltner decides not to run for reelection. In the gubernatorial election Maddox is pitted against Bo Callaway. Though Callaway wins the popular vote, he does not have the majority of votes because of a write-in campaign for Ellis Arnall. The Legislature chooses Maddox governor.

December 5
The Supreme Court upholds Julian Bond's right to sit in the Legislature.

Rep. Julian Bond (see Jan. 10)

Rep. Charles Weltner (see Fall/Winter)

Ellis Arnall (see Fall/Winter)

THIS YEAR IN THE NATION

Jan. 13: Robert C. Weaver, the first black to serve as cabinet officer, becomes Secretary of the newly created Department of Housing and Urban Development ... **Mar. 25:** Supreme Court rules that the poll tax in state elections is unconstitutional ... **May 11-16:** Sit-ins staged in several universities against the war in Vietnam ... **June 2:** First soft landing on the moon; Surveyor I sends back pictures of the lunar surface ... **June 7:** Charles Meredith shot while on march from Memphis, TN, to Jackson, MS ... **June 13:** Supreme Court rules in Miranda v. State of Arizona that an individual may not be interrogated by police until he has been informed of his constitutional rights to an attorney and to remain silent ... **July 1:** Medicare program that provides medical aid to elderly Americans goes into effect ... **July 17:** Richard Speck arrested in the murder of eight student nurses in Chicago ... **Aug. 1:** Gunman Charles Whitman murders 15 persons at the University of Texas before he is killed ... **Sept. 6:** Margaret Sanger dies at 83; a leader in providing birth control for women ... **Oct. 15:** Pres. Johnson signs legislation creating the Department of Transportation ... **Dec. 15:** Walt Disney dies at 65.

1967

May	Eugene Patterson, editor of The Atlanta Constitution, wins the Pulitzer Prize for his editorials.
May 1	Hyatt Regency Atlanta Hotel opens.
June 16	Six Flags Over Georgia opens.
June 19-20	Racial unrest follows the arrest of Stokely Carmichael and four other black men in west Atlanta. One black dies and three are seriously wounded before Mayor Allen declares a curfew for the area.
July 27	Pres. Lyndon Johnson names Atlanta's Police Chief Herbert Jenkins a member of the Kerner Riot Commission.
September	Confrontation breaks out between the Atlanta Board of Education and the black community. At the Board's September meeting black citizens led by Hosea Williams demand an end to double sessions in three high schools (due to overcrowding) and the appointment of more blacks to administrative jobs in the system.
November 7	Dr. Rufus Clement, president of Atlanta University since 1937 and member of the Board of Education, dies.
Fall	Steven Fuller and Jack Patterson begin to develop a project called Underground Atlanta; it opens in May, 1969.
November 17	Atlanta is one of 66 cities announced by the Department of Housing and Urban Development to receive planning grants under the U.S. Model City program. Atlanta's "model city area" encompasses 3000 acres and includes such areas as Grant Park, Atlanta Stadium, Candler Warehouse, Roosevelt High School, and the Key Golf Course. It includes four per cent of Atlanta's land area and 10 per cent of its population.

THIS YEAR IN THE NATION

Jan. 27: Three astronauts die in a fire while training at Cape Kennedy ... **Feb. 10:** 25th Amendment, which provides for the replacement of the Vice-President and for presidential disability, becomes effective ... **Mar. 1:** Adam C. Powell excluded from his seat in the House of Representatives ... **Apr. 15:** Huge anti-war rallies are held in New York and San Francisco ... **Apr. 21:** Stalin's daughter Svetlana Alliluyeva comes to the U.S. to live ... **May 9:** Muhammad Ali indicted by a grand jury for refusing induction in the army; he forfeits his world heavyweight title as well ... **July 22:** Author Carl Sandburg dies at 89 ... **July 23-30:** Race riots in Detroit ... **Oct. 2:** Thurgood Marshall becomes the first black to be a U.S. Supreme Court justice ... **Oct. 10:** Space treaty, which prohibits nuclear weapons in space and any territorial claims to the moon or the planets, goes into effect ... **Nov. 7:** Blacks win seats in state legislatures in Virginia, Mississippi and Louisiana for the first time since Reconstruction; voters in Gary, IN and Cleveland, OH elect black mayors ... **Nov. 20:** Census Bureau announces that the U.S. has a population of 200,000,000.

Hyatt Regency Hotel (see May 1)

Six Flags Over Georgia (see June 16)

Governor's Mansion: The West Paces Ferry Road abode opens in 1967 to its first occupant, Gov. Lester Maddox.

1968

January	The governor's residence, a neo-classical mansion on West Paces Ferry Road, is dedicated.
March 28	Cleveland Sellers of SNCC is convicted of draft evasion, an action he claims justifiable because of his stance against the war.
April 4	Dr. Martin Luther King, Jr. is shot in Memphis. Pres. Johnson proclaims a national day of mourning. On April 9 King is buried after a nationally televised funeral march through the streets of Atlanta.
June 11-12	Four convicts take 25 hostages after they fail to escape the federal penitentiary. After The Atlanta Journal publishes a list of prisoner complaints, the hostages are freed.
September 10	Rev. Ralph Abernathy, of SCLC, is arrested for encouraging 800 garbage workers to strike against Atlanta.
October 1	Eugene Patterson resigns as editor of The Atlanta Constitution. Despite his denials, rumors fly that Patterson felt management's concern with the financial well-being of the paper restricted editorial coverage. Patterson joins The Washington Post. Reg Murphy is named editor of The Constitution.
October 24-October 29	Two units of the $13 million Memorial Arts Center (now the Robert W. Woodruff Arts Center) are dedicated. Money is raised through private donations given in memory of those who died in the Paris' Orly Field crash of 1962.
October	Tom Cousins brings the St. Louis Hawks, a National Basketball Association team, to Atlanta. Early games are played at Georgia Tech's Alexander Memorial Coliseum.
November	In the race for U.S. Senator, Herman Talmadge defeats Maynard Jackson though Jackson carries Atlanta . . . Fulton and

DeKalb voters reject a proposal to underwrite the rapid transit system (MARTA) bonds with property taxes.

December	Due to the elimination of legal segregation, the passage of Civil Rights laws, the availability of other organizations, and a general lack of support, the Greater Atlanta Council on Human Relations, one of the most active white organizations promoting racial change in Atlanta, ceases to exist.

THIS YEAR IN THE NATION

Jan. 21-Apr. 5: Marine base in Khesanh, Vietnam is besieged but supplied by air until siege is lifted ... **Jan. 23:** Intelligence ship U.S.S. Pueblo captured by North Korea ... **Mar. 12:** In New Hampshire primary Sen. Eugene McCarthy captures 42% of the vote ... **Apr. 4:** Martin Luther King, Jr., is fatally shot in Memphis, TN ... **Apr. 4-6:** Riots break out in more than 100 cities as a result of Dr. King's assassination ... **Apr. 11:** Civil Rights Act covering discrimination in housing signed by Pres. Johnson ... **Apr. 23-30:** Students at Columbia University occupy several campus buildings ... **May 2-June 24:** Poor People's March in Washington ... **June 1:** Helen Keller dies at 87 ... **June 5:** Sen. Robert F. Kennedy is shot; he dies the next day ... **Aug. 5-8:** Republicans nominate Richard Nixon for President ... **Aug. 26-28:** At tumultuous convention, the Democrats nominate Hubert Humphrey for President ... **Nov. 5:** Richard Nixon elected President in a close popular vote ... **Dec. 20:** Author John Steinbeck dies at 66.

The Atlanta Civic Center is dedicated Apr. 2, 1968.

The Atlanta Memorial Arts Center is opened in October, 1968.

Funeral march for Dr. Martin Luther King, Jr.: Coffin in mule-pulled wagon passes state Capitol (see Apr. 4).

In the funeral march for Dr. Martin Luther King, Jr., were actors Sidney Poitier (left) and Sammy Davis, Jr. (right).

1969

January   Mayor Allen announces he will not seek a third term.

January 14   The Atlanta Municipal Theatre, whose initial production is the satire, "Red, White and Maddox," is briefly discontinued, but reorganizes in March.

February 4   Atlanta Constitution publisher Ralph McGill dies of a heart attack.

April   Peaceful demonstrations at the state Capitol mark the anniversary of Dr. Martin Luther King, Jr.'s death.

Spring   Students for a Democratic Society march on the state Capitol.

June 24   The Justice Department announces a suit against the West Peachtree Corporation for discriminatory rent policy. (During the year the Justice Department sues the Decatur School System along with the 80 other systems in Georgia. This suit is the fourth Metro area suit dealing with school integration.)

August   Altercations occur between police and members of Atlanta's hippie community during drug arrests near Piedmont Park.

October 21   Sam Massell defeats Rodney Cook to become the first Jewish mayor of Atlanta. His vice mayor, Maynard Jackson, is black, and black aldermen increase from one to five; three blacks, including Dr. Benjamin Mays, are elected to the Board of Education.

December   By year's end, 15 skyscrapers of 20 or more floors have been started since 1960 and over $1.3 billion of construction has been completed. Atlanta ranks in the top 10 in most growth categories over the last 10 years: downtown construction, bank clearings, air traffic, employment and mercantile construction.

Underground Atlanta opens in May, 1969: Shown is the entrance.

Ralph McGill (see Feb. 4)

Sam Massell (see Oct. 21)

THIS YEAR IN THE NATION

Jan. 20: Richard Nixon inaugurated as 37th President ... **Jan. 28:** Oil well in the Santa Barbara (CA) Channel blows out, causing oil to enter surrounding waters ... **Mar. 28:** Former Pres. Eisenhower dies at 78 ... **Apr. 7:** Supreme Court rules unconstitutional laws prohibiting the private possession of obscene materials ... **June 9:** Warren E. Burger confirmed by Senate as Chief Justice of the Supreme Court ... **June 22:** Singer-actress Judy Garland dies at 47 ... **July 19:** Sen. Edward Kennedy drives a car off a bridge on Chappaquiddick Island, MA, killing companion Mary Jo Kopechne ... **July 20:** Astronaut Neil Armstrong becomes the first person to set foot on the moon ... **Aug. 9:** Actress Sharon Tate and four friends found murdered in Los Angeles ... **Aug. 16-19:** Woodstock Rock Festival in New York state ... **Aug. 17:** Hurricane Camille strikes Gulf coast causing 150 deaths and a billion dollars' damage ... **Nov. 15:** 250,000 march in Washington against the war in Vietnam.

1970

January 7	Sam Massell takes office and during his first year appoints blacks as chairmen of Finance and the Police Committees.
March 1	Garbage workers, demanding a two-step wage increase, strike. The strike ends April 22 when Massell approves a pay raise for 2,300 city employees.
May	After 50 years' effort, the Confederate Memorial carving on Stone Mountain is finished.
May 9	Stone Mountain Memorial officially dedicated.
September 3-September 7	The First Congress of African People is held at Atlanta University.
November	Former State Sen. Jimmy Carter is elected governor.
	Also this year: Atlanta is the 20th largest city with a population of 497,421. Of the five hundred largest industrial firms in the nation, 430 have office plants or warehouses here. The 32-story, 596,666 square foot Equitable Life Building opens on the downtown site of the once-fashionable Piedmont Hotel.

THIS YEAR IN THE NATION

Feb. 18: "Chicago Seven" acquitted of conspiring to incite riot, though five of the seven are convicted of crossing state lines to incite a riot ... **Feb. 25:** Branch of Bank of America in Santa Barbara (CA) bombed ... **Mar. 11:** Author Erle Gardner dies at 80 ... **Apr. 30:** U.S. and South Vietnamese forces invade Cambodia ... **May 4:** National Guardsmen kill four war-protesting students on Kent State University campus ... **May 20:** One hundred thousand persons demonstrate support in New York for the Vietnam policy of Pres. Nixon ... **June 16:** Kenneth Gibson becomes the first black mayor of Newark, NJ ... **July 1:** New York adopts the most liberal abortion law in the nation ... **Aug. 7:** In Marin County (CA) courthouse Judge Harold J. Haley is killed after being taken hostage by black militants ... **Aug. 24:** One killed and four injured when bomb explodes at the Army Mathematics Research Center in Madison, WI ... **Sept. 28:** Author John Dos Passos dies at 74 ... **Oct. 2:** Environmental Protection Agency begins operation ... **Dec. 7:** Cartoonist Rube Goldberg dies at 87 ... **Dec. 27:** "Hello Dolly!" the then longest running Broadway musical, closes at 2,844 performances.

Stone Mountain (see May 9)

Musical Museum was a 1970 attraction in Underground Atlanta.

An attraction of Underground Atlanta: Dante's Down the Hatch Restaurant.

1971

February 22	William B. Hartsfield, former mayor of Atlanta for 23½ years, dies.
March 1	The aldermen pass an ordinance naming the airport the William B. Hartsfield Airport; six months later this name is changed to the William B. Hartsfield International Airport.
July 1	Eastern Airlines provides Atlanta with its first international nonstop flight - daily to Mexico City.
September 16	The Water Department is desegregated in accordance with Mayor Massell's 1970 directive that all departments "implement actions that will bring about a change with a goal of 50 per cent minority employment in all classifications within 40 months."
October 27	Mayor Massell announces he will have legislation introduced to expand the city limits to take in 50,000 persons, nearly all white, without a referendum. Massell cites the loss of inner-city businesses as the reason for this move. Black members charge racism. Massell's legislation dies in the state Senate when Gov. Maddox refuses to call the measure from the Senate calendar.
November	Atlanta, Fulton and DeKalb voters approve a 10-year four per cent sales tax to underwrite MARTA bonds. MARTA agrees to reduce the transit fare from 40 to 15 cents for the first seven years of its operation, to run a rail line to an outlying black area not included in its initial plans, and establish an aggressive affirmative action program. Voters in Gwinnett and Clayton counties defeat the measure for their areas.
December 16	Robert H. Brisbane becomes the first black member appointed to the Fulton County Civil Service Commission.
December	Atlanta unemployment is only 3.6 per cent for 1971, showing job gains of 25,000 yearly since 1961.

Gov. Lester Maddox rides a bicycle

THIS YEAR IN THE NATION

Feb. 9: Severe earthquake rocks southern California ... **Mar. 1:** Bomb explodes in the basement of the Capitol in Washington ... **Mar. 29:** Lt. William Calley, Jr., convicted in court martial for killing 22 civilians during My-Lai massacre in Vietnam ... **Apr. 6:** Russian-born composer Igor Stravinsky dies at 88 ... **Apr. 20:** In Swann v. Charlotte-Mecklenburg Board of Education, Supreme Court rules that busing is an acceptable method to achieve desegregation ... **June 30:** Supreme Court rules that newspapers have the right to print the once-classified "Pentagon Papers" ... **July 1:** Post Office Department becomes the U.S. Postal Service; the Cabinet position of Postmaster General is abolished ... **July 6:** Jazz musician Louis "Satchmo" Armstrong dies at 71 ... **July 25:** 26th Amendment, which lowers the voting age to 18, is ratified ... **Aug. 15:** Pres. Nixon announces a 90-day freeze on prices, wages and rents ... **Sept. 8:** John F. Kennedy Center for the Performing Arts opens in Washington ... **Sept. 13:** Riot and occupation of state prison in Attica, NY ends with 43 dead ... **Dec. 9:** Diplomat Ralph J. Bunche dies at 67.

1972

February 17   The Metropolitan Atlanta Rapid Transit Authority buys the Atlanta Transit Company for $12.8 million.

February   Mayor Massell dedicates a downtown commemorative gas light and placque honoring Atlanta's 125th anniversary as an incorporated town. (The idea was launched by "Atlanta" magazine editor Norman Shavin.)

March 20   After 40 years on the force (police chief since 1947), Herbert Jenkins retires. Mayor Massell appoints Lt. John Inman chief of police.

Spring   Ted Turner begins telecasting Braves' games.

June   The American Civil Liberties Union files suit on behalf of 26 black parents, asking that a metro-wide school desegregation plan be developed. Defendants are the superintendents and school boards of nine systems: Atlanta, Fulton County, Decatur, DeKalb County, Marietta, Cobb County, Buford, Gwinnett County and Clayton County.

August 1   Delta Air lines and Northeast Airlines merge.

September 20   Gwinnett County Commissioners reject a motion to place the rapid transit question before the voters. On November 8, Clayton County voters again oppose participation in MARTA (19,875 to 7,805). This was the last opportunity for both counties to participate in MARTA without bearing full costs for expansion in their counties.

October 14   The $17 million Omni Stadium opens.

November 9   Andrew Young is elected the South's first black congressman since Reconstruction.

THIS YEAR IN THE NATION

Feb. 21-27: Pres. Nixon visits China ... **Mar. 10-12:** First National Black Political Convention held in Gary, IN ... **Mar. 22:** Equal Rights Amendment passes both houses of Congress and is sent to the states for ratification ... **May 2:** FBI Director J. Edgar Hoover dies at 77 ... **May 8:** Pres. Nixon orders the mining of Haiphong Harbor ... **May 14:** Okinawa returned to Japan ... **May 15:** Alabama Gov. George C. Wallace shot by Arthur Bremer in Laurel, MD ... **June 4:** Angela Davis acquitted on charges based on a shootout in a San Rafael (CA) courthouse in 1970 ... **June 17:** Five men arrested in the Democratic National Committee offices in the Watergate complex ... **June 19-23:** Hurricane Agnes causes extensive flooding on the East coast, killing 134 and destroying over 100,000 homes ... **July 10-13:** Democrats nominate George McGovern for president ... **Aug. 3:** Senate ratifies SALT I treaty ... **Aug. 21-23:** Republicans nominate Pres. Nixon for a second term ... **Sept. 1:** Bobby Fischer becomes first American to hold world chess championship by beating Boris Spassky of the Soviet Union ... **Sept. 4:** Mark Spitz becomes the first person to win seven Olympic gold medals ... **Oct. 24:** Jackie Robinson dies at 53 ... **Nov. 7:** Pres. Nixon wins reelection in a landslide.

The Omni Stadium (see Oct. 14)

A commemorative gas light is installed downtown to mark Atlanta's 125th anniversary as an incorporated city (see February). Pictured (from left) are W. L. Lee, then president of the Atlanta Gas Light Co.; Norman Shavin, then editor of "Atlanta" magazine and originator of the idea; and former Mayor Sam Massell.

1973

January	A freezing ice storm disrupts power to 500,000 Atlanta residents for up to six days.
February 8	According to a report by the Chamber of Commerce, more than 88% of the nation's 500 largest industrial firms have established regional offices in Atlanta.
February 19	Negotiators announce a settlement of the Atlanta school desegregation lawsuit which would involve a small amount of busing to achieve at least 30 per cent black enrollment in all schools. Also involved in the plan are a black superintendent heading an integrated school administration, and an adjustment of the black-white faculty ratio in each school.
March 8	Southern Railways announces plans to construct an $18 million maintenance facility. It opens in 1976.
March 14	The Legislature approves a new charter for the city: 12 of the 18 councilmen are to be chosen from single-member districts and the other six would campaign at large, but for designated places based upon paired districts. (Under the old charter, all members had been elected at large.) The vice-mayor becomes president of the council with new legislative powers (approve all councilmanic committees, preside over council meetings and supervise the council's staff). Instead of aldermen supervising the day-to-day operations of city departments, the mayor is given sole function of supervision under a prescribed strict separation of powers between executive and legislative branches.
April	A federal court orders the busing of 2761 whites to integrate Atlanta's schools.
April 12	An estimated 200 demonstrators walk to Rich's downtown store to protest its alleged treatment of black employees; 92 demonstra-

tors are arrested. Rich's denies charges of discrimination.

April 16	The Robert Woodruff Foundation gives Coca-Cola stock whereby the City can create downtown Central Park (now Woodruff Park).
June 21-28	MARTA's bus drivers and mechanics walk off their jobs to protest contract negotiations. On July 13 employees approved a new contract.
July 3	Dr. Alonzo Crim becomes the first black superintendent of Atlanta Public Schools.
October 16	In an election marred by charges of racism on both sides, Maynard Jackson defeats Sam Massell to become Atlanta's first black mayor. Wyche Fowler defeats Hosea Williams for president of the city council (formerly the position of vice-mayor). Voters approve the new city charter.

Maynard Jackson (see Oct. 16)   *Dr. Alonzo Crim (see July 3)*

THIS YEAR IN THE NATION

War in Vietnam finally ends; clouds of Watergate darken Pres. Nixon's politial career ... **Jan. 22:** Supreme Court rules that a state may not restrict a woman from having an abortion during the first three months of pregnancy ... **Jan. 22:** Former Pres. Lyndon B. Johnson dies at 64 ... **Jan. 22:** George Foreman becomes world heavyweight boxing champion by beating Joe Frazier ... **Jan. 27:** Vietnam peace pact signed in Paris ... **Jan. 27:** End of military draft announced ... **Feb. 12:** A 10% devaluation of the dollar announced ... **May 29:** Thomas Bradley elected first black mayor of Los Angeles ... **June 16-25:** Soviet leader Leonid Brezhnev visits the U.S. ... **July 16:** In testimony before Senate committee Alexander Butterfield discloses the existence of White House tapes ... **Sept. 21:** Henry Kissinger confirmed as Secretary of State ... **Oct. 10:** Scandal-tainted Vice-President Spiro T. Agnew resigns ... **Oct. 17:** Arab oil-producing nations embargo oil shipments to the U.S. ... **Oct. 20:** Special Watergate prosecutor Archibald Cox fired ... **Nov. 1:** New Watergate prosecutor Leon Jaworski appointed ... **Nov. 16:** Legislation permitting the building of the Alaskan oil pipeline signed into law by Pres. Nixon ... **Dec. 25:** Gerald R. Ford sworn in as Vice-President under provisions of the 25th Amendment.

1974

January 7	Maynard Jackson, Atlanta's first black mayor, is sworn in. His council is 50 per cent black.
February 22	Groundbreaking ceremonies for MARTA are held.
April 1	After 71 years in Chattanooga, the Southern Newspaper Publishers Association relocates in Atlanta.
April 8	The Atlanta Braves' Hank Aaron breaks Babe Ruth's record of 714 home runs, hitting No. 715.
May-August	Mayor Jackson attempts to dismiss Police Chief Inman. Inman had been charged with racism, mismanagement and corruption. Inman argues that the new city charter is unconstitutional and maintains his post until he retires on pension. Inman's replacement, Reginald Eaves, is named public safety commissioner.
Summer/ Winter	A long and successful campaign begins to save the Fox Theatre from destruction. The Theatre was almost sold to Southern Bell to make way for its headquarters. Due to pressure from a group of Fox supporters (Landmarks, Inc.) and with the cooperation of Southern Bell, the Fox Theatre is saved.
June 18	The portrait of Dr. Martin Luther King, Jr., hung in the Capitol by Gov. Jimmy Carter, is defaced.
June 21	The Atlanta School Board rejects a textbook advancing the divine theory of creation.
June 30	Mrs. Martin Luther King, Sr., is murdered during services at Ebenezer Baptist Church.
July	Rev. Alice Henderson, the Army's first woman chaplain, is commissioned in Atlanta.

THIS YEAR IN THE NATION

Feb. 4: Patricia Hearst kidnapped from her California apartment by the Symbionese Liberation Army ... **Mar. 1:** Indictments handed down against seven Watergate defendants ... **Apr. 8:** Hank Aaron hits his 715th home run, breaking Babe Ruth's record ... **Apr. 30:** Pres. Nixon releases the transcripts of some White House tapes ... **May 9:** Impeachment hearings begin in House Judiciary Committee ... **May 16:** Former Attorney-General Richard Kleindienst pleads guilty to a misdemeanor and on June 7 receives a suspended sentence ... **July 9:** Former Chief Justice of the Supreme Court Earl Warren dies at 83 ... **July 13:** Senate Watergate Committee issued its final report ... **July 24:** Supreme Court rules that Pres. Nixon may not withhold the White House tapes from the special prosecutor ... **Aug. 9:** Pres. Nixon resigns the presidency ... **Sept. 4:** Diplomatic relations between the U.S. and East Germany are established ... **Sept. 8:** Pres. Ford pardons former Pres. Nixon for all crimes against the U.S. ... **Oct. 13:** TV personality Ed Sullivan dies at 73 ... **Oct. 30:** Muhammad Ali knocks out heavyweight champion George Foreman in the eighth round ... **Dec. 19:** Nelson Rockefeller is sworn in as Vice-President ... **Dec. 26:** Comedian Jack Benny dies at 80.

September 16	Major white opposition to the initiatives of Mayor Jackson surfaces. A letter from Central Atlanta Progress, organization of downtown business interests, to Maynard Jackson and Wyche Fowler expresses concern that some business operations are considering moving due to an increasing crime rate, the growing racial imbalance in the city, and the "perceived attitude that the mayor is anti-white."
September 26	At a forum white businessmen denounce "black racism as a coequal threat to the city." Black leaders are accused of being selfish and racist for opposing annexation and consolidation to maintain their political dominance.
October 30	Groundbreaking for the Georgia World Congress Center.
December	Atlanta is estimated to be 55 per cent black.

Hank Aaron (see Apr. 8)

George Busbee: elected governor in 1974.

Implosion of the Henry Grady Hotel (on downtown Peachtree St. next to present-day Macy's) made room for erection of the cylindrical Westin Peachtree Plaza Hotel.

1975

January	Over 2,000 unemployed people apply for 225 public service jobs.
January 2	After 44 years at Ebenezer Baptist Church, Rev. Martin Luther King, Sr., announces that he will retire as pastor in August.
January 15	Ground is broken for the Martin Luther King, Jr., Center for Non-Violent Social Change. The two-story frame house where King was born is recognized by the National Registry of Historic Places.
February	Resolutions are introduced in the Georgia Legislature to allow Atlanta to annex surrounding white suburbs.
February 11	Atlanta Stadium's name is changed to Atlanta-Fulton County Stadium after the County threatens to remove its financial support.
March 17	The new Buckhead Park is dedicated.
March 23	The Atlanta Constitution begins a seven-part series, "A City in Crisis." The series is basically critical of Mayor Jackson's administration.
March 24	Three are killed and several are injured when tornado hits Atlanta. Mayor Jackson calls for a state of emergency.
April 17	Despite charges of improprieties and departmental conflicts, Mayor Jackson reappoints Reginald Eaves as public safety commissioner.
May 1	Richard Rich, grandson of the founder of Rich's and top official of the store since 1949, dies.
June 17	Lockheed Air Terminal, Inc., opens a $5 million facility at Hartsfield International Airport, making it possible for the airport to quadruple its international charter flight business.

THIS YEAR IN THE NATION

Jan. 5: Pres. Ford names Vice-President Rockefeller to head a commission to study the domestic spying activities of the CIA ... **Feb. 21:** Three senior members of the Nixon administration are sentenced to prison ... **Feb. 25:** Elijah Mohammad, leader of the Black Muslims, dies at 77 ... **Mar. 1:** Bicentennial celebration, which will run to the end of 1976, begins ... **Mar. 7:** Senate reduces the needed majority to invoke cloture from 2/3 to 3/5 ... **Apr. 1:** Conrail goes into operation ... **Apr. 17:** John B. Connally, former Secretary of the Treasury, acquitted of accepting bribes ... **May 12-15:** Merchant ship Mayaguez seized by Cambodian army and then rescued by U.S. marines ... **June 10:** On the brink of bankruptcy, New York City surrenders its financial authority to the Municipal Assistance Corp. ... **June 26:** Two FBI agents are shot dead on Pine Ridge Reservation, South Dakota ... **July 17:** U.S. and Soviet space ships rendezvous in space ... **July 31:** Former teamster union president Jimmy Hoffa reported missing ... **Aug. 1:** Helsinki Accords signed; formally accept postwar European borders ... **Sept. 6 and Sept. 22:** Pres. Ford escapes two separate assassination attempts ... **Sept. 18:** Patricia Hearst and her two captors arrested by the FBI ... **Nov. 12:** Supreme Court Associate Justice William O. Douglas retires after serving on the court for a record 36 years.

June 18	The multifaceted deal to save the Fox Theatre for $1.9 million worth of property in the same area. Part of the property contains the proposed site of MARTA's North Avenue Station. MARTA agrees to purchase one remaining parcel on Peachtree Street and give it to Southern Bell.
September-October	Enrollment of white pupils in Atlanta's school system drops to 13 per cent. A teachers' strike damages the credibility of the school system.
October 23	U.S. Fifth Circuit Court approves of the out-of-court settlement reached between the Atlanta school system and black leaders.
December 1	The U.S. Justice Department files suit against Atlanta's Fire Department for discriminating against black employees. The lawsuit charges that the Department discriminated against blacks by refusing to hire them prior to 1964; by using unfair promotion tests, and by refusing to implement proper safeguards to prevent further discrimination.
December 9	A majority of Atlanta voters reject three sections of a controversial $48.9 million bond issue which would increase property taxes: three $10 million bond issues for sewers and drainage, the Atlanta Zoo and parks, and street improvements. A $18.9 million bond issue for a new library passes by a slim margin.

Birthplace of Martin Luther King, Jr. (see Jan. 15)

Steve Bartkowski, hired as the Atlanta Falcons' quarterback in 1975.

1976

January 6 — Ted Turner announces an agreement to buy the Atlanta Braves baseball team for $12 million.

January 28 — Veteran federal Judge Griffin Bell resigns from the Fifth Circuit Court of Appeals.

February 1 — Dr. Albert E. Manley, the first black and the first man to head Spelman College, announces he will retire in June. He was its president for 22 years.

April — Despite controversy that surrounds Reginald Eaves, statistics show a reduced crime rate in Atlanta and increased police training. The Atlanta police force grew from 952 officers in 1970 to 1,561 in 1975.

May 5 — Provisions of Atlanta's solicitation ordinances are declared unconstitutional, along with city code sections governing solicitation permits. The action stems from a suit filed by the International Society for Krishna Consciousness of Atlanta, the Hare Krishna religious sect. According to the court, the ordinance constituted prior restraint on religious freedom.

May 8 — Oakland Cemetery is placed on the National Register of Historic Places.

May 10 — Delta Airlines dedicates its regional air cargo terminal, one of the largest in the world.

August 17 — Georgia's $35 million World Congress Center opens. It includes the world's largest exhibition hall with 352,000 continuous square feet of display area.

December 16 — Andrew Young is nominated U.S. ambassador to the United Nations. On December 20 Griffin Bell is nominated U.S. Attorney General.

THIS YEAR IN THE NATION

Jan. 23: Singer-actor Paul Robeson dies at 77 ... **Apr. 5:** Billionaire industrialist Howard Hughes dies at 70 ... **May 24:** Supersonic Concorde lands in Washington on its first regularly scheduled flight ... **June 6:** Oilman J. Paul Getty dies at 83 ... **July 4:** U.S. celebrates its 200th birthday ... **July 15-16:** Democrats nominate Jimmy Carter for president ... **July 27-Aug. 5:** Outbreak of what becomes known as "legionnaire's disease" takes place at American Legion Convention in Philadelphia ... **Aug. 18-19:** Republicans nominate Pres. Ford for a full term ... **Sept. 3:** Spacecraft Viking II lands on Mars ... **Sept. 15-16:** Episcopal Church approves the ordination of women ... **Sept. 23:** First of three debates between Jimmy Carter and Pres. Ford ... **Sept. 30:** California becomes the first state to legalize living wills ... **Oct. 21:** Author Saul Bellow wins Nobel Prize for literature ... **Oct. 25:** Clarence Norris, the only remaining "Scottsboro Boy," is pardoned by Gov. George Wallace ... **Nov. 2:** Jimmy Carter is elected President ... **Nov. 11:** Sculptor Alexander Calder dies at 78.

Westin Peachtree Plaza Hotel — 73 stories, 743 feet tall, and designed by John Portman — opens officially on Feb. 27, 1976.

The Hilton Hotel and Towers opens Jan. 26, 1976.

World Congress Center (see Aug. 17)

"The World of Sid & Marty Krofft," an entertainment center inside the Omni complex, opens in 1976, but dies months later.

1977

January 4	Ted Turner buys his second professional sports team in Atlanta, the Hawks.
February-April	Garbage piles up as city workers strike to protest low wages.
February 16	Former Gov. Lester Maddox sells Pickrick Restaurant which he once closed rather than serve blacks.
March 17	Emory University chooses Dr. James T. Laney as president.
April 5	In the Democratic primary for the Fifth Congressional district, Wyche Fowler easily defeats John Lewis.
June 24	Instead of proclaiming a "gay pride" day, Mayor Jackson proclaims a "Liberties Day," honoring all minorities.
June 28	The City announces that the Cyclorama will close for two and a half years for renovation.
Fall	Mayor Jackson is reelected.
September	Ted Turner defends the jewel of the yachting world, the America's Cup.
October 10	5,000 employees strike at Lockheed-Georgia. The strike lasts until December.

Wyche Fowler (see Apr. 5)

Ted Turner (see September)

THIS YEAR IN THE NATION

Jan. 1: First female Episcopal minister ordained ... **Jan. 20:** Jimmy Carter inaugurated as 39th President ... **Jan. 30:** Largest TV audience ever watches adaptation of "Roots" ... **Apr. 21:** Pres. Carter proposes national energy program to reduce American dependence on foreign oil ... **July 13:** New York blackout results in over $135 million in property damage ... **July 28:** First oil sent through Alaska pipeline ... **Sept. 8:** Federal government charges Korean Tongsun Park with influence buying in Washington ... **Sept. 21:** Budget director Bert Lance resigns ... **Sept. 21:** Nuclear proliferation treaty signed by U.S. and Soviet Union ... **Nov. 6:** Earthen dam in Toccoa, GA collapses, killing 38 ... **Nov. 12:** First black mayor of New Orleans elected ... **Nov. 18:** Ku Klux Klansman convicted of bombing Birmingham, AL church in 1963.

1978

January 30	Loew's Grand Theatre, site of the premiere of *Gone With the Wind* is destroyed by fire. Eight people are injured in the blaze. On June 5 the site is sold for more than $3 million to a real-estate firm.
March 10	Mayor Jackson ousts Reginald Eaves as public safety commissioner and changes locks on police headquarter's doors. (Eaves is suspended for 90 days without pay until his letter of resignation takes effect June 7.) Eaves' ouster follows a report by lawyers investigating the massive cheating that occurred during the 1975 police promotion exams. Twenty-three officers, according to this report, were involved in the cheating or participated in its cover-up. The report claimed that Eaves knew, and possibly authorized, the cheating.
March 19	During a 25 minute speech on TV, Reginald Eaves denies he had any knowledge of the cheating, and accuses Mayor Jackson of breaking his agreement to hold his resignation until June 7 so he could clear his name. Eaves' appeal to City Council is later denied.
March 20	Because of the cheating scandal, City Council temporarily reinstates the office of Police Chief on the police organization chart. The police chief is given the same functions and duties as director of the Bureau of Police Services. He will be a deputy commissioner to give him authority over John Inman, director of the Bureau of Police Service who has kept his job due to his court battle against the City when Mayor Jackson tried to replace him as police chief.
March 28	The American Psychological Association reports it will switch its 1979 convention from Atlanta to New York because the Georgia Legislature has not ratified the Equal Right Amendment.
April 22	The Confederate Plaza at Stone Mountain Park is dedicated.
May 10	The Fox Theatre officially becomes an historic landmark.

June 6	George Napper wins the City Council's confirmation as new police chief. Lee Brown, "acting public service commissioner" since Reginald Eaves' departure, is made public safety commissioner.
June 19	City Council discusses a plan by Mayor Jackson to revamp City government. The City Council, among other changes, removes the responsibility of preparing the City's budget from the Finance Department, which answers to both the Council and the mayor, to the Budget and Planning Department which is accountable only to the mayor.
August 5	The Atlanta Daily World celebrates its 50 years as a newspaper.
September 2	Robert Woodruff gives $7 million to the Atlanta University Center for a new library. The gift is believed to be the largest contribution by an individual to black higher education. Of the $13 million raised by the school to this date, Woodruff has supplied $10 million.
October 20	Dr. Martin Luther King, Jr.'s neighborhood is named an historic site.

Also this year: Delta Air Lines initiates its first transAtlantic flights — to London.

Rafting on the Chattahoochee River (1978)

THIS YEAR IN THE NATION

Jan. 15: Former Vice-President and presidential candidate Hubert H. Humphrey dies at 66 ... **Mar. 27:** 112-day long coal miners strike ends ... **Apr. 6:** Margaret Brewer named first woman general in the Marine Corps ... **May 8:** David Berkowitz pleads guilty in the "Son of Sam" murders ... **May 28:** Postage for first-class letter goes from 13¢ to 15¢ ... **June 6:** Californians approve Proposition 13 to cut taxes ... **June 28:** In Bakke case Supreme Court rejects quotas but backs giving advantages to minorities ... **July 9:** American Nazis hold rally in Chicago ... **Sept. 17:** 13-day conference between Pres. Carter, Egyptian Pres. Anwar el-Sadat and Prime Minister Menachem Begin ends with the Camp David accords ... **Oct. 15:** Humphrey-Hawkins full-employment bill passes Congress ... **Nov. 8:** Mass murder-suicide takes place in Jonestown, Guyana ... **Dec. 15:** U.S. and China agree to establish full diplomatic relations.

1979

February/March The Atlanta Police Department begins a crackdown on prostitution. On March 19 Atlanta reinstates a prostitution law which allows policemen to arrest prostitutes or their clients based on certain gestures and verbal exchanges without having to overhear a proposition, as required by state law.

March 1 For the first time in seven years, MARTA increases its fare (15 to 25 cents). Prior to this date, Atlanta had the lowest bus fares in the nation.

April Two old buildings are sold this month —the Carnegie Building (to Ackerman and Co. for $1.2 million) and the Municipal Auditorium (to Georgia State University).

June 7 Gannett Co., Inc., acquires Combined Communication Corp. This merger is the largest in broadcast history and creates one of the largest communications conglomerates. Combined Communications Corp. owned WXIA-TV (Channel 11) in Atlanta.

June 21 A federal judge shelves Atlanta's "adult law" which required all adult entertainment establishments in Atlanta to be licensed by the City. The court found the wording of the ordinance too vague.

June 29 Atlanta City Councilman Arthur Langford, Jr., is acquitted of all three counts of a federal influence-peddling and perjury indictment. Langford had been charged with accepting money for himself and his United Youth Adult Conference from a promoter of the 1978 Southeastern Fair in exchange for an agreement that Langford would use his influence to intercede with City officials on behalf of the Fair.

July 18 United Airlines, the country's largest, announces it is pulling out of Hartsfield International Airport. On August 1 TWA announces that it too would pull out of Hartsfield.

August 27 WTCG-17, the Atlanta superstation owned by Ted Turner, changes its call letters to WTBS (the Turner Broadcasting System).

THIS YEAR IN THE NATION

Jan. 28-Feb. 5: Chinese Senior Deputy Prime Minister Deng Xiaoping visits U.S. ... **Mar. 28:** Accident at nuclear plant at Three Mile Island ... **Apr. 15:** Federal government bans aerosol propellants ... **June 14:** U.S. and Soviet Union sign the SALT II treaty ... **July 7:** U.S. and China sign three-year trade treaty ... **July 17:** Pres. Carter makes sweeping changes in cabinet and White House staff ... **Aug. 15:** Andrew Young resigns as U.S. ambassador to the U.N. ... **Sept. 1:** Spacecraft Pioneer II takes first close-up pictures of Saturn ... **Sept. 27:** Congress approves new cabinet-ranked Department of Education ... **Oct. 11:** Senate votes to censure Sen. Herman E. Talmadge of Georgia ... **Nov. 4:** U.S. embassy in Tehran and hostages seized by students ... **Dec. 3:** Eleven die in rock concert riot in Cincinnati.

September 1 Three hundred Klansmen gather at Stone Mountain for a cross-burning ceremony.

October/November The City reaches out-of-court settlements to racial discrimination suits brought against it by the police and fire departments. In both settlements the city agrees to pay back pay to officers discriminated against, use "good faith efforts" to achieve a racial balance, and provide safeguards to ensure that future applicants will not be discriminated against on the basis of race.

November 2 Architect John Portman's Atlanta Apparel Mart opens in a $42 million building.

November 8 Robert Woodruff donates $100 million worth of Coca-Cola Company stock to Emory University, the largest such single gift to any organization. Woodruff had previously given a total of $110 million to Emory.

November 13 The U.S. House of Representatives rejects a bill to establish Dr. Martin Luther King, Jr.'s, birthday as a national holiday.

Atlanta Apparel Mart (see Nov. 2)

John Portman (see Nov. 2)

1980

March 18   Among the 150 bills passed by the General Assembly is the "Great Park" bill authorizing Gov. Busbee to appoint a seven-member board to plan the redevelopment of 219 acres in northeast Atlanta.

April 30   Bert Lance is found not guilty of all but three bank fraud charges; these charges are later dismissed. Three co-defendents are also acquitted.

June 1   With the help of 300 employees, Ted Turner creates the world's first live 24-hour TV network (CNN).

August 1   Despite the protests of city officials and representatives of poor Atlantans, MARTA fares increase from 25 to 50 cents.

September 1   WSB-TV, one of Atlanta's most successful affiliates, switches to ABC; WXIA-TV becomes the NBC affiliate.

September 21   The Hartsfield airport terminal, one of the biggest in the world, opens.

October 13   The boiler at the Bowen Holmes Day Care Center explodes. Four children and a teacher are killed.

December 12   Three Morris Brown College football players are acquitted of rape charges filed by a Fulton County Grand Jury. They are convicted of simple battery in the case of a 19-year-old student who claimed the men assaulted her.

December 14   The Atlanta Falcons for the first time in their 16-year history win the Western Division of the NFC. On Jan. 3, 1981, Atlanta Falcons coach Leeman Bennett is named Coach of the Year. During this year, another professional team leaves Atlanta: The Flames, Atlanta's professional ice hockey team, are sold and move to Calgary.

Hartsfield Atlanta Airport (see Sept. 21)

Atlanta Public Library's main branch (downtown) opens May 27, 1980.

Joe T. LaBoon becomes president of Atlanta Gas Light Co. in 1980.

THIS YEAR IN THE NATION

Jan. 29: With Canadian help six U.S. embassy aides escape from Iran ... **Feb. 2:** FBI undercover operation Abscam ends with charges against public officials ... **Mar. 27:** Congress passes windfall profits tax on oil companies ... **Apr. 6:** Boatlift of thousands of Cubans to U.S. begins ... **Apr. 25:** U.S. raid to rescue Iranian hostages ends in disaster ... **Apr. 28:** Secretary of State Cyrus Vance resigns ... **Apr. 30:** Bert Lance acquitted on bank fraud charges ... **July 16-17:** Republicans nominate Ronald Reagan for President ... **Aug. 13-14:** Democrats nominate Pres. Carter for a second term ... **Nov. 4:** Ronald Reagan elected President ... **Nov. 8:** Spacecraft Voyager I discovers 15th moon of Saturn ... **Dec. 8:** Beatle John Lennon murdered in New York.

1981

January 4	Morris Brown College and Spelman College launch their 100th anniversary.
January 6	Dr. Benjamin Mays is elected to his twelfth term as head of the Atlanta Public School board.
January 7	Michael Lomax becomes the first black Fulton County commissioner.
January 8	Coca-Cola begins dismantling its downtown landmark sign which graced Margaret Mitchell Square for 32 years.
January 31	For the second straight season, the Atlanta Chiefs win the indoor eastern division championship of the North American Soccer League.
February 7	The White House announces that the government will provide Atlanta with advisors, but no funds, in the investigation of the city's missing and murdered children cases.
February 11	A suit is filed charging that more than 1,000 Cuban misfits in the Atlanta Penitentiary suffer mistreatment. The suit asks that they be released or the Prison meet standards.
February 21	Vice-Pres. George Bush announces the creation of a federal task force to aid Atlanta's police and citizens following the murder of 18 children. On March 5 Pres. Reagan announces that $979,000 in federal funds will be given the City for programs dealing with social and mental problems stemming from the murders.
March 7	New census figures show that Metro Atlanta has topped the 2 million mark, making it 16th on the list of most populous U.S. areas.
March 10	Four hundred marchers call on the Reagan administration to allocate more funds for the investigation of missing and murdered children. That same night, a benefit concert starring Frank Sinatra and Sammy Davis,

	Jr., raises more than $250,000 for the investigation.
March 13	Pres. Reagan provides Atlanta with $1.5 million for the investigation.
March 26	According to the U.S. census, Atlanta's population is 66 per cent black.
April 6	3500 Atlantans seek 150 post office jobs.
April 15	Coca-Cola production begins in Red China.
April	For the first four months of the year, Atlanta becomes the world's busiest airport, edging out Chicago's O'Hare by more than 10,000 passengers.
May 2	Dr. Clarence Bacote, distinguished black historian and civic leader, dies.
June 4	The Atlanta Chamber of Commerce votes to launch a $150,000 advertising and publicity campaign to brush up the city's image and spirits in the wake of the child killings. the campaign is titled "Let's Pull Together, Atlanta."
June 21	Wayne Williams, a 23-year-old black freelance cameraman, is arrested in the slaying of Nathaniel Cater, the last victim of the Atlanta child murders (No. 28). On July 17 the Grand Jury indicts Williams for the deaths of Jimmy Ray Payne and Nathaniel Cater.
July 1	MARTA fares are raised from 50 to 60 cents.

Michael Lomax (see Jan. 7)

THIS YEAR IN THE NATION

Jan. 7: Regularly scheduled air service established between U.S. and China ... **Jan. 18:** Iran agrees to free 52 hostages taken from U.S. embassy in Tehran ... **Jan. 20:** Ronald Reagan inaugurated as 40th President ... **Jan. 25:** Freed Iranian hostages arrive in the U.S. ... **Jan. 26:** Supreme Court approves the televising of state trials ... **Mar. 30:** Pres. Reagan wounded by gunman ... **Apr. 12:** Space shuttle Columbia makes first successful test flight ... **May 1:** Sen. Harrison Williams convicted in Abscam case ... **July 1:** United Auto Workers rejoin AFL-CIO ... **July 7:** Pres. Reagan nominates Sandra Day O'Connor as first female justice on Supreme Court ... **July 18:** Aerial walkway in Kansas City hotel collapses, killing 110 ... **July 31:** Baseball strike ends after seven weeks ... **Aug. 3:** Air-traffic controllers go out on strike ... **Dec. 28:** First test-tube baby born in U.S. hospital.

1982

January	Mayor Andrew Young, City Council Pres. Marvin Arrington, five new Councilmen and 13 incumbents are sworn in.
January 10	Atlanta is rated as the number one place to live in the United States.
January 12	A snow and ice storm hits Atlanta stranding over 100,000 motorists.
January 14	The Great Park Authority endorses the idea of having the Presidential Library and parkway in the Great Park area. Demonstrators march on the Capitol opposing the construction of the Jimmy Carter Presidential Parkway.
January 24	The Atlanta Journal and Constitution plan to combine news gathering operations to cover Metro Atlanta.
January 31	Atlanta police arrest 168 persons in a series of surprise raids. This action was part of Operation Clean-Up, the city's effort to crack down on street crime and harrassment.
February 11	The U.S. Justice Department rejects portions of Georgia's reapportionment plans for Congressional and legislative districts.
February 18	The Georgia Senate reapportionment committee votes unanimously to support Julian Bond's attempt to redraw Atlanta's Fourth and Fifth Congressional Districts. The Fifth District is drawn to create a black majority within the district. Bond's plan is eventually accepted.
February 28	Wayne Williams is convicted of murdering Nathaniel Cater and Jimmy Ray Payne and is sentenced to two consecutive life terms. The files of the other 26 victims are eventually closed by the police.
March 7	The nuclear submarine USS Atlanta is commissioned.
March 19	Gov. Busbee signs a bill giving City Council Pres. Arrington the right to vote on all matters before Council. The Council president had previously been limited to tie-breaking voting.

April 9	Mayor Young unveils his Great Park Plan which includes the Carter Presidential Library and a Presidential Parkway.
April 18	Two juveniles are arrested and charged with committing $500,000 to $1,000,000 worth of damage in Oakland Cemetery. Private and public drives are begun to raise money to repair and restore it.
April 24	Atlanta University's Woodruff Library is dedicated.
May 18	Dr. Ruth Schmidt is named first woman president of Agnes Scott College.
June 1	Atlanta's Cyclorama is reopened after renovation that took two years and cost $8.5 million.
June 21	Morehouse College's medical science building is dedicated.
August	The Church of the Immaculate Conception, one of Atlanta's oldest structures, catches on fire. It is eventually restored.
Summer	The Atlanta Braves win the Western Division of the National Baseball League, their first division title since 1969.
December	Throughout the year opposition grows to the construction of the Carter Presidential Parkway. Neighborhood organizations protest its construction.

The Crescent Ave. home of Margaret Mitchell, where she wrote most of "Gone With the Wind": an abandoned house in 1982.

THIS YEAR IN THE NATION

Jan. 29: Philadelphia Bulletin stops publication ... **June 21:** Would-be presidential assassin found not guilty due to insanity ... **June 25:** Secretary of State Alexander Haig resigns ... **June 30:** Equal Rights Amendment fails to be ratified ... **Sept. 14:** Princess Grace of Monaco dies in an automobile accident at 52 ... Pres. Reagan orders U.S. Marines to join Italian and French troops in peacekeeping operations in Lebanon ... **Oct. 6:** Deaths reported from cyanide-laced Tylenol ... **Nov. 21:** Football strike ends after eight weeks ... **Dec. 2:** First artificial heart implant, in Barney Clark.

Mayor Andrew Young (see January)

1983

January 6   Atlanta's new jail opens.

January 27   MARTA celebrates the opening of four new rail stations in Atlanta.

May 3   Mayor Young announces that Central City Park will re-open after $1 million in renovations.

May 11   The Fulton County Commission endorses extension of the North Atlanta Parkway.

May 16   Atlanta's City Council deadlocks on vote to extend the North Atlanta Parkway, thus killing the proposal.

June 16   A suit against the U.S. Government demands constitutional protection for Cuban refugees in the Atlanta Penitentiary.

July 1   The administration of the Atlanta Public Library system is transferred from the City to Fulton County.

October 19   The Atlanta Symphony Orchestra ends a seven week strike: Musicians will earn $560/week in 1983-84 and $585/week in 1984-85.

November   Pres. Reagan signs bill making Dr. Martin Luther King, Jr.'s, birthdate a federal holiday.

THIS YEAR IN THE NATION

Feb. 26: Queen Elizabeth II and Prince Philip begin tour of North America in San Diego ... **Mar. 21:** Congress passes $4.6 billion emergency job bill ... **Apr. 4:** U.S. grants asylum to Chinese tennis star Hu Na ... **Apr. 12:** Harold Washington becomes the first black elected mayor of Chicago ... **May 2:** Earthquake hits Coalinga, CA ... **May 24:** 100th anniversary of the opening of the Brooklyn Bridge ... **June 18:** Sally Ride becomes first American woman in space, aboard shuttle Challenger ... **Aug. 9:** Evidence of another solar system discovered by space telescope ... **Aug. 30:** Col. Guion S. Bluford, Jr., becomes the first black in space, aboard shuttle Challenger ... **Aug. 30:** Korean jet with Rep. Larry McDonald aboard shot down by Soviet fighter ... **Oct. 23:** 237 marines killed in terrorist bombing in Beirut ... **Oct. 25:** U.S. invades Grenada.

Gov. Joe Frank Harris inaugurated to first term on Jan. 11, 1983.

High Museum opens Oct. 15, 1983.

1984

January	Fear of a "flight war" mounts as some airlines announce their return to Atlanta. On January 4 TWA announces it will return to Atlanta with daily service to New York. United Airlines announces it will resume flights June 1. Air Atlanta makes its first flight in February, Eastern Metro Express inaugurates service from Hartsfield in April.
January 16	Hosea Williams and the Techwood Homes Tenant Association call for a federal investigation into the $17.2 million renovations done at Techwood. Williams and the Association charge there has been a misuse of funds.
January 20	Atlanta's first Ritz-Carlton Hotel opens in Buckhead. The Ritz-Carlton in downtown Atlanta opens in April.
February	Gwinnett Place Mall opens.
February 15	According to the American Humane Society, Grant Park Zoo is one of the worst in the nation.
March 28	Dr. Benjamin Mays, president of Morehouse College and head of the Atlanta Board of Education, dies.
April 3	Gov. Joe Frank Harris signs bill making Dr. Martin Luther King, Jr.'s birthday a state holiday.
April 19	Georgia Department of Transportation officials authorize the construction to widen Georgia 400 (the North Atlanta Parkway) from Interstate 285 to Holcomb Bridge Road in north Fulton County.
May	White Water Theme Park opens in Marietta.
May 25	Problems begin to plague Grant Park Zoo as a young elephant, Twinkles, dies. Investigations show that he illegally wound up with a traveling circus.
May 28	A computer malfunction causes a crash in "The Great Air Race," a ride at Six Flags Over Georgia; 33 persons are injured. On June 4 four people are shaken up when the Mindbender ride malfunctions.

THIS YEAR IN THE NATION

Jan. 1: A.T. & T. broken up into regional independent phone companies … **Jan. 3:** Syria frees Navy pilot Lt. Robert Goodman, Jr. … **Jan. 9:** Former EPA official Rita Lavelle sentenced to six months in prison … **Jan. 10:** U.S. and Vatican exchange diplomats … **Jan. 10:** U.S. and China sign accords on industrial cooperation … **Feb. 7:** Pres. Reagan orders Marines home from Lebanon … **May 10:** World Court rules against U.S. for mining Nicaraguan harbors … **July 11:** First compulsory seat-belt law enacted in New York … **July 16-19:** Democrats nominate ex-Vice-President Walter F. Mondale for President and Geraldine Ferraro for Vice-President; she becomes the first female so nominated by a major political party … **Aug. 20-25:** Republicans nominate Pres. Reagan for a second term … **Nov. 7:** Pres. Reagan reelected in a landslide.

June 1	The deaths of a tiger and lioness at Grant Park Zoo lead Mayor Young to call for an investigation.
September 3	Midtown Atlanta police arrest 26 in a prostitution sweep. Atlanta police officers dress as "johns" or hookers to make arrests.
September 30	Mayor Young announces he will seek a second term.
October/ November	Tensions rise among Cubans at the Atlanta Penitentiary. On October 14 inmates are locked in their cells after 75 Cubans demonstrate in a recreation yard. On October 29 lawyers for the Cubans call for an investigation of the conditions at the Penitentiary. On November 2 the Cubans begin an eight-hour siege of the prison protesting their treatment.
November 12	Rev. Martin Luther King, Sr., father of Martin and pastor of Ebenezer Baptist Church, dies.
December	MARTA opens five new stations and nine miles of track with free rides on buses and trains.

Lenox Square, as it looked in 1984, on its 25th anniversary.

The government complex, as viewed in 1984: The domed state Capitol (left) is flanked by state government buildings; beyond the dome is the square State Archives building; at top, Atlanta-Fulton County Stadium; in center, the towering City Hall; largest building below right is the Fulton County Courthouse. (Atlanta Airport is further south beyond the Stadium.)

1985

January	On January 11 a court orders the release of 107 Cuban prisoners. For the next four months the courts and the U.S. Government argue over the fates of these prisoners. The U.S. Government begins a program of deportation whereas the courts order their release, and 201 Cubans are deported by May 15.
February 21	City Council approves the idea of a "night mayor" to handle emergencies when City offices are closed. On March 2 City Council Pres. Arrington serves the first shift of this nighttime post.
February 27	City Council approves a resolution which calls for a halt to the construction of the Presidential Parkway.
March 7	Coca-Cola executive and philanthropist Robert W. Woodruff dies at 95.
April 3	Facing a federal contempt motion, the Fulton County Commission approves a tentative agreement to improve sanitary, safety and overcrowding conditions at Fulton County jail at a cost of at least $185,000.
July 9	Mayor Young signs a contract with Underground Festival Developing Company committing $125 million of City funds to create the Underground Atlanta entertainment area.
July 15	City Council approves funding for a renovation of the Grant Park Zoo for $25 million. The Fulton County Commission later agrees to help.
August 22	The Marriott Marquis Hotel opens.
September	Atlanta Life Insurance Company celebrates its 80th anniversary.
October	The Grant Park Zoo is renamed the Atlanta-Fulton County Zoo.
October 8	Atlanta re-elects Mayor Young with 83 per cent of the vote. A $38 million bond issue for Atlanta-Fulton County Library also passes.
October 9	The Georgia Supreme Court rules that the

City illegally transferred parkland to the State Department of Transportation, but the State could resume building the Presidential Parkway at its own risk.

October 17	Atlanta University celebrates its 120th anniversary.
October 22	To fight vandalism and crime in trains, buses and rail stations, MARTA establishes a hot-line to report vandals, adds increased police surveillance, and rewards people who report crimes.
October 29	Former State Rep. Hosea Williams beats Morris Finley in a run-off election for City Council.
December 6	Mayor Young publicly supports (for the first time) the extension of Georgia 400.
December 14	Despite the support for the construction of another stadium, the Atlanta-Fulton County Recreation Authority approves a $29 million revenue bond issue for improvements to Atlanta-Fulton County Stadium.

Marriott Marquis Hotel (see Aug. 22)

Rollout of the first C5-A at Lockheed-Georgia Corp., on July 12, 1985.

THIS YEAR IN THE NATION

Jan. 20: Pres. Reagan takes the oath of office for a second term ... **Feb. 17:** Price of a first-class letter goes from 20¢ to 22¢ ... **Feb. 18:** Gen. William Westmoreland sues CBS for libel ... **Mar. 15:** Secretary of Labor Raymond J. Donovan resigns; he is the first sitting cabinet officer to be indicted ... **Apr. 18-May 5:** Bitburg controversy; Pres. Reagan visits Bitburg, West Germany, cemetery where SS troops are buried ... **May 13:** Philadelphia police firebomb headquarters of MOVE organization; fire spreads, killing 11 and leaving many homeless ... **Aug. 9:** Arthur J. Walker convicted of spying for the Soviet Union ... **Oct. 8:** American Leon Klinghoffer killed by PLO terrorists on Italian ship Achille Lauro ... **Nov. 19-20:** Pres. Reagan and Soviet Premier Gorbachev meet in Geneva ... **Dec. 12:** Gramm-Rudman debt reduction bill signed by Pres. Reagan.

1986

January 2	City Councilman Hosea Williams charges that his drunken driving arrest is an attempt by "rednecks, Uncle Toms and sellouts" in the Atlanta Police Bureau to sabotage his effectiveness as a member of the Council. In March he is found innocent of drunken driving charges.
January 13	Because of increasing incidents of crime, MARTA hires additional police officers. In April it decides to hire private security guards.
January 16	An opening celebration is held at the Ibis Hotel on International Blvd.
February 20	The Georgia Senate passes legislation that would set up a commission to decide when state agencies should be allowed to condemn land. This legislation sets up the path for a continuation of the Presidential Parkway Project.
February 24	City Council approves a measure to prohibit discrimination against City employees based on sexual orientation. Attempts to repeal this measure in October fail.
March/April	Four elderly women who lived near each other in west Atlanta are killed. A suspect is caught.
April	City Council approves a new financing plan for Underground Atlanta. In May Superior Court approves of the bond issue. In July the Georgia Supreme Court approves the City's latest plan to finance a $135 million renovation and rebuilding of Underground Atlanta.
April 16	Mayor Young announces a sweeping package of cost-cutting measures for City Hall, including elimination of 157 jobs aimed at saving $8 to $10 million.
May 7-11	Coca-Cola celebrates its 100th anniversary with parades, addresses and entertainment programs.

THIS YEAR IN THE NATION

Oil prices break bringing economic relief to all but oil-producing countries ... **Jan. 28:** Space shuttle explodes, killing seven astronauts ... **Feb. 26:** Robert P. Warren named first poet laureate of the U.S. ... **Feb. 28:** Seven baseball players suspended for drug use ... **Mar. 11:** Atlanta's Leo Frank pardoned posthumously ... **Apr. 14:** U.S. airplanes bomb Libya in retaliation for the killing of a U.S. serviceman in a West Berlin discotheque ... **June 19:** Len Bias, University of Maryland basketball star, dies of drug overdose ... **July 3-6:** Statue of Liberty centennial celebration ... **Aug. 30:** Magazine correspondent Nicholas Daniloff arrested in Moscow; he is released Sept. 29 ... **Sept. 17:** William Rehnquist confirmed as 16th Chief Justice of the Supreme Court ... **Oct. 1:** Jimmy Carter Presidential Library dedicated in Atlanta ... **Oct. 22:** Pres. Reagan signs the most sweeping tax reform bill since World War II ... **Nov. 13:** Pres. Reagan acknowledges that U.S. secretly sold arms to Iran ... **Nov. 14:** Ivan Boesky agrees to pay fines of $100 million in Wall Street insider stock trading scandal ... **Dec. 23:** Voyager ends round-the-world flight without refueling.

May 24	City Council approves a three-month moratorium on permits to demolish so-called historic structures, but Mayor Young vetoes the resolution and is upheld.
June 2	John Lewis ends five years on the City Council as he resigns to qualify for the Fifth Congressional District race.
July	Air service between Atlanta and Tokyo is established by Delta Air Lines.
August 17	MARTA's north-south line grows by two miles and one station as East Point is added to the system.
September 22	MARTA board of directors vote on two new rail lines—one to run through the Georgia 400 highway corridor and the other to Proctor Creek Homes. The latter line is to honor a promise it made to the black community 15 years ago.
September	In a very divisive campaign within the black community, John Lewis defeats Julian Bond in the Democratic run-off for the Fifth Congressional District.
October 1-2	Dedication ceremonies are held at the Carter Presidential Center.
December 9	City Councilman James Howard is found guilty of two counts of income tax fraud. Howard resigns after state panels recommend he be suspended.
December 24	The apparent last obstacle to contruction of the controversial Presidential Parkway falls with a federal court ruling that environmental requirements about the road have been fulfilled.

Jimmy Carter Presidential Center (see Oct. 1)

Index to Sponsors

Honor Roll of Sponsors: Founding Dates

Below are listed the sponsors of this book in the order in which they were founded.

In the case of firms and/or institutions which merged with others, we use the launching year of their oldest component as their "founding date." As for multinational firms, we use the date of their founding, not the date they opened an Atlanta office.

Emory University	1836	Henrietta Egleston Hospital for Children	1928
Johnson & Higgins, Inc.	1845	Georgia Federal Bank, FSB	1928
Laing Properties	1848	Stewart Brothers	1932
Price Waterhouse	1849	Smith Ace Hardware	1935
Atlanta Gas Light Co.	1856	Aircond Corp.	1937
Rich's	1867	Mingledorff's, Inc.	1939
Graphic Industries, Inc.	1871	Callaway Gardens	1940
Marsh & McLennan, Inc.	1871	Selig Enterprises	1942
H. M. Patterson & Son	1880	Heery International, Inc.	1945
Southern Bell	1880	Hall's Flower Shops and Greenhouses	1946
The Sharp Boylston Companies	1881	Touche Ross	1947
Georgia Power	1883	The Portman Companies	1953
Maier & Berkele Jewelers	1887	Tempo Management, Inc.	1957
Manry & Heston, Inc.	1887	Gwinnett Hospital System	1958
Macy's	1890	Stone Mountain Park	1958
SouthernNet, Inc.	1896	Hitachi America, Ltd.	1959
Atlanta Coca-Cola Bottling Co.	1903	Georgia Lighting Co.	1960
Piedmont Hospital	1905	American Hotel	1962
Crawford Long Hospital of Emory University	1908	The Coach & Six	1962
Arthur Andersen & Co.	1913	DeKalb College	1964
Georgia State University	1913	Clopton Typography & Graphics, Inc.	1965
The Seydel Companies	1919	Phoenix Communications Co.	1975
WGST Radio	1922	Buckhead Life Restaurant Group	1979
Decatur Federal Savings & Loan Assn.	1926	Liberty House Restaurant Corp.	1979
Fulton Federal Savings & Loan Assn.	1927		

Aircond Corporation

It was 1937. Margaret Mitchell's "Gone With The Wind" won a Pulitzer Prize. Atlanta was celebrating its 100th anniversary. Dr. Willis Carrier had installed his first central air conditioning system in a

Fulton National Bank

New York City skyscraper.

It was now possible to air condition the tallest buildings built by man, and Carrier Atlanta, precursor of Aircond Corporation, was born. Its objective ... to bring heating and air conditioning installations, service and maintenance to commerce and industry.

In the early years, every installation was literally constructed from the ground up. Aircond technicians would pour the foundation, set the pump, cooling tower, compressors, duct work, wiring, and finally the water and refrigerant piping.

Aircond installed and serviced almost every major HVAC unit in Atlanta, including one in a mausoleum at Westview Cemetery.

Atlantic Steel, Coca-Cola, C&S Bank, Muse's, Maier & Berkele, J. P. Allen, the Haverty Building, Regensteins, Zachry's,

Cyclorama

furniture and food stores, trucking and manufacturing companies, executive offices and country clubs, notable early Atlantans Woodruff, Woolman, and Zachry ... all became Aircond's customers.

During the war years, Aircond's installations were limited to hospitals ... St. Joseph's, Grady, Emory, Crawford Long and Georgia Baptist ... and military installations: Robbins Air Force Base, and Bell Aircraft (later Lockheed Georgia.)

Afterward, the demand for comfortable working conditions and controlled environments accelerated. The new Ford and General Motors assembly plants, WSB's Biltmore Hotel studios, the Cyclorama, Fulton National Bank, Coastal States Insurance, even, unbelievably, the engine repair shop at Delta Airlines were air conditioned. Air conditioning was unique and people couldn't wait to show off and enjoy it.

In the '50s and '60s Belk's, W.T. Grant, and Davison's (now Macy's) were among the first with central air. Every A&P, Kroger and Colonial Store supermarket and all Reed's Drug stores had to have it. And on every entrance door was the company's decal, "Air Conditioned, Open."

As Mayor Ivan Allen's Forward Atlanta campaign moved through the '60s, and Executive Park's success brought a new kind of working environment into vogue, Freeway Office Park, Interstate North, Koger Center and others became clients of Aircond.

When Lenox Square was commissioned in 1958, Aircond handled installations in most of its shops. Then Greenbriar in '63, and Cumberland Mall in '69. It was no longer possible to be without conditioned comfort.

Carried on a wave of soaring oil prices into energy management in the late '70s, Aircond found a strong demand for systems that limited peak power demand and slashed energy usage. The Equitable, Plaza Towers, Monarch Plaza, and Peachtree Dunwoody Pavilion were first to see Aircond systems dramatically reduce energy costs, and pay for themselves quickly.

Large systems with huge cooling towers like those at Avon and GM required water treatment. In 1980 Aircond established a water treatment department. In 1981 Aircond formed a department to manufacture and replace the filters used by their 2200 service contract customers.

Over the past 50 years, Aircond has become an established authority ... the reliable source for specialists who focus on boiler performance, chemical water treatment, energy management, design, construction and renovation of central HVAC systems, planned preventive maintenance and thorough, professional service. Bringing single source responsibility to the people they serve ...

Atlanta and Aircond. Growing together.

Haverty Building

Phipps Plaza utilizes all of Aircond's services, a prime example of Aircond's Single Source Responsibility.

176

American Hotel

"It's just too good to be true," enthused The Atlanta Journal and Constitution when the Atlanta American Hotel officially opened its doors in 1962.

Two years earlier Dr. Marvin Goldstein, brother Irving, and their partners, Sol Golden and former Gov. Ellis Arnall, decided to turn a hole in the ground at the corner of Spring Street and Carnegie Way into the first hotel to be built in downtown Atlanta in more than 40 years.

The results lived up to everyone's expectations.

The hotel, now called The American, was built on the historic Walton Springs site. For many years, beginning when Atlanta was quite young, Walton Springs was one of the city's prime amusement sections, featuring carnivals and variety of entertainments. Today that same area is still in the heart of Atlanta's amusement section. Nightclubs, restaurants and hotels have sprung up around the American.

No strangers in the hotel industry, Dr. Goldstein and his brother owned and operated the Georgian Terrace Hotel, the Ponce de Leon Apartments and the Peachtree Manor.

This experience prompted them to combine the luxury of a hotel with the convenience of a motel in the heart of downtown Atlanta. The results took the city by storm.

The American offered the luxury of a south Florida country club in the heart of Atlanta, complete with all the special guest amenities that visitors had come to expect from the top tourist hotels in the country.

"We gave them a comfortable place to stay and play," explains Dr. Goldstein, "a philosophy we still adhere to after all these years."

Although the hotel is now called The American and has been completely renovated, the new philosophy is just as innovative.

"We have the only downtown luxury hotel at moderate prices, and that fills a need," explains Dr. Goldstein.

The original hotel featured a 125-seat night club on the roof called The Room at the Top which doubled as a meeting room by day.

Today this lounge is the city's acclaimed premier suite featuring a huge, round jacuzzi, steam bath and two bedrooms.

It was Dr. Goldstein who, during a trip to Jekyll Island, discovered the management genius of John Astarita and persuaded him to head up the hotel.

"Astarita immediately brought an unusual flair to the hotel," remembers Dr. Goldstein. From flaming sauces at tableside in The Golden Palm Restaurant (under the direction of Mr. Anthony), to a photographer on premises for conventions, Atlanta had never before experienced this kind of catering to the customer. Even Muzak in lobbies and elevators was new at the time.

Today The American Hotel has been completely remodeled, adding a concierge floor, a swimming pool, Gatsby's nightclub and restaurant, and state-of-the-art meeting rooms.

An active leader in Atlanta's community life, Dr. Goldstein is presently serving on the Governor's Historical Trust Commission and is professor of orthodontics at the Medical College of Georgia.

His past achievements run the gamut from service as president of the Atlanta Jewish Federation and B'nai Brith to past-president of the American Dental Fraternity Council and as Vice-President and Trustee of the Martin Luther King, Jr., Center for Non-Violent Social Change.

Dr. Marvin Goldstein

The acclaimed premier suite at the American—with sauna and two bedrooms

Arthur Andersen & Company

In 1940 William B. Nettles opened the Atlanta office of **Arthur Andersen & Co.** with eight people.

"When we first opened, the competition was rough," he reminisced recently. "There were six other firms in Atlanta and we were not known at all."

Forty-seven years later the Atlanta office of the public accounting firm of Arthur Andersen & Co. has 900 employees and has developed the largest professional practice of any firm in the southeastern United States.

With that decision over four decades ago to open the Atlanta office in the prestigious William-Oliver Building, Arthur Andersen & Co. knew Atlanta was destined to lead the Southeast into a new era, and it was committed to help make it happen.

In the forties Atlanta's milestones included its 100th birthday of incorporation, Hartsfield's new air terminal and the city's first TV station. By the end of the decade,

the Atlanta office of AA&Co. had 30 employees and began acquiring major clients that are still with the firm to this day.

In the fifties Atlanta saw its first freeways and its first shopping mall (Lenox Square). The AA&Co. office reached its first 100 employees.

The "times were a' changing" in the sixties. Atlanta was the "city too busy to hate"; it built a new airport, a new art museum and made Underground Atlanta an entertainment mecca.

Arthur Andersen & Co. saw changing times, too — new offices, first in the National Bank of Georgia Building in '61, then to the Trust Company Bank Building in '68.

Nettles, the founding partner of the Atlanta office, retired after over 20 years as managing partner and passed the baton to Albert J. Bows, Jr. By the end of the decade, the office had almost 300 employees and had spun off four new offices from its southeastern hub — Charlotte, Birming-

ham, Chattanooga and Tampa.

The seventies saw Atlanta established as one of the nation's top convention centers, enhanced by the Omni and the World Congress Center.

The Atlanta office of AA&Co. saw itself surge ahead in growth and productivity. It changed the reins of managing partner again to Samuel Hudgins and established a leadership position among accounting firms in Atlanta with almost 400 employees by the end of the decade.

In the eighties Atlanta's business is thriving, and Arthur Andersen & Co.'s is also. After another office move to the Georgia-Pacific Center and a new managing partner, James D. Edwards, the office has emerged as the leading accounting firm in the Southeast with over 900 employees in 1987.

On the brink of a new decade, Arthur Andersen & Co. has rededicated itself to an appreciation of its Atlanta heritage and a recognition of the role it can play in helping shape the future of this city.

William B. Nettles

Albert J. Bows, Jr.

Samuel Hudgins

James D. Edwards

Bottled Under Authority of "The Coca-Cola Company" By THE ATLANTA COCA-COLA BOTTLING COMPANY

Atlanta Gas Light Company

. . . the city's oldest corporate citizen

Company Chartered in 1856

When Atlanta Gas Light Company was chartered on February 16, 1856, a young City of Atlanta was its first and only customer. At that time, city officials were concerned about the city's dark, dangerous streets. So the new gas company was hired by the City to "light up Atlanta."

Gas was manufactured then, and for the next 75 years, from coal, pine knots, and other combustibles at the gas works, which was built on the site where the Georgia World Congress Center now stands. The number of gas lights in the city was still growing when the War Between the States pressed down on Atlanta. In 1864,

Sherman drove his Union soldiers into Georgia. The subsequent Battle of Atlanta and burning of the city so vividly depicted in the classic motion picture "Gone With the Wind" (1) devastated the city and destroyed the gas works. One of the city's 50 original street lights, complete with shell hole in its post and since named the Eternal Flame of the Confederacy, stands in downtown Atlanta as a reminder of the destruction (2).

In 1887, the City sold a portion of the stock it owned in the gas company and the money was used to buy lands on North Avenue — and build the Georgia Institute of Technology (3). When the 20th Century arrived, Atlanta Gas Light Company had weathered the War Between the States, several economic depressions and, in the 1880s, the introduction of electric lights. By 1916, gas cooking was popular in homes where gas was available. The first Old Stove Round Up, the company's longest continuous promotion, was held in 1929, when 1,058 gas ranges were sold in Atlanta alone. (Many people believe the Old Stove Round Up is the longest-running sales campaign in the United States.) One salesman in the first campaign, nicknamed Gasco Bill, rode around town selling ranges for three days, then left for parts unknown, horse and all! In 1930 the company provided another Gasco Bill, but this time he rode a "thief-proof" horse (4). Other successful campaigns followed. In 1933, the "House Warmer" campaign promoted gas radiant heaters. Young men wearing special uniforms went door-to-door offering heaters for 25 cents down (5).

But the most important development in the company's history occurred in 1930, when natural gas first arrived in Georgia through a pipeline from Louisiana. Atlanta officials celebrated the arrival at a commemora-

launched the annual Shining Light Award program to honor outstanding Georgians. Each year, a plaque bearing the honoree's name was placed on a gas lamp. In 1982, former U.S. Secretary of State Dean Rusk (8, center) accepted the award from Joe T. LaBoon (left), now chairman and chief executive officer of Atlanta Gas Light Company, and Michael J. Faherty, general manager and vice president of WSB radio.

tive ground breaking (6). The company has always shared in Atlanta's history. During World War II, for example, hundreds of Gasco employees fought for their country. At home, women took over meter reading jobs that were previously held only by men (7).

In 1956, Atlantans helped the gas company celebrate its 100th anniversary. And in 1963, the company, in conjunction with WSB radio,

Atlanta Gas Light Company is now the largest natural gas distribution company in the Southeast. A gold-plated meter (9) set in 1986 commemorated the addition of the company's one millionth customer. Throughout its history, the gas company has remained committed to Atlanta and, looking to the next 150 years, will continue "Growing with Georgia."

Illustration by R. T. Percivalle

181

Buckhead Life Restaurant Group:
Pano's & Paul's, The Fish Market, 103 West, Capriccio Ristorante, The Buckhead Diner

The Fish Market exudes comfortable elegance.

Born at opposite ends of the globe, two men met who were destined to provide Atlanta with the grandest of fine dining through their restaurant mini-dynasty, The Buckhead Life Restaurant Group, which includes Pano's & Paul's, The Fish Market, 103 West, Capriccio Ristorante, and The Buckhead Diner.

Originally from Savannah, GA, and son of a Greek immigrant, Pano Karatassos became one of his home state's premier restaurateurs. As a youngster he worked in his father's restaurant and import-food shop, and later worked in the food department while serving in the Navy. He graduated from the renowned Culinary Institute of America, and proceeded to apprentice and work at some of the finest restaurants and hotels in America and Switzerland.

Meanwhile, German-born Paul Albrecht was learning all aspects of the restaurant business at the Hotel and Restaurant School in Munich, and then at various gourmet restaurants in Germany and Switzerland. He moved to America in 1968 to continue his culinary career.

In 1968 Karatassos and Albrecht met while working in Washington, D.C. They greatly admired each other's talents and commitment to excellence, and decided to establish a restaurant of their own. After analyzing several popular markets in the Sun Belt, they decided on Atlanta, which they saw as the most success-oriented city in the South.

January of 1979 brought the grand opening of Pano's & Paul's, a restaurant which holds the distinction of being Atlanta's favorite continental restaurant from its early beginnings. Nestled in a shopping center amongst the Buckhead mansions, Pano's & Paul's has a posh yet comfortable "club" environment.

Its Victorian decor highlighting private dark green velvet-covered booths, attentive service, and impressive menus have made Pano's & Paul's a "hub" for Atlantans and a "must-see" for Atlanta visitors. The interior was devised by Atlanta's most prominent interior designer, Penny Goldwasser, who also decorated The Fish Market, 103 West, and Capriccio Ristorante.

Pano's & Paul's is the recipient of such prestigious awards as Restaurants & Institutions Ivy Award, Nation's Restaurant News Fine Dining Hall of Fame, Mobil Travel Guide Four-Star Restaurant, Atlanta Magazine's Best Continental and Overall Restaurant (1980-86), and American Express "My Favorite Restaurant" honor.

1981 began deliciously, for in January, Pano and Paul opened The Fish Market. Located in popular Lenox Square, The Fish Market offers one of the most opulent seafood dining experiences in the region.

While dining on batterfried lobstertails or Bouillabaisse, customers are surrounded by hues of pink, lavender, and gray, plus marble walls, domed skylights, and antique accessories.

Voted Atlanta's Best Seafood Restaurant in Atlanta Magazine (1984-86), The Fish Market has also been consistently selected as one of the top power-lunching spots in the city.

In October of 1982, the elegant doors of 103 West welcomed the world in. And the world came.

Situated in the heart of Buckhead, 103 West has established itself as one of

FOUNDING DATES

January, 1979: Opening of Pano's & Paul's Restaurant at 1232 West Paces Ferry Road

January, 1981: Opening of The Fish Market Restaurant at 3393 Peachtree Road

October, 1982: Opening of 103 West Restaurant at 103 West Paces Ferry Road

November, 1985: Opening of Capriccio Ristorante at 3018 Maple Drive at Pharr Road

September, 1987: Opening of The Buckhead Diner at 3069 Piedmont Road

Atlanta's grandest restaurants.

Offering a creative American cuisine with French influence, 103 West has a decor as interesting as its menu.

The luxurious details recapture the eclecticism typical of America's great homes and private clubs of the 1920's. Considered Atlanta's choice restaurant for special banquets and important events, 103 West has congregated some of the most powerful business/political leaders in our country — as well as hosted many of Atlanta's most poignant wedding, bar mitzvah, birthday and anniversary celebrations.

In November of 1985, while Americans were eating turkey for Thanksgiving, Atlanta began eating true Northern Italian cuisine at Capriccio Ristorante.

Within a few months of its opening, Capriccio had been applauded nationally for its unique pasta dishes, European-style service, menu authenticity, and sophisticated decor.

With the addition of a new co-owner/general manager of Italian descent (Genoa), Dino La Rosa brought the taste of Italy to a corner of Atlanta. Capriccio has received accolades in Playboy Magazine, New York Times, USA Today, Georgia Trend, CNN and NBC-TV, and was chosen as "Pasta Restaurant of the Year for Best Pasta in the City" by the National Pasta Association. Delicioso!

September of 1987 marks the grand opening of The Buckhead Diner, the fifth

Capriccio Ristorante manager/co-owner Dino La Rosa and a tray of polenta, a Capriccio original and specialty

eatery within the Buckhead Life Restaurant Group.

The "ritzy" Diner offers the same superb quality of the sister restaurants, only with a more casual flair. It features contemporary food for all times of the day and night in a variety of portion sizes, within a nostalgic decor reminiscent of the traditional diner concept.

The Buckhead Diner was developed with the assistance of internationally renowned

architect/designer Patrick Kuleto.

Celebrities have been common visitors at the Buckhead Life Restaurant Group.

Ted Turner, Prince Faisal, Anita Bryant, Mickey Mantle, Jimmy Carter, John Portman, Fran Tarkenton, and Hank Aaron are local frequenters, and the likes of Lee Iacocca, Bob Hope, Kris Kristofferson, and Oscar de la Renta make it a point to dine at these restaurants when in town.

Karatassos and Albrecht themselves have become local celebrities as they have been featured in all forms of media including being profiled in a CBS television program, "Glamour Jobs of Atlanta."

Charitable involvement is also important to the principals of the Buckhead Life Restaurant Group.

In 1987 Pano Karatassos was a key element in the coordination of Atlanta's Table, an aggressive effort to feed Atlanta's hungry; plus he is an active ambassador and fund raiser for his alma mater, Culinary Institute of America.

For his culinary and community contributions, Karatassos was selected as Georgia's Restaurateur of the Year in 1985 and Variety Club of Atlanta's Restaurateur of the Year in 1987.

The Buckhead Life Restaurant Group will continue to graciously entertain Atlanta diners, and will also serve Atlanta's desires for new restaurants through opening additional restaurants. History will soon tell of other exciting Buckhead Life Restaurant Group dimensions.

Pano & Paul are renowned for their gourmet delights at Pano's & Paul's.

The opulent decor of 103 West is evident even in its lobby.

Callaway Gardens

Aerial view of Hole #5 on Callaway Gardens' Lake View Golf Course flanked by The Gardens Restaurant (left) and the Callaway Gardens Inn

In mid-1940 textile industrialist Cason Callaway and his wife Virginia began creating the magnificent Callaway Gardens, near Pine Mountain, 70 miles south of Atlanta, as a labor of love to restore, preserve and protect the beauty of the natural landscape.

Callaway, whose life was distinguished by decades of advocacy of statewide land management reform, often expressed the belief that "every child ought to see something beautiful before becoming six years old."

Since opening in 1952, Callaway Gardens has provided that opportunity to thousands of children and visitors who annually enjoy its miles of scenic trails, acres of floral displays and year-round resort sports and leisure amenities.

Callaway Gardens encompasses over 12,000 acres of woodland preserve, 2,500 of which are a unique horticultural display of native Southeastern trees, plants, wildflowers and floral plantings. Its collections include the world's largest public display of holly and more than 700 varities of azaleas

— among these, the rare prunifolia, grown natively only within a 200 mile radius of the Gardens.

The rich red flower of the prunifolia remains a symbol of Callaway Gardens, which itself remains among few gardens resort properties owned and operated by a not-for-profit organization, The Ida Cason Callaway Foundation, named in honor of Callaway's mother. The Foundation continues to fulfill its mission, preserving and developing the Gardens, and, through an extensive educational program, promoting public understanding and appreciation of nature.

It also presents numerous arts and cultural activities at the Gardens and hosts benefit sporting and social events to aid other charitable endeavors.

In 1984 Callaway Gardens opened its innovative John A. Sibley Horticultural Center, among the first greenhouse facilities to combine indoor and outdoor environments, creating a unique interactive experience for visitors. The Center annually presents six seasonal floral displays, and its

lovely facilities are frequently used for civic and social events.

The nation's first live butterfly house, the Day Butterfly Center, opens at Callaway Gardens in 1988. Enabled by a gift from Mrs. Deen Day Smith of Atlanta and named in honor of Cecil B. Day, the center will serve as both a public display where visitors can view thousands of butterflies in lifecycle habitat, and as a research facility.

Within the acres of Callaway Gardens beautiful grounds are 13 stream-fed lakes. Its prime recreational lake, 65-acre Robin Lake, is bounded by a mile-long white sand beach (the longest inland man-made beach in the world) and sports lively summer family recreation of swimming, sailboating, water skiing, and rides on its Robin E. Lee Riverboat and Whistlin' Dixie Train. It has also been summer home to Florida State University's Flying High Circus, which performs under a canvas Big Top.

Also amid the lush woodlands are the award-winning Callaway Gardens resort restaurants, lodging, sports and conference facilities. Guests from around the world visit Callaway Gardens year-round to enjoy four championship golf courses, top-rated tennis, renowned Southern cooking and legendary hospitality.

As a meeting site, Callaway Gardens is the largest resort Convention Center in Georgia and also maintains a state-of-the-art Conference Center, Cottage Meeting Center, and Executive Lodge for business seminars and retreats.

In addition to guest rooms and suites at Callaway Gardens Inn, Callaway Gardens recently developed small woodland communities of contemporary Country Cottages and luxury Mountain Villa vacation homes to accommodate its many vacationing and meeting guests.

For the more than 750,000 people visiting Callaway Gardens each year, the beautifully restored environment and superb sports and leisure facilities are, as its founders intended, a place from which to take ... "nourishment for the soul, consolation for the heart, and inspiration for the mind."

One of 63 challenging holes of golf at Callaway Gardens Resort in Pine Mountain, Georgia

The John A. Sibley Horticultural Center attracts thousands of visitors annually to Callaway Gardens

185

The Coach & Six

When the Coach & Six turned 25 years old in July, 1987, the posh Atlanta eatery, known throughout the world and boasting some 3,000 house accounts, entered a select company of American restaurants.

A decidedly acquired taste for a city brought up on traditional Southern fare, "The Coach & Six," which premiered its mainstay menu of Continental American cuisine in 1962, is today considered among the grand dames of the retail food trade.

While a number of local restaurants are older, few, if any, have reached a third generation of customers with their vital signs so vigorous.

Now a sentimental favorite of locals and visitors with its uptown, clubby atmosphere and its unrestrained, elegant decor, The Coach & Six defies placement in any single category.

For a great many of the restaurant's well-heeled clientele, some of whose faces peer down from the restaurant's famed mural over the bar in the lounge, The Coach & Six is a place to be seen. Even among the city's socially prominent set, the competition for the Coach's favored tables, a tradition initiated by owner Beverlee Soloff Shere, is keen.

For other guests, The Coach is an equally great spot to hide away from the paparazzi and just enjoy a private, unheralded dinner. Regardless of motivations, The Coach & Six accommodates them all, from movie stars to movers and shakers in the world of sports and business, from prom goers, relishing their very first big night out on the town, to prominent politicos, whose names, faces and preferences are well known to the Coach's staff of 100.

Says Ms. Shere: "Our customers are our stars and they know it."

Today, owing to an unyielding commitment to both quality and excellence on the part of the hard-driving owner, The Coach maintains a preeminent position in the Atlanta restaurant community. This, despite an incredible proliferation of new and sophisticated dining establishments.

Over the years, the restaurant has received dozens of distinguished, fine dining awards, including the "500 Business Executive Dining Award," the "Travel Holiday Dining Award," the "Best of Atlanta," "World Famous Restaurants International," "The Ambassador 25 Award" and the "Silver Spoon Award."

In the 1980s The Coach emerged as a restaurant of national and international stature. Among the first restaurants in the city to offer its extensive menu in Japanese, Spanish, French and German, The Coach was one of only six American restaurants invited to participate in the kickoff party for the restoration of the Statute of Liberty.

Yet another distinct national honor came in 1984 when the Reagan Inaugural Committee asked the Coach to participate in the inaugural festivities honoring Pres. Ronald Reagan. A more recent demonstration of The Coach's clout resulted from the announcement last spring confirming Atlanta as the site of the 1988 Democratic National Convention.

"Within two hours of the announcement on television," remembers Ms. Shere, "we booked 64 reservations for the week of the convention."

Harbingers of success and prestige all, no single award or honor offers as clear or as compelling a picture of the Coach's ongoing success as its bottom line. The Coach first broke the $1 million mark in sales in 1974 and in 1987 is expected to post receipts in excess of $4.5 million.

Remarkably, success was not supposed to come the way of the Coach & Six Restaurant. Its demise should have been sealed in 1974 with the death of Hank Soloff, Ms. Shere's first husband and the lifeblood of the restaurant up to that point. His passing left a vacuum which no one expected his widow to want or even be capable of filling.

A New York native tricked by her husband into coming South "for just two weeks," Shere's background as a stand-up comic and a housewife and mother seemed ill-suited for the task of running a 200-seat restaurant. But despite her lack of experience, Ms. Shere held a meeting with the restaurant staff and emerged determined to give it a try. Says she: "I was never so frightened in my life."

With the hindsight of more than a dozen years of experience at the helm of The Coach & Six now behind her, Ms. Shere looks back to her early beginnings in the restaurant trade with both fondness and incredulity. No place for the naive, Ms. Shere counts her blessings. In a profession where change is perhaps the only constant, she considers herself lucky.

"Restaurants come and go," she remarks. "So few survive. When The Coach first opened, the business was 85 per cent beef. Today, it's 55 per cent fish and seafood."

A greater public awareness of the connection between health and diet has also led to butter-free, low cholesterol and no salt dishes being added to the menu at The Coach. For this, the restaurant was recently recognized by the American Heart Association.

Two additional symbols of ongoing change at The Coach are sons Richard, 22, a vice-president, and William, 27, a cook, both of whom are one day expected to carry on the family legacy. Both are a source of considerable pride to Ms. Shere. "How fortunate I am to have two sons who love the restaurant business," says she.

Currently, however, there are no plans for Beverlee Shere to turn over the reins at the Coach & Six. Undoubtedly, she could retire tomorrow and find her place in the restaurant's history secure. Everywhere, her outgoing personality and philosophy are writ large on her surroundings.

A philanthropist with a deep sense of social conviction, Ms. Shere's imagination even extends to the restaurant's cigarette machine. To aid in the fight against cancer and heart disease, she placed a 100 per cent surcharge on the cost of a pack of cigarettes in 1974, with the additional money going to heart and cancer research. To date, the machine has raised some $25,000.

Not surprisingly, the centerpiece of the Coach & Six's 25th anniversary celebration will also be charitable in nature. To show her appreciation to the infinite number of customers who have patronized the restaurant over the years, Ms. Shere will donate a considerable sum of money to Georgia Public Television.

"Now that we've reached our 25th year," says she, "I want to give something back to the city that made it all happen."

Coach & Six owner Beverlee Soloff Shere in front of her "celebrity bar"

Crawford Long Hospital of Emory University

Atlanta entered the 20th Century with a population of 90,000 struggling to raise their city from the devastation of war. The turn of the century brought the city's first public library, the immense popularity of Coca-Cola and a brand new hospital!

The 26-bed Davis-Fischer Sanatorium, founded in 1908, began the tradition of quality caring and progressive medical service that continues today as Crawford Long Hospital of Emory University.

One of Atlanta's first medical facilities, Crawford Long has kept pace with Atlanta's tremendous growth while maintaining its central location.

In 1911 the Davis-Fischer Sanatorium moved to the hospital's present site in the block bounded by Peachtree, West Peachtree, Linden Avenue and Prescott Street.

In 1931, after the death of co-founder Dr. E. C. Davis, the hospital became the Crawford W. Long Memorial Hospital, named for the Georgia physician who first used ether anesthetic during surgery.

In 1940, as the bed capacity exceeded 400, the facility became a division of Emory University and an ambitious building program was launched.

This well-planned expansion continued through the 1970's with the opening of the eight-story Glenn Building which houses physician, radiation therapy, and nuclear medicine offices and the medical library.

In 1973 the seven-floor Peachtree Patient Tower opened additional patient rooms and intensive care units.

The nationally recognized Carlyle Fraser Heart Center was established in 1975. The Center and its staff are dedicated to the prevention, care and treatment of heart and lung disorders.

In 1986 — Crawford Long's seventy-eighth year of achievement — several important property purchases marked a new surge of growth for the hospital.

These were acquisitions of the John Smith Chevrolet property on West Peachtree and the W. W. Orr complex, later renamed as the Robert W. Candler professional buildings.

The final acquisition in 1986 was that of the former Doctors Memorial Hospital on the corner of West Peachtree at Linden Avenue. That facility is now a comprehensive Outpatient Center connected to the hospital by an enclosed pedestrian walkway.

Outstanding leadership has consistently directed and contributed to the hospital's prosperous development. In 1953, after the death of co-founder Dr. Luther C. Fischer, Emory University Trustees appointed Medical Director Dr. Wadley R. Glenn as administrator.

Dr. Glenn, an extremely popular and efficient administrator, served in that position for over 30 years. A daily reminder of Dr. Glenn's dedication to medicine exists in the Wadley R. Glenn Operating Pavilion, consisting of 11 operating and cystoscopy suites.

With the death of Dr. Glenn in April, 1985, John D. Henry was named administrator and chief executive officer and Harold S. Ramos, M.D., was appointed medical director. They have overseen the recent expansion of facilities and medical services with the same thoughtful foresight that marked the repeated success of their predecessors.

Today Crawford Long Hospital of Emory University stands as a proud monument to all of the dedicated people whose dreams and hard work have made it a reality.

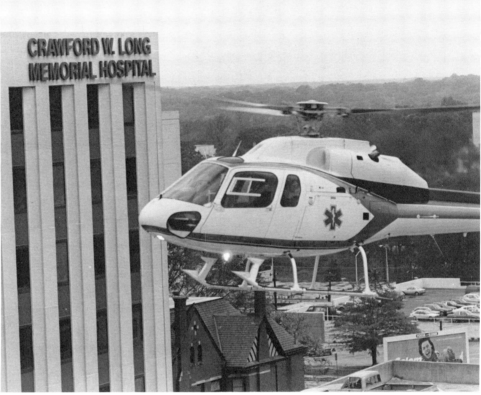

High above the Atlanta skyline, Crawford Long Hospital's helipad enables medical helicopter to transport patients smoothly to the hospital for attention.

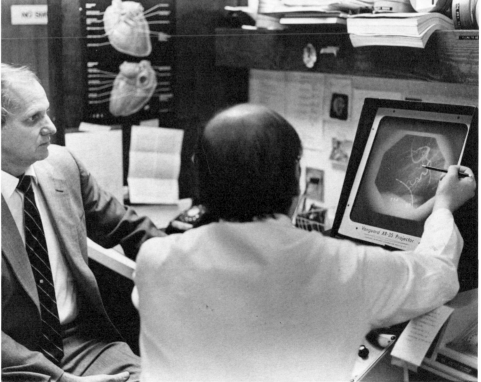

This Crawford Long patient understands a video recording of his own angiogram as it is explained by cardiologist Dr. Henry A. Liberman (right).

Decatur Federal Savings and Loan Association

At about the time television was being invented back in 1926, a group of far-sighted businessmen met together to form the Decatur Building and Loan Association in DeKalb County.

The founders of the Association, now Decatur Federal Savings and Loan Association, recognized that tremendous capital would be required to finance development of property and construction, and purchase of homes as DeKalb County was emerging from an agricultural economy into a semi-urban county oriented toward the fast-growing metropolis of Atlanta, six miles west of Decatur.

There were few institutions organized to encourage thrift and systematic savings. Mortgage funds were available only through brokers from the northern and eastern sections of the country. Furthermore, these funds were available only on very unsound terms.

J. Robin Harris

Now, 61 years later, Decatur Federal has become a vital force in providing the "good life" for many thousands of people in the Metro Atlanta area. Over the last 10 years, Decatur Federal has been the leading lender of funds for home financing in the six counties surrounding Atlanta and for the state of Georgia.

The first loan was approved in March, 1927 — two months after the building and loan was state chartered. It was in the amount of $2,250 for a home on Adair Street in Decatur. Assets at the time were $1,946.50, but at the end of the year had grown to $53,768.44.

The deep depression came along just three years after the Association had been organized. Homes throughout the country were being foreclosed, financial institutions were closing and near panic prevailed until Franklin D. Roosevelt declared a bank holiday. But Decatur Federal remained open.

The understanding and sympathetic attitude on the part of the directors made it possible for homeowners to retain ownership of their homes and eventually pay off their mortgages. To ease unemployment and provide some new homes during this period, the Association pioneered in making construction loans, which provided funds during construction.

Each decade brought new opportunities for Decatur Federal to confirm its commitment to help fulfill the dream of home ownership. Following World War II, the Association provided the only cache of local funds available for property development. The early 50's began a period of rapid growth and expansion of services for the people of the community, and Decatur Building and Loan became a federally-chartered institution to make this expansion possible.

In the 60's, attention was turned to greater activity in providing college education loans, home improvement loans and other types of lending, including efforts to serve the people in moderate- and low-income classifications needing adequate housing.

The decade of the 70's was marked with soaring interest rates and Decatur Federal consistently kept interest rates for borrowers lower than the majority of lenders. In May, 1980, the Association took a long stride into the 80's with a nationally-acclaimed move which rolled back interest rates on all loans to 12½ per cent.

The early 80's were difficult times for the industry, but Decatur Federal was able to withstand the effects of high rates paid on savings which were not matched with comparable loan rates, and survived those critical years.

Decatur Federal today reflects a finely-tuned approach to meet the dramatic changes in the savings and loan industry that came about because of deregulation. While continuing to pursue its objective of providing funds for home ownership, the Association turned to the secondary mortgage market and introduced many new products and services to maintain its position in the competitive environment. These included personal lines of credit, auto loans and automated services.

The third largest savings and loan in Georgia, Decatur Federal has assets of $1.9 billion, with a branch network of 27 offices throughout the Metro Atlanta area and in North Georgia.

Decatur Federal has maintained its identity as a conservative organization more concerned with security and service for its customers than with achieving rapid growth. This has been affirmed by its reputation with customers who have a loyal allegiance, which has contributed to the Association's progress and success.

DeKalb College

Over 300,000 students in the Metropolitan Atlanta area have attended DeKalb College during its 23-year history.

Founded by the citizens of DeKalb County for the purpose of providing DeKalb residents with the opportunity for quality education beyond the secondary level, DeKalb College is the only public junior college in the state which was established under the Georgia Junior College Act of 1958 which allowed a local board of education to finance and operate a junior college.

DeKalb College continued as a part of the DeKalb County School System from 1964 when its Central Campus in Clarkston opened until July 1, 1986, when the college became the 34th unit of the University System of Georgia.

As the Atlanta area grew, so did DeKalb College. In 1972, DeKalb's South Campus near Decatur was completed. In the same year, DeKalb College entered into an agreement with DeKalb Area Technical School to allow students to enroll in both collegiate and vocational programs.

As a result of the agreement, the College was designated DeKalb Community College by the DeKalb County Board of Education. In 1979, the college's North Campus opened in Dunwoody.

Throughout its history, DeKalb College has responded to the changing educational needs of the Atlanta community, designing its programs to meet current and future career demands.

The College's curriculum offers both a comprehensive developmental program for those students who need to improve basic skills and an honors program which has received national recognition. Students may earn associate in arts and associate in science degrees in 38 college transfer programs or associate in science and associate in applied science degrees in 25 career programs.

In addition to traditional academic pro-

DeKalb College's Central Campus is one of the College's three campuses.

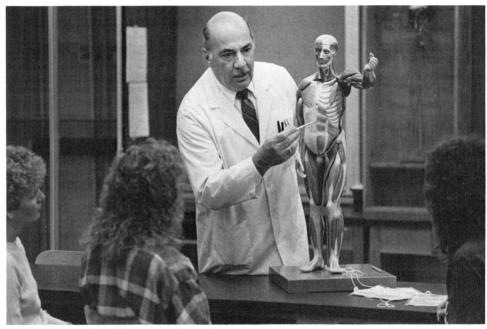
Anatomy and physiology laboratory at DeKalb College.

DeKalb College students prepare to meet the demands of the future.

grams, DeKalb College offers instructional programs in Japanese, Chinese and Arabic as it keeps pace with Atlanta's growing international role. Through its Continuing Education Program, DeKalb College provides training opportunities to the business community, career planning and development services, and a broad range of courses for life enrichment for all ages.

Although a large number of DeKalb College students are recent high school graduates, a significant number are older than the traditional college-age student. Consequently, DeKalb College places a strong emphasis on services for non-traditional students through support groups, seminars, and counseling to help them in coping with college, home, and work responsibilities.

DeKalb College sponsors musical and theatrical groups which include both students and community members as participants. The DeKalb Symphony Orchestra, now in its twenty-third year,

numbers over 500 Atlanta residents among its past and present members. DeKalb College is also the home of *The James Dickey Newsletter*, which serves as a national forum for scholarship concerning the works of the Atlanta author and poet.

DeKalb College has pioneered in Georgia in open door admissions, personalized approaches to instruction, and community-related curricula. Its students have excelled in professions, arts, government, education, technology and business. Many of DeKalb's students continue their education at four-year colleges and universities throughout Georgia.

Much of DeKalb College's success can be credited to its leaders who have included Jim Cherry, superintendent of DeKalb County Schools at the time of the College's founding, and its presidents - Dr. Thad W. Hollingsworth (1964-1967), James H. Hinson, Jr. (1967-1976), Dr. W. Wayne Scott (1976-1981), and Dr. Marvin M. Cole (1981 to present).

Henrietta Egleston Hospital for Children

"I bequeath and devise the sum of One Hundred Thousand (100,000) Dollars ... for the purchase of a lot, and the erection thereon a Hospital for Children" ... — From the will of Thomas Robert Egleston, Jr., Atlanta, Georgia, November 22, 1912

"To treat sick children, to encourage scientific investigation into medical problems of children, and to provide instruction in the diseases and care of children."

That was the dream of Thomas R. Egleston, a prominent Atlanta businessman whose generous bequest of $100,000 in 1916 laid the foundation for Henrietta Egleston Hospital for Children.

His dream was a memorial to his mother, Henrietta Holmes Egleston, who knew the tragedy of having four of her five children die in early childhood. She was known as a friend of children throughout her life.

When Egleston opened its doors on October 15, 1928, on Forrest Avenue, the first young patients and their parents arrived to find a building of classic elegance sitting amid 15 acres of verdant and tranquil beauty.

They also met a dedicated and disciplined staff, led by M. Hines Roberts, M.D., the medical director, and Jessie Maria Candlish, R.N., superintendent and nursing director. The medical staff was comprised of 21 physicians from the community and two residents.

In May, 1928, five months before the hospital opened, 39 enthusiastic Atlanta women attended a meeting at the home of Mrs. W. R. Prescott on West Paces Ferry Road to organize an auxiliary for the hospital. Their single purpose was to meet the needs of sick children.

The auxiliary's contributions in the early days included staffing the hospital office six days a week, sewing linens, performing many patient-related duties, and supporting a 10-bed ward at a cost of $6,000 per year through fund-raising activities. Hundreds of volunteers helped collect milk and tend a garden to provide home-grown foods for the patients.

The staff and volunteers' diligence helped to compensate for the limitations of a budget that allowed only half of the 52 beds to be utilized. Even harder times were coming; the next year, the Great Depression fell upon the nation.

Each year in Georgia alone, 2,000 children died from a dozen communicable diseases and other major illnesses associated with malnutrition and insanitary practices. All too frequently a child would be returned to health and home, only to be promptly readmitted because of an unhealthful environment. Doctors and nurses could do little but ease pain, provide supportive care — and pray.

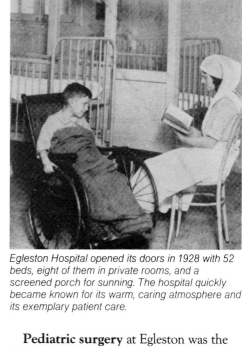

Egleston Hospital opened its doors in 1928 with 52 beds, eight of them in private rooms, and a screened porch for sunning. The hospital quickly became known for its warm, caring atmosphere and its exemplary patient care.

Pediatric surgery at Egleston was the best in the area, but so many conditions were inoperable. Among 466 procedures performed in 1928-29, there were only two brain surgeries and 10 chest surgeries, compared with 294 operations to remove tonsils and adenoids.

In his report for 1929, Dr. Roberts stated: "The work done during the first (full) year of the Hospital's existence leaves much to be desired, but I feel that much has been accomplished. By continually striving to improve each department, we undoubtedly will come nearer each year to the goal of perfection."

Thus, this group of extraordinary people used their talents and other resources well and instituted a tradition of never being satisfied with less than superb performance.

The 30's and 40's ushered in an era of new diagnostic procedures, drugs, surgical techniques and preventive measures. As the old foes of child health slipped in both real and statistical importance, pediatric medicine found new freedom to attack conditions affecting smaller numbers of children.

These included lethal diseases — leukemia and cystic fibrosis, for example — and limiting and debilitating conditions such as congenital heart problems, kidney diseases and metabolic and glandular disorders.

More illnesses — in greater diversity — were being diagnosed and treated by the child's community physician, and it became clearer that neither one person nor one discipline could begin to master the whole spectrum of pediatric care. It logically followed that increasing numbers of acutely ill children and those with uncommon and rare problems would require the expertise of super-specialists working together in a children's hospital.

Mrs. Blake Van Leer (Ella Wall) was representative of so many wonderful volunteers who faithfully served Egleston's patients as "Pink Ladies." Until her death in 1986 she served Egleston for 27 years as an auxilian, employee and trustee.

By the 1950's, the population of the Atlanta community had grown tremendously, and Egleston's 50-bed facility was no longer adequate to meet the city's needs. Several bequests, along with five acres of land donated by Emory University, enabled Egleston to move to its present-day Clifton Road location in 1959 and become an active affiliate of the Robert W. Woodruff Health Sciences Center of Emory University.

The on-site director of professional services was Joseph H. Patterson, M.D., chief physician. Associated with him then and for the next 11 years was Margaret P. Bodeker, R.N., M.P.H., director of nursing.

Egleston Hospital's role rapidly began to change upon its move to the Emory University campus. It became a regional referral center for the care of critically ill children. Through the leadership of the Emory University School of Medicine Egleston began a long tradition of providing education and training for thousands of medical students, resident physicians, nurses and allied health professionals.

The new 100-bed hospital in all its aspects — building, furnishings, equipment, philosophy, and techniques —

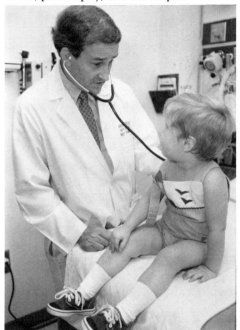

Three-year-old Nathan Henning was born with a small hole in his heart. The problem is not severe, and Dr. Joseph A. Snitzer, III, assistant chief of pediatrics at Egleston Hospital, hopes that the hole will eventually close on its own. In the meantime, Nathan visits the Egleston Children's Health Center near his home in Gwinnett County regularly for EKG testing and chest X-rays.

focused on children and their families.

Egleston Hospital pioneered a program for enhancing parent participation in the healing process. The vital relationships of parents and child, and especially mother and infant, were protected by allowing a parent to spend the night in the room.

In addition, parents were permitted in isolation areas (protective practices were required); and even in the intensive care units, short, periodic visits were encouraged.

Egleston's auxiliary played a vital role in meeting the increasing costs of care,

Egleston Hospital is committed to employing technology and exercising humanity in every phase of care. After taking an extensive infant training course designed for volunteers, auxilian Elizabeth Jamison devotes her time to rocking tiny babies to sleep in the infant nursery.

equipment, and services. Innumerable hours of volunteer service were given to provide funds for those patients whose families were unable to pay the cost of their care and to provide the latest medical equipment for the young patients.

To meet the needs of more and more children as Atlanta and Egleston grew, the hospital auxiliary began to take on fund-raising projects of much larger scope such as the Festival of Trees and the Georgia-Pacific Atlanta Golf Classic.

Over the years, many important community leaders have taken a special interest in the health care of the critically ill children at Egleston. On the occasion of philanthropists George and Irene Woodruff's 50th wedding anniversary in 1967, Mr. Woodruff made a special gift to Egleston honoring Mrs. Woodruff who dedicated much of her life to helping Egleston's sick children.

Fifteen years later in May, 1981, a $25 million 65-bed addition to Egleston Hospital was named the George and Irene Woodruff Pavilion honoring the couple.

Egleston Hospital is now the largest and most comprehensive children's medical facility in the state. All medical and surgical sub-specialties are represented by Egleston's 400-member medical staff. Over half of Egleston's physicians are faculty members of the Emory University School of Medicine.

Included in Egleston's full range of services are renal dialysis, kidney transplants and bone marrow transplants. Housing one of the largest cardiology and cardiovascular surgery programs for children in the country, Egleston is a leader in diagnostic and treatment procedures for childhood diseases and life-threatening illnesses.

Research also plays an important role at Egleston. The formation of the Emory-Egleston Children's Research Center in 1985 combined the expertise of investigators in the Emory University School of Medicine with the 59-year commitment of Egleston Hospital to improve the quality of children's lives.

To meet the growing needs of pediatricians and families in Gwinnett County and surrounding areas, the hospital opened its first outpatient satellite facility in September, 1986: Egleston Children's Health Center.

The original Egleston staff frequently found itself with little to offer but compassion. The current staff has a vast repertory of specialized instruments, computerized equipment that appears to think for itself, almost miraculous drugs, and scientific and technical know-how that boggles the mind.

Despite the onrushing developments, the need for compassionate concern in the care of patients continues unabated. The Egleston staff is committed to employing technology and exercising humanity.

Today, Egleston Hospital is guided by the leadership of Selena D. Dunn, hospital administrator; George W. Brumley, M.D., medical director, and Horace H. Sibley, chairman of the board.

Egleston's history has been filled with the works of thousands of leading Atlanta citizens and community members dedicated to one purpose — providing high quality pediatric medical and nursing care in surroundings created especially for children.

Four-year-old Leigh Ann Moore of Riverdale, Georgia, refers to Egleston as her hospital and thinks of the staff as a second family. Through the course of her treatment at Egleston, she developed a close relationship with her primary nurse, Gay Maloney, RN.

A Great City Deserves a Great University

and Atlanta has one...EMORY.

Emory provides Atlanta with an economic boost, enriches the cultural lives of its citizens, and is a significant provider of health care in Atlanta.

Economic Impact

Emory has sent some 25,000 graduates into Georgia and some 18,000 now reside in Atlanta. These graduates have become scholars and statesmen, business leaders and lawyers, ministers, nurses, physicians, and dentists.

Emory's annual revenues of $453.4 million rank it among the top twenty companies in Georgia. Emory is the second largest employer in DeKalb County and one of the largest private-sector employers in Atlanta.

Since 1969, Emory faculty at Grady Memorial Hospital secured more than $100 million in grants for patient care and research. Last year, Emory health science center researchers received more than $43.5 million from federal and private sponsored research. The number of faculty devoted to such research will double by 1990, from 95 to 195.

Local contractors are reaping the benefits of Emory's current construction boom. In late 1986, sixteen major construction projects with a total value of $151.3 million were planned or in progress at the university.

Health Care

Last year, Emory University Hospital and Crawford Long Hospital admitted roughly 20,000 patients each, with another 35,000 seen as emergency room/clinic patients at Crawford Long

and 7,500 seen in Emory's treatment room. The Emory Clinic was visited by more than a quarter of a million patients from virtually every American state and thirty-four foreign countries.

Emory is the only hospital in Georgia to transplant livers. Emory's heart transplantation program is among the most successful of the newer programs with more than fifty transplants in two years.

Fifteen percent of all the physicians and more than half of all the dentists in Georgia received their medical/dental degrees from Emory, and numerous others took their specialized residency training here. More than 1,500 graduates of the nursing school work in Georgia.

Individual Enrichment

Each year, 9,000 Atlantans enroll in Evening at Emory classes, an enrichment program for adults which offers 480 classes a year ranging from foreign language instruction to courses for singles.

Emory's professional schools offer continuing education programs for practicing professionals.

Cultural Enrichment

Last year, Emory's music department's workshops, seminars, recitals and concerts were attended by 32,000 people. Theater Emory's sixty-two performances and fifteen student productions were attended by 3500 people. The Museum of Art and Archaeology in the Michael C. Carlos Hall, was visited by 26,000 people last year—3,000 of them Georgia school children. Cannon Chapel hosted cultural events, from lectures to organ recitals which enriched the lives of 50,000 people.

Volunteerism

In 1986, Volunteer Emory, a student-run organization that each year matches 200 student volunteers with the needs of more than forty of Atlanta's social service agencies, received the Georgia Governor's Community Service Award as one of the state's top volunteer organizations.

The Future is Bright

Atlanta is destined to become one of the leading cities in the nation and as Emory and Atlanta look toward the twenty-first century, the future is bright. Emory is determined to be one of the nation's strongest and most distinctive universities. After all, a great city deserves a great university.

Fulton Federal Savings and Loan Association

1927 Atlanta attorney Granger Hansell organizes Fulton Federal, then known as the First National Savings Syndicate.

1933 Hansell applies for a federal charter for a savings and loan association, after reading in The New York Times that such charters are available. He and William Scurry sell subscriptions for savings shares in their company. They are granted the first federal charter for a savings and loan association in Georgia on November 25, 1933, making Fulton Federal the oldest S&L in the state. The association's name officially becomes Fulton County Federal Savings and Loan Association.

1950 Fulton Federal becomes the first S&L to develop a branch system, opening an office at 106 Thompson Avenue in East Point, on June 30.

1956 The word "county" is dropped from the legal name.

1957 Fulton Federal is the first S&L to build high-rise office headquarters in Atlanta, located at Edgewood Avenue and Pryor Street.

1959 Fulton Federal begins using a punch card system of bookkeeping, the initiation of data processing into Georgia's S&L industry.

1964 Fulton Federal's first branch outside metropolitan Atlanta is opened in McDonough.

1972 Fulton Federal takes its first step toward becoming a statewide S&L by merging with First Federal of Waycross.

1975 Fulton Federal introduces automated teller machines; the first Georgia S&L to do so.

1978 Assets top the $1 billion mark.

1981 Fulton Federal begins the transition from a traditional savings and loan association to a family financial center in the wake of the Financial Deregulation Act of 1980, which allows S&Ls to offer new services. Interest-earning checking accounts, VISA credit cards and consumer loans are marketed, changing the image of Georgia's second largest savings and loan.

1982 Fulton Federal actively pursues mergers in markets outside metro Atlanta, expanding its presence to include Athens, Augusta, Cairo, Cartersville, Claxton, Columbus, Douglas, Fitzgerald, Hogansville, LaGrange, Macon, Madison, McRae and Statesboro.

Fulton Federal was the first S&L to build high-rise office headquarters in Atlanta, in 1957. The Association still maintains its Main Office located at Edgewood and Park Place South, overlooking Woodruff Park.

1984 Fulton Federal looks to the future by adding electronic banking services. It joins the statewide AVAIL network as a founding charter member; participates in two home banking networks, TranstexT and Harbinger's The Promise; and supports BUYPASS point-of-sale system.

1986 Assets reach $2 billion.

1987 Fulton Federal converts from mutual to stock ownership, selling 4.2 million shares of common stock.

1988 Fulton Federal continues to provide customers with innovative services in a courteous and efficient manner.

Through the years, Fulton Federal's time and temperature sign at the Main Office in Atlanta has guided hundreds of people daily, helping to keep them warm in the winter and on time for appointments.

Georgia Federal Bank, FSB

Original building, Marietta at Broad

Georgia Federal Bank, FSB, one of the state's largest and strongest financial institutions, had a humble beginning in 1928 when the tallest building in Atlanta was 17 stories, women wore hats and white gloves to shop in the city, and the nation enjoyed prosperity.

At that time a group of professional and business men met daily for lunch at Mrs. Blackburn's Tearoom in downtown Atlanta, for conversation as much as the meal. Subjects ranged from politics to religion. They did not agree on all issues, but they did agree that most loans on real estate in Georgia came from out-of-state lenders and interest on those loans was not reinvested in Georgia.

From the luncheon forums came the idea to establish a mutual building and loan organization in Atlanta to encourage thrift and promote home ownership. It would contribute to the growth of the community through the construction of more homes, create employment and enhance the demand for building materials.

Rawson Collier, an executive with Georgia Power Company, was president of the newly-formed Atlanta Building and Loan Association for the first three years, until business interests took him from the city. He was succeeded in 1931 by Walter McElreath, an eminent attorney and one of the founders of the Atlanta Historical Society.

After Atlanta Building and Loan Association became Atlanta Federal in 1935, he continued to serve as its president until 1950, then as chairman until his death. McElreath was instrumental in bringing W. O. DuVall, the third president, into the organization.

DuVall provided more than 50 years of extraordinary leadership. He served as legal advisor to the bank from its beginning, as secretary 1921-1949, as president 1950-1966, chairman of the board 1966-1975, and now as chairman emeritus.

Other distinguished citizens who played significant roles in Georgia Federal's growth include Robert W. Davis, a food broker; E. H. Ginn, a General Electric vice president; W. L. Blackett, a retired oil executive, and Charles A. Adair, an appraiser and contractor.

Bill C. Wainwright joined the bank in 1945 and served as president from 1966 to 1977, and as chairman from 1975 until his retirement in 1981.

John B. Zellars, the current chairman of the board, has provided outstanding leadership for more than 35 years, and directed the firm's statewide expansion and conversion to stock ownership.

Richard D. Jackson now serves as president and chief executive officer, having joined Georgia Federal in July, 1986, after 12 years as president of First Georgia Bank (now First Union Corp. of Georgia) in Atlanta.

The company's corporate headquarters were relocated in 1935 from 74 Plaza Way to the 22 Marietta St. Building, formerly occupied by the Third National Bank. The 17-story building was purchased in 1950, followed by the purchase in 1958 of the adjoining building at 18 Marietta St., the old Fulton National Bank Building. In 1966 the two buildings were renovated and joined to become 20 Marietta St., the current corporate headquarters at Five Points.

Statewide expansion began in 1972 when Home Federal of Augusta joined Atlanta Federal. Subsequent mergers of Glynn Federal in Brunswick, First Federal in Dublin, and Home Federal in Savannah brought into focus the need for a new name for the statewide, Atlanta-born institution. So, Atlanta Federal became Georgia Federal Savings and Loan in 1976.

Additional locations since have joined the growing Georgia Federal network of more than 70 offices: Columbus, Perry, Macon, Albany, Moultrie and Marietta. In 1985 the bank acquired First Family Financial Services, a consumer finance company which now operates about 150 offices in eight southeastern states.

In July, 1983, the company changed its federal charter to a mutual savings bank in order to maximize its retail banking and consumer lending opportunities. At that time, the company name was changed to Georgia Federal Bank, FSB. On Feb. 1, 1984, the bank converted from mutual to stock ownership by issuing 7.9 million shares of common stock.

Georgia Federal's statewide franchise attracted the interest of well-known businessman and investor J. B. Fuqua, who acquired a personal stake of almost 10 per cent of the stock of the bank after it went public. In April, 1986, his *Fortune 500* company, Fuqua Industries, Inc., acquired Georgia Federal for $223 million in cash. Georgia Federal now operates as a wholly owned subsidiary of Fuqua, which has other profitable interests in lawn and garden equipment, photofinishing and sporting goods companies.

From modest assets of $46,471.51 in 1928, resources of Georgia Federal have grown to more than $3.3 billion as of March 31, 1987.

Company management takes pride in Georgia Federal's financial strength and its recent record earnings performance. For over 50 years the company's primary purpose was to promote thrift and home ownership.

Supplementing that heritage, the purpose today is to satisfy the increasingly diverse range of consumer banking needs and also to serve small and medium-sized businesses through a new corporate banking division started in October, 1986.

With its combination of geographic location, market position, strong capitalization, asset base and management team, Georgia Federal is well prepared to meet the challenges of the future.

Georgia Lighting Company

Throughout history the practical need for illumination has been blended with the decorative and artistic impulses of civilization. It was over 25 years ago that Harry L. Gilham, Jr. first became fascinated with the idea that lighting can be a delightful synthesis of the practical and the aesthetic.

After graduation from Emory University and a stint in the Navy, Harry worked for a large electrical wholesale company. He was asked to set up a lighting department, and his new-found fascination with lighting kindled his entrepreneurial spirit.

Sizing up the Atlanta market, Harry saw a need for a service that would meet the needs of building and electrical contractors as well as interior designers and the general public. **Georgia Lighting opened** its doors in 1960 with three employees. It now employs over 100 people and is the largest single-location lighting company in the U.S. and the leading importer of fine quality chandeliers and lamps. Its combined resources make it the nation's largest decorative lighting company.

Georgia Lighting is unique in the excellence and diversity of its project offerings. Buyers travel the world seeking out the few remaining skilled artisans who can execute delicate blown glass or hand-chased bronze. Avoiding mass production facilities, they explore the byways of Italy, France, Spain and Austria to find the small shops where the masters still ply these ancient crafts.

Georgia Lighting then actively coordinates the work, blending dimensions and technical requirements of modern fixtures to the timeless beauty of European designs.

"**Many designs** are created exclusively for us," Harry explains, "and some even have numbered parts which only fit that single piece. This creates a truly individual work of art. Other designs are accurate reproductions of original antiques, modified only to meet safety standards. We commission custom molds and glass designs to create our own exclusive lines."

To more fully develop the European import market, in 1967 a separate division called World Imports was inaugurated. World Imports occupies a 50,000 square-foot building on Ellsworth Industrial Blvd. Imported fixtures are assembled and through agents are sold to most lighting stores in the U.S.

Georgia Lighting has provided fixtures for many homes of historical significance, including the President's Home at the University of Georgia, the original Georgia Capitol in Milledgeville, and the Henry Grady House in Athens. Large commercial fixtures from Georgia Lighting illuminate hotels throughout the world, including Marriott, Hilton and Sheraton properties.

Georgia Lighting's product lines are displayed in the largest showroom in the Southeast, at 530 14th Street NW. The facility recently underwent its second expansion and now encompasses 65,000 square feet.

"A building of this scope is required since our philosophy is to carry a very large inventory to accommodate builders and contractors," Harry explains. The showroom also houses decorative accessories for interior design including hand carved wood and Venetian mirrors.

But, as with all businesses, the ultimate responsibility for success rests with people. The highly trained Georgia Lighting staff is service-oriented and well prepared to assist, whether it be a homeowner seeking guidance on decor, or a contractor setting specifications for track and recessed lighting.

The Senior Management Team is composed of Harry Gilham, President; Ray Gardner, General Manager; John White, Vice President of Operations, and Anna L. Gilham, Vice President of Sales, and Harry's mother.

The industry has recognized both Harry and Ray Gardner for their knowledge and success in the lighting industry.

Harry is past president of the American Home Lighting Institute and in 1978 was named Lighting Person of the Year. This award is bestowed by the trade association comprised of 600 lighting showrooms throughout the U.S. and Canada. Ray Gardner was first Vice President of the American Home Lighting Institute and served as President in 1986.

For the past 25 years the people, products and facilities of Georgia Lighting have accurately mirrored Harry Gilham's initial view of the purpose of lighting: to blend the practical and the beautiful into an aesthetic whole which creates comfort and pleasure for people.

Ready to greet customers in the spacious lobby of the Georgia Lighting Company showroom are (from left) Harry L. Gilham, President; Ray Gardner, General Manager, and the receptionist.

Georgia Lighting Company's 65,000 square-foot showroom at 530 14th St., NW, is the largest decorative-lighting showroom in the Southeast.

Georgia Power

Morgan Falls Hydroelectric Plant, the South's first construction job to use a power-operated rock crusher and concrete mixer, has changed little since it was built in 1902-04. Though small by today's power plant standards, it is still an important part of the Georgia Power system.

Georgia Power's energy-award-winning Atlanta headquarters building has the largest solar system for climate control and water heating of any commercial structure in the U.S. The 24-story office tower exemplifies the Company's ongoing commitment to alternate energy research.

In 1883 the original company in Georgia Power's ancestral line, the Georgia Electric Light Company of Atlanta, was granted a charter to provide electricity for lighting purposes only.

Its first order of business was to furnish the city with street lighting. Atlantans were skeptical of the venture as they regarded electric lighting as a doubtful substitute for gas lamps then in use.

The Company persevered and, in 1891, it was purchased by the Georgia Electric Light Company, which had just been formed by H. M. Atkinson. A newcomer to Atlanta, Atkinson had a vision of the electric industry's future possibilities. In his acquisition, improvement and expansion of properties owned by Georgia Electric Light and succeeding companies, he became a leader of electric development in Atlanta and Georgia.

The Atlanta Constitution said of his Company on June 6, 1894: "There is not a better lighted city in America than Atlanta ... The City is to be congratulated that the lighting service is in the hands of a Company that performs its duty so faithfully."

Atkinson organized the Atlanta Rapid Transit Company in 1901 and soon controlled all street railway, electrical and steam-heat properties in the city.

Merging his interests in 1902, he formed the Georgia Railway and Electric Company. (Electricity was then used mainly for street lighting, lighting homes and businesses in the city, and powering small motors in elevators and plants. Most domestic

appliances and labor-saving devices commonly used today had not even been dreamed of.)

Atkinson served as chairman of the new Company and his lawyer, Preston S. Arkwright, was named president. Joining them on the board were several influential Atlantans, including Thomas Egleston, founder of the Henrietta Egleston Hospital for Children.

In 1904 the Company provided Atlanta with its first source of hydroelectric power when the Morgan Falls Plant, located north of the city, became operational. Most of the dam's 10,500-kilowatt output was initially used to run the Atlanta street car system.

Another merger in 1911 led to the formation of the Georgia Railway and Power Company. To meet the ever-growing demand for electricity, the Company opened the Tallulah Falls Hydroelectric Plant in 1913, bringing its total system output to 94,200 kilowatts.

Increased electrical demands during World War I led to the construction of five more north Georgia hydro plants in the early 20's.

The Company brought the state its first radio station in 1920, but soon turned it over to *The Atlanta Constitution*. The newspaper later gave the station to Georgia Tech where it was operated as WGST for more than 50 years.

After consolidation in 1927 of several power and railway systems across the state, the modern Georgia Power Company was

formed. Atkinson became chairman of the board and Arkwright, president and CEO. (Arkwright, who coined the Georgia Power slogan, "A citizen wherever we serve," personified the Company in the public's eyes until his death in 1946.)

The Company continued to acquire and integrate electric systems in Georgia while furthering its transmission and distribution facilities across the state.

During the 40's and 50's, Georgia Power divested itself of all street transportation systems and embarked upon a program of steam-electric power plant construction and use that has continued to the present. The 70's marked the start-up of Plant Bowen, one of the largest such power plants in the country, and Plant Hatch, the Company's first nuclear-powered generating station. A second was completed in 1987.

With 33 generating plants, Georgia Power is today one of the largest investor-owned electric utilities in America. Its 16,000-megawatt system supplies electricity to 97% of the state, serving more than 1.4 million customers.

Under the leadership of Robert W. Scherer, board chairman and CEO, the Company continues its tradition of growth and progress. His vigor and foresight are major reasons a study ordered in 1981 by the Georgia Public Service Commission called the Company's management "progressive and energetic."

Georgia Power is a unit of The Southern Company, which owns an integrated system of power companies across the Southeast.

Georgia State University

In 1913, just as Atlanta had completed her 75th birthday celebration, classes in "the new business of science" were held in rented spaces in downtown Atlanta.

Today, poised against the backdrop of the gold dome of the Georgia state capitol, yet only two blocks from the hub of activity at Five Points, Georgia State University has grown from a few classes in borrowed space to become the second largest institution of higher education in the state of Georgia.

Atlanta is its campus.

The 75-year history of GSU is one of outreach to Atlanta and her surrounding communities. It is also the story of a rich heritage that reflects foresight, determination and leadership.

As Atlanta grew from the ashes of the Civil War to enter the 20th Century, GSU began to evolve from its beginnings as a unit to its present status today as a whole, thriving institution that continues to grow for the future.

The Georgia Institute of Technology founded "the Georgia Tech Evening School of Commerce" in 1913. The classes were greeted with interest, and enrollment increases forced four relocations throughout the first 18 years. In 1916, a group of seven young men became the school's first graduating class.

Dr. Wayne S. Kell, on loan from Georgia Tech, was the first director of the school and remained at the helm of the school until 1918. He was succeeded as director by John M. Watters, then Fred. B. Wenn.

In 1928, at the face of the Great Depression, Dr. George McIntosh Sparks assumed leadership of the school. Through Dr. Sparks, the school raised enough funds to purchase in 1931 its own building, the Sheltering Arms Building on Luckie and Walton Streets.

In 1933, the school began to offer the bachelor of arts degree in addition to the business degree. Another building, also on Luckie Street (moving early students to say they went to "LSU—Luckie Street University") was acquired in 1938. Enrollment that year topped 1,700.

Eight years later, in 1946, Sparks negotiated the purchase of a parking garage at 24 Ivy Street to accommodate the influx of World War II veterans. Soon after, the 4,000 students moved in. The building, Kell Hall, became the first building in the GSU campus of today.

In 1947, some 17 years after the formation of the University System of Georgia Board of Regents, the school was incorporated into the University of Georgia and became the "Atlanta Division of the University of Georgia." But this move lasted less than eight years.

In 1955, as the second building on campus, Sparks Hall, was being constructed, the Regents recognized the momentum of the school and separated it. The Georgia State College of Business Administration was born. Dr. George M. Sparks was named president of the newest college in the system.

In 1957 Dr. Sparks retired and Noah Langdale, Jr., a young lawyer from Valdosta, GA, became president of the college.

Langdale continued to initiate the changes begun by his predecessor. Enrollment continued to increase, and in 1961 the Regents dropped "of Business Administration" and the name became Georgia State College.

More degrees — including the doctorate degree — were added. Schools of general studies, allied health sciences and education joined business administration and arts and sciences. In 1969 the Board of Regents recognized the tremendous growth and the college became Georgia State University.

The growth did not stop when GSU became a university. Throughout the 1970s GSU saw its greatest jumps in enrollment. More buildings, beginning with the J.C. Camp Student Center built in 1964, were constructed, bringing the total of the buildings on the downtown campus today

to 14.

This building growth mirrored the growth of the GSU program. The University now has six colleges — business administration, education, arts and sciences, public and urban affairs, health sciences, and law. More than 3,500 degrees — from associates to doctorate — are conferred each year.

Under Langdale's leadership the reputation of GSU has spread across the nation. The University has gained the respect of educators as one of the premier urban universities in the country.

Enrollment in the Master of Business Administration program in the College of Business Administration is the sixth largest nationwide. The College of Education boasts the third largest teacher education program in the Southeast. The William Russell Pullen library has acquired 1 million volumes with the addition of a first edition of Adam Smith's *The Wealth of Nations.*

The faculty of GSU is known nationally for its research, and the University was a pioneer in the initiation of telephone registration of students. When he took a leave of absence from the presidency of GSU in June, 1987, Dr. Langdale had the longest tenure of any college president in the United States.

Although GSU has grown, it still is able to meet its primary goal — educating students. Enrollment has topped 21,000, with some 2,000 classes offered each quarter from 7 a.m. to after 10 p.m. While a majority of students still come from the metro Atlanta area, GSU attracts more students from across America and nearly 100 foreign countries each year.

In 1988 Georgia State University will celebrate 75 years of educational excellence. From rented space to more than 24 acres, GSU has grown to meet the needs of an ever-expanding Atlanta.

Graphic Industries, Inc.

From a one-man Atlanta print shop in 1922, Graphic Industries, Inc., has emerged as one of the leading 50 commercial printing companies in North America.

By 1987 Graphic had grown into a publicly held NASDAQ listed company with 29 operating companies and 2,100 employees in major U. S. market regions, including the Northeast, Midwest, Southeast and Southwest.

Graphic's 31 plants produce commercial, corporate and financial printing, direct mail, point-of-purchase, graphic communications and reprographic services in Atlanta, New York, Boston, Chicago, Detroit, Miami, Houston, Dallas, Charlotte, Raleigh and other cities.

Sales for the year ended January 31, 1987 were a record $168 million. In the three years after its initial public offering, Graphic increased sales three and one-half times and tripled net income. Over a 10-year period the Company achieved compounded annual growth in sales of 28%, net income of 27.8% and shareholders' equity of 33.9%.

Graphic's predecessor was Williams Printing Company, founded in Atlanta by Jesse R. Williams in 1922. To launch his venture, Williams worked nights as a printer for the Atlanta Journal & Constitution and turned out business stationery at his small shop during the day. In the next three decades, the enterprise prospered as annual sales grew to more than $250,000 in 1948.

Mark C. Pope III began at Williams in 1949 and was promoted to president in 1955, serving in that capacity for the next 22 years. Under his guidance the company became a leader in applying new technology to printing, and Pope began to plan a major nationwide operation. He envisioned a network of separate yet complementary companies, providing all types of printing and graphic communications services throughout the United States.

The first step was the acquisition of Atlanta Blue Print Company in 1962. During the next 20 years Atlanta Blue expanded into the largest reprographic firm in the Southeast with nine divisions and blue-printing and photographic services and a national clientele.

Next came the acquisition of Rybert Printing Co., now Ryco, Inc., a general commercial printer founded in Atlanta in 1912. The firm became known for fast turnaround of medium to short-run, multi-color printing.

Graphic Industries, Inc., was organized as a holding company for the group of businesses in 1970 to provide the structure and financial base for Mark Pope's planned nationwide enterprise. In 1977 Graphic almost doubled its capacity and staff by acquiring Atlanta's Stein Printing Company, founded in 1924 by James S. Stein as a specialty printer of railroad tariffs. Today it is a regional leader in financial and corporate printing.

Graphic subsequently added 25 more operating companies to the corporate group, following Pope's concept of acquiring well-established firms, often family-owned businesses, with reputations for quality and with strong management.

Acquisition of the W. E. Andrews Co. gave Graphic entry into New England and Florida markets, while Wetmore & Company in Houston and Heritage Press in Dallas added the Southwest. Entry into the Midwest and direct mail came with the acquisition of Printing Service, Inc., in Detroit and A. J. Kennedy & Co. in Chicago.

The major Graphic Industries companies by their founding dates include:

1871: Edwards & Broughton Company of Raleigh, NC.

1906: A. J. Kennedy & Co., Inc., Elmhurst, IL (Chicago).

1912: Ryco, Inc., Atlanta.

1919: Atlanta Blue Print Company.

1922: Williams Printing Company, Atlanta.

1923: Heritage Press, Inc., Dallas.

1924: The Stein Printing Company, Atlanta.

1939: Printing Service, Inc., Madison Heights (Detroit), MI.

1947: Wetmore & Company, Houston.

1953: W. E. Andrews Co., Inc., Boston, MA; Hartford, CT. and Miami, FL.

1957: Craftsman Printing Company, Charlotte, NC.

1973: IPD Printing & Distributing, Inc., Atlanta.

Jesse R. Williams, founder of Williams Printing Company, predecessor of Graphic Industries, Inc.

Old Stein Printing Company building, 161 Luckie Street, NW, was purchased for $22,500 in 1933.

From left: Carter Pope, vice president, Atlanta Blue Print; John Pope, leading account representative for Williams Printing Company; Mark C. Pope III, founder and chairman of Graphic Industries, Inc., and Mark C. Pope IV, president, Williams Printing Company.

Old Atlanta Blue Print building at 112 Spring Street, NW, in 1938; it was destroyed by fire in 1956.

Gwinnett Hospital System

January 23, 1958, was an important date for the 200 people who gathered at the site of a former county work camp in Lawrenceville.

They witnessed the groundbreaking for a new facility — a general acute-care hospital owned and operated by the recently formed Hospital Authority of Gwinnett County.

Nineteen months later, on August 12, 1959, Gov. Ernest Vandiver dedicated Button Gwinnett Hospital saying, "Modern, efficient hospitals serve as an attraction to new industries. Perhaps it would be better to say necessity since new industries mean more people and there must be adequate provision for the health of all people."

Vandiver and the 500 people attending the dedication ceremony could not have predicted how quickly the 35-bed hospital would grow into a vital progressive health-care system.

Button Gwinnett Hospital increased in size to a 79-bed hospital, then became one part of a hospital system when the Hospital Authority acquired two other facilities.

Joan Glancy Memorial Hospital in Duluth joined the system in 1966. The Joan Glancy Memorial Hospital was originally built as a private clinic in 1941 by the Glancy family in memory of "Little Joan," their daughter who died when she was six years old.

Also in 1966 the Hospital Authority opened a newly constructed hospital in Buford. Buford Hospital offers quality care for substance abuse patients and emergency services for local residents.

The combination of the three facilities became known as Gwinnett Hospital System.

On December 29, 1984, Gwinnett residents witnessed the beginning of a new health-care era. At the same moment Button Gwinnett Hospital's doors closed, the doors to the nine-story, 190-bed Gwinnett Medical Center in Lawrenceville opened.

Together with Buford Hospital and Joan Glancy Memorial Hospital, Gwinnett Medical Center formed a health-care system which offered a wide range of services to Gwinnett residents.

Medical technology changed dramatically from the 1950's to the 1980's.

Cardiac catherization, lithotripsy, magnetic resonance imaging, CT scanning, nuclear medicine, outpatient surgery and laser surgery are just a few of the services offered by Gwinnett Hospital System in 1987 which Gov. Vandiver and others at the Button Gwinnett Hospital's dedication could not have predicted.

Rather than relaxing and simply enjoying the growth and success of the hospital system in the mid-1980's, the Gwinnett Hospital system is constantly striving to look into the future, to prepare for changes and growth in the upcoming years with long range planning and constant monitoring of trends in health care.

Gwinnett Hospital Authority member L. O. Hinton, of Dacula, dug the first shovel of dirt to break ground for the Button Gwinnett Hospital in 1958.

The progress and evolution of health-care is visibly demonstrated in the architectural differences in the first and the most recent hospital opened by the Hospital Authority of Gwinnett County. Twenty-five years separated the two openings.

Hall's Flower Shops and Greenhouses

Mildred Hall

Wayne H. Hall

At the age of 12 Wayne H. Hall had already started on the career and hobby that has become his life's work—and play. Working for 10¢ per hour for a local greenhouse, Wayne was so enthralled with the business that he talked his father Wayne C. Hall, into opening his own greenhouse. You might say "He grew up in the business."

In November, 1946, even before they were married, Wayne H. opened the first Hall's Flower Shop at 1947 Boulevard Drive, SE, with the former Mildred Shirley working with him, and his mother helping out. In February, 1947, they were married.

Through the first years the business and the family grew slowly and solidly. The concept was and is excellent quality, courteous personnel, comparable pricing and good service.

While raising children and seeing to the needs of their customers, Wayne and Mildred also found time to work in the community, become active and involved in their church and attend seminars and schools to increase their knowledge of the art of floral care, arranging, management, buying, growing, etc.

This commitment to excellence has continued through the years.

In 1961, due to the changing population, a new location in the Decatur/Belvedere area was acquired and a building designed and built. This is still one of the active flower shops and is managed by John Cannon, an employee of 20 years. As this area grew and became one of the prime shopping areas in DeKalb County, so grew Hall's Flower Shop.

Again in 1972 the population change and the growth of the shop made it desirable to find an additional location further out into suburbia. Naturally, with the Belvedere shop on Memorial Drive, it was logical to move further out Memorial

Drive into the rapidly expanding Stone Mountain area.

A beautiful existing home situated on five acres complete with swimming pool and recreation area was purchased. (The pool and recreation area have been retained for the use of the employees and their families on weekends along with special community events.)

An additional eight acres of adjoining land was later purchased and four additions to the houses have been added, still retaining the original layout and charm of rooms now used for the convenience of separate show rooms for gifts, bridal and consultations, fresh flower arrangements, work rooms, plus silk and dried arrangements and stems.

Finally, during the early Seventies, the greenhouses began to appear. At first only one was open to the public, then two, and now four. Another five greenhouses for growing plus several at Wayne's home have brought him full circle to his first love, the growing and tending of flowers.

Home-grown poinsettias, lilies, hydrangeas, azaleas and a variety of novelty pot plants and perennials regularly appear in the retail greenhouses and cut-flower areas of the shops.

A Christmas Open House in November and a Spring Greenhouse Open House, usually in late March, invite the public to view the season's best to come. One spring open house found six inches of snow atop the bedding plants while another winter ice storm caved in the roof of one of the greenhouses. The Halls take these setbacks in stride and push on to bigger and better things.

Their youngest son, Kenneth, has been the greenhouse manager in charge of growing for the past three years. He seems to be following in his father's footsteps. Daisy Swann, an employee of 20 years is the manager of the Stone Mountain Flower Shop with 35 employees under her direction.

The two shops have grown from the original two-person operation into a work force of 55 employees. The Halls belong to the floral wire services, local and national floral organizations, a central floral delivery service and many church and civic organizations. Many days the volume of business in the two shops and the greenhouses is in excess of three times the total first year's business. They just keep on growing.

In the center, Wayne H. Hall and Mildred Hall, seated, with their first child, Wayne, Jr. Standing, center right, are Mr. and Mrs. Wayne C. Hall, parents of Wayne H. Also shown are the parttime help used during Hall's second Easter in business.

Children
Of Atlanta

Sidney Reid (early 1890s)

Hugh M. Dorsey (governor, 1917-1921)

Heery International, Inc.

The Robert W. Woodruff Rotunda, The Central Reception Building, Headquarters Complex of The Coca-Cola Company, Atlanta.

Heery is **Heery International, Inc.** an organization of design and professional practices serving clients throughout the United States and Europe.

The founding company was established in 1945 by C. Wilmer Heery, AIA, an Atlanta native, in Athens, Georgia, for the practice of architecture. The firm became Heery & Heery in 1952 when his son, George Heery, began his practice in Atlanta. Today, that practice is the design group of Heery International, and is the largest architectural and engineering firm in Georgia specializing in **architecture, planning, interior and graphic design, strategic facilities planning and facilities management for health, sports, and commercial and institutional facilities.**

Heery integrates architectural services with **civil, mechanical, electrical, and structural engineering, land planning, landscape architecture, and energy consulting:** however, each service may be performed independently for a client.

The firm has been a national leader in developing the concept of professional **construction program management.** Fast, ambitious schedules are established and maintained to control construction costs for design and construction activities, and usually saves more money for owners than the relatively low costs of this service.

Heery International is ranked among the top fifty architectural, engineering and related professional services firms in the United States. Five hundred people work to assure client satisfaction.

999 Peachtree at Peachtree Place, Atlanta

George T. Heery, FAIA, RIBA, Chairman and Chief Executive Officer - Heery International, Inc.

The Dorothy C. Fuqua Conservatory, Atlanta Botanical Garden.

At this time of Atlanta's 150th Anniversary, three of the firm's recent design projects are illustrated. The Dorothy C. Fuqua Conservatory, Atlanta Botanical Garden, is scheduled to open in the Fall of 1988. Heery International celebrated the revitalization of Midtown Atlanta by relocating its Corporate Headquarters to 999 Peachtree in the Summer of 1987. The Central Reception Building and new office tower (not pictured) are projects designed for The Coca-Cola Company.

Corporate Headquarters, Georgia Power Company, Atlanta's most energy efficient high-rise office building.

Herman Miller, Inc., The Roswell, Georgia Facility.

Computer Aided Design Waterpark Plan

White Water, Atlanta

Launching a program management project

Point Loma Wastewater Treatment Plant, San Diego, California

Hitachi America, Ltd.

Namihei Odaira and Thomas Edison never met. But had they done so, it seems certain the legendary American inventor and industrialist and the founder of Hitachi, Ltd., would have shared a common vision.

The first products of Hitachi, Ltd., were three small five-horsepower electric motors, produced in the repair shop of a mining company in 1910. Today, Hitachi is one of the largest manufacturers of electronic and electrical products in the world.

These products include computers, integrated circuits, telecommunications equipment, consumer products, electrical utilities, industrial machinery, metal, chemical, wire and cables, as well as other products.

From its modest beginnings, Hitachi has grown to become the world's 21st largest corporation and now the Hitachi name is recognized in every corner of the globe as a standard-bearer of quality and reliability.

Recognizing that growth depends upon the forging of strong economic links throughout the world, Hitachi America, Ltd., was founded in 1959. The company started with only six employees, but as it enters its second quarter century, it has developed into a billion dollar corporation with 11 divisions, hundreds of employees and products serving key industries throughout America.

One of these divisions, Telecommunications, of Norcross, GA, provides Hitachi's telecommunications products. Started in 1969, this division was established to market PBX systems in the U.S. It has not

Mr. Namihei Odaira (left), founder of Hitachi, Ltd., shown with an early work crew, circa 1908.

only developed new products, but has sold and serviced communications systems for hundreds of satisfied customers in many diverse areas of commerce.

In 1980 the Telecom Division initiated a Research and Development Group which produced the "DX Series" of communication systems. 1985 saw the addition of the small HD-200 PBX, as well as a line of facsimile machines to the product group.

The DX Series Communication Systems consist of:

WelCOMM™, Hitachi's premier PBX designed especially for hotels and motels. It continues to lead the industry in quality

and technology. These feature-rich systems allow hotels to turn their communication systems into profit centers by reselling telephone service to their guests.

HealthCOMM™, for hospitals, nursing homes and other healthcare institutions, combines reliable communications with built-in emergency and messaging features.

COMMerce™, serving such diverse business endeavors as manufacturing plants, educational institutions and long distance trucking firms, is a telephone system that can be configured to meet most traffic capacity requirements.

The WelCOMM, HealthCOMM and COMMerce communication systems are all supported by the Inteliset II™, a sophisticated, yet easy-to-use multiline telephone with all the capabilities, but not the bulk, of a key system.

Hitachi also markets the HD200, a fully digital PBX that is a compact, modular one-cabinet system designed for small-to-medium businesses or hotels.

Facsimile machines, the new boon to businesses all over the world, are offered by Hitachi in its "HIFAX Series." Some of the HIFAX models offer more than 20 features, including gray scale for transmission of photographs and high-speed transmission to cut communication costs.

Hitachi's mission is to bring the company's high standards of quality, technology and dependability to the American communications field, as well as to remain a caring and involved member of the greater Atlanta community throughout its next 150-year history.

Hitachi America's headquarters, 1987.

Johnson & Higgins, Inc.

Johnson & Higgins was founded in New York City in 1845 by two young marine-loss adjusters, Henry W. Johnson and Andrew F. Higgins. They saw a need to fill the void in professional assistance in settling losses.

In providing this service the two men also found themselves negotiating insurance contracts for clients. Their activities led them to establish the first insurance brokerage firm in the United States.

Previously a buyer had to handle insurance matters directly with the insurance companies. Service to the client rather than allegiance to one particular company remains the hallmark of Johnson & Higgins.

As a marine-oriented firm, the new insurance brokers' business from the outset was tied to the marine industry, and soon they opened a second office on the West Coast. Over the years, however, the firm has expanded into all areas of insurance and established a network of offices in major cities throughout the country.

In 1956 the firm made the decision to enter the southeastern insurance market. The area was emerging as a fast-developing region of the country and was attracting an increasing number of businesses. Since Atlanta was the transportation hub as well as an important business and financial center, firm officials decided to initiate service to the Southeast through an Atlanta location, a move which no doubt would have pleased founder Andrew Higgins, a native of Macon, GA.

To open the Atlanta office, Johnson & Higgins merged with the firm of DuBose-Egleston, a well-established local agency which had been founded in 1876, only 31 years later than Johnson & Higgins. The principal of the agency, Beverly M. DuBose Jr., was named head of the newly created subsidiary, Johnson & Higgins of Georgia, Inc.

The southeastern territory included eight southern states from Virginia to Florida and Louisiana. The firm quickly determined the need for the many services provided by a major insurance brokerage firm in the Southeast, and it became apparent that more offices would be required to carry out the pledge of providing the best service.

In the 1960s and 1970s offices of Johnson & Higgins were established in Richmond, VA; New Orleans, LA; Miami, FL; and Charlotte, NC.

In 1968 the Atlanta office acquired the important local firm of Lipscomb-Ellis, founded in 1898, thus merging Atlanta's two oldest agencies into one. Charles Sims Bray, president of Lipscomb-Ellis, became president of Johnson & Higgins of Georgia Inc., and Beverly DuBose Jr. was elected chairman of the board.

As the Atlanta office continued to grow, more services were provided. The Johnson & Higgins organization became a major U.S. broker in the international field, with a network of more than 36 overseas offices. Access to those facilities was offered the clients in the Southeast.

The Atlanta office typifies the Johnson & Higgins goal to provide full service in insurance in each of the company's offices throughout its system. This was a goal set in 1845 when the company was founded. As a firm, Johnson & Higgins pioneered in several areas of service such as employee benefits and actuarial consulting. The founders strove to remain in step with the times and today the company still follows their example.

In 1980 a new office was opened in Birmingham, AL, and a year later an office was created in Nashville to serve Tennessee. The Atlanta office, now under the leadership of Albert S. McGhee, has developed into a major branch of Johnson & Higgins. After almost a century and half, the oldest and only major privately held insurance brokerage firm in the country looks forward to the challenges of the future.

Henry Ward Johnson

Andrew F. Higgins

Laing Properties

Laing's international ties were emphasized when Her Royal Highness, Princess Anne participated in the Grand Opening Ceremony of Laing's Lakeside Centre. Joining her in the dedication ceremony is George L. Aulbach, President of Laing Properties, Inc.

A house still stands in Cumbria, England, bearing a plaque with the legend "JAL 1848". This marks the date that John A. Laing founded John Laing and Son Limited. Major contract work was achieved during 1889 and formal incorporation was established in 1920. The company celebrated its centennial in 1948.

In 1978 John Laing and Son Limited, by then one of the largest U.K.-based international general contractors with a substantial property activity, went through a restructuring, whereby two new companies were formed.

One of the companies, Laing Properties, plc, was to be primarily involved with the development and retention of property investments, with operating subsidiaries in Atlanta and Vancouver, British Columbia, in addition to their main U.K. operation.

With their expertise and proven financial capability, Laing was committed to this objective: "To build an investment portfolio by developing and acquiring income producing properties for retention."

Since then, Laing Properties, Inc., the U.S. subsidiary in Atlanta, has actively pursued this objective, building an impressive portfolio consisting of both commercial and residential properties. The commercial portfolio includes Lenox Towers, Newmarket Business Park, Lakeside Centre, Palisades, Interchange and the NW Atlanta Hilton. In south Atlanta a 1987 groundbreaking is scheduled for a 150-acre business park on Camp Creek Parkway.

On the residential side, Laing has developed Huntcliff Summit, a $27 million luxury retirement community in North Fulton County. The 410,000 square-foot project comprises 236 one-and-two-bedroom units set in 14 heavily landscaped acres. The company has also formed several joint ventures which will develop apartment communities in Atlanta and the southeast.

Laing Properties can parallel a certain aspect of its growth with that of Atlanta's; both entities have served as magnets for international business development.

Consider Laing's Newmarket Business Park, an award-winning property located in Cobb County. There you will find Telemecanique, a French concern, and Sweden-based ProComp, a paper manufacturer. Newmarket is "home" to West Germany's Amoena Corporation, Gunold & Stickma of America, and Buderus Corporation. Japan is also represented at Newmarket by U.S. Amada, Ltd.

Laing's Buckhead property, Lenox Towers, is also part of this "United Nations." Antwerp Sales International, a wholesale jewelry firm out of Belgium, has been a tenant in the 3390 Tower since 1979. The 3400 Tower serves as a base of operations for two major international airlines, AeroMexico and Lufthansa.

Swiss entry is at Laing's Lakeside Centre on Northlake Parkway. Roche Biomedical Laboratories, Inc., a reference laboratory, is a division of Hoffman-LaRoche, a pharmaceutical firm.

The international flavor of Laing Properties continues in the firm's Palisades property on Peachtree Dunwoody Road. Palisades is the location for Alcan Aluminum of Montreal, Canada, and serves as division headquarters for Alcan Cable. Another Palisades veteran is UG U.S.A., Inc., a uranium trading company whose parent firm is located in Frankfurt, West Germany.

Laing Properties, Inc., recognized from the beginning that the philosophy of its successful tradition must be carried forward — a philosophy of building first quality products with people in mind. By developing projects from an investment standpoint, Laing makes a long-term commitment to each project. And this means lasting dedication to their customers and developments — which is what "The Laing Standard" is all about.

The U.S. subsidiary of Laing is headquartered at the company's Interchange property in north Atlanta. The British-based company was founded in 1848 by John A. Laing.

Liberty House Restaurant Corporation

Friday, July 27, 1979: Bone's Steak and Seafood, Liberty House's first Atlanta restaurant, opens its doors.

February, 1980: THE ATLANTA BUSINESS CHRONICLE: "Atlanta is fortunate to have Bone's, a new restaurant that can be compared to great steak houses anywhere."

March, 1980: ATLANTA MAGAZINE: "Bone's — The Best Little Steakhouse in Georgia! Bone's quest to re-establish fine beef as haute cuisine is a success."

November 10, 1982: Liberty House premieres its second restaurant, Trotters Restaurant, the South's answer to New York's "21" Club.

December, 1982: CUISINE MAGAZINE's editor-in-chief applauds Trotters and sends "Compliments to the Chef!"

February, 1983: THE NORTHSIDE NEIGHBOR newspaper praises Trotters' sophisticated, clubby decor. "While atmosphere is a big plus, the food is what keeps customers coming back."

February, 1983: THE ATLANTA BUSINESS CHRONICLE extols Trotters as "Atlanta's best restaurant" and adds, "Trotters serves food so good it exhausts superlatives."

May, 1983: "Trotters, sibling of the successful Bone's steak palace, is out of the gate with an auspicious flourish," declares ATLANTA MAGAZINE.

May, 1983: Bone's receives the prized AMERICAN AUTOMOBILE ASSOCIATION's "Official Appointment," an honor bestowed on fewer than 10% of the nation's restaurants.

June, 1983: Bone's is applauded by MOBIL TRAVEL GUIDE and given a rating of "Excellent," a title reserved for a handful of American restaurants.

July, 1983: SALES & MARKETING MANAGEMENT MAGAZINE selects Trotters as the definitive choice for travelers to Atlanta.

August, 1983: ATLANTA MAGAZINE names Trotters Atlanta's "Most Promising Major New Restaurant."

November, 1983: RESTAURANT HOSPITALITY honors both Bone's and Trotters with prized Top of the Table Awards.

March, 1984: THE NEW YORK TIMES singles out "Bone's … for the best steaks and lamb chops in the Southeast."

April, 1984: ESQUIRE MAGAZINE hails Liberty House proprietors Susan DeRose and Richard Lewis as the two instrumental forces in the refinement of the Atlanta dining scene. Bone's and Trotters are lauded as Atlanta's two most celebrated restaurants.

April, 1984: THE INTERNATIONAL HERALD TRIBUNE, London, cites Bone's and Trotters as two of the mandatory stops on a visit to the United States.

May, 1984: GENTLEMEN'S QUARTERLY MAGAZINE selects Bone's as one of the country's top 10 steakhouses.

May, 1984: The editors of METROPOLITAN HOME endorse Trotters and Bone's as two of the nation's finest restaurants, and identifies them as the "places to be" when in Atlanta.

December, 1984: BUSINESS ATLANTA endorses Bone's as "<u>the</u> power lunch in Atlanta."

May, 1985: RESTAURANT HOSPITALITY commends Susan DeRose and Richard Lewis, the owners of Bone's and Trotters, as Atlanta's "two most innovative restaurateurs."

June 27, 1985: Pearls Fish Cafe, the third gem in Liberty House's crown of achievement, opens its doors.

July, 1985: THE ATLANTA JOURNAL/CONSTITUTION cheers Liberty House partners DeRose and Lewis in a feature article, and makes special note of Pearls as Atlanta's "hottest new dining spot."

August, 1985: ATLANTA BUSINESS CHRONICLE compliments Bone's, Trotters and Pearls as offering "a dining trilogy unsurpassed."

September, 1985: CREATIVE LOAFING says "Quality draws quality . . . Pearls is packing in the town's classiest crowd."

January, 1986: USA TODAY honors Bone's as one of the nation's "prime spots" for beef.

April, 1986: THE ATLANTA JOURNAL/CONSTITUTION selects Trotters as one of the 10 Atlanta restaurants where "the elite meet to eat."

May, 1986: NATION'S RESTAURANT NEWS names Pearls Fish Cafe as one of the country's "hottest restaurants" in operation today.

October, 1986: Trotters is named "Best Overall Restaurant" at Guest Quarters BEST OF ATLANTA party.

December, 1986: Bone's and Trotters each receive coveted TRAVEL/HOLIDAY Fine Dining Awards for the third year in a row.

December, 1986: THE ST. LOUIS POST DISPATCH SAYS "Pun or no pun, Pearls is a true gem."

January, 1987: Bone's is named the pre-eminent winner in the ATLANTA JOURNAL/CONSTITUTION's "search for the best upscale steakhouse."

Where it all began: From these beginnings at Bone's on Piedmont Road, Liberty House Restaurant Corporation has grown to become Atlanta's premier restaurant company.

Macy's

A Milestone in the Development of Macy's

In 1890 a water well for horses near Five Points was the primary factor for Douglass-Thomas & Company's decision to locate their dry goods store on Whitehall Street.

The years that followed brought about many changes: The horses and watering wells disappeared and the first automobiles clamored down Peachtree Street. And the tiny dry goods store on Whitehall Street kept pace with Atlanta's new-found growth.

Partners of the store changed and so did the name.

By 1901 the store had moved one block north of its original location and was now called Davison-Paxon-Stokes Co. The city of Atlanta evolved with the means and enthusiasm to support an upscale department store, and Davison-Paxon-Stokes Co. prospered because of it.

By 1920, Atlanta had reached the 200,000 population mark and the rest of the country was beginning to take note of the South's fastest growing city. A New York firm by the name of R. H. Macy & Co. took an interest in the store because the owners of Macy's — Jesse, Percy and Herbert Straus — had family roots in Talbotton, Georgia. They decided to join forces with the growing retail enterprise in Atlanta.

R. H. Macy & Co. purchased Davison-Paxon-Stokes Co. on April 25, 1925, and the following day announced plans for a mammoth six-story department store to be built at 180 Peachtree Street, between Henry Grady Hotel (now the site of the Westin Peachtree Plaza Hotel) and Ellis Street.

On the block which previously was the site of four of Atlanta's most fashionable and prestigious homes, the Davison-Paxon-Stokes Co. would replace the glorious

Victorian residences of the past with the most modern and luxurious department store of its time.

General contractor Asa G. Candler erected one of the most fashionable department stores of the day at a grand total of 600,000 square feet and a cost of $6,000,000. It boasted the largest store window expanse in the country, the most modern facilities to be found in any store and a quaint vaudeville theatre which entertained loyal customers for 20 years.

Fine ornamental plastering by Italian artisans echoed the opulence of the age and a 37-foot penthouse, then the highest point in Atlanta, stood as a pinnacle to success to be challenged by ensuing Atlanta businesses. All of Atlanta waited in astonishment for opening day on March 21, 1927.

Davison-Paxon was one of the first businesses to make this northward move, away from the security of the thriving railroad district. As history proved, others would follow their direction.

Seventeen years later, Davison-Paxon ventured even farther and began its advancement in Georgia and into the prospering northern and southern suburbs of the city.

By 1963 the name was shortened to Davison's and in 1985 changed to Macy's. What began as a small store run by 30 employees has developed into a 17-store

chain of over 6,500 employees. Today, the recently renovated Macy's flagship on Peachtree Street is a gleaming milestone of the past, present and future of Atlanta.

Early in 1987 Macy's continuing commitment to downtown Atlanta was recognized when it was presented an award for "outstanding rehabilitation of a non-residential structure for its original use" by the Georgia Trust for Historic Preservation, Inc.

To this day, Macy's has kept pace with Atlanta's progressive growth, always maintaining its tradition of quality and service. And now, as in past years, Macy's is still proud to be a part of Atlanta's life.

Maier & Berkele Jewelers

Interior of the first Maier & Berkele store, 31 Whitehall Street

Three generations of the Maier family (from left): Gordon C. Maier, Executive Vice-President; Frank H. Maier Sr., Chairman of the Board; portrait of founder H. Armin Maier; and Frank H. Maier, Jr., President.

The happy ending to thousands of love stories, the Maier & Berkele diamond engagement ring

Maier & Berkele Jewelers comes to its 100th Anniversary with a sense of Atlanta tradition and celebration. It is the city's oldest jeweler, a hallmark of fine jewelry, and still a family-run business.

Since the enthusiastic young Armin Maier began his jewelry business in 1887, the store has played a part in the history of the City and the State.

The company designed commemorative silver spoons for the Cotton States and International Exposition of 1895 and created a plaque ordered by the Georgia General Assembly to be presented to Theodore Roosevelt. The current Great Seal of Georgia was engraved by a Maier & Berkele employee, J. W. Kreeger.

H. Armin Maier's original jewelry repair business, known as Delkin & Maier, soon underwent a change of company name as well as location to Maier & Berkele at 31 Whitehall Street. The new store had elaborate mahogany showcases, crystal chandeliers, and a new department featuring fine art, china, crystal and giftwares.

Among the most popular items were rings, lavalieres, watches, brooches and fraternal jewelry. Prices were low, usually $1 to $3. In those days a $10 sales was a big one.

The pocket watches of a century ago have given way to fashion timepieces. Maier & Berkele is one of the South's leading dealers of famous Rolex watches.

No gift has been traditionally more special than the Maier & Berkele Diamond Ring, worn with pride by four generations of Atlanta brides. The Bridal Registry showcases the very best china, crystal, and flatware, with a computerized Bridal Service that includes toll-free numbers for brides who expect to receive gifts from out of town.

Today, Maier & Berkele strives to design fashion jewelry with the emphasis on color; precious and semi-precious stones, like tourmaline, amethyst, topaz and exotic varieties of pearl are offered along with extraordinary selections of diamonds.

Many Atlantans choose to update their heirloom jewelry by having the Maier & Berkele custom jewelry designer execute new, original pieces from older settings.

The staff of Maier & Berkele delight in their tradition and service to the Atlanta community. As the special events of the Anniversary celebration unfold, Maier & Berkele employees and customers reflect on what makes an Atlanta tradition.

The president, Frank H. Maier, Jr., served in the industry's highest office, the presidency of the American Gem Society.

The Gemological Institute of America awarded the title of Registered Jeweler to 14 of the firm's employees, the title of Certified Gemologist to seven, and the newest title, Certified Gemologist Appraiser, to one employee. These honors and Maier & Berkele's quality are the foundation of their tradition.

Maier & Berkele starts its second century with sales 30 times larger than they were 30 years ago. It has over 160 employees now as compared to about 20 then. In addition to salespeople, designers, and jewelry makers, the staff includes specialists in appraisals, insurance replacement and corporate sales.

The business philosophy of founder H. Armin Maier is still the guide for daily operations: "The reputation we have earned is something that is our privilege to give. It must never be charged for."

Manry & Heston, Inc.

Board of Directors of Manry & Heston (from left), B. Fred Hedges; Jim D. Cherry, CIC; Jack B. Deal, CIC; James C. Young, CPCU, CIC, and W. Dan McDonald, CPCU.

Entering its second century of service as Atlanta's oldest full-line agency, Manry & Heston, Inc., looks back on a remarkable 100-year record of stability and success.

Because its progress has been based on an enduring philosophy of commitment to service, Manry & Heston today ranks in the top one per cent of all insurance agencies in the United States.

This commitment to customer service was established the day W. F. and J. M. Manry opened for business at 30 Broad Street in downtown Atlanta. Even in 1887, they knew the success of the agency would depend on customer satisfaction based on the service aspect of the insurance business.

Only with such deliberate intent could the founders of the company be sure to consistently fulfill the insurance needs of their clients.

Manry & Heston is still driven by that same philosophy. The thousands of Manry

& Heston clients can be sure of service provided by people who care and are knowledgeable. All service representatives, who are licensed and trained professionals, are assigned specific clients for total service after the sale.

Claims are managed by the same Account Representative who services all other areas of the insurance program. This

individual attention clearly separates Manry & Heston from many other large insurance agencies.

All insurance needs are not the same and a high level of professionalism and expertise is required to determine proper coverage and the correct kinds and amounts of protection. To address the variety of customer needs, Manry & Heston maintains three divisions, each specializing in specific areas.

The personal division covers insurance for home, auto, and personal property.

The commercial division is responsible for business insurance such as liability, property, workers compensation, equipment and business interruption.

The financial service division offers employee insurance benefits including life, health, major medical, dental, pension and profit sharing plans.

Along with this level of professional qualification of employees comes an attitude toward performance. Simply stated, Manry & Heston hires the best people available and insists on high standards of achievement and continued education.

Employees enjoy high morale through constant training, special seminar programs to keep ahead of a fast changing industry and a performance review by management every 6 months. Therefore, Manry & Heston customers work with a well motivated staff ready to serve all their insurance needs.

Manry & Heston offers an unlimited range of financial products and insurance services covering every aspect of both business and family needs. Backed by leading insurance companies with combined assets of over $15 billion, Manry & Heston is able to continue to broaden its position as a leader in the Atlanta insurance community.

As Manry & Heston completes its first century of continuous operation, it recalls a proud tradition of serving three generations of Atlantans and reaffirms its commitment to the opportunities and challenges of the next 100 years.

1895 photograph shows the original office site at 30 Broad Street at the intersection of Marietta Street. The northbound streetcars are headed for the 1895 Exposition at Piedmont Park. In 1898 the agency moved to the Grant Building (shown in the background of this photograph). The agency was located in this area for 79 years.

Marsh & McLennan, Inc.

Marsh & McLennan, Incorporated, the world's largest insurance broker, traces its origins to a small insurance agency founded in Chicago within a month of the great fire which devastated that city in 1871. The firm, like the nation, grew quickly as the 19th Century drew to a close and the 20th Century began.

It was an era of rapid industrial innovation and expansion in America, and the firm's founders, Henry N. Marsh and Donald R. McLennan, were quick to respond to the changing insurance needs of their corporate clients.

It was Marsh who pioneered the concept of the insurance brokerage working on behalf of the client rather than the underwriter. The practice, which required a broker to negotiate with as many underwriters as necessary to fulfill a client's insurance needs, was both radical and timely.

By 1906, Marsh & McLennan was the largest insurance broker in the world, a distinction it continues to hold by a wide margin.

What Messrs. Marsh and McLennan were practicing then—the identification, analysis and transfer of risk—reshaped not only the way clients were served, but the insurance industry itself. This concept proved to be a solid foundation upon which our worldwide insurance transactions and marketing strength are built, and their sound solutions to the complex problems associated with progress attracted an outstanding list of clients.

It wasn't until 1952 that Marsh & McLennan came to Atlanta. Even so, it was the first insurance brokerage to locate in the Southeast. The company chose a proven professional, Frank M. Ridley, to manage the new office.

Ridley opened the Atlanta branch of Marsh & McLennan with a staff of two, counting himself. The first account transferred to the new office was Tuskegee Institute of Alabama. An ascendent Atlanta firm, Haverty Furniture Co., was the first local client.

During Ridley's 15-year tenure, word of the unique service of first analyzing the risks of the client and then finding the best risk transfer mechanism provided by Marsh & McLennan spread throughout business circles in the region, and its Southern client base matured into a broad spread of service and industrial clients, both privately and publicly-owned.

Ridley was succeeded in 1967 by D. Robert Marsden. Under Marsden's leadership, Marsh & McLennan continued to expand throughout the Southeast. Today, the office is headed by managing director H. Cartan Clarke.

In 1982, a worldwide insurance brokerage was formed, merging all brokerage operations into Marsh & McLennan, Incorporated, with 11,500 employees operating out of 268 offices in 80 nations. The Atlanta office alone employs more than 100 persons.

Throughout its history, Marsh & McLennan has been an innovator in the insurance industry, pioneering coverages that made possible many of the technological and economic developments of the last 100 years. For example, more than 40 years ago it devised the first umbrella liability insurance form and, almost a century after its birth, the firm brokered the first coverage for telecommunications satellites.

Marsh & McLennan was the first American insurance broker to establish strong, continuing ties with Lloyd's of London and remains the world's largest supplier of insurance business to Lloyd's.

In 1962, Marsh & McLennan, Incorporated, went public. In 1969, it became a subsidiary of the parent company, Marsh & McLennan Companies, Inc., which has grown into a corporate family of separately managed subsidiaries with an enormous range of financial services.

Today, insurance brokerage challenges are tougher than ever. Property and casualty markets have been affected by high costs, restricted coverage and lack of capacity. The number of underwriters for large unpredictable risks—such as those faced by the space, energy and chemical industries—has shrunk rapidly. Yet, the true test of performance of an insurance broker is the ability to deliver in difficult and challenging times.

In 1986, for example, Marsh & McLennan negotiated and placed just less than $10 billion of premium for clients worldwide. Moreover, Marsh & McLennan has guided its clients through every market turn since 1871.

Service to the client has been the hallmark of Marsh & McLennan since Henry N. Marsh and Donald R. McLennan formed a partnership that continues to thrive today.

Henry N. Marsh

Donald R. McLennan

Mingledorff's, Inc.

Joe Budreau was a French-Canadian native of Quebec. He made his fortune in the 1930's as a potato broker in Savannah, GA. But he never did get used to the heat and humidity of Georgia's coastlands.

In 1939 Mr. Budreau decided to build his dream home on Abercorn Street in Savannah. But he wanted it cool and comfortable. He wrote to the Carrier Air Conditioning Company in Syracuse, NY, a firm started by Dr. Willis H. Carrier, the inventor of air conditioning, and explained his problem.

There were not many air conditioned homes around in those days, so Carrier was immediately interested. The company sent an engineer to Savannah to see Mr. Budreau and look over the house plans. Mr. Budreau asked his son-in-law, Lee Mingledorff, a recent graduate of Georgia Tech, to sit in on the meeting.

By the time the three men had finished, an agreement was made to air condition Mr. Budreau's new home, and Lee Mingledorff had agreed to be Carrier's representative in the southeastern part of our state. It was a fortunate beginning for what is now one of Atlanta's largest privately held corporations: Mingledorff's, Inc.

Mr. Budreau's home at 2909 Abercorn Street is still standing; its Carrier air conditioning system is still running. Mingledorff's, Inc., now occupying a 116,000 square foot building in the Peachtree Corners area, is also still going strong, having become a major distributor for Carrier and other air conditioning products with sales of $70 million in 1986.

Originally a contracting firm which designed and installed air conditioning and heating systems, Mingledorff's, Inc., like many other businesses, became dormant during the World War II years.

The company was re-organized in 1946 as a direct Carrier distributor/contractor with responsibility for sales in the southern half of the state. In 1948 Carrier, recognizing the growing need for air conditioning equipment, requested that its distributor/contractors form wholesale departments and establish air conditioning dealers in their territories to meet the demand for keeping Georgians cool.

In 1958 the expanding air conditioning business brought about another change for Mingledorff's, Inc.; this one was decided, literally, by the toss of a coin. Carrier now wanted its representatives to be either contractors or wholesalers.

Lee Mingledorff flipped a coin with another major Carrier distributor/contractor and won the wholesaling end of the business. The win required locating in Atlanta, so the company sold its Savannah contracting and service organization and made the move, assuming responsibility for wholesaling Carrier equipment in most of Georgia and parts of Alabama and South Carolina.

Lee Mingledorff did not come to Atlanta; he stayed in Savannah. He was, in fact, that city's mayor, a post he filled from 1954 through 1960. The former Executive Vice President, Ed Eckles, was named President and Lee Mingledorff became Chairman of the Board.

Locating in Atlanta and becoming a wholesaler also meant hiring a number of new people. Among them was a young salesman named Bob Kesterton. Once again it was a fortunate event. Bob Kesterton became Dealer Sales Manager in 1960.

In 1969, when Ed Eckles went into semi-retirement as Vice Chairman of the Board, Bob Kesterton was named as President. He still heads the company, having guided it through a period of rapid expansion and growth and making it into the second largest independent Carrier distributor in the nation. In the years 1983 and 1984, Mingledorff's, Inc. won Carrier's top award for distribution excellence.

The primary goal established by Mingledorff's, Inc., as an equipment wholesaler was to develop a strong base of dealer/contractors throughout its sales territory. Those dealers were needed, since the air conditioning business was a rapidly growing one and, with the new construction boom of the 1960's and 1970's, a central cooling system had become almost as necessary as a heating system.

Today that goal has been accomplished, as dealer/contractors representing Carrier can be found in almost every Georgia community.

Air conditioning for homes is only a part of the business. Initially it was a very small part, but today residential equipment sales accounts for about 60% of the company's dollar volume in sales. In addition, Mingledorff's, Inc. sells the Carrier equipment needed to air condition commercial, industrial and institutional buildings.

The growth of the air conditioning business can be dramatically illustrated by comparing the sales volumes achieved by Mingledorff's, Inc. in the years since it became an Atlanta-based wholesaler. In 1958 sales are approximately $2,000,000; for 1987 they are predicted to exceed $75,000,000.

The home of Joe Budreau at 2909 Abercorn Street in Savannah. Mr. Budreau's desire for home cooling led to the formation of a Carrier distributorship in Georgia by his son-in-law, Lee Mingledorff.

Two relocations were required during this time. From the original office and warehouse space at 215 Chester Avenue, S.E., Mingledorff's, Inc. moved to 159 Armour Drive, N.E., in 1961. In 1985 another relocation was made to the present facilities at 6675 Jones Mill Court in Norcross.

The company currently serves over 3,000 customers. About 600 of those customers are dealers and mechanical contractors purchasing equipment; the remainder are those who purchase parts.

Mingledorff's, Inc., now employs more than 130 people, among them being Joe Budreau's grandson, L. Budreau "Bud" Mingledorff, who serves as Sales Administration Manager and Corporate Secretary.

There are fully staffed sales offices in Macon and Savannah, and the distributorship operates eight parts stores, five in the Metro Atlanta area and others in Macon, Augusta and Savannah. There are also two equipment warehousing facilities in Atlanta to handle peak summer inventories which currently may go as high as $18,000,000.

In addition to the Carrier line, Mingledorff's, Inc., represents over 40 manufacturers of products related to air conditioning, heating and ventilating. Its services include sales, sales assistance, advertising and sales promotion programs, engineering, service training, business management assistance, technical help and parts supply.

As simply stated by the company's president, Bob Kesterton, the growth and success of Mingledorff's, Inc., has been built on a marketing philosophy that "encourages a very close-knit, professional relationship between the manufacturer, the distributor, and the dealer, thereby assuring customer satisfaction with both product and service."

The modern, 116,000 square foot building currently occupied by Mingledorff's, Inc. at 6675 Jones Mill Court in Norcross. The building includes offices, a parts store and 85,000 square feet of warehouse space.

H. M. Patterson & Son

H. M. Patterson & Son, as a business, came into being in Atlanta in 1880 when the late H. M. Patterson, who came to Atlanta from Ohio as a very young man the year before, purchased the business of George R. Boaz.

At that time the business was located at 16 Loyd Street, the old Markham House block.

In 1896 the building in which the business was located was destroyed by fire and Mr. Patterson moved to 32 Peachtree Street, NE, at Five Points, the present location of the William-Oliver Building.

He operated successfully in this location until 1904, by which time the town of Atlanta had grown to such an extent that the Five Points area became quite congested.

In 1904 Mr. Patterson constructed a building at 110 N. Forsyth Street, which was next to the Carnegie Library. This was the first building in the South erected especially for a Funeral Directing Business, having in it a chapel, state rooms, reception rooms, offices, adequate garage space and every modern convenience of that day.

In 1905 Mr. Patterson took his son, Frederick W. Patterson, into the business as a partner, and the firm became known as H. M. Patterson & Son. The firm operated in this location until 1928.

At that time Mr. Fred Patterson, having become head of the firm following the death of his father in 1923, decided that the downtown area was entirely unsuited for the proper operation of a funeral business.

He began plans for the construction of Spring Hill, to be located at 1020 Spring Street, NW, this street being one of the main north and south arteries of Atlanta. This magnificent structure, known as one of the finest buildings of its kind in the entire country, was built as a memorial to the late H. M. Patterson.

It stands today as an emblem of the heritage of service to mankind so strongly exemplified in the life of this great Atlantan.

In 1961 Mr. Fred Patterson built two more facilities: Oglethorpe Hill near Oglethorpe University in north Atlanta, and Cascade Hill at Utoy Springs and Cascade Road on the southwest side of the city.

These locations were chosen to meet the needs of the people of this ever-growing metropolitan city. Thus two fine new mortuaries, with the same elegant surroundings, and the same high standards of service, as Spring Hill.

The high ideals of service, first established by H. M. Patterson and continued by his son Fred W. Patterson (deceased 1972), Brannon B. Lesesne (deceased 1981) and Dan Allen (deceased 1984), are successfully continued today by Mr. "Fred's" daughter, Lee Patterson-Allen, and her sons, Dan, Fred, Hugh and Jack.

We pledge to continue these standards of service to the Greater Atlanta community.

Original firm established in 1880 at 16 Loyd St., now Central Ave., was known as the old Markham House Block.

32 Peachtree St., NE, at Five Points, from 1896 to 1904

110 N. Forsyth St., next to the old Carnegie Library, 1904-1928.

Phoenix Communications, Inc.

Phoenix Communications, Inc., and its affiliated companies, Phoenix Periodicals, Inc., and Market Impact, Inc., are engaged in creative printing, publishing, institutional marketing and multi-media communications.

The Phoenix group is recognized nationally as an organization that seeks any challenge involving the printed word.

The company was founded in the mid-1970's. In 1977, Mendel Segal and Cary Rosenthal brought to the fledgling firm the management techniques, extended client base and necessary investment capital to set in motion what has become one of the premier graphic arts companies in the region.

The Phoenix team is led by Mendel Segal, chairman of the board; Cary Rosenthal, president; Mackey Whitmire, executive vice president; and Joseph Segal, secretary-treasurer and president of the publishing company, Phoenix Periodicals.

Their combined talents make them uniquely qualified. Mendel Segal's 50 years of leadership in the printing industry, coupled with his reputation as an author and the person who developed the "creative printing" concept, give Phoenix stability.

Cary Rosenthal's extensive background in marketing and sales management, his reputation as a public speaker, and his growing responsibility in the printing industry, demonstrated by his recent election as president of the Printing Association of Georgia, give Phoenix viability.

Joseph Segal, with his strong academic background as a *magna cum laude* undergraduate and a Master in Business Administration from the Emory University School of Business, his long experience in financial planning and management, as well as his

development of Phoenix Periodicals, Inc. — with its current roster of three monthly and three annual publications — give Phoenix diversity.

Mackey Whitmire, a leader in the complex world of high volume printing sales, gives Phoenix depth.

The Phoenix creative department, maintaining a permanent staff of writers, art directors, designers, production artists, and typesetters, is capable of fulfilling the needs of communications in print.

Developed originally to serve the marketing needs of educational institutions throughout the U.S.A., the creative staff also aids in the production of annual reports, industrial catalogs, manuals for the high-tech industry and promotional literature such as brochures, direct mail publications, posters, magazines, house organs and corporate identity programs.

Phoenix Communications enjoys an excellent reputation as a sophisticated purveyor of printing services to corporations, educational institutions, advertising agencies, government agencies, financial institutions, real estate developers and small businesses.

With an employee roster approaching 125 (up from 17 in a period of eight years), with computer-aided typesetting, state-of-the-art plate-making equipment, a convenient mix of multi-dimensional bindery services, this growing company has the balance needed to serve a diverse clientele.

From the kernel of an idea to the final delivery of the printed product, Phoenix Communications demonstrates how a full service "under-one-roof" creative organization can change the perception of a printing company in every sense of the word.

This photography, representative of the many elements which go into the creative printing process, hangs in the lobby of the Phoenix Communications building. It carries the motto, "Creative Minds At Work For You."

PIEDMONT HOSPITAL

1968 Peachtree Road, NW
Atlanta, Georgia 30309

Piedmont
Sanatorium
Capitol Avenue
1905–1957

Piedmont
Hospital
Peachtree Road
1957–1987

The hospital Atlantans have
traditionally relied on for
generations of quality care.

The Portman Companies

The Portman Companies and Atlanta have grown side by side during the past four decades.

The history of Atlanta's development is punctuated by dates which are significant to the growth of The Portman Companies from a two-man architectural firm in 1953 to a group of 10 companies with over 800 employees and projects throughout the world.

Founded by John C. Portman, Jr., the firm merged in 1956 with the firm of Griffith Edwards and was known as Edwards and Portman until Edwards' retirement in 1968; at that time it became John Portman & Associates.

The early years were filled with a variety of architectural projects, including over a dozen schools in the city of Atlanta and DeKalb County, the Dana Fine Arts Center at Agnes Scott and Georgia Tech's Infirmary.

ATLANTA MARKET CENTER: 1961 marked a major development for Atlanta and The Portman Companies. It was in this year that JP&A completed the Atlanta Merchandise Mart, which emphatically established Atlanta as the dominant market center for the southeast. The original 1 million square foot facility was doubled in size in 1968 and expanded again in 1979 with the construction of the Atlanta Apparel Mart.

The Merchandise Mart added another 600,000 square feet in 1985 to accommodate the contract furnishings industry. In 1987, construction began on INFORUM, a 1.5 million square foot market facility for the telecommunications industry.

The total complex, now known as the Atlanta Market Center, generates 27 per cent of the tourism trade, or over 300,000 visitors to Atlanta annually. Studies calculate that the Market Center has a $142.7 million annual impact on Atlanta's economy.

The second significant development was the beginning of Peachtree Center. This, the first of Atlanta's mixed-use complexes, has grown to include seven office towers, totalling 2.7 million square feet, three major hotels, the Atlanta Market Center and over 200,000 square feet of retail space.

Portman designed, developed and manages Peachtree Center; it reflects the Portman commitment to the strength and vitality of Atlanta's Central Business District.

HOTELS: No buildings, however, have received more acclaim at Peachtree Center than the hotels. In 1967 Portman revolutionized contemporary hotel design with the Hyatt Regency Atlanta. Its 22-story atrium, glass-cabbed elevator and revolving Polaris restaurant was a dramatic departure from the typical hotels of the day. It has since become a prototype of successful hotel design.

In 1976 Atlanta added to its skyline America's s tallest hotel — the 743-foot tall Westin Peachtree Plaza.

In 1985 the completion of the 1,674-room Marriott Marquis gave Atlanta the largest convention hotel in the Southeast.

THE EIGHTIES: The Eighties marked the firm's first major venture into the suburbs. Northpark Town Center, a 100-acre mixed-use complex at Georgia 400 and Abernathy Road, will bring focus to Atlanta's ever-expanding suburban office/retail market. The pedestrian-oriented complex is creating a town-like center for north Atlanta.

Two buildings at Emory University have been completed which have significantly enhanced the quality of student life there. The George W. Woodruff Physical Education Building opened in 1983 and the R. Howard Dobbs University Center, in 1986.

As Atlanta has developed internationally, so have The Portman Companies. The two-man architectural firm has grown to include Portman Properties, Portman Barry Investments, Inc., Portman Overseas, the Atlanta Market Center, Portman Hotel Company, Peachtree Center Management Company, Atlasia, Peachtree International and Portman Capital Company.

These companies combine a thorough knowledge of the marketplace with a commitment to quality service. Meeting the demands of the complex and competitive world of real estate, The Portman Companies are proud to be a part of Atlanta's growth.

Peachtree Center, Atlanta

Marriott Marquis Hotel, Atlanta

Hyatt Regency Hotel, Atlanta

Atlanta Apparel Mart

Price Waterhouse

Price Waterhouse, the international public accounting and consulting firm, began its commitment to the Southeast in 1928 with the opening of its Atlanta office by Alabama native Thornton Goodloe Douglas.

Today, the Atlanta practice has two offices, located at 3700 First Atlanta Tower and in the 200 Galleria Parkway building, and is the headquarters for Price Waterhouse's Southeast Region.

From a 16-person office serving all of Georgia, Alabama, Florida, Tennessee and North and South Carolina in 1955, the Atlanta office has grown to a staff approaching 300 professionals, including 18 partners, serving Georgia clients.

John P. O'Brien became partner-in-charge of the Atlanta office in July of 1987, replacing Edward C. Harris who had charted the office's growth for the preceding decade.

O'Brien came to Atlanta in 1985 as partner-in-charge of Price Waterhouse's Southeast Region offices, establishing Atlanta as the headquarters for the region. Price Waterhouse's Southeast Region now includes 10 offices in Georgia, Alabama, Tennessee and North and South Carolina, with 40 partners and a staff of 700.

Price Waterhouse had its origins with the London, England, accounting practice established by Samuel Lowell Price in 1849. The practice, which was expanded in 1865 to include William Hopkins Holyland and Edwin Waterhouse, was principally devoted to liquidations, bankruptcies, arbitrations and some auditing in its early years.

The Industrial Revolution created a need for more sophisticated accounting methods and innovative financial management techniques in a variety of industries worldwide. As the need grew, so did Price Waterhouse.

An increasing amount of work for American companies on the London Stock Exchange led to the establishment of the first U.S. office in New York in 1890. The firm's reputation spread, additional offices were opened and the separate U.S. firm was established in 1895.

In 1986, Price Waterhouse worldwide had over 28,000 staff in more than 360 offices in 95 countries and territories, serving leading businesses around the globe.

The U.S. firm's prominence is highlighted by its position as auditor of the largest percentages of *Fortune 500* clients, but the backbone of the Price Waterhouse practice — in Atlanta and worldwide — is the medium-size and small business.

Clients of the Atlanta offices are involved in virtually every kind of commercial endeavor, including the agribusiness, banking, communications, transportation, manufacturing, insurance, real estate and many others. The office works with a growing number of clients having international operations, as well as with government agencies and nonprofit organizations.

To address the unique needs of Georgia's entrepreneurs, the Atlanta practice's Galleria office has special Comprehensive Professional Service practitioners dedicated to serving smaller businesses and specially trained in taxation, business systems and business planning to handle their special needs.

Price Waterhouse's partners and staff are committed to their community, serving leading roles in a variety of civic activities and public service endeavors in Atlanta and Georgia.

Through its history of public service and professional accounting, auditing, tax, management advisory services and service to small businesses, Price Waterhouse has distinguished itself as a growing and important partner in Atlanta's business community.

John O'Brien, Partner-In-Charge, Atlanta Office

Bob Watson, Partner-In-Charge, Tax Services

Wayne Pace, Partner-In-Charge, Audit Services

John Fridley, Partner-In-Charge, Management Consulting Services

Rich's

Every Thanksgiving evening, in a traditional finale to a day spent with family and friends, all Atlanta and vicinity usher in the Christmas season with the lighting of the Great Tree on Rich's Crystal Bridge.

Rich's has a long history of community involvement in Atlanta.

Since the store was founded in 1867 by Morris Rich, it has played two roles in the city — that of retail business and that of a philanthropic institution. Atlantans feel a sense of patriotism to the store — civic pride for a local success story.

The original store opened on Whitehall Street with five employees. By 1924 Rich's had 75 departments and 800 employees and moved to 45 Broad Street, the present site of Rich's Downtown. Today Rich's is an internationally recognized retailer with 14 stores in the metropolitan Atlanta area and a total of 20 stores in the Southeast.

It has always been the philosophy of the store that people are more important than things. In the 1930's when the City of Atlanta was too broke to pay the school-teachers, Walter Rich, nephew of Morris Rich, suggested that the teachers be paid in scrip which Rich's would cash.

In 1945 when the army's time-locked vault would not open to pay Fort McPherson troops who were being discharged over the weekend, Rich's advanced the money for the payroll so the soldiers could go home.

After World War II, Richard H. Rich, "Mr. Dick," joined his grandfather's store. Many changes took place. The Rich Foundation was established in 1943. This foundation built the Emory Business School, donated a radio station, WABE, to the city, built a computer center at Georgia Tech, an outpatient clinic at Georgia Baptist Hospital and a wing at St. Joseph's Infirmary.

Continuing in the tradition of the founding fathers, the store's philosophy has not changed. Rich's maintains its reputation as a distinguished retailer known for its outstanding customer service, liberal credit policies and fair price convictions.

Since 1948 Rich's has ushered in the Christmas season with the annual "Lighting of the Great Tree" atop the four-story Crystal Bridge of the Downtown Store. This event is celebrated by several hundred thousand people each Thanksgiving Night and is televised in a one-hour program.

Rich's Fashionata, a major Fall fashion presentation for Atlanta since 1956, has raised thousands of dollars for cultural, health and civic organizations.

In 1982, in response to a critical need, Rich's, in conjunction with the Atlanta Public Schools and Exodus, initiated the Rich's Academy. Rich's Academy is an alternative high school program for youths not successful in a usual school setting. Located in the Downtown Rich's store, over 100 students attend daily.

The Downtown Child Development Center is an example of Atlanta businesses working together to solve a modern-day problem.

Five major employers in the downtown area including the Atlanta Journal and Constitution, The Federal Reserve Bank of Atlanta, First Atlanta Corporation, Georgia-Pacific Corporation and Rich's opened the Downtown Child Development Center in January, 1986. The center is a non-profit child care facility located on the Plaza Level of Rich's Downtown.

To further emphasize its faith in the future of Atlanta, Rich's recently undertook a multi-million dollar renovation of the Downtown Atlanta store built in 1924 by Philip Shutze. The renovation was complete in Spring, 1987, the year of Atlanta's sesquicentennial.

Rich's is intricately woven into the fabric of Atlanta's past and continues to shape her future. Rich's executives are actively involved in Central Atlanta Progress and have given leadership support to the Underground Atlanta Project. There is a feeling of pride for the city, for the accomplishments that have been made, and an optimism and faith in the future.

Artist's conception of Morris Rich's original store which opened on Whitehall Street in 1867.

Selig Enterprises

No story on Atlanta real estate and development would be complete without mention of the saga of Selig Enterprises, Inc., which started its history in 1942 as CMS Realty Company, named after its major stockholder, Caroline Massell Selig.

The name was changed to Selig Enterprises, Inc., in 1968 when Simon S. Selig, Jr., and his son, S. Stephen Selig, III, the current chairman and president, took over the complete management of its operation.

CMS Realty Company was founded by Ben J. Massell, father of Caroline M. Selig, and operated by him until his death in 1962. Massell was known to all Atlanta as "the father of Atlanta's skyline."

He was called "a one man boom" by the late Atlanta Mayor William B. Hartsfield. During his lifetime, Ben Massell was responsible for construction of more than 1,000 buildings of all sizes from one-story, single-tenant structures to today's Merchandise Mart on Peachtree Street.

When Ben Massell died in 1962, son-in-law Simon Selig divided his time between the Massell Company and Selig Chemical Industries, a budding giant in the chemical specialties field. The dual responsibility was too much.

Selig sold the chemical company to National Service Industries and went full time with CMS Realty Company, the operating company Massell had started. Upon his death, Massell's holdings were divided between the Massell Company (then operated by Ben Massell, Jr.) and CMS Realty Company.

CMS Realty Company, under Simon Selig's direction, eventually reacquired all of the properties which were divided at the time of Massell's death. It was Selig's guidance, leadership and business acumen that enabled CMS Realty (ultimately Selig Enterprises, Inc.) through countless acquisitions and new developments, to spark the type of growth which had not been seen in the Atlanta real estate community in many years.

Now under the direction of S. Stephen Selig, III, Selig Enterprises continues to build on a well established reputation as a leader in the real estate market. This burgeoning real estate empire, a constellation of office buildings, industrial complexes and shopping centers, not only polka-dots the Atlanta landscape but stretches as well from North Carolina to Tennessee and from Florida to Puerto Rico.

Selig's portfolio of over 200 properties remains one of the largest and most diverse in the Southeast. The company's dramatic growth is shown by the increase in the number of properties developed or acquired over the past several years.

Selig Enterprises today encompasses the full spectrum of retail, office and industrial real estate holdings. Selig's corporate headquarters are located in one of its modern office buildings at 1100 Spring Street, NW, where its senior staff consists of officers heading up the financial, leasing, administrative, development, construction, property management and appraisal operations.

Selig Enterprises, Inc.'s, success "key" is growth — growing with Atlanta and helping Atlanta grow. Selig's proven commitment to the growth and prosperity of Atlanta are also reflected by Stephen Selig's active participation in the arts, civic affairs, and charitable and political activities in the area. Community responsibility and awareness have made Stephen Selig one of Atlanta's most prominent civic leaders.

S. Stephen Selig, III

The Seydel Companies

Founded in Atlanta in 1919 by Dr. Paul B. Seydel and later joined by his father-in-law Dr. Vassar Woolley, The Seydel Companies is distinguished by both a long history of family management and employee participation in ownership.

Founded as Seydel-Thomas and later renamed Seydel-Woolley & Company, the process chemical manufacturer prospered as the first to be located in the Southeast specializing in serving the textile industry.

The founders' sons, Vassar Woolley and Paul and John Seydel, took terms at the helm during a steady growth course that kept the firm at the forefront of its field for 50 years. John then spun off the family's Seydel International group to its employees, including his son Scott, and merged the domestic firm with AZ Products of Lakeland, FL, to form AZS Corporation which he chaired.

In an interesting twist, AZS Corporation then merged with Toyo Soda of Tokyo, Japan, in 1980 and five years later the Seydel family bought back the Atlanta-based Seydel-Woolley group.

The Seydel Companies now comprises the Seydel International and Seydel-Woolley subsidiaries as well as several other domestic and international subsidiaries. Additionally, the firm is involved as licensor and joint-venture partner with firms manufacturing its chemicals and machinery in two dozen international locations.

Scott Seydel presides and is joined by Raimundo Mejia as president of Seydel International; Steve Adams, president of Seydel-Woolley & Company; Claude Mayfield, president of SICO, S.A.; Bill Letbetter, president of International Precision, and Lynn Rose as corporate treasurer.

In May, 1987, The Seydel Companies completed its new corporate office building on the Chattahoochee River and the Seydel-Woolley group initiated construction of a new polymer production unit in north Georgia.

In the same year Seydel International commissioned manufacturing units in Korea, Africa and India using Seydel's processes, and Industrial Precision began worldwide marketing of a patented chemical application device that reduces yarn processing costs significantly.

The group's SEYCO® process chemicals are now manufactured in Europe, Asia, Latin America, Australia and Africa for distribution in more than 50 countries, and are employed in the manufacture of textiles, paper, paint and adhesives.

Scott insists that his grandmother, Mildred Seydell, is the more newsworthy family member. As an international journalist, she interviewed such international leaders as Benito Mussolini and Winston Churchill for the old Atlanta Georgian newspaper and the Hearst syndicate.

It was the proceeds from the sale of her 1926 Buick which helped purchase husband Paul's first manufacturing plant.

Vassar Woolley, Jr.

John R. Seydel, Jr., Chairman of the Board

Paul B. Seydel, Sr.

First Seydel-Woolley plant, financed partly from the sale of Mrs. Mildred Seydel's 1926 Buick.

220

The Sharp Boylston Companies

The Sharp Boylston Companies, Atlanta's oldest real estate firm, was founded in 1881, the same year that the city was preparing to host the International Cotton Exposition, the most significant cultural and commercial event in Atlanta's brief history.

The Cotton Exposition was destined to focus national attention on Atlanta as the capital of the New South, effectively underscoring the city's growing influence as a major transportation, distribution, and manufacturing center.

It was during this auspicious period in Atlanta's history, a full five years before the first glass of Coca-Cola was served at Jacob's Pharmacy, that Sir John J. Woodside founded the real estate company which, after a series of mergers and acquisitions, would become known as The Sharp Boylston Companies.

Since its founding 106 years ago, Sharp Boylston has been involved in some of Atlanta's most significant real estate transactions including:

- The original land sale underneath the Galleria office complex in northwest Atlanta
- The original land sales underneath the Circle 75 Office Park in Cobb County
- Original land sales underneath Akers Mill Square, Emerson Center and the Parkway 75 mixed-use development
- The $17,000,000 real estate exchange whereby both Georgia Power Company and Genuine Parts Co. acquired their present corporate headquarters locations.

In June of 1986, Richard R. Felker, President of Richard Felker Company and one of Atlanta's most successful real estate investors, acquired Sharp Boylston from Marion Blackwell and Warren Chilton, two of the city's most respected investment and land brokerage specialists, both of whom remained with Sharp Boylston as senior vice presidents.

Richard Felker has long been active in Atlanta business and civic affairs, having served as organizer and director of several banks, director of Central Atlanta Progress and the Atlanta Chamber of Commerce, president and director of a number of industry associations and a trustee of Darlington School.

As Sharp Boylston's Chairman and Chief Executive Office, Mr. Felker immediately began laying the foundation for a new period of growth and expansion, based upon a commitment to provide a full range of brokerage and management services to the firm's clients.

In January of 1987, David S. Branch joined the company as only the sixth president in the firm's 106-year history, after a distinguished brokerage career at Coldwell Banker, where he ranked as either the number one or number two producer for four straight years.

Mr. Branch has been involved in the negotiations of some of Atlanta's most significant real estate deals, including the ground lease beneath IBM's new 50-story midtown headquarters, the assemblage of Homart Development Co.'s Securities Centre office complex in Buckhead, and the original land sale beneath Cadillac Fairview's new Signature Center development near the I-75/I-285 intersection, as well as a number of major corporate and regional headquarters relocations for such tenants as Merrill Lynch, General Dynamics, Technicon Data Systems and Southern Electric International.

The Sharp Boylston Companies, after being located within a four block radius of the Equitable Building downtown for over 106 years, are now relocating to Buckhead in order to be more centrally located to expanding markets along the north perimeter, while still remaining close to the

dynamic central business district and the rapidly expanding midtown market.

Sharp Boylston provides its clients with a full range of office, industrial, retail, acreage and investment properties brokerage. Special areas of emphasis include high level tenant representation for corporate and regional headquarters relocations, land assemblages, and the sale of major investment properties.

The Sharp Boylston Management Co., under the leadership of David Archer, currently manages a portfolio of over $130 million of commercial real estate and is actively expanding its asset management capabilities.

As Atlanta prepares to meet the civic, political and commercial challenges of the 1990s, The Sharp Boylston Companies are preparing to meet the challenges inherent in its commitment to remain one of the city's preeminent privately-held real estate brokerage firms.

Richard R. Felker (left), Chairman and Chief Executive Officer, and David S. Branch, President and Chief Operating Officer

Smith Ace Hardware

Smith Hardware Company in 1935

William Commins and Robert Nemo

As Atlanta experienced growth and change, so did Smith Hardware.

In 1935, when Smith Hardware opened its doors, it began with the philosophy of giving its customers what they wanted. Horse collars, cotton scales, belly bands, pitch forks and cast iron skillets were all standard stock at that time.

Today, Smith Hardware still gives its customers what they want, though the inventory has changed somewhat. Lawn mowers, generators, power tools, brass fixtures, food processors, German crystal and greeting cards all stand as silent testimonial to the change.

Started in a small building off Decatur Square, Smith Hardware was eventually moved to a 7,500 square foot facility on East College Avenue, and enlarged to 25,000 square feet in the early 1970s. In 1974 it was purchased by William Commins and Robert Nemo, both longtime residents of Atlanta.

They saw the growth that the city was experiencing and the need for a hardware store that could be a vital part of that growth. The store on East College Avenue was further expanded to 35,000 square feet, more than quadruple its original size.

Four other Smith Hardware stores were added in Buckhead, East Cobb, Marietta and Alpharetta, bringing the-store-that-caters-to-its-customers within easy reach of most Atlantans. This growth pattern is continuing with a new store currently in the planning stages.

Location, product lines and personnel have changed in the last 50 years, but not so Smith Hardware's attitude toward its customers.

"We sell over 30,000 different items — almost anything you need — but what really sells the customers on us is service. It's even a part of our logo. Home repairs have gotten more complicated and fewer people have the confidence to try them, which is why we staff our stores with experts who can answer their questions and help them solve their problems," says Robert Nemo. "Our staff greets customers, answers their questions, special orders hard to find items and even helps them carry purchases to their cars. That kind of concern is what makes us different."

Another difference is the neighborhood store attitude. The stores are not mass merchandised; each store buys for its own customers in its particular location. One store may be frequented by large numbers of contractors and maintenance personnel, so its merchandise runs more towards professional equipment. Another store may cater to a more rural community, and thus carry animal feed and farm supplies. That way customers get what they are looking for.

Apparently this attitude has paid off. (Over a million customers visit Smith Hardware every year.)

In addition, the stores have been recognized repeatedly as The Best of Atlanta in annual polls by "Atlanta" magazine, listed as The Best of Cobb County by "Inside Cobb Magazine," and referenced in several articles in the "Journal/Constitution."

So, as Atlanta continues to grow and prosper, Atlantans can rest assured that Smith Hardware will be right there with personal attention and quality products.

Children
Of Atlanta

Sisters Israella (left) and Rebecca Ella Solomons (circa 1860): The latter becomes Mrs. Julian M. Alexander (whose son Henry was one of the lawyers defending Leo Frank in his 1913 murder trial). She was also the paternal grandmother of present-day architect Cecil Alexander.

A young, unidentified woman of the 1880s

Southern Bell

In 1947, directory assistance operators at Southern Bell's office on Ivy Street in Atlanta located directory information on vertical index files. Today, directory assistance operators use computerized records instead.

When Alexander Graham Bell invented the telephone on March 10, 1876, the South's economy was slowly beginning to recover from the ravages of the Civil War.

Farming remained the chief source of income, cotton and tobacco being the two principal crops. Manufacturing plants were few, and many articles in common use were produced by hand. Travel between cities was difficult and slow.

Communication, though, was in somewhat better shape. Western Union Telegraph Company had already extended its system to most of the South's larger cities. Nevertheless, the largely rural South hungered for a more personal means of communication.

Atlanta's first telephone was installed in 1877, connecting, on a private basis, the Western and Atlantic freight depot with Durand's restaurant in the Union Passenger Station. The first telephone exchange opened for business in Atlanta in 1879.

Southern Bell's story, however, began a bit later in 1879, when a group of investors negotiated a contract among themselves, Western Union and the National Bell company to spread the benefits of Bell's invention to the southeastern United States.

The new company, Southern Bell Telephone & Telegraph Company, officially opened for business in 1880 with offices in Virginia, North Carolina, South Carolina and Alabama. Its top management remained in New York, where it was incorporated.

Southern Bell opened offices in Atlanta, later to be the site of the company's headquarters, in 1882. By 1884, the company had approximately 400 subscrib-

ers in Atlanta and one long distance line, extending to Decatur. This was the beginning of an extensive system of intercity lines terminating in Atlanta.

During these early years, though, Southern Bell concentrated almost exclusively on local service, partly as a result of the lack of long distance amplification equipment. Even at that, connections were not always assured.

Twice during the 1880s, most of the telephone equipment in Atlanta was destroyed — once by ice storm, the other time by fire. Later, in 1892, construction was begun on a fireproof building for the

Atlanta exchange. And none too soon. Four months before completion of the new office, the old one burned to the ground.

The next day, one of the earliest tributes paid to telephone operators by newspapers was printed in The Atlanta Constitution: "Service was rendered until blazes burst into the operating room. The operators even informed parties making inquiries as to the location of the fire that the telephone building was the place."

Growth and expansion, with a strong emphasis on good public relations and quality service, characterized Southern Bell's formative years. Southern Bell listened to its customers. Young boys, who hitherto had handled the switching of telephone calls, were replaced by young women. Customers had complained that the boy operators were too excitable and used foul language. Women, it was hoped, would prove more appropriately genteel.

In recognition of the growth and of the need for closer involvement in the company's day-to-day activities, the company's base of operations was moved from New York to Atlanta in 1909. By 1912, Southern Bell served a nine-state region comprised of Alabama, Florida, Georgia, Kentucky, Louisiana, Mississippi, North Carolina, South Carolina and Tennessee.

In 1917, America entered World War I, and in 1941 the country joined its Allies again following the Japanese attack on Pearl Harbor.

Southern Bell responded to world conflicts by sending vast numbers of its work force into the armed services. While its men fought abroad, Southern Bell people on the home front established emergency phone service in local military

Southern Bell used company cars to test new mobile equipment. Visible at left in the background is Atlanta's Hurt Building, the company's headquarters until 1981.

The construction of Southern Bell's new headquarters in Atlanta was a major undertaking. The 45-story structure and its support building opened in 1981.

nated in an agreement between the parties in 1982. Under the terms of the settlement, AT&T agreed to divest itself of its 22 wholly-owned operating companies—among them Southern Bell—by January 1, 1984.

Later in 1982, the parties agreed upon a plan of reorganization, which divided the Bell operating companies into seven regions, each roughly equal in terms of number of employees and assets. The Southeast region includes the operating territories of Southern Bell and South Central Bell. BellSouth Corporation, newly headquartered at the Campanile Building, is the parent company of these two entities.

As Southern Bell moves beyond these events toward the 21st Century, it continues to focus on providing telecommunications services of the highest quality for its customers. And it continues to experience unprecedented growth. In 1986, Southern Bell exceeded even its own projections, gaining a record number of lines in service.

In Atlanta, the company continues to demonstrate its commitment to its customers, introducing digital services and fiber optic transmission facilities, as well as initiating in 1986 Enhanced 911 emergency telephone service in portions of the metropolitan area, the largest area in the Southeast served by an E911 system.

Atlanta is not just growing fast, it's moving fast, and it demands the best. Southern Bell and its more than 10,500 people in Atlanta are determined to make it, quite simply, the best there is for communications technology and services.

training camps. Overall, the war years were periods of slow growth for Southern Bell. The end of each war, however, found the company with large backlogs of orders for new telephones.

Continued, unsurpassed growth marked the postwar years, and that growth continues today. It had taken 50 years for Southern Bell to reach its first million telephones, from 1879 until 1929, and 17 years to reach the second million in 1946. By comparison, the third million was reached in 1949; the fourth in 1953; and the fifth million in 1956. Today, Southern Bell is one of the larger telephone companies in the United States.

In 1968, in order to maintain quality of service and close contact with customers, the one company was divided into two: Southern Bell, which now serves Florida, Georgia, North Carolina and South Carolina; and South Central Bell, which now serves Alabama, Kentucky, Louisiana, Mississippi and Tennessee.

The postwar years also saw a number of technical firsts for the Southern Bell

region. In 1957, Southern Bell introduced direct distance dialing, and three years later, a less popular innovation—all-number calling. No more HEmlock, JAckson and WAlnut prefixes for Atlanta's telephone numbers. A decade later, Atlanta was the site for one of Southern Bell's first electronic switching offices.

When the company celebrated its 100th anniversary on December 20, 1979, nearly half of its customers were served by electronic switching, and plans were under way for Southern Bell Center, the new corporate headquarters on West Peachtree Street in midtown Atlanta, which opened in 1981.

As Southern Bell continued to introduce new technologies, other events at the national level would soon have a profound effect on the way it would do business with its customers. The advent of competition in both the telephone equipment and long distance service markets resulted in a national debate in the Seventies about competition in the telecommunications industry.

That debate led to a suit by the Department of Justice against AT&T, which culmi-

This woman is using an early open telephone booth in front of the Hurt Building.

SouthernNet, Inc.

The city of Atlanta and SouthernNet go back a long way. Before there was any such thing as fiber optics, an 18-year-old boy named J. Smith Lanier left home to attend the Cotton States Exposition in Atlanta's Piedmont Park.

The year was 1895. At the Exposition, J. Smith Lanier saw a new invention called the telephone.

It impressed J. Smith Lanier so much that he went home to West Point, GA, and began building his own telephone exchange. Called the Interstate Telephone Company, it opened for business in the spring of 1896 with 36 subscribers. As the years passed, Mr. Lanier made improvements to his system. He was the first to use a battery operated switchboard. An idea so new in its time, he had to consult with Thomas Edison himself to have the batteries he needed specially designed.

Edison told the young J. Smith Lanier, "Young man, my batteries have never been used in a telephone system, but if you install them, you will be gray haired before they come out." The batteries lasted for over 30 years.

J. Smith Lanier died in 1972. The company he founded expanded and merged with other telephone companies and is today affiliated with SouthernNet, Inc., based in Atlanta and serving six states of the Southeast.

The Bettmann Archive

Today, SouthernNet serves a rapidly growing base of over 180,000 customers with a brand new technology called Fiber Optics. A clear and precise method of transmitting voice or data by pulsing light through fiber optic strands, SouthernNet links businesses in the Southeast with the entire nation.

SouthernNet salutes the City of Atlanta on its 150th birthday. We hope to play as large a role in the city's future as we have in its past.

SOUTHERNNET®

61 Perimeter Park Drive, N.E., Atlanta, GA 30341/404-458-4927

Stewart Brothers, Inc., Paving Contractors

Following a five-year term as Fulton County Commissioner, Walter B. Stewart founded Stewart Asphalt Products in 1932.

During his term on the Commission, Stewart and his fellow commissioners were instrumental in the early development of Candler Field, which later became Hartsfield International Airport.

As a resident of Hapeville and active Southside businessman, Stewart understood the long-range significance of having a first-class airport. Stewart and his fellow commissioners were responsible for the grading and extending of the airfield runways, and were continually counted on by the City of Atlanta to lend manpower and equipment to the construction of Candler Field.

With the start of Stewart Asphalt Products, the company was involved in road construction and paving throughout Atlanta and the Southeast. Early projects included work at Candler Field, Naval Air Station-Atlanta (later to become Dekalb Peachtree Airport), and the Bell Bomber Plant (present day Lockheed-Dobbins Complex).

The company's original offices and plant were off Jefferson Street across the street from Fulton County Bellwood Road Maintenance Camp. During the 40's and 50's the company was located in the heart of downtown Atlanta on Cain Street (now International Boulevard) between Courtland and Ivy Street (now Peachtree Center Ave.).

During the war years of the 40's, Stewart's business expanded and the company paved airfields throughout Florida and Georgia including Deland Naval Air station near Daytona and Lawson Field at Fort Benning.

With two sons entering the business early on, Walter B. Stewart turned the operation over to William C. Stewart who served as president and Donald B. Stewart as vice-president in 1946. At that time the company changed its name to Stewart Brothers to reflect the change in ownership.

In 1952 Stewart Brothers was called on to repave the Five Points area of downtown Atlanta and to remove the trolley tracks that criss-crossed this area of the city.

With wartime experience gained in paving airfields and military facilities, Stewart Brothers repaved the Glynn Co. Naval Air Station Blimp Base in 1951. As the years passed, Stewart Brothers focused their attention on the burgeoning Atlanta area, paving hundreds of miles of streets and highways and the expanding parking areas that served Atlanta's growing automobile population.

Continuing the tradition of continuous family ownership, William C. Stewart retired in 1962 and Donald B. Stewart took over as president. As Atlanta accelerated its expansion, Stewart Brothers has kept pace paving Perimeter Mall and a wide variety of residential projects throughout the Atlanta area, as well as roads and highways.

Like his father, Donald B. Stewart had sons that grew up in the business. In 1971, following graduation from college, Donald B. Stewart, Jr., joined the firm, and in 1974 William M. Stewart entered the business.

Today the family tradition continues. Donald B. Stewart serves as chairman of the company with Donald B. Stewart, Jr., serving as president and William M. Stewart as vice-president.

The firm's corporate headquarters are located on Pleasantdale Road in Doraville, with the company's three asphalt plants located in Conley, Doraville and Buford.

Vintage paving equipment from the early 1940's

Stone Mountain Park

Small Problems

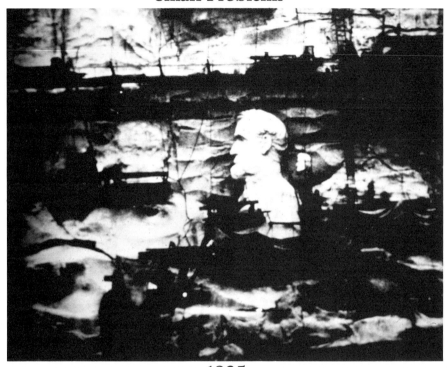

1925

Can't "Stonewall" Great Achievements

1970

Stone Mountain Park acknowledges the magnificent achievements of its neighbor city, Atlanta, for the past 150 years ... and sends best wishes for the next.

Georgia's Stone Mountain Park™

Tempo Management, Inc.

With the same kind of enterprise and energy which have historically characterized successful Atlanta firms, nationally-respected Tempo Management, Inc., has emerged as one of the largest owners and managers of apartment units in Metro Atlanta.

With such visibility in the Metro Atlanta area, its motto is justified: "You can't look at Atlanta without looking at Tempo."

Tempo Management, Inc., is today a $30 million firm which has the majority ownership in more than 4,300 rental units involving more than 30 apartment communities, and manages more than 25 other apartment communities representing an additional 5,000 units.

But 30 years ago, when the concept for Tempo Management was first seeded, its president Jerry Blonder and secretary-treasurer Dave Berkman made a modest beginning, managing a few apartment units. Until 1974 Tempo was solely a builder-owner of apartment communities. But that year owners of such communities—including individuals, life insurance firms, REITs and mortgage bankers—began asking Tempo to manage their properties.

They had studied Tempo's track record, and liked what they saw: a successful growth company which had surmounted the adverse economic conditions of the early 1970s and had grown by adhering to certain philosophies.

Its guidelines included quality growth, dedication to detail and sound professional management, and a thorough understanding of the needs of residents and clients.

The Company, which displays its "We Care" attitude in its relationships, has also benefitted from the fact that its executive leadership has been with the firm since its inception. Another key officer is Charles Felix, Financial Vice-President.

Headquarters of Tempo Management, Inc., 2190 Plaster Road, NE, Atlanta.

For more than two decades Tempo has also utilized the top-quality services of Royal Developers, its own construction arm, as the exclusive contractor for multi-housing communities. Royal Developers, which is also available to build for others under contract, is a cost-efficient company whose professionalism has won the admiration of other contractors.

The dominant growth of Tempo Management, Inc., has been in the past 13 years, during which the company's leadership has taken it into the management and/or ownership of properties in other states, including Alabama, Florida, South Carolina, Ohio, Texas and Kentucky. The firm has dealt successfully with mortgage firms in Georgia, life insurance companies in Virginia and Connecticut, and investment firms in Pennsylvania, Illinois, New York, Canada and West Germany.

Today, Tempo manages almost 10,000 apartment units, and considers its growth less remarkable than what it envisions. Tempo plans to manage, acquire and develop additional apartment communities, and enlarge its commercial real estate holdings.

"We believe we have proven that we can manage multi-housing developments to achieve any client's goals," said Blonder. "We've achieved our own objectives, and continue to set new ones. Because of careful management of our own properties, we can do the same for others since we're more than mere rent collectors. Tempo is composed of business people—owners and investors whose goals are akin to ours.

"Our business philosophy," said Blonder "is that we don't develop, build or buy monuments. We are in the business to make money the time-tested way; by creating or managing quality properties, and caring deeply about every aspect of our operations."

Touche Ross

When the 33 founding partners of Touche Ross gathered at the first partners' meeting in 1947, they were working out of 10 offices. They had seven or eight national clients, visionary leadership, and the ambition to grow and compete as a major accounting firm.

And Touche Ross has grown — dramatically. Today Touche Ross has 85 U.S. practice offices located in major metropolitan areas, a national office in midtown Manhattan, a financial services center on Wall Street, and a Washington service center in the nation's capital.

The national firm is a member of Touche Ross International, which is composed of 54 member firms operating in 90 countries through 471 offices worldwide. Over the years, Touche Ross International has become one of the world's most respected professional services firm.

The firm has grown because of the quality of its people and its ability to perceive and respond to the needs of its clients and the trends of the time. Nowhere is that more clearly demonstrated than in the history of the firm's Atlanta office.

Touche Ross decided to break into the southern market when Rich's department store began looking for a new accounting firm. Obtaining the account, the firm opened its doors in the First National Bank Building in July, 1958, with a staff of seven professionals. Soon after its entrance into the market, Touche Ross expanded its client list.

From the Atlanta office, Touche Ross professionals moved into the southeastern region, opening offices in Mississippi, Alabama, North Carolina, Tennessee and Kentucky to serve an ever-increasing client base and a growing region.

Today, with a staff numbering 225, Touche Ross Atlanta serves some 200 clients, including Rich's, its original client, Aaron Rents, Days Inns of America, Elson's Holdings, and FFMC. Audit, Tax, Emerging Business, and Management Consulting departments give the Atlanta office full service accounting, tax, and consulting capabilities.

The Management Consulting Department is nationally recognized for its services in these important areas: Telecommunications, Strategic Planning, Financial and Accounting Management and Operations/ Productivity Management. The Emerging Business Department known as the Enterprise Group, provides responsive service to emerging businesses through a special group of professionals with finance, accounting, tax and computer backgrounds.

A wholly-owned subsidiary, Garr Consulting Group, Inc., provides specialized management engineering and consulting services to a number of clients from its Marietta headquarters.

The firm's resources and its people have been committed to providing quality client service. In addition they have been committed to the Atlanta community.

Community participation has characterized the firm's leadership over the years. Over half of the firm's 21 partners participate on community boards, including the Atlanta Symphony, Alliance Theatre, Atlanta Ballet, Atlanta Kiwanis Club, and the Atlanta Jewish Federation.

Such leadership began with former managing partners, Alfred E. Garber, Fred W. Nichols, Robert E. Minnear and David J. Vander Broek. Under their stewardship, for example, Touche Ross employees have given at the highest level possible to the United Way for 23 uninterrupted years. In recognition of this fact the firm was presented the John A. Sibley Award in 1983.

The tradition of civic contribution continues with Ira Hefter, the current Managing Partner of the Atlanta practice. Mr. Hefter participates on a variety of community boards and is serving his second year as Chairman of the New Peach Bowl.

A commitment to client service and to Atlanta — a tradition that characterized Touche Ross' first 29 years in Atlanta and one that will continue into its future.

Ira Hefter, managing partner (1983-present)

Former managing partners Alfred E. Garber and Fred W. Nichols at the opening of the Fulton Industrial Park

▲ **Touche Ross**

WGST Radio

The turn of the century brought profound, rapid changes to the world, and radio—still in its infancy—was what Atlantans relied on to stay informed.

WGST combined the ability to inform and entertain when, in 1922, an enterprising Georgia Tech student named Arthur Murray broadcast the first radio dance music to dancers with headsets, on the rooftop garden of an Atlanta hotel. This event marked the beginning of a tradition of innovative programming and a dedication to news and public service.

WGST was owned and operated by The Atlanta Constitution in the early Twenties. In 1924 the Constitution donated the station to the Georgia Institute of Technology, under which it operated during the school year, using the air slogan, "The Southern Technical School with a National Reputation."

Six years later, WGST joined the Columbia Broadcasting System (CBS) and became a commercial station, but reserved air time for special broadcasts from Georgia Tech. In May, 1931, WGST went on the air around the clock from the Ansley Hotel.

During its CBS years, WGST aired network shows like The Lux Radio Theatre hosted by Cecil B. DeMille, soap operas including The Guiding Light, and such family radio favorites as Fred Allen and Jack Benny. The station's staff orchestra played dance music and provided backup tunes for shows including Chuck Wagon and Notes and Nuggets from 1937 until 1943.

Quiz shows captured the airwaves in the pre-World War II era, and WGST broadcast Atlanta's first—The Jackpot—in 1941. It was followed by WGST's Star Quiz, a show that gave contestants a chance to win cash prizes for naming a mystery movie star.

Hollywood also came to Atlanta via WGST's broadcast of The Texize Movie Man in 1948, featuring a local announcer who would become a national star: Bert Parks got 18 months' experience as a WGST announcer at age 16. Meanwhile, the locally-sponsored J.P. Allen 219 Quiz for teenage girls and The Basement Boys, shopper interviews from Rich's department store, enjoyed wide popularity.

From the beginning, news coverage has anchored WGST's hold on Atlanta radio audiences. WGST was one of only three local stations reporting on World War II. Over the years its news department has prided itself on first reports of Franklin Delano Roosevelt's funeral in 1945, John F. Kennedy's assassination in 1963 and the major U.S. space launches.

It was a natural progression for WGST to become a 24-hour news station in 1977, following Georgia Tech's sale of the station to the Meredith Corporation a few years earlier. Five years later, operating under vice president and general manager John Lauer,

Atlantans listened to WGST for coverage of the 1939 "Gone With the Wind" movie premiere. Pictured (left to right) are actors Ann Rutherford and Howard Dietz.

WGST's news staff boasted 37 persons, a number greater than all other Atlanta radio news staffs combined.

WGST NewsRadio 92 ushered in the Eighties with other "firsts." It was the nation's first radio station to broadcast a monthly town meeting with the mayor, during which listeners received immediate response to their concerns.

In July, 1985 Jacor Communications of Cincinnati purchased WGST, sister station WPCH, and the Georgia Radio News Service.

Widely recognized as the South's most honored radio news station, WGST's reporters canvass the city to bring Atlanta news first whenever and wherever it happens. WGST augments news coverage with a variety of features emphasizing community improvement, along with an

ongoing commitment to strong editorials and hard-hitting investigative reporting.

With talk shows like the informative and sometimes controversial Neal Boortz program to the provocative Ed Tyll show, and Counterpoint with Tom Houck, WGST keeps the pulse of the public on local and national stories affecting Atlanta. All the Atlanta Hawks basketball games can be heard exclusively on WGST and the Hawks radio network, and WGST is Atlanta's leader for pro and college sports coverage regionally and nationally.

As the flagship station of the Georgia Radio News Service, WGST broadcasts firsthand news reports through its 143 affiliates across the state. From Atlanta's first "radio dance station," WGST has earned its position as "Atlanta's news station."

Data Sources

In the development of the chronology data, a great many sources were used for basic information as well as double-checking. The primary ones include:

The Blue Flame (history of the Atlanta Gas Light Co., Tate)
Microfilm of The Atlanta Journal-Constitution
Atlanta and Environs (Garrett)
Story of Atlanta University
Peachtree Street, Atlanta (Williford)
Illustrated History of Atlanta (Clarke)
The Atlanta Century (Shavin)
Atlanta (Hornaday)
The First Hundred Years (a history of King & Spalding)
Fort McPherson, The First 100 Years

Images & Memories, Georgia Tech 1885-1985
Atlanta and Its Builders (Martin)
The Coca-Cola Company Chronology
Dictionary of Georgia Biography
Atlanta (Reed)
Atlanta Constitution Chronology
Governors of Georgia (Cook)
The American Almanac (Linton)
History of Atlanta and Its Pioneers
Atlanta Chamber of Commerce Chronology

The Cadillac truck used by Excelsior Laundry Co. in Atlanta in 1906—first truck in the city.